POLITICS, POLICY, AND FINANCE
UNDER HENRY III
1216–1245

Politics, Policy, and Finance under Henry III 1216–1245

ROBERT C. STACEY

CLARENDON PRESS · OXFORD
1987

Oxford University Press, Walton Street, Oxford OX2 6DP
Oxford New York Toronto Melbourne Auckland
Delhi Bombay Calcutta Madras Karachi
Petaling Jaya Singapore Hong Kong Tokyo
Nairobi Dar es Salaam Cape Town
Associated companies in Beirut Berlin Ibadan Nicosia
Oxford is a trade mark of Oxford University Press

Published in the United States
by Oxford University Press, New York

British Library Cataloguing in Publication Data
Stacey, Robert C.
Politics, policy and finance under Henry III,
1216–1245.
1. Great Britain—History—Henry III,
1216–1272
I. Title
942.03′4 DA227
ISBN 0-19-820086-2

Library of Congress Cataloging in Publication Data
Stacey, Robert C.
Politics, policy, and finance under Henry III,
1216–1245.
Originally presented as the author's thesis (doctoral—Yale University).
Bibliography: p.
Includes index.
1. Great Britain—Politics and government—1216–1272.
I. Title.
DA227.S73 1987 942.03′4 87–1630
ISBN 0-19-820086-2

Printed and bound by Butler & Tanner Ltd
Frome and London

FOR ROBIN

PREFACE

HENRY III ruled England for fifty-six years, longer than any English monarch until George III. The son of King John, he had to learn to live with the concessions his father had granted in Magna Carta. Yet for all the historical interest which the Great Charter has inspired, we know surprisingly little about the king under whom it in fact became the law of the land. Modern study of Henry III effectively ended in 1947, when F. M. Powicke published his magisterial two-volume work, *King Henry III and the Lord Edward: The Community of the Realm in the Thirteenth Century*. Powicke sought to write history 'from the heart of a subject, by what people thought and said and felt' (p.v) at the time, an aim for which his unsurpassed knowledge of thirteenth-century chronicles and genealogies equipped him magnificently. But in its aims no less than its methods, Powicke's work owed more to the influence of Stubbs than it did to the careful archival studies pioneered by T. F. Tout. The result has been that an air of vaguely Victorian constitutionalism has continued to cling to Henry's reign, long after such clouds were dispersed from the reigns of his father and his son. Despite the massive quantities of financial, legal, and administrative documents which exist for Henry's reign, we are still forced to write textbooks based on Powicke and the chronicles because so little of this archival evidence has been digested. In recent years, however, the governmental records of Henry's reign have at last begun to attract researchers. Much of this work is still unpublished, but it does now appear that Henry III will receive the same detailed examination long accorded to King John and to King Edward I. This study is a contribution to these efforts.

I have incurred many debts in preparing this study, which it is a pleasure to acknowledge. For financial assistance, I am indebted to Yale University, to its Council on West European Studies, its Concilium on International and Area Studies, and especially to the Mrs Giles Whiting Foundation, which generously supported me during my final year of research. I am also very grateful to the Fulbright/Hays Fellowship programme, which by supporting my wife as a Fulbright Scholar enabled her dependent spouse to spend an additional year in the archives. For archival assistance, Dr David Crook, Dr John Post, and Mrs Halford of the Public Record Office were indispensable. All transcripts and translations of Crown copyright records in the PRO appear by permission of the Controller of Her Majesty's Stationery Office.

Dr Paul Hyams of Pembroke College, Oxford, helped me with innumerable stimulating conversations and a generous flow of references, as did Dr David Carpenter of Queen Mary College, University of London, and Dr John Maddicott of Exeter College, Oxford. At a later stage in the proceedings, Professor Michael Clanchy's criticisms were invaluable. The influence of James Campbell, my undergraduate tutor at Worcester College, Oxford, and a scholar of astounding depth and breadth, will be apparent on every page to those who know him. The errors, of course, I added myself.

This book began life as a Yale University Ph.D. thesis, supervised by Professor Harry Miskimin with unflagging enthusiasm and goodwill. Along the way, it also benefited from the suggestions and criticisms of Professors Conrad Russell (now of the University of London), John Boswell, and Jaroslav Pelikan. I would also like to record my gratitude to the staffs of the Bodleian Library, the British Library, the Sterling Memorial Library, and the Oxford University History Faculty Library.

My greatest debt I acknowledge by the dedication.

New Haven, Connecticut RCS
May 1986

CONTENTS

LIST OF TABLES

ABBREVIATIONS

AM	*Annales Monastici*
BIHR	*Bulletin of the Institute of Historical Research*
BNB	*Bracton's NoteBook*
Book of Fees	*Liber Feodorum: The Book of Fees*
Charter Rolls 1226–57	*Calendar of Charter Rolls*, vol. i: *Henry III, 1226–1257*
CLR	*Calendar of Liberate Rolls, Henry III*
Cl.R.	*Close Rolls of the Reign of Henry III*
CM	*Matthaei Parisiensis Chronica Majora*
CPR	*Calendar of Patent Rolls, Henry III*
CRR	*Curia Regis Rolls*
Diplomatic Documents	*Diplomatic Documents*, vol. i: *1101–1272*
Ec.H.R.	*Economic History Review*
EHR	*English Historical Review*
Foedera	*Foedera, Conventiones, Litterae, etc.; or Rymer's Foedera* (London, 1816–69).
Glanvill	*Tractatus de Legibus et consuetudinibus regni Anglie qui Glanvilla vocatur*, ed. G. D. G. Hall (London, 1965).
Meekings, 1235 Surrey Eyre	*The 1235 Surrey Eyre*, vol. i, ed. C. A. F. Meekings (Surrey Record Society 31, 1979)
Patent Rolls	*Patent Rolls, Henry III*
PBA	*Proceedings of the British Academy*
PRO	Public Record Office, London
PRS n.s.	Pipe Roll Society, new series
Red Book	*Liber Rubeus de Scaccario. The Red Book of the Exchequer*
Rott. Litt. Claus.	*Rotuli Litterarum Clausarum in Turri Londinensi Asservati*
Royal Letters	*Royal and Other Historical Letters Illustrative of the Reign of Henry III*
Stubbs, *Select Charters*	*Select Charters and Other Illustrations of English Constitutional History*, ed. William Stubbs, 9th edn., revised by H. W. C. Davis

Thorne, *Bracton*	*De Legibus et Consuetudinibus Angliae*, ed. G. E. Woodbine, revised and translated by S. E. Thorne, 4 vols. (Cambridge, Mass., 1968, 1977)
TRHS	*Transactions of the Royal Historical Society*
Walter of Coventry	*Memoriale Walteri de Coventria*

I

The Inheritance of the Minority
1216–1236

ON the 28th day of October, 1216, Henry III was crowned king of England. Neither the ceremony nor its circumstances augured well for the new regime. The archbishop of Canterbury, whose right it was to crown the new king, was still in Rome, appealing against his suspension by the pope. The crown itself and most of the regalia had been lost—whether to the late king's creditors, to his death-bed attendants, or to the enveloping waters of the Wash, we cannot now be sure.[1] The great men of the realm, who ought to have witnessed the coronation, were mostly in rebellion, as were the citizens of London, whose acclamation should have confirmed it. Of the hereditary household stewards, only Earl Ranulf of Chester remained loyal, and he had not yet arrived from his campaigns in the northern marches of Wales. The justiciar, meanwhile, was shut up in Dover Castle, besieged by Prince Louis of France. Even Gloucester, the site of this unlikely crowning, was an expedient, made necessary by the loss of Westminster Abbey to the rebels. In the south-east and in the north, a few royal castles still held out; but otherwise, the most populous half of the new king's realm had already transferred its allegiance to a pretender, Prince Louis of France.

In his favour, the new King Henry had the unstinting loyalty of his father's military captains and castellans: Fawkes de Breauté, Engelard de Cigogné, Philip Mark, Peter de Maulay, and a host of others, who between them controlled the midlands and the sea-coast castles. He had the two greatest magnates in England, William the Marshal, earl of Pembroke and Striguil, and Earl Ranulf of Chester, both of whom had fought for Henry's grandfather, and for every Angevin since. Between them, these two earls commanded the Welsh Marches and

[1] J. C. Holt, 'King John's Disaster in the Wash', *Nottingham Medieval Studies* 5 (1961), 75–86; A. V. Jenkinson, 'The Jewels Lost in the Wash', *History* 8 (1923), 161–8.

the marcher lords. Henry had also the near-unanimous support of the English episcopate; and he had the powerful moral and diplomatic weight of the papacy and a resident papal legate behind him. And he also had time, although time must have seemed very short in October of 1216. On his coronation day, the new king of England was only nine years old.[2]

A royal minority was a new experience in Angevin England. To all intents and purposes, it was unprecedented. Philip II of France had been only fourteen years old when, in 1179, his father had had him crowned co-king, and associated him with himself on the throne. But when Louis VII died a year later, his son ruled alone from that date. Richard of England had ruled Aquitaine from the age of about fourteen, without any official restrictions on his powers, but under the effective, albeit intermittent, supervision of his father.[3] A fourteen-year-old king might thus be able to rule; but a nine-year-old king certainly could not.[4] The need for a regent was obvious to all. Legally, the wardship of the heir to England belonged to the papacy, from whom since 1213 King John had held England as a fief. In more settled times, the papal legate Gualo might well have chosen to exercise the claim to the regency which thus devolved upon him.[5] In the circumstances of October 1216, he could not and did not. The paramount concern of the men who gathered at Gloucester to crown the young king was to end the civil war which raged around them. To win the war, the royal party had to be able to recall to its allegiance at least some of the great men who had deserted King John during the last three months of his reign.[6] The only man in England whose

[2] The standard accounts of the minority are still Kate Norgate, *The Minority of Henry III* (London, 1912); J. H. Ramsay, *The Dawn of the Constitution, 1216–1307* (London, 1908); and F. M. Powicke, *King Henry III and the Lord Edward* (Oxford, 1947). The interpretation offered here differs considerably from these earlier accounts, but since the narrative of events is not in dispute, I have not cited contemporary chronicle references where these can be easily traced through Norgate, Ramsay, or Powicke.

[3] John Gillingham, *Richard the Lionheart* (New York, 1978), 51–98; W. L. Warren, *Henry II* (Berkeley, 1973), 120–1, 564–80.

[4] Later French custom seems to have presumed that the heir to the throne came of age at fourteen: cf. Joseph R. Strayer, *The Reign of Philip the Fair* (Princeton, 1980), 6.

[5] Gualo was recognized as the presumptive head of the government even while the Marshal served as *rector regis et regni*: cf. Hubert de Burgh's 1238 description of Gualo's position in *CM*, vol. vi, 65.

[6] On the arrival of Prince Louis of France in late May 1216, the earls of Salisbury, Arundel and Warenne, the count of Aumâle, and a number of important barons, including Hugh de Nevill and Warin fitzGerold, had all abandoned King John to join the rebels: cf. Sidney Painter, *The Reign of King John* (Baltimore, 1949), 374–7; W. L. Warren, *King John* (London, 1961), 252.

political influence and personal stature were adequate to this task was the Earl Marshal. In military power and financial resources, only the earl of Chester could rival him. Chester, however, had never played the role at court which had been the Marshal's through three previous reigns, nor could he command the personal reverence, even awe, which friend and foe alike reserved for the Marshal. With Chester's approval, the elderly Marshal reluctantly accepted the charge of king and kingdom from the legate Gualo. The young king's person Earl William immediately committed to Peter des Roches, bishop of Winchester and the boy's tutor. The assembly then turned its collective attention to the task of ending the war.

Two weeks later, in an assembly at Bristol which brought together almost all the young king's key supporters, the royalist party issued its manifesto. In 1215, the Great Charter which King John accepted at Runnymede had been an attempt at peace which instead produced a war.[7] In the autumn of 1215, it had been formally annulled by the papacy at King John's request. By November of 1216, when Henry's supporters issued a revised version of the Charter in the young king's name over the seals of the legate and the Marshal, the Charter had again become their best hope for a lasting peace, and hence for the continuation of Angevin rule in England. To see the 1216 Charter as a product of the war is not to suggest that those who issued it were personally or politically opposed to the concessions it contained.[8] Nor is it to suggest that the reissued Charter was a hasty patchwork, cobbled together from the wreckage of the 1215 original. It was, however, a tentative document, and self-confessedly so.[9] First and foremost, it was an expression of good faith by the new king's supporters, a statement of the principles and minimum concessions on the basis of which they proposed to rule the realm on behalf of the nine-year-old king. It was also a plea to the rebels to join with them in revising these principles and concessions so as to re-found royal government on lines which would be acceptable to all. It was put forward by the royalist party as a foundation upon which terms of peace between the king and the rebels might be negotiated. It was not intended as a definitive statement of the terms themselves, a fact which

[7] The best discussion of how this occurred is in J. C. Holt, *Magna Carta* (Cambridge, 1975), 149–74, 242–68.
[8] They were not, as Holt, *Magna Carta*, 269–72, makes clear.
[9] Holt, *Magna Carta*, 272, takes a different view, suggesting that the 1216 Charter reflects 'a remarkable confidence in the outcome of the war. These men were already building for the future.'

the final provision of the new Charter stated explicitly.[10] The plea for fuller counsel which this provision contained can only have been directed at the rebels; all the men who mattered from the king's party were already witnesses to the Charter at Bristol.[11] In this respect, the 1216 Charter looked forward to a situation much like that which had produced the 1215 Charter: two hostile sides, neither militarily strong enough to impose its own terms on the other, coming to a negotiated peace. In 1216, however, there were to be two crucial differences from that unhappy precedent: the terms of a final peace would be determined only after the rebel barons had renewed their fealty to the king; and the king and his advisers would enter into the negotiations in good faith, with a basic minimum of concessions and a statement of fundamental principles already agreed and conceded by the king.

In the event, the 1216 Charter accomplished both less and more than the royalist party had hoped. Soon after its issue, William Longsword, earl of Salisbury and uncle of the new king, and William Marshal, son and heir of the great Marshal, returned to the royal camp. Over the next several months, a trickle of fellow rebels joined them. But the reissue of the Charter did not bring in the rebels as a group to negotiate an end to the war. In that respect, it was a failure. Instead, the war ended with a crushing and totally unpredictable victory for the royalist forces at Lincoln in May 1217, followed almost immediately by the defeat of a French fleet conveying reinforcements to Louis in the south-east. The result of the royalists' unforeseeable military victory was thus to give an unexpected and indeed unintended permanence to the terms of the 1216 Charter. Although the Treaty of Kingston specified that King Henry would grant all of the liberties the barons had demanded, by their military defeat the former rebels had lost the corporate leverage by which they might have forced major revisions in the terms of the 1216 offer. Provisions which had been dropped in 1216 from the 1215 original therefore remained dropped, preserved only in the popular memory and in the terms of some unofficial versions of the Charter.[12] A few further changes were made in the 1217 reissue, but except for some clauses in the new Forest

---

[10] Stubbs, *Select Charters*, 339 (cap. 42).

[11] Even Hubert de Burgh had escaped from Dover Castle for the occasion: see the witness list appended to the 1216 Bristol Charter in Stubbs, *Select Charters*, 336.

[12] Holt, *Magna Carta*, 211–12, 286–92; J. C. Holt, 'The St Albans Chroniclers and Magna Carta', *TRHS* 5th s. 14 (1964), 67–88; J. C. Holt, 'A Vernacular French Text of Magna Carta, 1215', *EHR* 89 (1974), 346–64.

Charter, none significantly limited the powers of the Crown.[13] With the Treaty of Kingston, what had been in 1216 a statement of the minimum concessions the king was willing to offer his subjects became, instead, a final statement of the principles and limitations which the regency government would observe in ruling England.

The restrictions which the 1217 Charter imposed on royal government were therefore rather less than those which might ultimately have emerged from the 1216 reissue. But even these restrictions were real enough. The fundamental claim advanced in 1215 the royalists had already accepted. By reissuing the Charter after John's death, they recognized that the Great Charter had been not merely an indictment of John's reign, but of certain features of Angevin kingship as it had evolved since 1154.[14] The Angevins had accustomed England to rule by custom; henceforth, the royal *vis et voluntas* would also be bounded by a written statement of its customs. The restrictive effects of this fundamental concession were clearest in the 1217 Charter's regulations concerning the feudal rights of the king over his tenants-in-chief, and in the king's control over his forests.

Provisions governing the king's conduct as feudal lord were adopted wholesale from the 1215 original by all subsequent versions of the Charter. Such changes as were made in these sections appear to have been intended only to clarify and make more precise their meaning and intent. Reliefs henceforth were to be fixed, at £100 for an earldom or a barony, and 100s. per knight's fee; no fine or relief was to be paid to recover land held by the king in wardship; lands in wardship or custody were not to be wasted; widows were to be given their dowers freely, without delay or payment, and were not to be forced to marry against their will. No heirs or heiresses in the king's custody were to be committed to a disparaging marriage. The services due to the Crown from knights' fees and from escheated honours and baronies were not to be increased, nor could the king claim the custody of vacant abbeys founded by baronial families. The king's rights as a war-lord, however, remained untouched. Gone were all the 1216 restrictions on the king's freedom to bring foreign mercenaries into the realm, and limiting the manner in which and the occasions when he could levy scutages and

---

[13] These changes are most easily followed in Stubbs, *Select Charters*, 336–48. They are discussed in Holt, *Magna Carta*, 272–5.

[14] J. C. Holt, 'The Barons and the Great Charter', *EHR* 70 (1955), 1–24; Holt, *Magna Carta*, 19–42, esp. 38; and from a rather different point of view, J. E. A. Jolliffe, *The Constitutional History of Medieval England*, 4th edn. (London, 1961), 246–63, and *Angevin Kingship*, 2nd edn. (London, 1963), *passim*.

aids. Scutage henceforth was to be taken as it has been under Henry II—a meaningless restriction. Only the royal right to compel those who owed castle-guard to commute their obligations into a monetary payment was abolished. The king's right to claim and enforce castle-guard itself was untouched.[15]

The king's role as judge ordinary in his realm was even less restricted. Henry's right to deny royal justice to a freeman was specifically proscribed by the Charter, but his ability to extend that justice was, if anything, enhanced. Only 1215 cap. 34 represented any limitation on the scope of royal justice, and although it reappeared in all reissues of the Charter, it remained to all intents and purposes a dead letter. By prohibiting general writs *praecipe*, the provision succeeded only in guaranteeing a future for the new writs of entry, which accomplished even more efficiently the same purpose served by *praecipe*, of transferring cases directly into the royal courts which otherwise would have arrived there only with difficulty, after a tedious series of transfers by tolt and pone, from seigneurial and local courts.[16] Otherwise, the judicial provisions of Magna Carta 1215 had attempted to extend, but above all to regularize, the existing operations of royal justice, an intention which all subsequent versions of the Charter continued to reflect.

The Charter did, however, significantly restrict the king's hitherto unfettered power to deny his justice to any free man, or to apply it arbitrarily without judgement of his court. Writs of inquisition of life and limb were hereafter to run *de cursu*. No one was to be seized or imprisoned except by the judgement of his peers or else in accordance with the law of the land. Amercements were to be proportionate to the gravity of the offence, and could not be set at a level which would threaten the livelihood or status of the man amerced. The general tenor of the Charter's judicial provisions was well summarized in 1215 cap. 40, which all subsequent versions of the Charter repeated: 'To no one will we sell, to no one will we deny or delay right or justice.' All the other judicial provisions of the Charter were a gloss on this basic principle. In this respect, the Charter demanded a common law; a law, that is, which would guarantee a regular and predictable justice, and

---

[15] On the interpretation of these clauses, see William S. McKechnie, *Magna Carta*, 2nd edn. (Glasgow, 1914); Holt, *Magna Carta*, 201–41.

[16] Naomi Hurnard, 'Magna Carta, Clause 34', in *Studies in Medieval History presented to F. M. Powicke* (Oxford, 1948), 157–79; Michael T. Clanchy, 'Magna Carta, Clause 34', *EHR* 79 (1964), 542–8; and S. F. C. Milsom, *The Legal Framework of English Feudalism* (Cambridge, 1976), 68–71.

which would offer a certain number of remedies accessible to all free men.[17] It did not, however, envision either a law or a judiciary which would be independent of the king's will. The Charter restricted the scope of that will's operation, but will remained an essential feature of Angevin royal justice.[18] The courts were still the king's courts, and the judges still royal officials, answerable before all other concerns for the preservation of their royal master's interests. Magna Carta promised judgement, and judgement in the king's court guaranteed a hearing. It did not guarantee an impartial verdict. This was as it should be. To the men of Henry's minority, a justice without prejudice towards the interests of the king and his faithful men would have been no true justice at all.

The area in which the greatest and most unprecedented restrictions were placed on the new king's government in 1217 was in the forest. Before 1215, the Angevins had administered the forest law essentially unchecked by the emerging legal customs of the king's other courts. In the 1217 Forest Charter, however, the royalists and the former rebels set out together to define the legal customs of the forest, and to define the geographical boundaries within which forest custom should run.[19] In the first aim, they were largely successful. In the following decades, 'the Forest Charter became part of the law of the land cited in courts of law and appealed to in disputes over rights'.[20] But in defining the bounds of the forest, the new Charter engendered controversy and rancour for fully a century. The Charter asserted that forest customs were to be as they had been at the first coronation of Henry II in 1154. It made no such explicit declaration concerning the forest boundaries. According to the new charter, all forests created *de novo* by King Richard or King John outside the royal demesne were now to be disafforested. Since neither king created much new forest, and since

---

[17] It should not be presumed that Magna Carta established a 'common law'. On the evolution of such a concept, see Paul R. Hyams, 'The Origins of the English Common Law', presented to the 1981 Legal History Conference at Bristol.

[18] The classic expression of this point of view is Jolliffe, *Angevin Kingship*. See also Ralph V. Turner, *The King and his Courts* (Ithaca, 1968), and Holt, *Magna Carta*, 63–104.

[19] The text of the 1217 Forest Charter is reprinted in Stubbs, *Select Charters*, 344–8; the 1225 Forest Charter by Holt, *Magna Carta*, 359–62. For discussion, see Holt, *Magna Carta*, 235–7; J. C. Holt, *The Northerners* (Oxford, 1961), 157–64; Charles R. Young, *The Royal Forests of Medieval England* (Philadelphia, 1979), 60–73; and now J. R. Maddicott, 'Magna Carta and the Local Community, 1215–1259', *Past and Present* 102 (1984), esp. 36–40.

[20] Young, *Royal Forests*, 68.

both kings disafforested much previously existing forest, this provision caused few problems.[21] Henry II's reign, however, presented major difficulties: were royal woods lost under Stephen and then 'reafforested' by Henry II after 1154 now to be considered forest or common? Ninety years later, even a local jury acting in good faith might not know with certainty whether a given tract of land had been forest in 1135, and there was copious evidence that not all these local juries acted in good faith when declaring the forest bounds.[22] Among Henry III's first acts upon declaring his full majority in 1227 was to order a complete review of all the disafforestations which had been carried out under the terms of the Charter during his minority. The action aroused much ill feeling, but it produced overwhelming evidence that many royal rights had been lost as a result of these local inquests. A new perambulation of the forest bounds was ordered, and many boundaries readjusted, but the issue was never fully resolved. Henry apparently remained convinced that many legitimate royal rights had been lost, and in the decades which followed his minority, he came increasingly to claim as forest all lands which had been held as forest in 1215 by King John. Henry's subjects, meanwhile, saw such claims as direct violations of the 1217 Charter, reissued and reconfirmed in 1225 in return for a fifteenth on moveables granted to the king. The ambiguity of the Charters' provisions thus helped to ensure that forest issues would remain a political irritant between the king and his subjects until the end of the century.[23]

Despite these modifications and restrictions, however, in its essentials the Angevin administrative system was unimpaired by the 1217 Charters, a fact which became apparent as soon as the regency government restored it to proper working order after the war. The exchequer had been closed since the spring of 1215. The last full set of accounts it had prepared ended with Michaelmas 1214. But by the autumn of 1218, the exchequer officials were again auditing the accounts of the shires, and attempting to call in the debts owing from the years of war.[24] Magna Carta had insisted only that, in collecting its debts, the exchequer distrain first on a man's chattels before distraining on his

---

[21] Ibid., 18–32, 65–73; Holt, Magna Carta, 235–7.
[22] David Crook, 'The Struggle over Forest Boundaries in Nottinghamshire, 1218–27', Transactions of the Thoroton Society 83 (1979), 36.
[23] Young, Royal Forests, 69–73; Powicke, Henry III, 71; Maddicott, 'Magna Carta and the Local Community', passim.
[24] Introduction to Pipe Roll 3 Henry III, ed. Brian E. Harris, PRS n.s. 42 (London, 1976), xiv–xvi.

land.[25] It had not limited the exchequer's ultimate right of distraint to collect the king's debts. Fines made with King John by defeated rebels returning to his peace were enrolled by the exchequer and were summoned for payment, as were the sums still owing from the 1214 Poitevin scutage.[26] Scattered debts owed by a single debtor were again gathered together under a single heading on the pipe rolls, and terms set for their combined payment, just as they had been under John.[27] Debts owed to Jews which had subsequently fallen into the exchequer (known technically as *debita Judeorum*) were also summoned, despite the opposition to such practices in 1215. The provisions of the 1215 Charter limiting such debts to the principal only, and excluding any accumulated interest from the king's collectors, were among those left out of the 1216 reissue, and were therefore never observed.[28] The exchequer moved more hesitantly now in attempting to compel the payment of such debts, but the powers by which it could so if it chose were unrestrained.

The general eyre which began in the autumn of 1218 pointed dramatically to another aspect of Angevin administration which continued unchecked after the Charters. Magna Carta had demanded more justice, not less, a demand which the regency government made every effort to meet. There were several reasons for the speed with which this first eyre was initiated. The war had left a large backlog of claims unheard, and had added to them a tremendous number of new disputes over tenures. Disputes between fellow royalists were common. Those between rebels and royalists were even more numerous, and even more of a threat to the king's peace. But beyond the obvious need to resolve such cases, a general eyre was also among the most reliable devices the king possessed by which to raise funds, and funds were sorely needed in 1218–19.

The eyre also served a third purpose, in the long run no less important than doing justice or raising money. It also maintained that essential contact between the king's court and the shires, and that essential control over the activities of curial officials in the shires, on which Angevin government fundamentally depended. These *curiales* posed a

---

[25] 1215 Magna Carta cap. 9.

[26] *Pipe Roll 3 Henry III*, xvii, xxiii. On the opposition to this scutage in 1214, see Holt, *Northerners*, 88–102.

[27] *Pipe Roll 3 Henry III*, xiv–xv; Holt, *Northerners*, 170–1.

[28] 1215 Magna Carta caps. 10, 11. The substance of these two provisions was, however, re-enacted in 1236 by the Statute of Merton, as Holt, *Magna Carta*, 234 and n. 1, points out.

general problem for any royal government. As sheriffs, castellans, and bailiffs, these men of the court played an integral role in governing the shires, guaranteeing the loyalty of their areas in time of war, and guaranteeing also that royal policies would be publicized and implemented in peacetime. There was, however, no expectation that they should be disinterested servants of the Crown. Local office was profitable, and as such it was the expected reward of an able royal supporter at court. A delicate balance had to be struck, however, between these court-based officials and the great men of the locality in adjudicating their respective claims to office, power, and patronage within their localities. An over-powerful curial official was likely to raise opposition in the shire, and could also pose a threat to the very royal control which his presence was intended to facilitate. The king had to be on guard constantly to ensure that the men he raised up to local prominence did not entrench themselves too deeply in their local offices. At the same time, he had to guard against these same men monopolizing the local wardships, custodies, and marriages which were distributed through the king's court. Knowing the localities yet frequently in attendance at court, *curiales* were ideally placed to enrich their own local connections at the king's expense. Where patronage travelled too easily and too often through the hands of a specific royal official into the countryside, there was a constant danger that the local men thus enriched would owe their allegiance, not to the king, but to their curial patron. Much of the political purpose behind the distribution of such patronage might thus be dangerously misdirected.

These problems were intrinsic to Angevin government, but they were particularly acute in the years after 1217. Competing claims to patronage, influence, and local office were bound to create tensions in any minority government. John, however, had exacerbated these tensions by his own failure to balance such claims effectively during his reign.[29] Even without the civil war, his legacy to his son would therefore have been a troubled one. The war, however, had compounded these problems enormously. Royalist commanders had had ample opportunity during the war to capture and retain the lands, offices, and castles of defeated rebels and even of absent royalists.[30] Having won the war for the young king, they had every reason to expect to retain these prizes at least until the king's majority. Some of

---

[29] Holt, *Northerners*, 217–50; David Carpenter, 'The Fall of Hubert de Burgh', *Journal of British Studies* 19 (1980), 1–17.

[30] For examples, see Holt, *Northerners*, 241–50.

the royalist castellans even claimed to have taken oaths to King John to this effect, swearing to surrender their commands only to the young king himself, and only when he was of full age.[31] Fawkes de Breauté is the best example of the scale of the problem posed by these men. In 1219 he was the sheriff of six contiguous Midland counties; he was the castellan of at least seven castles, and the farmer of an enormous number of royal manors and hundreds.[32] But his example is far from unique. Hubert de Burgh held three counties and at least six castles, William Longsword two counties and at least eight royal manors, and the earl of Chester three counties with their attendant castles, in addition to his earldom.[33] In the autumn of 1218, 'half a dozen barons and military experts ruled from their strongholds nearly a score of shires in the midlands and west of England'.[34]

Such concentrations of power were dangerous, less so for fear of incipient rebellion (although such fears were real enough) than for the insidious threat they posed to royal control within the localities thus administered. Above all else, a royal sheriff was charged with the maintenance of royal rights within his bailiwick. These rights—to view of frankpledge, to deliver writs within private hundreds, and to many other such privileges and local imposts—were rarely matters of written record in the early thirteenth century. Their maintenance in the king's hands therefore depended on their forceful and continuing exercise by his officials. A long-serving sheriff with local interests to further might thus be able to create a *de facto* liberty for himself and his heirs simply by failing to exercise the king's rights within his own private lands. When a new sheriff finally did take over, the customary liberty thus established could prove very difficult indeed to recover from the king. Royal hundreds might become private hundreds, royal

[31] Norgate, *Minority of Henry III*, 280–6; Powicke, *Henry III*, 55 and n. 1. See also G. J. Turner, 'The Minority of Henry III', *TRHS* n.s. 18 (1904), 245–95, and 3rd s. 1 (1907), 205–62.

[32] Fawkes held Bedfordshire, Buckinghamshire, Cambridgeshire, Huntingdonshire, Northamptonshire, and Oxfordshire, along with the custody of Rutland: cf. *Pipe Roll 3 Henry III*, 52, 62, 77, 86, and, for Rutland, Norgate, *Minority of Henry III*, 149.

[33] De Burgh held Norfolk and Suffolk, and Kent, along with the Tower of London, Dover Castle, Oreford, Norwich, Canterbury, and Rochester castles: cf. Powicke, *Henry III*, 55. Longsword was sheriff of Wiltshire and Lincolnshire, and held the royal manors of Bromsgrove, Aura, Brampton, Andover, Ludingland, Finedon, Clive and Writtle, along with the revenues from the town of Southampton: cf. *Pipe Roll 3 Henry III*, 13, 117, 1, 7, 20, 24, 37, 77, 103–4, 25. Chester held Shropshire, Staffordshire, and Lancashire, along with the castles at Lancaster, Shrewsbury, and Bridgnorth, in addition to his own contiguous earldom of Cheshire: cf. *Pipe Roll 3 Henry III*, 5, 3, 153.

[34] Powicke, *Henry III*, 55.

woods become private woods, and royal rights to frankpledge or sheriff's aid might lapse, all by a similar process of usurpation and neglect. The damage to royal power and to the king's shire revenues could prove irreparable.[35]

There were therefore clear reasons of policy why even a selfless and disinterested minority government might order a general redistribution of these offices, custodies, and castles. Without such an effort, a long minority might otherwise accomplish what Magna Carta had not: a permanent and irreparable weakening of the Angevin monarchy's capacity to rule England. But there were other motives too which urged such a redistribution upon Henry's regents, motives which had less to do with policy than with patronage and political power. Office and land were the expected and necessary rewards of royal service. Even in the best of times, there were never enough to go around. There were even fewer such rewards available when so many were in the hands of a few of King John's wartime supporters, whose hold on the country the minority threatened to make permanent.[36] The need to provide such patronage was, moreover, rendered even more acute by a minority government in which a number of great men, each with their own followers to satisfy, all claimed a hand in government and its rewards. Factional strife within the regency government and outside it followed as an almost inevitable consequence. As factions grew, so too did the pressure to redistribute these wartime prizes. Eventually, for reasons which are now an indistinguishable amalgam of policy and self-interested patronage, the pressure became irresistible.

So long as the elder Marshal lived, however, these factional struggles for place and local influence were kept fairly well in check. Partly this was because the Marshal's government attempted no major redistributions of office or power during its tenure; partly because the Marshal himself was a fair-minded man; and partly too because no one else could compete with the Marshal on even terms in the struggle for place. When the Marshal's bailiffs seized the lands of the earl of Huntingdon from Fawkes de Breauté, who claimed as sheriff to have the custody of them, Fawkes wrote to the justiciar, Hubert de Burgh, to seek redress. 'I would bear this', wrote Fawkes, 'from no one

---

[35] David Carpenter has illustrated these dangers particularly clearly with respect to Fawkes de Breauté's tenure as sheriff of Oxfordshire. See his unpublished University of Oxford D.Phil. thesis, 'Sheriffs of Oxfordshire and their Subordinates, 1194–1236' (1973), 148–98. I am grateful to Dr Carpenter for permission to use his thesis.

[36] Powicke, *Henry III*, 49–51; compare the views of Turner, 'Minority of Henry III', *passim*.

except the Marshal.' But because the Marshal was involved, he sought instructions.[37] Several of his most faithful men the Marshal promoted into royal service. His nephew John Marshal became chief justice of the royal forests, as well as bailiff in fee of Chippenham, Devizes, and Rowde in Wiltshire.[38] Ralph Musard, a Marshal ally, had already become sheriff of Gloucestershire and constable of Gloucester Castle in 1215, replacing Engelard de Cigogné, who was moved to Berkshire.[39] Walter de Verdon, another of the Marshal's marcher connections, became under-sheriff to the Marshal in Essex and Hertfordshire.[40] Other Marshal allies were the recipients of royal favours. Alan Basset of Wycombe, for example, paid five marks for a grant of a Friday market at his manor of Wootton in Wiltshire, despite the clear understanding that no grants in perpetuity could be made while the king was a minor.[41]

As soon as the great Marshal died, however, on 14 May 1219, the factional struggles in court and countryside broke out in earnest. Minor changes in local office followed quickly: Philip d'Albini, for example, a close associate of the bishop of Winchester and the young king's tutor in knightly pursuits, immediately replaced John Marshal in Chippenham, Devizes, and Rowde.[42] Much more serious, however, were the conflicts over castle custodies which soon erupted. Within nine months of the regent's death, the king's government was faced with no less than five separate refusals to obey royal orders to surrender castles to new custodians. The count of Aumâle had held the castles at Rockingham and Sauvey since 1216, when King John had granted them to him to hold until he could recover his own lands from the rebels. By February 1218, the count's lands had long since been restored to him, and the regent therefore ordered Aumâle to hand over these castles to Fawkes de Breauté. Aumâle ignored these orders, and con-

[37] *Royal Letters*, vol. i, 4–5.
[38] *Patent Rolls 1216–25*, 162; *Pipe Roll 3 Henry III*, 14–15.
[39] On the connections between Ralph Musard and William the Marshal, see *Histoire de Guillaume le Maréchal*, ed. Paul Meyer, 3 vols. (Paris, 1891–1901), ll. 15611–30. Control of Gloucestershire had been taken from the Marshal in Jan. 1208, when Engelard's kinsman Gerard d'Athée replaced the Marshal supporter Richard de Mucegros as sheriff. The appointment of Ralph Musard in 1215 returned the shire to the control of the Marshals. See F. W. Maitland, *Pleas of the Crown for the County of Gloucester A. D. 1221* (London, 1884), xiv–xvi, xx–xxi.
[40] He became sheriff in his own right at Michaelmas 1218: cf. *Pipe Roll 3 Henry III*, 102, 104.
[41] Ibid., 18. Such grants appear to have been extremely common by 1219; at least twenty-one new grants of fairs and markets appear on this pipe roll alone.
[42] *Pipe Roll 3 Henry III*, 14–15.

tinued to ignore them, despite excommunication in November 1219
for his contumacy. By the spring of 1220, he had reconciled himself
with the Church by taking the Cross, but he still held the two castles
which had been the grounds for his initial excommunication.[43] William
Marshal the younger, now earl of Pembroke and Earl Marshal after
his father's death, continued to retain Fotheringay Castle despite a
direct order by the king's government to surrender it to the countess
of Huntingdon in dower. He also retained the royal castle at Marlborough, which he had first claimed from Prince Louis, and which he had
been granted in custody by his father's government when he returned
to the king's allegiance. Moreover, in the spring of 1220 he was busily
fortifying the castle without royal permission, a violation not only of
its status as a royal castle, but also of the king's long-established right
to license all crenellations in England, whether private or royal.[44]
Meanwhile, on the Welsh Marches, Hugh de Vivona had flatly refused
an order in February 1220 to hand over Bristol Castle to the earl of
Gloucester.[45]

The most serious such dispute, however, was the small-scale private
war which threatened to break out between Fawkes de Breauté and
William Longsword over the custody of Lincoln Castle. Bad feeling
between the two men probably went back at least to 1215, when King
John married Fawkes to the widow of the heir to the earldom of
Devon. In March 1218, William the Marshal had awarded Plympton
Castle and all the Devonshire lands of the Redvers earldom to Fawkes
and his reluctant bride in dower. This established the upstart Fawkes
in an area in which Longsword had long cherished interests, interests
which had been further encouraged by Longsword's appointment as
sheriff of Devon and Somerset in August 1217.[46] Trouble between the
two, however, broke out first, not in the south-west, but in Lincoln,
over the rival claims of Longsword and the redoubtable dowager
Nicholaa de la Haye to the constableship of Lincoln Castle. Longsword
claimed the castle as appurtenant to the sheriffdom of Lincoln, which
he also held, and for a few months in 1217 he may indeed have held
the two together. Dame Nicholaa, however, had held the castle and

[43] Ralph V. Turner, 'William de Forz, Count of Aumâle: An Early Thirteenth-Century
Baron', *Proceedings of the American Philosophical Society* 115 (1971), 221–49, esp. 232–
9; Norgate, *Minority of Henry III*, 121–3.
[44] For references, see Norgate, *Minority of Henry III*, 150–3.
[45] *Royal Letters*, vol. i, 90–1.
[46] *Patent Rolls 1216–25*, 86, 87. Powicke suggests Longsword may have hoped to
create a palatinate in Devon and Somerset: cf. *Henry III*, 50.

the shrievalty for twenty years as the hereditary right of her family, and in the autumn of 1217 it was ordered that she be reinstated in her inheritance. Longsword, however, was soon thereafter restored to the sheriffdom, but this time without the castle, which remained in Nicholaa's hands. This result Longsword never accepted. As soon as the great Marshal died, he renewed his efforts to evict Dame Nicholaa from the castle. To defend her rights, the king's government ordered Fawkes de Breauté to garrison the castle with his own men, and to defend it from Longsword. Fawkes's presence preserved the castle for its castellan, but it confirmed the enmity between him and the influential earl of Salisbury.

No government could ignore such open defiance for long, especially not when the example set by men like the younger Marshal and William Longsword was being aped by relative lightweights like Hugh de Vivona. Nor could the king's finances endure much longer the hearty disdain which custodians like the count of Aumâle regularly showed to exchequer summonses. The count had paid not a penny on the farm of Sauvey or Rockingham Castles since the day he had received them from King John.[47] There is, moreover, evidence that the scale of the king's debts was causing mounting concern in this period, especially to Pandulf, the new papal legate and titular head of the regency government after the Marshal's death. There is an air of secrecy about the legate's preparations in the spring of 1220, but the letters which passed between the legate, de Burgh, and des Roches during these months do make clear that it was Pandulf who was behind the careful plans which were then being made to resolve the related problems of the castle custodies and the king's finances.[48]

The first step in Pandulf's plans was accomplished with the re-coronation of the king at Westminster on 17 May 1220. Even more significant than the ceremony, however, was the oath which the Dunstable annalist claims was taken on the following morning by the barons who had assembled for the coronation.

The barons who were present swore that they would resign their castles and wardenships at the will of the king, and would render at the exchequer a faithful account of their farms; and also that if any rebel should resist the king, and should not make satisfaction within forty days after being excom-

[47] *Patent Rolls 1216–25*, 240; Norgate, *Minority of Henry III*, 155–6.
[48] *Royal Letters*, vol. i, 116–21.

municated by the legate, they would make war upon him at the king's bidding, that the rebel might be disinherited without the option of a fine.[49]

No immediate steps were taken to enforce the terms of this oath, but it strengthened the legate's hand for his next move. After the coronation, the young king, accompanied by the justiciar, went on a progress through the midlands, solemnly entering the castles as a sign of royal ownership. The route of the royal party meandered somewhat, probably so as to allow the count of Aumâle time to make up his mind to surrender Sauvey and Rockingham Castles when the king arrived. But there can be no doubt that the legate intended from the outset to include Sauvey and Rockingham in the progress. When the king finally did arrive before their gates, the count had left the garrisons to shift for themselves. After a token show of resistance, both garrisons capitulated before the threat of a royal siege.[50] An important point about the castles had been made; but, for the moment, the other castellans remained undisturbed in their custodies.

Pandulf laid these plans, but it was Hubert de Burgh, the royal justiciar, who carried them out; and from this point on, it is the justiciar's influence within the government which becomes steadily more apparent. In 1219, the dying Earl Marshal had committed his responsibility for king and kingdom to Pandulf, remarking as he did so that 'in no land are the folk of so many different minds as in England; and if I committed him to one, the others, you may be sure, would be envious'.[51] The remark may be apocryphal, but the perception it expressed is accurate enough. As the titular head of the government, Pandulf exercised a general supervision over its activities. He was not a reluctant participant in the government, and when the situation demanded, he was not hesitant about ordering the justiciar or the vice-chancellor around in a most peremptory fashion. But his influence outside the narrow circle of the royal council remained small, except perhaps over the prelates. The attention of those desiring favours from the young king's government therefore tended to focus either on the justiciar, Hubert de Burgh, or on the king's personal guardian, Peter des Roches, the bishop of Winchester. In the contest which ensued between these two for predominance within the govern-

[49] Annals of Dunstable, *AM*, vol. iii, 57. I have adapted Norgate's translation in *Minority of Henry III*, 146.

[50] See the Barnwell chronicler, preserved in *Walter of Coventry*, vol. ii, 244–5.

[51] Norgate's translation (*Minority of Henry III*, 105) of *Histoire de Guillaume le Maréchal*, ll. 18038–46.

ment, de Burgh's office gave him overwhelming advantages. As the head of the judicial system, he moved by far the greatest number of royal writs giving force to judicial decisions. This in itself was a source of enormous power. The only man with even remotely comparable influence over the courts was the acting chancellor (in fact, the vice-chancellor), Ralph de Nevill; significantly, he too attracted something of a curial following, especially among the professional justices and their clerks.[52] Nevill certainly used his official position to facilitate the management of his private estates; he was a good patron, uncovering vacant offices and promoting his own men into them; and occasionally, his help was sought by his Nevill relations, to change the venue of a plea, to frustrate the designs of a family enemy at court, or to procure a writ.[53] But Ralph de Nevill seems to have confined his interests to a comparatively narrow sphere. He either made no real attempt to extend his influence at court, or else his attempts were unsuccessful. He steered a generally independent line in the conflicts between de Burgh and his enemies during his years at court. Perhaps as a result, he outlasted them all, and died in office.[54] But he never attempted to direct royal policy, or to build up a party in the shires. He was therefore never a primary player in the struggle to control the young king's government.

For ubiquity of influence at court, no one could match de Burgh. Head of the judicial apparatus, he was also a baron of the exchequer, sheriff of three counties, and the man in charge of Irish and Poitevin affairs for the government. As justiciar, he also had a direct and official interest in royal policy toward the castles. Moreover, he was a shrewd political infighter. He carefully cultivated his relationship with the king's favourite uncle, William Longsword, the troublesome earl of Salisbury, who became de Burgh's strongest ally within the regency

[52] C. A. F. Meekings, 'Six Letters concerning the Eyres of 1226–8', *EHR* 65 (1950), 492–504; Carpenter, 'Fall of Hubert de Burgh', 5.

[53] Nevill's correspondence is preserved in PRO Special Collections (SC 1), vol. vi, letters 1–162. *Royal Letters*, vol. i, contains a representative selection from this correspondence, including a series of letters between Nevill and his estate steward Simon de Seinliz (271–2, 276–82, 288–9), and a letter from his relative Hugh de Nevill seeking Ralph's help in transferring an assize of false judgement from Nottinghamshire to Leicestershire, so as to remove the plea from the influence of Hugh's enemy, Walter Mauclerc, bishop of Carlisle and the king's treasurer (68).

[54] Carpenter, 'Fall of Hubert de Burgh', 5. Nevill did lose custody of the Great Seal in August 1238, in a quarrel with the king over Nevill's disputed election to the bishopric of Winchester: cf. pp. 129–30 below. He recovered possession of the Seal in May 1242, in the general reconciliation which preceded Henry's expedition to Poitou, and died in office in Feb. 1244.

council.[55] In return, de Burgh lent his tacit support to Longsword's various schemes. In 1221, when the private war between Longsword and Fawkes de Breauté spilled over from Lincolnshire into Devon, the earl of Salisbury recruited a group of local knights which included the acting sheriff of Devon, Robert de Courtenay, to attack and lay waste Fawkes's lands in that county. At the last minute, Salisbury apparently called them off, deciding instead to concentrate his attacks in Lincolnshire. Nonetheless, de Courtenay laid an embargo on all supplies and munitions destined for Fawkes's principal Devonshire castle of Plympton. When challenged by Fawkes's bailiffs, de Courtenay replied that he had a royal warrant for his actions. Fawkes wrote to de Burgh to protest.[56] De Courtenay may have been lying; no such warrant is enrolled on the chancery rolls. But there is no reason to think that such a writ, if indeed it was issued, would ever have been enrolled in the first place. When de Courtenay wrote to de Burgh, he addressed the justiciar as his 'most loved and special friend', an impression suggested also by the tone and nature of their communications.[57] De Burgh's hand cannot be proved to have been behind this embargo, but the circumstances strongly suggest that it was. Fawkes may well have thought so too. Although his letter to de Burgh complains strongly of de Courtenay's actions, it nowhere casts doubt upon de Courtenay's claim to have a royal warrant authorizing them. Fawkes suggests merely that de Burgh, in accordance with 'sound ... and fruitful counsel', should issue orders to de Courtenay to cease and desist from his activities, and to release Fawkes's servants whom he had captured.[58] The curiously flat tone of Fawkes's letter, on which Miss Norgate has remarked,[59] may reflect not so much an acceptance of the legitimacy of private war as an accurate assessment of where the responsibility for de Courtenay's depredations actually lay.

De Burgh's relations with the new Earl Marshal were more complex. Marshal and Longsword were long-standing friends and allies. They had returned together to the royal allegiance in the spring of 1217,

---

[55] It is not clear just when this relationship began. The very warm letter reprinted in *Royal Letters*, vol. i, 135–6 (June 1220?) may reflect a developing relationship rather than a long-standing one. De Burgh's evident reluctance to act against William Longsword in the complicated dispute over Mere in Wiltshire (on which see Holt, *Northerners*, 244–5) may, however, suggest that Longsword and de Burgh were already allies in 1218–19.

[56] We have only Fawkes's version of these events: *Royal Letters*, vol. i, 172–3 (Mar./Apr. 1221?).

[57] 'carissimo et speciali amico': ibid., 160 (1220?).

[58] 'sanum ... consilium et fructuosum': ibid., 173.

[59] Norgate, *Minority of Henry III*, 183.

they had fought together in the Marches of Wales, and they may also have shared a dislike of Fawkes de Breauté's presence in the south-west.[60] There are signs, however, that in the early 1220s the relationship between these two old friends was occasionally strained by Long-sword's exuberant disregard for the laws of the kingdom. In at least one such instance, the Marshal called on de Burgh to mediate, remind-ing him that Longsword had recently sworn, in the justiciar's presence, to disturb the peace of the realm no more.[61] De Burgh's role in formulating Irish policy made him an important man for the Marshal to cultivate, but de Burgh's own family interests there made him for the Marshal at least as much a potential enemy as an ally.[62] De Burgh did play an important role in negotiating the Marshal's marriage with the king's younger sister Eleanor;[63] whether he was also responsible for delaying the marriage almost three years is not known. This marriage was offered to the Marshal partly in compensation for a marriage he had intended to make with the sister of Count Robert of Dreux, which the royal council apparently quashed, and also as a device by which to recover possession of Marlborough Castle and the nearby manor of Ludgershall for the king, both still retained by the Marshal.[64] This mixture of motives, of favouritism and uncertainty, characterized most of de Burgh's relations with the younger Marshal. Although there is no suggestion that the earl was unhappy with the marriage bargain, there are hints during this period that the council remained uncertain of his reliability as a supporter.[65] He was by no means a de Burgh opponent, but he was no firm ally either.

De Burgh's rise to predominance within the minority government was facilitated also by the absence of Earl Ranulf of Chester on crusade. The earl left England in June of 1218, with the great Marshal firmly in command of the country. He did not return until the late

[60] Fawkes and the young Marshal were certainly in conflict in Bedfordshire: cf. *Royal Letters*, vol. i, 175–6; Carpenter, 'Fall of Hubert de Burgh', 4.

[61] *Royal Letters*, vol. i, 178–9. Thomas de Berkeley, heir to the honour of Berkeley, had married a niece of the Marshal. Longsword, however, continued to retain Berkeley Castle in his own hands, refusing to hand it over to Thomas. William Marshal wrote to de Burgh to complain, reminding him that Longsword's oath had been sworn in the justiciar's presence.

[62] J. F. Lydon, *The Lordship of Ireland in the Middle Ages* (Dublin, 1972), 70–8, offers a good short treatment.

[63] *Diplomatic Documents*, no. 140.

[64] Norgate, *Minority of Henry III*, 167–9; Powicke, *Henry III*, 157–8.

[65] *Royal Letters*, vol. i, 244–5, 170–1; Powicke, *Henry III*, 54, n. 1; Noël Denholm-Young, 'A Letter from the Council to Pope Honorius III, 1220–1221', *EHR* 60 (1945), 88–96.

summer or early autumn of 1220. His return added new complications
to court politics, and posed a particular threat to de Burgh, whom
Chester loathed. Chester's animosity towards the *parvenu* de Burgh
may well have been renewed by a complex series of arrangements
made in June and October 1220 between the kings of England and
Scotland, arrangements in which de Burgh played a prominent role,
and by which he profited greatly.[66] The kings of Scotland had a
traditional claim to hold the three northern counties of Northumberland, Cumberland, and Westmoreland. The claim dated back to the
reign of King Stephen, and although it had been abrogated by Henry
II, it had thereafter provoked a number of Scottish incursions into the
area in support of one or another of the English rebellions. In 1209
King John tried to resolve this claim by arranging a marriage between
his son Henry, then rather less than two years of age, and the Scottish
king's sister, Margaret, who was then at least fifteen. Margaret's dowry
was to be the three disputed counties, plus 15,000 marks paid in
advance to King John. Margaret was then sent to the English court to
await her marriage, accompanied by her younger sister Isabella, who
went as a 'spare' should Margaret die before the young Prince Henry
came of age.[67] Ever since, the marriage had been a thorn in relations
between the two courts. With John now dead, no marriage could be
contracted for Henry until his majority; but the Lady Margaret still
required a husband, and the question of the northern counties still
hung fire. The agreement reached between the two kings in June 1220
attempted to resolve these problems.[68] Alexander II was to marry
Henry's sister Joan. Henry would in turn find suitable marriages for
Margaret and her sister Isabella, and provide them with dowries out of
the 15,000 marks the Scottish king had already paid John. If these ladies
could not be appropriately married by October 1221, they were to be
returned to their brother's care in Scotland. Although not a part of
the written treaty, it was apparently also agreed that, in return for
this, Henry would turn over to Alexander custody of the English lands

[66] For an overview of these negotiations and their background, see Norgate, *Minority
of Henry III*, 126–8; E. L. G. Stones, *Anglo-Scottish Relations 1174–1328* (Oxford, 1970),
xlv–xlviii.

[67] Isabella may have been intended as a bride for King John's second son, Richard:
see Stones, *Anglo-Scottish Relations*, xlvi. But in Henry's 1239 charges against Hubert
de Burgh (*CM* vol. vi, 70–1), he states only that Richard was to marry Margaret if
Henry died beforehand. In recounting the terms of this 1220 agreement, Henry said
nothing about Richard marrying Isabella. In 1225, Henry married her to Roger Bigod,
heir to the earldom of Norfolk.

[68] *Foedera*, vol. i, pt. 1, 160–1.

of the late earl of Huntingdon, the Scottish king's uncle, along with the wardship of his heir and his widow.[69] It was at this point that the interests of de Burgh and Chester collided.

The date on which the marriage of Margaret to Hubert de Burgh was proposed is unknown, but it was probably approved in October 1220, when the two kings again met at York.[70] Earl Ranulf had a dual interest in this development. Through his sister Maud, now the widow of the earl of Huntingdon and thus the aunt of Margaret, Chester himself had direct family connections to the Scottish court,[71] and he may well have regarded the marriage itself as disparaging. For this supposition, there is no proof. There are, however, clear signs that he was concerned about the disposition of the custody of the lands, widow, and heir of the earl of Huntingdon, now in the gift of Alexander. There is also reason to think that Alexander planned to grant this custody to Hubert de Burgh. The chief castle of the Huntingdon honour was Fotheringay, which had been in the custody of William Marshal the younger since 1217. The rest of the honour had been handed back to the earl of Huntingdon in 1217, and on his death had passed to the king of England in custody. The Marshal, nevertheless, retained Fotheringay until late November 1220. When finally he did hand over the castle, however, it was not to King Alexander, but to a representative of Hubert de Burgh, who must have had the Scottish king's permission to receive and hold it.[72] This

[69] *Patent Rolls 1216–25*, 236; *Rot. Litt. Claus.*, vol. i, 429b. In 1237, when the next earl of Huntingdon died, custody of the Huntingdon honour and its caput at Fotheringay was immediately recognized as belonging to the king of Scots: cf. *CPR 1232–47*, 186.

[70] The principal purpose of this second meeting was to hand over to Alexander his promised bride, Joan, who had been detained by her mother in Poitou as a hostage against the latter's dower claims. Joan did not, in fact, arrive back in England in time for the Oct. meeting, and her marriage was therefore delayed until June 1221, when it was celebrated at York. Hubert de Burgh married Margaret of Scotland in York at the same time. De Burgh's marriage had obviously been arranged at some date prior to June 1221, and since the two kings did not meet between Oct. 1220 and the following June, the former becomes the most likely date when the match between de Burgh and the lady Margaret might have been agreed. On the date of de Burgh's marriage, see *Walter of Coventry*, vol. ii, 250 (the Barnwell chronicler); *CM*, vol. iii, 66–7.

[71] A fact noted by the Barnwell chronicler in connection with his account of the subsequent revolt of the count of Aumâle: cf. *Walter of Coventry*, vol. ii, 248. The Barnwell chronicler is by far our most reliable source for these years.

[72] Norgate presumes, and I agree, that Gregory de la Tour was a representative of Hubert de Burgh: *Minority of Henry III*, 163. Gregory received custody of the castle from William Marshal on 23 or 24 Nov. 1220: cf. *Patent Rolls 1216–25*, 272; *Rot. Litt. Claus.*, vol. i, 442. De Burgh had custody of the castle when Aumâle seized it in Jan. 1221: *Walter of Coventry*, vol. ii, 247. For further evidence that it was Alexander, and

development must in turn have raised Chester's anxieties about the ultimate guardianship of his sister and nephew, especially if, as seems likely, the marriage between de Burgh and Margaret of Scotland had already been agreed.

This background sheds new light on the otherwise quite baffling revolt of the count of Aumâle in December and January 1220–1. As with so many of the disturbances in these years, this one had its origins in a dispute over the custody of a castle, in this case Bytham Castle in Lincolnshire.[73] Historians have tended to discount the threat to the realm which this very curious incident posed. Powicke's verdict on the count is typical: 'There was no substance in him or his cause. A little plain speaking and a little firm action were sufficient to overthrow him.'[74] To be sure, when one knows that it failed, the revolt does have its absurd aspects. A solitary rebel, without allies, incapable of taking three of the four castles he attacked, who nonetheless issued letters of peace to all the merchants of England to pass freely between his castles, must invite derision.[75] Contemporary chroniclers, however, portray the revolt as a much more closely run thing than it has subsequently appeared to its historians.[76] The key to Aumâle's failure was his inability to attract allies to his cause. The Barnwell chronicler, however, did not believe that in the beginning Aumâle had acted alone: 'He did this, however, so it is said, by the counsel of many of the magnates of England, both native and foreign....'[77] Who these magnates were is nowhere stated, and one cannot be certain that they existed. But there is reason to think that Aumâle may have pinned his hopes on Chester siding with him. Why else would he have bothered to attack Fotheringay Castle, rout the garrison which de Burgh had installed there, and install his own? And why too would he have abandoned it, without damage, immediately upon hearing that a royal army, accompanied by Chester, was advancing against him? The castle had no strategic importance in the context of Aumâle's revolt, and

---

not Henry, who committed Fotheringay to de Burgh, see *CPR 1232–47*, 186; and *CM*, vol. iii, 618–20.

[73] The clearest narrative of this revolt is Turner, 'William de Forz', 238–41.

[74] Powicke, *Henry III*, 54.

[75] *Walter of Coventry*, vol. ii, 247.

[76] The only two chronicles which contain a reliable record of this revolt are from Barnwell (*Walter of Coventry*, vol. ii, 247–8) and Dunstable (*AM*, vol. iii, 63–4). The account given by Roger of Wendover is hopelessly confused with the events of 1223–4, and must be ignored.

[77] 'Hoc autem faciebat, ut dicebatur, per consilium plurimorum magnatum Angliae tam indigenarum quam alienigenarum ...': *Walter of Coventry*, vol. ii, 247.

had no bearing at all on the question of the custody of Bytham Castle, which had been the catalyst for the rebellion. It is of course possible that Aumâle's motive in attacking Fotheringay was simply to revenge himself upon de Burgh for the judicial decision which had deprived him of Bytham. But if Aumâle knew, as he must have known (he was present at the June 1220 negotiations, and at the October meeting at York), that Chester suspected de Burgh of attempting to seize the custody of Fotheringay Castle and the honour of Huntingdon, he may well have attacked Fotheringay on the gamble that, by so doing, he would bring Chester into the struggle on his side.

In the event, Aumâle guessed wrong. Chester joined in excommunicating Aumâle, and played a key military role in suppressing his revolt. But the tone of the Barnwell chronicler's account of Chester's decision suggests that matters were very delicately poised at this moment, and that the royal council and the countryside alike were waiting to see how the newly returned Chester would decide to act in this circumstance.[78] Had he thrown his weight behind Aumâle, the count might well have won his case. But once Chester decided against him, his cause was lost. Aside from Aumâle's excommunication, which probably weighed more heavily with the chronicler than it did with Chester, the motives ascribed to the latter in deciding as he did are plausible enough: anger at Aumâle's evident contempt for royal authority, and anger also at the attack on Fotheringay, which still belonged of right to Chester's nephew, whether or not it was temporarily in the hands of de Burgh. The Fotheringay gambit therefore backfired on Aumâle; but in so far as no one could be entirely sure what role the newly returned earl of Chester might decide to play in the royal council, the gamble may still have been worth taking. In the end, Aumâle's revolt benefited Chester. Within a month, the king of Scots had granted

---

[78] 'Quod cernentes quidam regni proceres, et comitem ab errore suo revocare sperantes, ad reformandam pacem inter dominum regem et illum mediatores se exhibuerunt. Sed illis inaniter laborantibus, comes Cestrensis, qui cum aliis proceribus in hoc concilio praesens aderat, audita comitis excommunicati et suorum obstinatione et violentia tam divitum quam pauperum depraedatione, multipliciter exacerbatus est, tum quia cernebat dominum suum regem propter ipsius juventutum contemptui haberi, tum propter castelli de Fodringhe [Fotheringay], quod jus haereditarium erat nepotis sui, fraudulentam occupationem. Unde domino legato et regi fideliter promisit, quod omnes vires suas exponeret ad comitis praefati et suorum expugnationem. Set et quamplures Angliae magnates ipsius commendabilem audientes compromissionem fidelemque constantiam, pari modo ad regis obsequium se devoverunt, quia comes excommunicatus et sui a multo tempore exosi habebantur tam ab ecclesiasticis quam a saecularibus personis, quibus damna et contumelias graves ingesserant, nullo existente qui errata corrigeret.' *Walter of Coventry*, vol. ii, 248.

him the custody of his sister, his nephew, and the honour of Huntingdon, including Fotheringay Castle.[79] De Burgh seems never to have
recovered custody of Fotheringay after Aumâle took it from him.[80]

This was, however, but a temporary set-back for the justiciar.
Chester's readiness to stand by the young king may even have embold-
ened de Burgh in his next moves against his principal rival on the
council, the bishop of Winchester. Philip d'Albini, the bishop's firmest
ally on the council, took the Cross early in 1221, intending to set out
for the Holy Land as soon as the bishop returned from his own
pilgrimage to Compostella. This eliminated one de Burgh opponent,
at least for the foreseeable future. While the bishop was in Spain, de
Burgh took steps to remove two more of the bishop's supporters in
the shires. Peter de Maulay had been custodian of Corfe Castle since
1215, where he guarded not only King Henry's brother Richard but
also the king's first cousin, Eleanor of Brittany, whose claim to the
English throne was arguably stronger than Henry's own.[81] At the
Whitsun court in 1221, Richard de Mucegros, a Dorsetshire knight,
suddenly brought treason charges against de Maulay and the absent
bishop of Winchester, alleging that the two of them had conspired to
release Eleanor from Corfe Castle and spirit her away to France. The
bishop's pilgrimage, it was alleged, was only a ruse to conceal his real
intentions in travelling out of the kingdom.[82] Fawkes de Breauté later
claimed that this charge had been manufactured at the instigation of
de Burgh, 'with his accomplices'.[83] There is no direct proof for this,
but the circumstances of the charge must raise that suspicion. De
Maulay was compelled to resign his custody of Corfe Castle with all
its contents into the hands of the king through the justiciar, Longsword,
the Earl Marshal, and William Brewer.[84] He was left in possession of
the sheriffdom of Dorset and Somerset, but only until November, when
he cleared himself of all charges, but was forced nonetheless to resign
his shrievalty to Roger de la Forde, a local shire knight. In January

---

[79] *Patent Rolls 1216–25*, 285.

[80] When the royal army, accompanied by Chester but not by de Burgh, recaptured
Fotheringay, temporary custody of the castle was entrusted to Fawkes de Breauté: AM,
vol. iii, 64.

[81] Eleanor was the daughter of Geoffrey of Brittany, son of Henry II. Geoffrey was
the next elder brother to John.

[82] *Walter of Coventry*, vol. ii, 250–1; AM, vol. iii, 75. The bishop's pilgrimage is
confirmed in the Annals of Winchester, AM, vol. ii, 84.

[83] '... cum complicibus suis': *Walter of Coventry*, vol. ii, 259–60 (Fawkes's *Querimonia* to the pope).

[84] *Patent Rolls 1216–25*, 320.

1222, he was deprived of his final office, the custody of Sherborne Castle in Dorset. Thereafter, he remained out of favour at court until 1232, when the fall of Hubert de Burgh paved the way for de Maulay's return.

Engelard de Cigogné, another of John's Poitevin captains and also a des Roches ally, was arrested about the same time as de Maulay.[85] Engelard, however, was quickly released from prison after giving security that he would resign custody of Windsor Castle at the king's command. Four months later, he was sent on an embassy to Poitou. But he was not called upon actually to surrender the castle at Windsor until almost two years later.

The charges against both de Maulay and de Cigogné were groundless, but they served their purpose. When Peter des Roches returned from his pilgrimage, the council declared his tutelage of the king to be at an end. From that date on, complained Fawkes afterward, 'the king began to adhere firmly to the counsels of the justiciar and his accomplices'.[86] Within a month, Pandulf had resigned his legation, and de Burgh stood alone at the head of the king's government. The reins of power were now firmly in his hands.

De Burgh had attained this position by skilfully playing upon the strengths inherent in his offices, and by carefully fostering the interest of William Longsword and the younger Marshal. He maintained his position with the powerful and at times decisive support of the archbishop of Canterbury, Stephen Langton. Langton's overriding personal objective in the years after Pandulf's resignation was to prevent the return of a papal legate to England.[87] Langton did of course have an interest in preserving domestic peace and in creating a stable foundation for royal government; but these wider, 'national' interests, so often emphasized by his biographers, were nonetheless precisely the conditions which would best guarantee that no new legate would be sent to England to threaten Langton's ecclesiastical primacy.[88] But to des Roches, the earl of Chester, and the other great men displaced

---

[85] *AM*, vol. iii, 68.

[86] '... coepit idem rex justiciarii complicumque suorum consiliis inhaerere': *Walter of Coventry*, vol. ii, 260 (Fawkes's *Querimonia*).

[87] The Dunstable annalist says that Langton obtained a papal privilege to this effect in Rome in 1221: *AM*, vol. iii, 74.

[88] Compare F. M. Powicke, *Stephen Langton* (Oxford, 1928), 145–60, esp. 145–7, for a different explanation for Langton's efforts to bring Pandulf's legation to an end. Opposition to papal legates was a very long-standing policy at Canterbury; it should not be surprising that Langton shared this attitude.

during the next few years by de Burgh and his followers, a new papal legate began to seem the only potential counterweight to the justiciar's primacy in the royal council. Their efforts to secure the appointment of such a legate pushed Langton ever more firmly into de Burgh's camp.[89]

By Christmas 1221, the tensions resulting from this change in the balance of power on the council were evident to all. The Christmas court, as in past years, was held at Winchester. But this year, for the first time, the king and his party stayed, not at the bishop's palace, but rather in the royal palace, which was specially refurbished for the occasion. During the festivities, a violent quarrel broke out between the earl of Salisbury on the one hand, supported by de Burgh, and the earl of Chester on the other. What started the quarrel we are not told. The Barnwell chronicler is our only authority for the episode, and he hints darkly at the influence of 'foreigners' on Chester. It was, however, a serious matter. Longsword and de Burgh, described by the chronicler as 'regis rectores et regni' (a significant plural), prepared their 'followers' (*sequela*) for battle with Chester.[90] Langton brought the two sides together by pronouncing a general excommunication, with his suffragan bishops, against all disturbers of the king's peace. But the hostility which existed between the contending parties could not be so easily swept away.

By the end of 1222, the divisions at court had begun to affect not only the shires and shire office but, much more importantly, the relations of the English court with Llewellyn of Wales. In November 1222, de Burgh sent an order to William Marshal, requesting that he resign his custody of Caerleon Castle to the king. The Marshal may already have been in Ireland, preparing to spend the winter on his lands there; at any rate, he ignored the order. While the Marshal was away, however, Llewellyn of Wales took the opportunity to launch a full-scale assault on the Marches of Wales. De Burgh and a royal army marched to Shrewsbury, but delayed when the earl of Chester offered to act as surety for Llewellyn's appearance in the king's court to answer for his attacks. Soon after, the Earl Marshal arrived in south Wales from Ireland with a large army. When Llewellyn failed to appear on the promised day, the Earl Marshal attacked and took both Cardigan and Carmarthen Castles from him. These were royal castles, which the Marshal's father had entrusted to Llewellyn as custodian during

---

[89] *Walter of Coventry*, vol. ii, 261–2.
[90] Ibid., 251; notice the factional connotations of the noun *sequela*.

the regency. The war between the Marshal and Llewellyn continued throughout the rest of 1223, in most respects a typical marcher war.[91] It became rather more than that, however, by virtue of the influence which court politics had on it. William Longsword and William Marshal jointly led a force into south Wales, composed indifferently of Marshal retainers and royally summoned troops. Hubert de Burgh brought the king himself into the campaign, and began building a new royal castle at Montgomery, under his own direct control. Chester, however, played little or no role in the campaigns. His nephew, heir to the earldom of Huntingdon, was married to a daughter of Llewellyn. Moreover, he had no great desire to secure the interests of his own greatest rival on the Marches, the Earl Marshal, in a war against Llewellyn. The successful results of this royal campaign on the Marches, combined with the grant to the Earl Marshal of the custody of Cardigan and Carmarthen Castles in November 1223, sealed the alliance between the Marshal and de Burgh,[92] and completed the isolation of Chester from the court.

Events now moved swiftly to their factional climax. In April 1223, the pope had sent four virtually identical letters to England, one addressed jointly to de Burgh, des Roches, and William Brewer, one to the earl of Chester, one to the other earls, barons, and freemen of England, and a fourth, dealing specifically with matters affecting the great seal, to Ralph de Nevill, the acting chancellor.[93] These letters declared Henry to be of age; they gave him full control over the royal seal, and they ordered all those who held lands or castles from the king to resign their custodies to him. Although these letters were not formally proclaimed until early December 1223,[94] word of their contents had probably leaked out well before then, especially if the earl of Chester had in fact received the copy of the letter addressed to him. Otherwise, it is hard to understand why the revocation of the custodies of Gloucester and Hereford Castles in November 1223 stirred up so much resistance on the part of Chester and his supporters. They

---

[91] The best account of these campaigns is in R. F. Walker, 'The Anglo-Welsh Wars, 1217–1267' (unpublished University of Oxford D. Phil. thesis, 1954). See also the same author's article on 'Hubert de Burgh and Wales, 1218–1232' *EHR* 87 (1972), 465–94. I am grateful to Dr Walker for permission to use his thesis.

[92] See also Carpenter, 'Fall of Hubert de Burgh', 4–5. In May 1224, de Burgh sent William Marshal to Ireland as the new justiciar for that kingdom: *Patent Rolls 1216–25*, 437.

[93] These letters are misdated in the *Red Book of the Exchequer*; for important commentary on them, see Norgate, *Minority of Henry III*, 202–3, 286–90.

[94] Compare Norgate, *Minority of Henry III*, 202–7, with Powicke, *Henry III*, 57–9.

had accepted such individual resumptions before, albeit grudgingly; but this time these two resumptions drove them into open revolt. They must have had some reason to believe that, with the Welsh war now over, these two revocations were but the first drops of rain in an approaching storm which would soon wash away almost all their custodies and castles.

The interests of William Marshal bulked large in both of these critical resumptions. Walter de Lacy, the dispossessed constable of Hereford Castle, was the brother of the exiled earl of Ulster, Hugh de Lacy, who had recently returned to Ireland illegally from enforced exile. Hugh de Lacy was the principal rival to the Marshal interests in Ireland; it was to control the revolt Hugh de Lacy had stirred up that William Marshal had journeyed to Ireland in the winter of 1222–3.[95] On 15 November 1223, Walter de Lacy was compelled to hand over Hereford Castle to the household steward Ralph fitz Nicholas. Six weeks later, it was in the hands of the justiciar.[96] Gloucester Castle, however, was held, not by a Marshal enemy, but by Ralph Musard, an old Marshal retainer and one of the elder Marshal's most intimate advisers. It is not clear why de Burgh revoked this castle also. It may have been to give an impression of even-handedness in his treatment of Walter de Lacy. What is clear is that the order to revoke Gloucester Castle was never enforced. When in early December 1223 an armed uprising by Chester and his party threatened the justiciar's safety, he and the young king retreated to the security of Gloucester Castle, still safely held for them by Ralph Musard.[97] Musard remained in unmolested custody of Gloucester until 1225.

For whatever reason, the orders revoking these two castles appear to have been the final straw for Chester and his allies. While de Burgh and the king were shut up in Gloucester Castle, the earl of Chester, joined by the earl of Gloucester and the count of Aumâle, and by Fawkes de Breauté, Engelard de Cigogné, Brian de Lisle, Robert de Vieuxpont, John de Lacy, Peter de Maulay, Philip Mark, William Cantilupe, and his son William, made an armed demonstration against the Tower of London.[98] This brought de Burgh and the king back to

[95] Lydon, *Lordship of Ireland*, 72–3.

[96] *Patent Rolls 1216–25*, 414, 419. Fawkes de Breauté is our only literary source for these incidents: *Walter of Coventry*, vol. ii, 261. See also Norgate, *Minority of Henry III*, 203–4.

[97] *Patent Rolls 1216–25*, 71.

[98] The fullest account of these events is in the Annals of Dunstable, *AM*, vol. iii, 83–4. There is additional information in *Walter of Coventry*, vol. ii, 252–3; in Fawkes's

London, where the archbishop of Canterbury brought the two sides together at a council. Chester and his allies demanded the dismissal of de Burgh, accusing him of wasting the king's treasure and of oppressing the kingdom with unjust laws. At this point a violent altercation broke out between Peter des Roches and de Burgh. De Burgh accused the bishop of being the author of all the troubles which had disturbed the realm since the death of John. Des Roches replied by declaring that if it cost him all he had, he would bring de Burgh to his knees. With this, des Roches stalked from the council chamber, followed by the barons and earls of Chester's party. Langton arranged a truce to last until mid-January; but the real test of strength between the two sides came with their rival Christmas courts. De Burgh's party, aided by the Marshal, Longsword, the Earl Warenne, and most of the other English earls, decisively outnumbered the followers whom Chester was able to gather at Leicester.[99] On 29 December, after receiving assurances from Langton that any resignations and redistributions of castles would be handled fairly and equally, Chester's party capitulated. A few weeks later, they sent Robert Passelewe and the knight Robert of Kent to Rome to plead for a papal legate to be sent to England.[100]

The massive redistribution of castle custodies and shrievalties which followed the surrender of Chester's party marks a watershed in the history of the minority.[101] Changes on this scale were clearly desirable, not only to preserve royal rights in the localities, but also to safeguard the private rights of local men from oppression by a too long-serving royal official. Moreover, there is much evidence to suggest that some of John's old wartime captains were particularly rapacious administrators in the shires.[102] Their removal from office cleared the way for aggrieved local men to bring charges against them. So long as the sheriff against whom complaints were made was himself the man who executed the writs of complaint, there was little future in trying to

Querimonia, ibid., 261–2; in Ralph of Coggeshall, *Chronicon Anglicanum*, ed. Joseph Stevenson (London, 1875), 203–4; and in *CM*, vol. iii, 83.

[99] Carpenter, 'Fall of Hubert de Burgh', 3–4.

[100] *Walter of Coventry*, vol. ii, 262 (Fawkes's *Querimonia*); Annals of Dunstable, *AM*, vol. iii, 89; *Diplomatic Documents*, no. 136.

[101] There is a useful table of these changes in an appendix to *Royal Letters*, vol. i, 508–16.

[102] Turner, 'Minority of Henry III', underestimated these dangers, which have been most clearly pointed out by Carpenter, 'Sheriffs of Oxfordshire', 148–89. See also Maitland, *Pleas of the Crown for Gloucester*, xvi–xvii; J. C. Holt, 'Philip Mark and the Shrievalty of Nottinghamshire and Derbyshire', *Transactions of the Thoroton Society* 56 (1952), 18ff.; and Holt, *Northerners*, 228–30.

right such wrongs. The removal of men like Fawkes de Breauté brought a flood of charges of local abuse into the courts against them. That relatively few such charges were brought against the displaced allies of de Burgh might suggest that their standards of conduct in local office were generally higher. Perhaps they were, but it is more likely that the charges brought in 1224 reflected the accuracy of local men's perceptions as to the chances of winning the cases they brought. The changes in 1223–4 left no doubt whose party was in, and whose was out. This was the time for those with complaints against the losers to bring them forward. A chance to complain of abuses by those now in power might perhaps come later.

This spate of judicial cases against the displaced administrators came in to a judicial system headed by de Burgh. Most of the complainants probably needed no specific urging by the justiciar to come forward, but some of the complaints against Fawkes de Breauté do bear the marks of the justiciar's orchestration. In a council held at London in April 1224, Langton had secured promises of reconciliation and forgiveness from all the parties involved in the recent disputes. Three days later, an eight-year-old charge of murder was laid before the king himself against Fawkes de Breauté. Writs were immediately issued by de Burgh, ordering the new sheriff of Bedfordshire to compel Fawkes to stand trial concerning the charge.[103] Soon thereafter, de Burgh assigned as royal justice on assize a well-known enemy of Fawkes and his brother William to hear sixteen separate cases of novel disseisin which had been brought in Bedfordshire alone against the de Breauté brothers. The judge found against them on every single one.[104] In the meantime, de Burgh had received two virtually identical letters, one from William Marshal, the other from William Longsword, each complaining that Fawkes had disseised John Marshal of his lands and forest at Norton, and alleging that Fawkes had declared he would pay no attention if John Marshal brought thirty pairs of royal letters ordering his reinstatement. These two letters are so similar that they can only have been prepared from a common original.[105] Longsword and Marshal may have prepared the letters themselves, or else de

---

[103] Fawkes's *Querimonia* in *Walter of Coventry*, vol. ii, 263–4, confirmed by the writs entered on *Rott. Litt. Claus.*, vol. ii, 72b, 73. On these writs, see the discussion by Norgate, *Minority of Henry III*, 230 n. 2.

[104] *Querimonia* in *Walter of Coventry*, vol. ii, 264; Coggeshall, *Chronicon Anglicanum*, 204–8; and see Norgate, *Minority of Henry III*, 230–1. The irregularity of these cases is well brought out in Turner, *The King and his Courts*, 206–7.

[105] *Royal Letters*, vol. i, 220–2.

Burgh may have solicited them. But the impression of a co-ordinated attack on Fawkes de Breauté, stage-managed by de Burgh, is difficult to avoid.

A royal army had already mustered at Northampton when the news reached court that William de Breauté had kidnapped the royal judge who had pronounced the sixteen verdicts against him, and had imprisoned him in Bedford Castle. This army had been summoned to Northampton ostensibly to go to the aid of Poitou, at that moment being overrun by the armies of Louis VIII of France. But in fact, as Miss Norgate has shown, 'The barons were summoned to Northampton because their help was wanted in the execution of a project predetermined in the royal Council, for the ruin of Faulkes de Breauté'.[106] Langton and his suffragan bishops of Bath and Salisbury immediately excommunicated Fawkes, the legal castellan of Bedford, as a disturber of the peace, even though he was not personally involved in the judge's kidnapping. The royal army then invested the castle. During the eight-week siege that followed, Poitou was lost to Louis, a fact not lost on the pope, who complained in strong terms both to the king and to Langton that it was foolish to expend so much energy on civil war when the defence of the king's lands was in jeopardy.[107]

The siege of Bedford demonstrated the rifts which by now divided the great men of the land, and which would continue to divide them until 1236.[108] Fawkes, now a fugitive, sought through the earl of Chester and the bishop of Winchester a respite from the king's court in which to answer the charges against him. Their request was refused. Chester, Aumâle, des Roches, William de Cantilupe, Brian de Lisle, Peter de Maulay, and others of the participants in the November 1223 demonstration against the Tower answered the king's summons to Northampton, and accompanied the army to Bedford. But on finding that their voices went unheard in the king's councils, the bishop and Chester left the army and returned home, accompanied by their followers. As the siege dragged on into August, Earl Ranulf sent a civil and gracious letter to King Henry, declaring that he remained the king's loyal servant on the Marches as elsewhere, but that he believed Henry's anger against Fawkes to be unjustified.[109] When the royal army finally did take Bedford, Henry hanged the entire garrison, except

---

[106] Norgate, *Minority of Henry III*, 236. On the loss of Poitou, see Ch. 5 below.

[107] *Royal Letters*, vol. i, 543–45.

[108] Carpenter, 'Fall of Hubert de Burgh', *passim*.

[109] *Royal Letters*, vol. i, 233–5.

for three men whom he cut down and sent to join the Templars in the Holy Land. Fawkes threw himself on the king's mercy and was exiled from the realm, after first giving an oath to Langton that he would not appeal to the pope against this sentence, or seek to introduce a papal legate into the realm.[110] Fawkes went to Rome nonetheless; in his plea to the pope, he portrayed Stephen Langton as the villain of the plot which brought him down, aided and abetted in this design by two other unnamed bishops, probably Jocelyn of Bath and Wells, and Richard le Poore, bishop of Salisbury.[111] The pope took Fawkes's side in the dispute, and sent several critical letters to Langton and the king, decrying this unnecessary attack against a loyal servant of the king. But it did no good, and Fawkes died before the campaign for his reinstatement could progress very far.[112]

De Burgh and Langton had swept all opposition before them.[113] The purge of 1223–4 extended not only to the shires and the castles, but even to the offices of the king's household.[114] The result was that de Burgh was now free, if he chose, to take fairly radical measures to reform the financial system at Westminster and in the shires, as a first step toward resolving the chronic poverty which had dogged the king's government throughout the minority. That de Burgh did not do so says much about the man, but even more about the extent to which the factional struggles of the preceding years continued to circumscribe the policies of the king's ministers, even after the triumph of the justiciar's faction at court. The few procedural changes which de Burgh did introduce at the exchequer after 1224 were in fact a return to procedures which more venturesome administrators had previously abandoned.[115] De Burgh's fundamentally conservative approach to financing royal government did have some advantages. It did not raise opposition in the shires, and it did not press too heavily upon the great

[110] Fawkes's *Querimonia* in *Walter of Coventry*, vol. ii, 270.

[111] The bishop of Bath appears almost as frequently as the archbishop of Canterbury in Fawkes's *Querimonia*: cf. especially 267–8, 270 in *Walter of Coventry*, vol. ii. After Langton, Bath and Salisbury were the two most prominent bishops at court during these years, and were closely involved in the events at Northampton and Bedford: cf. *Diplomatic Documents*, no. 149. Both were close allies of de Burgh: cf. Carpenter, 'Fall of Hubert de Burgh', 4.

[112] *Diplomatic Documents*, nos. 149, 153, 182–5, 190, 203.

[113] Carpenter, 'Fall of Hubert de Burgh', 2–4.

[114] T. F. Tout, *Chapters in the Administrative History of Mediaeval England* (6 vols., Manchester, 1920–33), vol. i, 188–91.

[115] Mabel H. Mills, 'Experiments in Exchequer Procedure, 1200–1232', *TRHS*, 4th s., 8 (1925), 165–6.

men of the land.[116] It did not, therefore, repeat the mistakes of John's reign. Nor did it threaten de Burgh's own personal control over the government by raising the spectre of revolt. To this extent, it may be judged a success. But it did not resolve the problem of the king's poverty either, and in this respect, de Burgh's regime was a dismal failure, a fact which even the king himself finally came to recognize. When he did, de Burgh's fall followed swiftly.

The only major financial reform imposed by de Burgh after 1224 was to add a separate, additional sum, known as 'profits', to the established shire farms owed yearly by the sheriffs.[117] This policy had been followed with considerable financial success for a few years after 1204 by King John, but it had met with opposition not only from the men of the shires, who indirectly had to pay these increments, but also from the great curial officials, for whom a shrievalty was a source of profit and local patronage.[118] In the 1215 version of Magna Carta, the king's right to impose such profits had been abolished. But this clause was dropped in the 1216 reissue, and hence from all subsequent versions of the Charter. De Burgh's reintroduction of the policy in 1224 was a positive step, but a characteristically hesitant one. He could not afford to abandon the shires as sources of patronage for his supporters. He could not, therefore, raise the profits to levels which would preclude his supporters from making an appropriate personal gain from their shrieval offices. De Burgh's increments were therefore very modest; and in cases where the shire was held by an important curial official, the allowance granted the sheriff for keeping the shire usually matched most, if not all, of the profits he owed beyond the farm.[119] The king's finances therefore showed little overall improvement from de Burgh's new increments. The grant of a fifteenth from both clergy and laity in 1225, in return for royal confirmation of the charters, eased the financial squeeze somewhat.[120] But the financial system of the minority could not support the costs involved in a major war. Even the relatively modest operation mounted in 1225 to attempt

---

[116] David A. Carpenter, 'The Decline of the Curial Sheriff in England, 1194–1258', *EHR* 91 (1976), 1–32; Maddicott, 'Magna Carta and the Local Community', 28–30, 40.

[117] Mills, 'Experiments ... 1200–1232', 166–8.

[118] Brian E. Harris, 'King John and the Sheriffs' Farms', *EHR* 79 (1964), 532–42; and pp. 49–51 below.

[119] Carpenter, 'Curial Sheriff', 10–13.

[120] Fred A. Cazel, Jr., 'The Fifteenth of 1225', *BIHR* 34 (1961), 67–81. Most of the proceeds from this tax went to defray the costs of Richard of Cornwall's 1225–7 Gascon expedition.

the recovery of Poitou strained the royal finances to their limits.[121] The king's campaign in Brittany in 1230 brought a complete financial collapse.

The changes of 1223–4 also brought change in the personnel who dominated the king's council at Westminster. The earl of Chester and the bishop of Winchester ceased to be influential figures at court. The Earl Marshal, meanwhile, had never been a regular attender on the king, and in the years after 1223 his interests in Ireland and on the Marches kept him away from the court even more. The earl of Salisbury was ageing and unwell; a year in Gascony, followed by many weeks of misery crossing the sea, completed his demise. He died early in 1226. Except for de Burgh, the great men who had made up the royal council in the early years of the minority were thus gone by 1225. Their place was taken by a rising and ambitious group of household stewards: Ralph fitz Nicholas, Godfrey de Craucombe, and William de Cantilupe.[122] These were the men who benefited most from de Burgh's government after 1225, acquiring on favourable terms shrievalties, castle custodies, farms of Crown lands, and keeperships of royal manors. They served occasionally as judges, frequently as diplomatic envoys, and, with the king's majority in January 1227, as witnesses to royal charters. They did not have the influence of de Burgh, Ralph de Nevill, or perhaps even of Walter Mauclerc, bishop of Carlisle and royal treasurer, with respect to the greatest offices. They were, however, an important and accessible link between local society in the shires and the royal court. As such, they were influential people in both worlds, a source of patronage and promotion for local worthies, and a barometer of local political opinion for de Burgh and the king.

Henry III declared his majority in January 1227, but the declaration changed little with respect to the power which de Burgh and the household stewards wielded over his government. The immediate

[121] The expedition comprised fewer than seventy knights, but still cost the English exchequer about £36,000, a sum which consumed almost the entire proceeds of the fifteenth: cf. Noël Denholm-Young, *Richard of Cornwall* (Oxford, 1947), 4–8; Sydney Knox Mitchell, *Studies in Taxation under John and Henry III*, (New Haven, 1914), 168–9; and for the yield of the fifteenth Cazel, 'The Fifteenth of 1225', 67–81, who finds it to have been about £39,200.

[122] The late C. A. F. Meekings compiled detailed biographical studies of Henry III's stewards. A small portion of this material appears in the introduction to *CRR*, vol. 15, xxxvii–xxxix; at present the rest are available only in manuscript at the PRO in London. The only other adequate study of a household steward is Dr Carpenter's treatment of Godfrey de Craucombe in 'Sheriffs of Oxfordshire', 214–46, 255–74. The pioneering account by Tout, *Chapters*, vol. i, 201–5, is unreliable.

purpose of the declaration may even have been to raise money, by calling in all extant royal charters for confirmation and re-sealing. The only policy change occasioned by the king's majority was the series of inquests which Henry himself launched into the bounds of the royal forest. In keeping with the terms of the 1217 Forest Charter, renewed along with the Great Charter in 1225, the forest bounds had been perambulated and defined by juries of local knights. The young king suspected that much royal forest had been lost in these proceedings, and over the next twelve months he forced numerous revisions in the forest boundaries, inspiring much popular ill will in the process. But to the 'structure of politics' at court, the king's majority made little immediate difference. Partly this was because Henry came of age so gradually, and so often.[123] Factional struggles had time with each stage to adjust to the new circumstances of a slightly more powerful king, and to try to bend the new situation to their advantage. Partly, too, it was because the young king brought no independent party with him to power in 1227. He therefore had no choice but to rule through the men already established in office. His majority did, however, offer entirely new prospects for promotion and advancement. The king could now confer permanent titles and dignities, and make grants in perpetuity. An unseemly scramble ensued in the early months of 1227 to secure as many of the newly available prizes as possible. Characteristically, de Burgh came away with the biggest prize. On 14 February, Henry created him earl of Kent.

Henry's majority had one other effect. For the first time since 1216, it re-created a royal household distinct from the justiciarship. In this respect, it created a new and potentially deadly threat to de Burgh's control over the government. After 1227, there would always be at least two avenues of approach to the king, one leading through the justiciar, the other leading directly to the king through his own servants and household men. Wielding influence at court therefore became more complicated after 1227, and began to require almost continuous attention. The question of who was in attendance on the king on any given day becomes an increasingly important one, as the men around the court fought either to acquire or to retain favour and office. The king's own volatile temper, coupled with a tendency to be swayed by the last advice he had taken or by the saddest story he heard from a

---

[123] Partial declarations of the king's majority were made in 1220, 1221, 1223, and perhaps also in 1225, with the reissue of the Charters. See Norgate, *Minority of Henry III, passim.*

competing claimant, further increased the uncertainties of office-holding around his court. Even life-grants, renewed at frequent intervals by the king himself, were insufficient to allay the general sense of insecurity which resulted among the king's officials. Such insecurities aggravated further the scramble for office and favour, and thus contributed to the general atmosphere of uncertainty around the court.

The deleterious effect of this struggle on the tottering royal finances is writ large across the records of these years. Henry's expenses, meanwhile, were steadily mounting. In 1225 he had created his brother Richard earl of Cornwall, and alienated the revenues of the county to him. The war in Gascony was a continuous drain on the royal purse between 1225 and 1227. When a truce was finally sealed, the money which previously had gone to Gascony was redirected instead to pay the fees of the king's household knights, a force which Henry began to reconstitute soon after his declaration of majority.[124] Some kind of financial equilibrium seems to have been maintained, but only so long as the kingdom could avoid war in Wales or, worse, on the Continent. De Burgh may have realized this fact. Henry, if he did, did not care. His 1230 attempt to recover Brittany and the other French lands lost by his father was a failure. In 1229 de Burgh made insufficient preparations for the expedition, forcing its postponement; in 1230, when the force finally did depart, the chance was wasted.[125] When the king returned, penniless, he was faced immediately with war on the Marches. The royal finances, structured primarily to ensure the continuance of de Burgh's control over the government, were simply inadequate to cope with these new demands. By the spring of 1232, the king's government was in a state of complete financial collapse.[126]

In the end, de Burgh's regime fell victim to its own fiscal paralysis, itself the product of the essentially factional nature of his position at court. De Burgh could not provide the funds Henry needed even to defend his borders against the Welsh, much less to recover the overseas lands of his ancestors, except at the cost of reforms which would put at risk the justiciar's support at court or in the countryside. De Burgh's failure in March 1232 to win approval from the magnates for a fortieth on moveables for the king emphasized the precarious nature of his position, at a time when the king's own military failures in Brittany and Wales, combined with his now desperate poverty, were lending a

---

[124] Walker, 'Anglo-Welsh Wars', 79.
[125] On this expedition, see Ch. 5 below.
[126] Carpenter, 'Fall of Hubert de Burgh', 7.

particular urgency to his search for an alternative to de Burgh. It was in these auspicious circumstances that the bishop of Winchester returned to court after a five-year absence on crusade. Publicly he preached to the king the need for radical reform of the king's finances; privately he schemed to depose his long-standing personal enemy, and to reverse the verdict of the 1223–4 factional struggles.

The fall of Hubert de Burgh has been recently re-examined by Carpenter, and need not detain us here. De Burgh himself was widely unpopular in the countryside by 1232, as his failure to secure the fortieth on moveables reveals. He was also dangerously isolated at court. The archbishopric of Canterbury was vacant, William the Marshal was dead, and his successor, Richard Marshal, suspected de Burgh of poisoning the king's mind against him. When Hubert finally lost the support of the king, he was an easy target for des Roches. But many of the great men who helped to displace de Burgh in 1232 had benefited greatly from his years in office. They had profited in no small measure from the lands and offices which the bishop of Winchester's men had lost in 1223–4, and they had no intention, in deposing de Burgh, of substituting an even more narrowly based court faction in his place. Nor had they any intention of allowing the new regime to threaten the personal gains they had made under de Burgh. Des Roches, however, brought with him into power almost all the survivors of the 1223–4 purge: Earl Ranulf of Chester, Brian de Lisle, Peter de Maulay, Engelard de Cigogné, and his own nephew Peter des Riveaux, who was soon granted an unparalleled monopoly over almost all the most profitable court offices. These men had scores to settle, and long-standing claims to resurrect. Satisfaction of their claims would require the reversal of verdicts which de Burgh had rendered over many years with respect to castle custodies, shrievalties, and the possession of royal manors. But with the reins of power now firmly in their hands, des Roches and his nephew set about restoring their supporters to their lands.

Had the bishop's regime been able to repay its factional debts solely out of the losses sustained by de Burgh's court supporters, his government might have survived long enough either to justify or to betray the promises of financial reform he had made to the king. The evidence of its achievements, however, is not encouraging. Financially, the regime's solitary success lay in securing the grant of a fortieth in the autumn of 1232. Otherwise, des Riveaux's extraordinary concentration of offices—by the summer of 1232 he was treasurer of the household, keeper of the wardrobe, custodian of the Jews, keeper of the mint, administrator of all custodies and escheats, and the sheriff of twenty-one counties—had far more decisive effects in facilitating the distribution of patronage than it did in improving the king's finances.[127] Despite the regime's promises, and despite its radical programme of administrative centralization, the factional inheritance of the minority restricted des Roches's freedom to extract the maximum financial return from the king's resources no less than it had de Burgh's. Indeed, with so many debts to repay to their factional supporters, the Poitevin 'reformers' were even less free than de Burgh had been to increase the king's share of his own revenues.

The extent to which the ties of faction determined the policies of des Roches's and des Riveaux's government is well illustrated in the sequence of events which brought them down.[128] During the civil war, King John had entrusted Upavon manor in Wiltshire to Peter de Maulay, a supporter of the bishop of Winchester and one of the big losers in the 1223–4 purge. After the war had ended, de Maulay was summoned before de Burgh to show his warrant for the manor. De Maulay conceded that he held the manor *de ballio regis*; it was therefore transferable at the king's will. King Henry, through de Burgh, then transferred it to Gilbert Basset, a household knight, an intimate friend of the Marshal Earls of Pembroke, and a de Burgh supporter. Several years later, in 1229, King Henry granted the manor to Gilbert Basset and his heirs forever, and gave them a royal charter for it. There the matter rested until 1233, when de Maulay renewed his claim under the favourable auspices of the bishop of Winchester's regime. De Maulay denied that he had resigned the manor willingly before de Burgh. He claimed that King John had given him the manor in perpetuity, and that it was only 'through fear and threats made to him

---

[127] Compare Carpenter's verdict on the Poitevin 'reformers' in 'Curial Sheriff', 13–15, with the earlier account by Mabel H. Mills, 'The Reforms at the Exchequer, 1232–42', *TRHS*, 4th s. 10 (1927), 111–33. Mills's views were accepted by Powicke, *Henry III*, 84–108, and by S. B. Chrimes, *An Introduction to the Administrative History of Mediaeval England*, 3rd edn. (Oxford, 1966), 90–6. Bertie Wilkinson, 'The Council and the Crisis of 1233–4', *Bulletin of the John Rylands Library* 27 (1943–4), 384–93, accepted Mills's claims that the Poitevins were financial reformers, but denied that their reforms were the cause of their downfall, as Mills had suggested. Aside from Carpenter, Wilkinson is the only one of these authors who seems to have appreciated the fundamentally factional nature of the royal government between 1217 and 1234.

[128] The only coherent account of the years between 1232 and 1236 is by C. A. F. Meekings, in the introduction to *CRR*, vol. 15, xxiii–xxxvii; for the fall of the Poitevins, see xxiii–xxviii. The analysis offered here follows Meekings's account closely.

by H. de Burgh then justiciar of England and his fellows, who threatened him that unless he returned that manor he would put him in such a position that he would not see his hands or feet',[129] that he had resigned the manor. He therefore sought its return. Gilbert Basset responded that any threats which might have accompanied de Maulay's resignation were not his doing, and asked the king to warrant the charter he had made him. De Maulay, asked for some documentary evidence to substantiate his claims, could provide none, except to produce suit to attest to the threats which had been made against him. Basset replied again that these threats were none of his doing, and besought the king to warrant his charter, which he now produced. The case was then transferred from the court to the council. Like the court, however, the council declined to rule on a royal charter, and left the case up to the king. Henry, *per voluntatem suam*, then disseised Gilbert, and restored the manor to de Maulay, offering Gilbert Basset no compensation at all.[130]

Henry's refusal to warrant the charter he had made, and his consequent refusal to offer Gilbert Basset an adequate exchange for Upavon, was a fundamental violation of the essential requirements of good lordship, and propelled the Bassets into open revolt. They were quickly joined by Earl Richard Marshal, and a small-scale war erupted in the Marches, the south-west, and the southern Midlands. The war continued throughout the winter of 1233–4, and eventually spread to Ireland. Edmund Rich, the new archbishop of Canterbury, sought to mediate the dispute. In April 1234, both des Roches and des Riveaux were removed from office, and negotiations were arranged between the king's men and the Marshal. But when the Marshal was treacherously murdered in Ireland, in a deed in which the king or his closest advisers appeared to be implicated, the situation threatened to explode again. Henry now turned on the remaining supporters of the Poitevin regime, and in yet another purge dismissed them all from office. De Burgh was restored to favour, although not to office, and de Maulay was again disseised of Upavon, which was returned to Gilbert Basset. Under the careful supervision of the archbishop of Canterbury, and under the watchful judicial eye of William de Ralegh, the new chief justice of

---

[129] '... per timorem et minas ei illatas ab H. de Burgo tunc justiciario Anglie et suis, qui illi minati fuerunt quod nisi illud redderet illum in tali loco poneret quod non videret manus nec pedes ... ' *CRR*, vol. 15, no. 131.

[130] Ibid., supplemented by *BNB*, vol. ii, no. 857, where the conclusion to the case can be inferred from the record of its reversal in May 1234: cf. Meekings's note in *CRR*, vol. 15, 28, n. 2.

the court *coram rege*, the situation eventually cooled. No new justiciar was appointed, perhaps because no suitable candidate, unconnected with either of the warring factions, was available.[131] Control of the government during the following two years fell, almost by default, to the household stewards, Ralph fitz Nicholas, Godfrey de Craucombe, John fitz Philip and Amaury de St Amand.[132] It is greatly to their credit that the next two years of government were largely uneventful.

Uneventful they may have been; unimportant they were not. The years between 1234 and 1236 were a watershed which divided the politics of the minority from the problems and policies which would preoccupy Henry's government in the decades to follow. The king's personal rule has usually been dated from 1236, but the characteristics of that rule first began to emerge in 1234, after the departure of the Poitevins. With the fall of de Burgh and then des Roches, the factions which had dominated court politics since the death of John were both decapitated. Their dissolution followed quickly. For the next few years, the king's council was dominated by the unexceptionable figures of the archbishop of Canterbury and the earls of Cornwall and Lincoln.[133] Meanwhile, there began to emerge alongside them a body of household men who owed their promotion, not to their service to King John, but rather to their loyalty to his son. Henry drew these men indifferently from the ranks of the Poitevins and from their opponents, as well as from his own royal clerks and household knights. By and large they were younger men, like the king himself, who, despite their associations with des Roches or de Burgh in years past, had not themselves been direct participants either in the troubles of John's reign or in the factional struggles which followed it.[134] The emergence of this 'king's party' within the household was paralleled in the ranks of the earls. By 1235, half of the sixteen earls were under thirty years of age. The earls who would dominate the remainder of the reign—Leicester, Gloucester, Cornwall, Norfolk, and Hereford—

---

[131] Compare Meekings, *CRR*, vol. 15, xxviii.

[132] Carpenter, 'Curial Sheriff', 15–16.

[133] See Ch. 3 below for a more elaborate discussion of the composition of the king's council during these years.

[134] Robert Passelewe is a good example of these new men. He started out in the service of Fawkes de Breauté, and then transferred his services to the bishop of Winchester's regime in 1232–4. But he only found permanent employment around the king's court after 1236. Equally important figures like Walter de Merton, Silvester de Everdon, John Mansel, and John de Gatesden also appear at the king's court for the first time between 1234 and 1237.

all grew to maturity along with the king. King John was for them only a memory.

These same two years also witnessed a marked increase in the departmental professionalism of the king's administration. The justices of the Bench had grown into a consciously professional body during the minority;[135] the legal compilation we know as Bracton is an expression of their pride in this achievement. The court *coram rege*, however, was not re-established until the king's full majority in 1227. Even then, it laboured long under the shadow of the Bench. Its membership varied markedly, as did its sessions and its jurisdiction. 'It is not until the winter of 1235–6 that the court [*coram rege*] seems to reach its full jurisdictional stature beside the Bench … and only from 1236 onwards that the scope and relationship of the two central courts seems to be once more comparable with what had obtained between 1204 and 1209.'[136] The maturity of the court *coram rege* owed much to the stature of its chief justice, William de Ralegh, whose appointment in May 1234 was yet another consequence of the collapse of the Poitevin regime. But it owed something too to the increasing self-confidence of the king's household stewards, with whom the *coram rege* justices regularly sat to hear pleas.[137] After a long apprenticeship, the king's own men were establishing a role for themselves in the government.

Similar developments were also under way at the exchequer. Despite the claims which have been made for des Roches and des Riveaux as financial reformers, it is only after their fall that one can trace the re-emergence of a consciously independent body of exchequer barons, with their own departmental methods, records, mysteries, and traditions. This change seems to coincide with the July 1234 appointment of Alexander de Swereford as chief baron. The exchequer had functioned adequately under the guidance of de Burgh, and had struggled mightily to cope with the dizzying speed of change under des Riveaux. But it was only under Swereford that it really found its feet again. New classes of records began, and old classes were kept in far better order after 1234 than had been the case before. Swereford himself searched through the miscellanea of the exchequer for returns which ought to be preserved in the archives of his department. We have them today only because his memoranda book survived as the

---

[135] See now Ralph V. Turner, *The English Judiciary in the Age of Glanvill and Bracton, c. 1176–1239* (Cambridge, 1985), 126–38, 191–205.
[136] Meekings, introduction to *CRR*, vol. 15, xxiii.
[137] Ibid., xxi–xxiii, xxxi–xxxix.

Red Book of the Exchequer. By 1236 he had reformed the exchequer into a department capable of coping with whatever administrative changes the king's council might demand. The success of the council's financial reforms after 1236 was in no small measure due to the success of Swereford's reorganizational efforts at the exchequer in 1234 and 1235.

Finance, however, remained the critical problem facing Henry's government. The fortieth of 1232 sufficed to pay off the debts remaining from the Brittany campaign of 1230, but provided no financial reserve from which Henry could meet his continuing obligations on the Continent. Between 1230 and 1234, the king spent more than the total proceeds of the fortieth on Breton subsidies alone.[138] Between 1234 and 1236, although the Breton subsidies stopped, the defence of Gascony, combined with the yearly fees Henry paid to his Gascon and Poitevin retainers, cost the king an additional £15,000 per year in continuing expenses.[139] Henry's revenues could not keep pace with these demands. His cash receipts from the shire farms were still badly crippled by the allowances his sheriffs received for keeping them, while the value of the royal demesne manors was similarly reduced by the favourable terms on which most of them were held by various factional favourites. Between 1232 and 1234, royal receipts were even further reduced by the financial anarchy occasioned by the Poitevin regime. In 1232, the confusion at court created by the Poitevins' accession forced cancellation of a scheduled judicial eyre, cutting deeply into the king's judicial revenues. As soon as peace was restored in 1234, the eyre visitations were resumed.[140] Although the eyre produced about £19,000 in cash receipts between 1234 and 1236,[141] even this sum did no more than rescue the king from his debts. Improvements in exchequer accounting after 1234 helped to guarantee that the king's accounts would at least be properly audited, but the exchequer itself could do no more. Responsibility for actually increasing the king's revenues lay,

---

[138] Henry's Breton subsidies amounted to between £15,000 and £20,000: cf. Sidney Painter, *The Scourge of the Clergy: Peter of Dreux, Duke of Brittany* (New York, 1969), 82. The fortieth apparently produced about £16,475 (Mitchell, *Studies*, 205, citing *Red Book*, vol. iii, 1064), although the enrolled accounts show total receipts of slightly less than £13,000: cf. *Foreign Accounts Henry III, 1219–34*, ed. Fred A. Cazel, Jr., PRS n.s. 44 (London, 1982), 63–73 (my computation).

[139] The Poitevin fees amounted to about £2,000 p.a., the Gascon expenses to about £3,000 p.a. during these years. See Ch. 5 below.

[140] Meekings, *CRR*, vol. 15, xviii. On the financial importance of the general eyre to the king's judicial revenues, see Ch. 6 below.

[141] Meekings, *1235 Surrey Eyre*, 135.

not with the exchequer, but with the council. And in the aftermath of the Poitevin débâcle, there was little immediate likelihood that the king's remaining councillors would risk the dangers of too thoroughgoing a financial reform.

Events, however, were soon to force their hand. In 1235, Henry secured his greatest diplomatic triumph to date, when he betrothed his sister Isabella to Emperor Frederick II of Germany. Henry promised the bride a dowry of £20,000, to be paid in three six-monthly instalments. The marriage was a good one for Henry, offering him for the first time a serious ally against King Louis IX of France in the struggle to recover his ancestral lands.[142] But the extreme efforts necessary to provide this dowry underscored the inflexibility and fundamental weakness of the king's financial resources, and emphasized yet again the need for a thoroughgoing overhaul of his financial system.[143] Henry's own marriage, in January 1236, brought immediate festival costs, and promised additional long-term increases in the king's domestic expenses. Royal houses and castles needed to be rebuilt to accommodate the queen; her own and eventually her children's expenses would need to be met. Nor had Henry abandoned his ambitions to recover his Continental territories from the Capetians. After the failure of the 1230 campaign, however, both the king and his advisers realized that recovery of the French lands would require the expenditure of sums substantially greater than those which had bankrupted him in 1230. The financial system created by the factional conflicts of the minority could not cope with even these existing demands. It could not begin to supply the costs of a new military expedition to the Continent. If Henry was to find these sums, a new approach to the management of the king's resources would clearly be required.

By the spring of 1236, the mounting pressures on the king's purse finally brought home to Henry and his councillors the urgency of his financial situation. In response to this crisis, the king's council began a comprehensive investigation and rehabilitation of almost all his existing sources of income. The systematic scope of this four-year undertaking, and the resolve with which it was carried through, find no adequate parallels elsewhere in the history of thirteenth-century English administration. The resulting reforms, and their consequences for both king and kingdom, are the subject of this volume. It is important at the outset, however, to see these reforms in their proper

---

[142] For the diplomatic context of this marriage, see Ch. 5 below.
[143] For the king's difficulties in paying this dowry, see Ch. 3 below.

context. By limiting the king's capacity to raise revenues from his tenants-in-chief through arbitrary fines and amercements, Magna Carta certainly contributed to the chronic financial problems which provoked these reforms; and to that extent, the Charters may be said to lie behind those problems. Henry's most important fiscal resources, however—the shire farms, the royal demesne manors, taxation, and the profits of justice—were unimpaired by the Charters. What had crippled royal finance in the two decades prior to 1236 was not so much the Charters as the minority itself, and the easygoing fiscal arrangements to which its factionalism had given rise. These were the arrangements the council set out in 1236 to overturn. And since the impact of the minority had nowhere been more severe than on the king's receipts from the shire farms and from the royal demesne, it was therefore to the reform of these two resources that the council turned its attention first in the spring of 1236.

2

The Management of the Shire and Manorial Farms

I. The Exploitation of the Shire Farms

THE farms paid by the royal sheriffs for the shires they controlled were among the most ancient, and the most regular, of all Henry III's sources of revenue. By 1236, however, these farms bore little relationship to the real value of the shires. Henry II had fixed most of these farms during the 1160s, at levels which appear not to have differed greatly from those in force under Henry I.[1] Thereafter, the farms changed little. Although Henry II attempted a few adjustments in the decades which followed, only in the double counties of Norfolk and Suffolk did he effect any considerable increase in a shire farm. Substantial reductions after the 1160s were equally unusual. London purchased a reduction from £500 to £300 in its yearly farm with Middlesex from Richard I during the sale of privileges which followed his coronation in 1189. But among the regular shires, only Nottingham and Derby had its farm reduced after the 1160s, and this was to take account of an alienation. Elsewhere, however, the Angevins usually preferred to allow the value of such alienated manors to the sheriff as a deduction against the shire farm, rather than to reduce the farm itself from its fixed, 'ancient' level. As alienations continued, the value of these deductions mounted. By 1236, such deductions exceeded the total value of the shire farms in at least seven shires.

Although the farms themselves thus remained fixed, the constituents of these farms changed profoundly in the century which separated Henry I from Henry III. In the early twelfth century, the shire farms were made up principally from the proceeds of the royal demesne manors, most of which were entrusted to the sheriff's care. But such revenues were never the only resource from which sheriffs drew their farms. Sheriffs played an active and profitable role in justice, presiding

---

[1] For what follows, see G. J. Turner, 'The Sheriff's Farm', *TRHS* n.s. 12 (1898), 117–49, especially the appendix, 142–9.

directly over the monthly shire courts, and through bailiffs over the tri-weekly hundred courts. Even in 1086 the revenues from such local jurisdictions could be substantial. In Domesday Book, the sheriff of Worcester owed the king yearly £17 by weight and £16 by count for the farm of such pleas, beyond the farms of the royal manors.[2] Sheriffs also collected a number of customary local levies, whose incidence and amount varied markedly from shire to shire and probably from sheriff to sheriff. The origins of such payments were obscure, but sheriff's aid was being collected in some shires at least during the 1160s,[3] and probably predates the reign of Henry II. Similar such payments, including hundred pennies, ward pennies, and payments for view of frankpledge, were being collected by early thirteenth-century sheriffs, and are also probably older than our records reveal. But because shrieval revenues were all lumped together on the pipe rolls into a single, undifferentiated shire farm, we cannot judge precisely the relative importance of manorial issues, customary levies, and judicial perquisites in making up the farms paid by the twelfth-century sheriffs.

As the population of England grew during the twelfth century, however, and as royal alienations reduced the number of manors under direct shrieval control, the proportion of the shire farms represented by such non-agricultural revenues probably increased. By the late 1170s, judicial revenues already made up a great part of the farms, as the author of the *Dialogue of the Exchequer* noted.[4] The enormous expansion in the scope of royal justice which occurred under Henry II and his sons, and the concomitant extension of the king's justice further and further down the social ladder, must in turn have accelerated this shift dramatically. These effects, however, were very inadequately reflected in the revenues the Angevins drew from their sheriffs. The shire farms themselves remained fixed at their traditional levels, and although Henry II did impose additional payments on four of his sheriffs beyond their farms, these increments amounted to less than 250 marks in all.[5]

Throughout the twelfth century, therefore, it was a profitable busi-

---

[2] Judith A. Green, 'Some Aspects of Royal Administration in England during the Reign of Henry I' (unpublished Oxford University D.Phil. thesis, 1975), 11, citing *Domesday Book* (London, 1783–1816), vol. i, ff. 64b–65b. I am grateful to Dr Green for permission to use her thesis.

[3] Judith A. Green, 'The Last Century of Danegeld', *EHR* 96 (1981), 255–7.

[4] '... tota non exurgit ex fundorum redditibus set ex magna parte de placitis.' *Dialogus de Scaccario*, ed. Charles Johnson (London, 1950), 64.

[5] Harris, 'King John and the Sheriffs' Farms', 533 n. 1.

ness indeed to be a royal sheriff. Losses occasioned by the alienation of royal manors were compensated, while the gains accruing to the sheriffs from the profits of justice, sheriff's aids, and other less respectable exactions and *douceurs* remained largely in the sheriffs' own hands. Nor were the values of the manors which remained in shrieval hands accurately reflected in the rigid shire farms. The price of grain and other agricultural produce rose gradually during the first three-quarters of the century, and rose rapidly in the half-century of inflation which followed.[6] Sheriffs, meanwhile, were free to exploit these manors by whatever methods proved most profitable to themselves in the changing agricultural conditions. They could lease an entire manor, often at a rate higher than the farm they owed the exchequer for it; they could exploit the manor directly; or they could let the manorial lands out in small parcels at rent. This freedom left an intelligent sheriff well-placed to benefit from the agricultural conditions prevailing in his locality. There is no way of knowing how many sheriffs took advantage of this freedom. But the prospects for private profit were clearly enormous.

The scale of this profit is indirectly suggested by the number of important curial officials who held sheriffdoms during the twelfth century. Like the royal demesne manors, shrievalties were an important source of patronage, from which the king's servants might legitimately expect to draw a private income.[7] On the other hand, the king had an obvious interest in diverting such profits, or at least a significant percentage of them, into his own hands. There were, after all, many other ways in which *curiales* might be supported at significantly less cost to the king. Efforts to redirect these private profits into the king's

---

[6] P. D. A. Harvey, 'The English Inflation of 1180–1220', *Past and Present* 61 (1973), 3–30; Edward Miller and John Hatcher, *Medieval England: Rural Society and Economic Change, 1086–1348* (London, 1978), 64–9; but compare now A. R. Bridbury, 'Thirteenth-Century Prices and the Money Supply', *Agricultural History Review* 33 (1985), 1–21, who thinks prices may have remained relatively stable between 1220 and 1270.

[7] Robert C. Palmer, *The County Courts of Medieval England, 1150–1350* (Princeton, 1982), 30–2, argues that financial motives were not principally what propelled the king's curial officials into shrievalties, suggesting instead that the Angevin curial sheriffs were appointed to unify variant county customs through their supervisory role in the shire courts. Although this may have played some role in the appointment of judicial specialists such as Geoffrey fitz Peter and Hubert de Burgh to a series of sheriffdoms, it cannot by itself explain the numbers of curial officials who held shrieval office in the late twelfth century. Most of these curial sheriffs had no significant judicial experience, and it is unlikely the majority were even resident in the shires over which they presided. Primarily, they sought shrieval office because it was profitable, and because it provided them with an influential position in county society.

treasury therefore began very early. In 1129–30, Henry I appointed Aubrey de Vere and Richard Basset to be joint sheriffs over eleven shires. He charged them to pay into the exchequer not only the farms of their shires, but also any additional profits they could raise, as custodians, beyond the farms. On the pipe roll for 30 Henry I, they cleared the entirety of their eleven farms, and paid in a surplus of 1000 marks.[8]

Henry II renewed the effort to increase royal revenues from the shire farms, but did so in a far less thoroughgoing manner than his grandfather had done. His attempt in 1163 to convert sheriffs' aid into an annual levy payable to the Crown was apparently foiled by the opposition of Archbishop Becket,[9] and his cautious attempts to add increments to the farms of four shires produced less than £175 per year in additional income. It was therefore not until 1194, in the general sale of offices which accompanied Richard's second coronation, that the imposition of increments on the sheriffs produced a sum to match the 1000 marks Henry I had received in 1130.[10]

Even then, it does not appear that the ten new increments imposed by King Richard in 1194 were the fruits of any long-considered attempt by the king or his exchequer to get better value from the shire farms. The sheriffs were changed in 1194 as part of the general redistribution of offices which Richard carried through in preparation for his war with Philip Augustus. The only consistent motive behind this policy was one of granting office to the man who paid the highest price to obtain it. Increments, amounting to 1070 marks beyond the approximately 250 marks in 'ancient' increments imposed by Henry II, were part of the price which ten of the sheriffs newly appointed in 1194 agreed to pay for their offices, sometimes in lieu of a fine, sometimes in addition to one. These increments were not regarded, either by the sheriffs or by county society, as a permanent increase in the shire farms.[11] Succeeding sheriffs in particular tended to regard the 1194 increments as arrangements made solely with the outgoing sheriffs, which the successors were not bound to pay. In some cases their arguments succeeded, especially when the incoming sheriff was an

[8] Judith A. Green, 'William Rufus, Henry I and the Royal Demesne', *History* 64 (1979), 349–50.

[9] Judith A. Green, 'The Last Century of Danegeld', 255–7.

[10] Doris M. Stenton, introduction to *Pipe Roll 6 Richard I*, PRS n.s. 5 (London, 1928), xix–xx, and Harris, 'King John and the Sheriffs' Farms', 533 and n. 2.

[11] The analysis which follows differs in emphasis, but is based on the evidence assembled in Harris, 'King John and the Sheriffs' Farms', *passim*.

important figure at court. More often, the exchequer managed to extract at least some portion of the 1194 increment from succeeding sheriffs, despite their claims to exemption.[12] But even when succeeding sheriffs accepted the obligation to pay these increments, they continued to regard them as a private arrangement made with each man upon his entry into office, which the sheriff assumed in addition to the shire farm, but not as an essential part of it. The exchequer, of course, took a different view, but there is some evidence that King John's view was closer to that of his sheriffs. He pardoned increments to curial sheriffs and imposed additional ones on new sheriffs as part of the bargain whereby they took up office.[13] The exchequer therefore never succeeded in transforming these new increments into a permanent feature of the shire farms. In the countryside especially, they continued to be regarded as an unpopular novelty, and in the 1215 version of Magna Carta, they were abolished (cap. 25).

By that date, however, the fertile financial brain of King John had already seized upon a more efficient scheme for extracting revenues from the shires in addition to the ancient farms. Custodians had long been a familiar feature in the administration of escheats under the Angevins. In 1194, King Richard began to entrust some of the royal demesne manors to them also.[14] King John expanded their application yet again, and in 1204 began entrusting entire shires to custodial sheriffs.[15] These new sheriffs answered not only for the shire farms and ancient increments, but also for all the revenues they could extract beyond them. Some of them received in turn a fixed salary to defray their expenses, but this was by the king's generosity and not 'of right'. Most of the custodial sheriffs appear to have served the king at their own expense.[16]

The new custodial system did not affect all the shires, but in the nineteen shires which were affected it brought an immediate exodus of curial sheriffs from office. As Carpenter has pointed out, this result

[12] William Marshal made the argument stick in Gloucestershire, and paid no increment. In Somerset and Dorset, sheriffs generally paid a portion of the increment to be quit of the remainder. See Harris, 'King John and the Sheriffs' Farms', 533-4 and notes.

[13] Carpenter, 'Curial Sheriff', 7-10, and Harris, 'King John and the Sheriffs' Farms', 534-5.

[14] Stenton, introduction to *Pipe Roll 6 Richard I*, xx-xxi.

[15] The fullest account of this new policy is in Harris, 'King John and the Sheriffs' Farms', but see also Painter, *Reign of King John*, 115-24, and Carpenter, 'Curial Sheriff', 7-10. There are obvious parallels here with Henry I's scheme in 1129-30.

[16] Carpenter, 'Curial Sheriff', 10 n. 5.

cannot have been either accidental or unintended.[17] The king's government had clearly decided that *curiales* would not make the most
satisfactory custodians. The great men who were thus displaced did
not, however, remain long in the wilderness. Two of them managed
to recover their shrievalties within a year, in each case as a farmer
rather than a custodian.[18] Between 1207 and 1209, many more such
modifications followed. Sidney Painter has suggested that the quick
reappearance of these curial sheriffs in their old offices, and the abandonment of the custodial system in several other shires in favour of a
return to fixed increments, resulted from a general opposition to the
new policy, especially among some of the great men of the land
like William Marshal, with whom John's relations were particularly
strained during 1207–8.[19] This may be so;[20] but as Harris has pointed
out, it is wrong to speak of the custodial policy as having been
abandoned altogether after 1207.[21] The modifications in the custodial
system which occurred between 1207 and 1209 emphasized the continuing importance of shrieval office as a source of patronage for
curiales, which King John could not afford to abandon completely. It
reflected also the importance of having nationally prominent men in
control of the shires during a period of political disaffection and
potential rebellion. But within the essentially political constraints thus
imposed upon him, the changes also reflected the king's resolve to
secure the maximum possible return from the remaining shires. Kent,
Lincolnshire, Worcestershire, Hampshire, Wiltshire, Dorset and
Somerset, and Sussex were returned to the hands of farmers in 1207–
8; but in the following two years Yorkshire was newly placed in the
hands of a custodian, along with Devon, Rutland, and Essex and
Hertfordshire. Cambridgeshire and Huntingdonshire, Hampshire,
Lincolnshire, Sussex, and Warwickshire and Leicestershire were later
returned to custodial hands after a period in the hands of farmers,
some of whom paid increments, and some of whom did not.[22]

John's approach to extracting profits beyond the shire farms was

[17] Ibid., 8.

[18] Ibid., 8 and n. 8.

[19] Painter, *Reign of King John*, 122–3. For the king's relations with William Marshal
during these years, see the same author's *William the Marshal: Knight-errant, Baron,
and Regent of England* (Baltimore, 1933), 136–69.

[20] Carpenter, 'Curial Sheriff', 9–10, finds more merit in the suggestion than does
Harris, 'King John and the Sheriffs' Farms', 538–9.

[21] Harris, 'King John and the Sheriffs' Farms', 538 n. 12.

[22] Details of these changes appear in Harris, 'King John and the Sheriffs' Farms',
538–9, and in Carpenter, 'Curial Sheriff', 8–9.

thus extremely flexible. It seems to have mattered little to him whether the payments he exacted were labelled *proficui* ('profits', as payments by custodial sheriffs were technically known) or *crementa* ('fixed increments') by the exchequer. What mattered to John was the revenue they produced. In this respect, the new custodial 'system' was entirely unsystematic. Shires moved in and out of custodial control, sometimes paying profits, sometimes increments, sometimes both, and sometimes paying a fine to avoid paying either. What is clear, however, is the increasing financial pressure on the countryside which the new exactions, by whatever name, represented. By the spring of 1213, when mounting political opposition forced the abandonment of both profits and increments, the king was collecting at least £1500 per year from this source, despite the fact that the system had never been extended to at least a third of the counties of England.[23] After deductions for *terris datis* and other yearly payments assigned on the farms, the shire farms themselves were worth only about £3000 per year in cash to the king.[24] If fully paid, the profits and increments thus represented a 50 per cent increase in the king's net receipts from the shire farms.

Although the clause in Magna Carta 1215 which prohibited increments was omitted from all subsequent reissues of the Charter, it was not until Hubert de Burgh gained an unquestioned ascendancy over the government with the shrieval changes of January 1224 that the regency government felt itself strong enough to reintroduce profits and increments in a thoroughgoing way.[25] During the five years which followed, most of the shires were placed again under custodial sheriffs. In contrast to the practice under John, however, these new custodians were granted sizeable allowances to defray the costs of their administration. In many shires, these allowances effectively eliminated any financial gain to the exchequer which the profits ought to have produced. The shires therefore remained a lucrative source of support for de Burgh's supporters at court. In 1229, the profits of ten shires were converted into modest fixed sums, and the sheriffs ceased to be custodians, although the additional amounts for which they now answered continued to be described as *'proficui'* on the pipe rolls.[26]

[23] See the table presented in Harris, 'King John and the Sheriffs' Farms', 542. Notice, however, that these tables record the sums charged to the sheriffs as profits, not the amounts actually cleared by the sheriffs on the pipe rolls through payments or credits.
[24] I have computed this figure from *Pipe Roll 13 John*, ed. Doris M. Stenton, PRS n.s. 28 (London, 1953).
[25] Mills, 'Experiments ... 1200–32', 167–8; Carpenter, 'Curial Sheriff', 10.
[26] Carpenter, 'Curial Sheriff', 10–13.

From this date on, the terminological distinction between profits and increments ceases to have any official significance. The four ancient increments imposed by Henry II were still described as *crementa*. All other payments by a sheriff beyond the farm, whether fixed or variable, were described as *proficui*, and it is as 'profits' that we shall hereafter refer to them.

The regime of the Bishop of Winchester and his nephew, Peter des Riveaux, had no significant effect on the exploitation of the shire farms. The new regime had a great many factional debts to repay, and simply could not forego the patronage possibilities inherent in the shire farms, despite its promises of fiscal reform. Their passing in 1234 therefore made as little impression upon the administration of the shire farms as did the return of the curial sheriffs between 1234 and 1236.[27]

It was not until the spring of 1236, therefore, that the king's government launched its first truly systematic attempt to redirect the private profits of its sheriffs into the royal treasury. In sophistication and thoroughness, the new policy was unprecedented. In the six months between April and October 1236, all but five of the twenty-seven English counties were placed in the hands of custodial sheriffs.[28] In most of these shires, the king combined these appointments (or in some cases, reappointments) with a provision retaining all the royal demesne manors in his own hand, outside the shire farms.[29] These the king entrusted to three specially appointed manorial keepers, who were to exploit the lands as profitably as possible, and who were to answer for all their issues directly to the exchequer.[30] The new custodial sheriffs, meanwhile, were required not only to answer for all the issues

---

[27] Carpenter, 'Curial Sheriff', 13–16; 'Sheriffs of Oxfordshire', 255–7, 265–8.

[28] London and Middlesex paid no profits as a result of the fine made with King Richard in 1190, nor did Worcestershire, which was held heritably by William de Beauchamp. The sheriff of Lincoln paid a fixed increment of £200 per year, in return for remitting all his claims against the king for services he had done King John: cf. Fine Roll 20 Henry III (C. 60/35 m. 16). In Cambridgeshire, Jeremiah de Caxton fined with the king to respond for a fixed 50 mark profit for 20 Henry III (C. 60/35 m. 2). Thereafter, Cambridgeshire was also placed in custody. In Kent, Bertram de Cryoll paid a fixed £40 per year profit between Michaelmas 1234 and Easter 1239, but while the earl of Essex and Hereford held the shire (from Easter 1239 to Michaelmas 1241) no profits were charged. I omit Westmoreland (held heritably by Robert de Vieuxpont), Cornwall (held by the king's brother Richard) and Rutland (dower land of the queen mother, held by Richard of Cornwall) from these calculations, as all three were anomalous counties.

[29] The fullest versions of these appointments are given not on the Patent Roll (*CPR 1232–47*, 141–7), but on the unpublished Fine Roll for 20 Henry III (C. 60/35 mms. 11–9).

[30] For discussion of these manorial reforms, see section III below.

of their shires, but also to file with the exchequer a yearly record of these issues and their constituents. Although such records, known as *rotuli de particule proficui comitatuum* or simply as *particule*, had been filed occasionally by custodial sheriffs before 1236, only three such accounts survive which pre-date the 1236 custodial experiment. Between 1236 and 1240, when the shires were returned to farmers, more than forty survive from what was once an unbroken series.[31] These *particule* provide us with our first detailed view of the revenues which made up the shire farms and profits.

The *particule* were drawn up locally by the sheriffs' clerks, and therefore show great variations in organization and presentation. Once submitted to the exchequer, however, they were all audited in a broadly similar way. The shire farms were first reduced by all fixed deductions for lands alienated from the sheriff's control (*terris datis*) and by all fixed alms and other customary payments. In several shires, the entire shire farm was wiped out by these fixed deductions; elsewhere, a certain sum remained owing on the shire farm.[32] This revised debt was then further reduced by the discretionary payments which the king had authorized the sheriff to make during the year. Sometimes the sheriff's total payments and deductions exceeded the amount he owed the king for the shire farm. In this case, the excess would be credited to the sheriff as a 'surplus' on his account. In other cases, some portion of the shire farm would still be owing, even after all the sheriff's deductions had been allowed. The calculation of this credit or debit completed the audit of 'the body of the shire' (*corpus comitatus*).

Attention now turned to the *particule*. If the sheriff had a surplus from the body of the shire, then the gross total of the receipts on the *particule* would be recorded on the pipe roll as 'the profits of the shire'. The sheriff could then choose whether to have his surplus credited to him against the sum he now owed as 'profits', or against another debt he might owe the king on the pipe rolls. If, however, the sheriff's account for the body of the shire showed a debit, this debit had first to be made good before the profits of the shire beyond the farm could be computed. The amount still owing on the shire farm would therefore be deducted from the gross sum of the receipts on the *particule* 'in order to complete the farm of the shire' (*ad perficiendum corpus*

---

[31] A complete listing of the extant *particule*, arranged chronologically by counties, is available in the Round Room of the Public Record Office, Chancery Lane, benchmark 7:40.

[32] See Ch. 6, Table 6.6 below.

comitatus).[33] The net sum remaining on the *particule* after this reduction would then be recorded on the pipe roll as profits. If the receipts recorded on the *particule* did not even suffice to complete the shire farm, the pipe roll would record a notation to this effect, and no profits would be recorded for that year.[34]

Taken by themselves, however, the sums recorded on the pipe rolls as profits do not provide an accurate measure of the king's gains from the new custodial policy. With a few exceptions, all the custodial sheriffs received an allowance for their expenses. These allowances were not recorded on the *particule*; instead, they were recorded as a deduction against the profits on the pipe rolls. The king's net return from the shires was therefore reduced by the amount of these shrieval allowances. Even after making this deduction, however, we are still some way from an accurate computation of net profits. The size of this allowance, and the expenses which were included and excluded from it, were matters for negotiation between the king and each individual sheriff. The terms struck by successive sheriffs could vary significantly, especially in shires where the sheriff also served as constable of one or more royal castles. One sheriff might undertake to keep the royal castles at his own expense; his successor might receive a fee for keeping the castle in addition to his fee for keeping the shire.[35] One sheriff might undertake to respond *ut custos* (as a custodian) for the castle-guard receipts, while another might retain them to defray the costs of his constableship.[36] In some cases, the sheriff or another royally appointed constable might even agree to pay the king a farm in order to hold a castle the tenure of which had previously been a part of the undifferentiated shire farm.[37] Mill proceeds were another

---

[33] In the four shires which owed ancient increments, the amount of these increments would also be deducted from the *particule* receipts at this point in the account.

[34] The foregoing is based on a study of all the extant *particule* between 1236 and 1240, and a comparison of them with the associated accounts on the pipe rolls. The account offered by Mills, 'Reforms ... 1232–42', 125–6, is inaccurate even after the corrections by Carpenter, 'Curial Sheriff', 21 n. 3.

[35] In Somerset and Dorset, for example, Hugh de Vivona received a fee of 40 marks per year for keeping Corfe Castle after Michaelmas 1240, a fee which exactly balanced the notional 40 marks per annum profits the exchequer continued to charge against the shires. Between 1236 and 1240, all the previous sheriffs had held Corfe at their own expense.

[36] In Norfolk and Suffolk, Thomas de Ingoldesthorp, custodial sheriff between 1236 and 1238, responded separately for the wards of Norwich Castle in addition to the profits of the shires. His successor, Robert de Brus, responded for these castle-guard receipts as part of the shire profits.

[37] Until 1239, custody of Harston Castle was included as part of the shire farm and profits of Nottingham and Derby. After that date, the castle was farmed to the sheriff

source of income which was sometimes included and sometimes excluded from the shire proceeds.[38] Each of these arrangements will affect the computation of the king's net return from the shire.

In calculating the king's total net profits from this new policy, it is also necessary to keep careful track of the manors which the king removed from shrieval control in 1236–7 into the hands of the manorial keepers. The 1236 reforms come at the end of a forty-year period during which manors once held as part of an undifferentiated shire farm had been gradually leased out at farm and fee-farm either to the sheriff himself, to the men of the manors concerned, or to other royally appointed farmers.[39] The reforms of 1236–7 therefore removed relatively few royal manors directly from the shire farms.[40] Of the fifty-seven manors placed in the custody of the manorial keepers at some date between 1236 and 1240, only six had been indisputably a part of the shire farms until 1236.[41] Four additional manors, all in Lancashire, may have been.[42] Most of the manors entrusted to the special keepers had already been removed from the body of the shire before 1230, and were held in 1236 at farm, either by the sheriff himself (five),[43] by the men of the manor (nine),[44] or by a royally appointed farmer (eighteen).[45] Fourteen had previously been held by custodians.[46]

for £11 15s. 7d. per year. A similar situation existed with respect to Rockingham Castle in Northamptonshire. Until the fall of 1237, it had been held as part of the shire farm. Thereafter, it was farmed for 20 marks per year.

[38] Mill issues were included in the farm of Oxfordshire in 1229–30 as a favour to the king's household steward Godfrey de Craucombe, then sheriff of the county. The mill was excluded from the profits in 1236 and all subsequent years.

[39] Robert S. Hoyt, *The Royal Demesne in English Constitutional History, 1066–1272* (Ithaca, 1950), 134–56.

[40] Compare Palmer's claim (*County Courts*, 28), that 'Prior to 1236, sheriffs had also been responsible for the supervision of royal estates, and this had constituted the single most profitable aspect of the office.'

[41] Acornbury, Dilwyn, Lugwardine, and Marden (Hereford), Somerton (Som.), and Melksham (Wilts.).

[42] Skerton, Slyne, Overton, and Singleton.

[43] Brill (Bucks.), Newnham (Gloucs.), Brocton (Lancs.), Pickering (Yorks.), and the combined manor of Wirresdale, Lonsdale, and Amounderness (Lancs.).

[44] Dymock (Gloucs.), Andover and Basingstoke (Hants.), King's Cliffe (Northants.), Bridport and Dorchester (Dorset), Feckenham (Worcs.), and Scalleby and Clopton (Yorks.).

[45] Bray, Cookham and Windsor (Berks.), Hatfield and Newport (Essex), Winchcombe (Gloucs.), Abthorpe, Brigstock, Finedon, Geddington, Silverstone, and Thorpe (Northants.), Fordington (Dorset), Devizes and Rowde (Wilts.), Bromsgrove (Worcs.), Easingwold and Falsgrave (Yorks.).

[46] Langwatheby, Penred, Salkill, Scoteby, Stanweys, and Weriholm (Cumb.), Writtle (Essex), Barton Gloucester, Minsterworth, Rodley, and Slaughter (Gloucs.), Alton (Hants), Ospringe (Kent), and Kempton (Middx.).

In theory, the sheriffs should have been compensated for the loss of these remaining manors by having their value deducted from the shire farms they owed. But in practice, they did not always receive such allowances. Where manors or castles were removed from the shire farms without such an allowance being made, this represented a net increase in the shire farm for which the sheriff responded. The same thing happened when the deduction conceded to the sheriff in order to compensate him for the loss of a manor represented far less than the actual value of the manorial issues. The sheriffs of Herefordshire suffered particularly from such hidden increases between 1236 and 1240. In the autumn of 1237, Acornbury, Marden, and Lugwardine were removed from the shire farm, and placed in the hands of the manorial keeper Walter de Burgo. For Acornbury, the sheriff received no allowance at all. For Lugwardine and Marden, he was allowed a total of £40. De Burgo, however, drew more than £90 net from these two manors in his first year of custody, and took another £6 in net receipts from Acornbury.[47] Net profits from Herefordshire, however, rose from less than £20 to more than £40 during the same year.[48] The total gain for the king was therefore approximately £82. The *particule* for Herefordshire have not survived, and so it is not possible to explain exactly how this remarkable result was achieved. It did not, however, prove to be repeatable. In 1239 the manor of Dilwyn was similarly removed from the sheriff's hands, again without compensation. But this time the net profits from the shire dropped by the approximate value of the manor, about £40. This is the result one would expect under a custodial system, if indeed the new sheriffs were accurately responding for every penny they collected, if they were already exploiting fully the financial resources of their shires, and if the *particule* record all the sources from which they drew their shire revenues. In Herefordshire at least, the surprising elasticity of the sheriff's resources between 1236 and 1238 must suggest that at least one of these assumptions is probably wrong, and therefore that the custodial sheriffs may have continued to have sources of income on which they drew, beyond the allowances the king granted them for keeping the shires, which did not always find their way onto the *particule proficui comitatus.*

---

[47] Pipe Roll 22 Henry III (E. 372/82 rots. 1–3d).

[48] Pipe Roll 21 Henry III (E. 372/81 rot. 6) vs. Pipe Roll 22 Henry III (E. 372/82 rot. 5).

Financially, the new custodial policy in the shires was strikingly successful.[49] Taking 1230 as a 'base' year, the 1236 reforms tripled the exchequer's gross receipts from profits, from about £600 to about £1800 per year, and doubled the king's net profits, from about £600 to about £1200 per year. Shrieval allowances accounted for the £600 to £700 differential between gross and net receipts. These increases are even more remarkable when considered as a percentage of the king's total shire revenues. Although the shire farms were notionally valued at about £10,000 per annum, in fact more than two-thirds of this sum was wiped out by deductions for lands alienated from shrieval control. When fixed alms and other customary payments are also deducted, the king's yearly revenues from the shire farms, including the four ancient increments, amounted to only about £1900 per year.[50] The new profits policy thus produced an approximate 60 per cent increase in the king's annual net shire revenues.

The impact of these reforms on shrieval oppression in the shires is more difficult to assess. The new custodial system aimed to squeeze out the private, unreported profits which previously had accrued to the sheriffs, but it did not necessarily attempt to increase the total amount of money collected yearly by the sheriffs from the shires. So long as the new custodial sheriffs were content with their allowances, they were under no compulsion to exploit the men of the shire any more ruthlessly than their predecessors had done. It is on this basis that historians have hailed the new custodial system as marking an important financial compromise between the competing financial interests of the king and of county society.[51] But did the system actually work this way? Or did the sheriffs continue to collect and retain sums of money, beyond their allowances, which they never reported on the *particule*? And if the new sheriffs did continue to collect unreported profits, does this mean that the new custodial system in fact increased the fiscal pressure exerted by the sheriffs on the countryside?

On the whole, the custodial sheriffs were probably more careful administrators than the officials they replaced in 1236. On these grounds alone it is likely, therefore, that they did in fact collect more

[49] Year by year and shire by shire computations of the yield from shire profits between 1236 and 1250 are provided in Robert C. Stacey, 'Crown Finance and English Government under Henry III, 1236–45' (unpublished Yale University Ph.D. thesis, 1983), 472–92, on which the following general conclusions are based.

[50] See Table 6.7 below.

[51] Carpenter, 'Curial Sheriff', 20–1, 29; Maddicott, 'Magna Carta and Local Community', 44–6.

money from the shires after 1236 than had been customary before that
date. We do not, however, have any accurate means of judging the
size of the private profits pocketed by the shrieval farmers before 1236.
We cannot, therefore, determine arithmetically the extent to which the
1236 reforms actually increased the direct financial pressure exerted
by the sheriffs on the localities. All we can say is that, after 1236, a
higher percentage of the sheriffs' total revenues was now being reported
to the king.

The *particule* do, however, provide some basis on which to speculate
as to the relationship between the exchequer's demands for profits and
the level of shrieval oppression in the countryside.[52] In a general way,
some such relationship may appear to be intuitively obvious; but the
directness of the relationship will be determined in each individual
shire by the diversity and expansibility[53] of the sheriff's revenue-
producing resources. By removing a number of the royal demesne
manors from shrieval control, the reforms of 1236 reduced both, and
in this respect, the reforms may thus have removed an important buffer
between the men of the shires and the exchequer's financial demands
on the sheriffs. After 1236, all increases in the shire farms or profits
would have to come directly out of the pockets of local men, and not
from the increasing value of the king's manors.

On the other hand, however, this was an aspect of the reforms
which did not affect all the shires equally. Devon, Northumberland,
Shropshire and Staffordshire, Surrey, Sussex, and Warwickshire and
Leicestershire were never included in the new manorial system at all,
although all were placed under custodial sheriffs. In some of these
shires, it is possible that insufficient royal demesne remained by 1236
to repay the attentions of manorial custodians, but in Shropshire and
Staffordshire[54] and in Northumberland[55] this was not the case. Some

---

[52] Carpenter argues strongly for such a direct relationship in 'Curial Sheriff', 22 and
passim: 'shrieval abuse in the period before 1258 ... was ... in considerable part the
baleful product of exchequer demands.'

[53] I use 'expansibility' here to refer to the relative ease with which revenues from a
given shrieval resource could be increased by changes either in the methods or the
intensity of its exploitation, without transgressing the bounds of legality.

[54] In Shropshire and Staffordshire, the sheriff continued to hold Worfield, Wol-
verhampton, and Withington as part of the shire farm until early 1238, when these
manors were granted to Henry de Hastings and his wife in part exchange for her claims
on the earldom of Cheshire lands: cf. *Cl.R.* 1237–42, 60. After the death of John fitz
Philip in 1237, the sheriff also held Bernerby, Claverley, and Kinver at farm; all three
were royal demesne manors which previously John had held in fee-farm (Claverley and
Kinver) or in free alms (Bernerby). In addition, the sheriff farmed Kingswinford and
Tettenhall outside the shire farm, except in 1238–9, when Tettenhall appears among

of the custodial sheriffs thus retained a role in the administration of the royal demesne despite the professed intentions of the 1236 reforms to eliminate this practice. The sheriff of Herefordshire, for example, held Dilwyn until 1239, although loss of all the *particule* for the county makes it impossible to say on what terms he held it. The sheriff of Nottingham and Derby held Harston until 1239, and responded for it among his other shire profits at a set farm.[56] The sheriff of Leicestershire held the manor of Welham without interruption, but seems never to have responded for it among the profits of the shire. We do not know where the revenue from it went.[57] Kent was never placed under custodial sheriffs, although the sheriff did respond for a fixed £40 per annum profit from 1234–9, and again from Michaelmas 1241. The royal manor of Milton, however, remained continuously in his custody until 1249.[58] In several other shires also, the sheriffs continued to hold one or more royal manors at farm, outside the farm of the shire.[59] Possession of such agricultural revenues gave sheriffs an opportunity to raise additional sums which did not derive directly from the cash payments of local men to the sheriff. To this extent, these continuing agricultural resources may thus have cushioned the men of some shires from the full effects of the exchequer's demands.

In very few shires, however, did manorial revenues produce a large percentage of the sheriffs' total incomes by 1236. The extent to which

---

the profits of the shire: cf. Pipe Roll 23 Henry III (E. 372/83 rot. 12) and E. 370/6/10. Ford, which Carpenter lists among the manors in the sheriff's hands ('Curial Sheriff', 19 n. 3) was in fact held in perpetual fee farm by Henry de Audley: cf. *Pipe Roll 14 Henry III*, ed. Chalfant Robinson, PRS n.s. 4 (London, 1927), 229; and the unpublished Pipe Rolls for 20–25 Henry III (E. 372/80 rot. 12; E. 372/81 rot. 6d; E. 372/82 rot. 15; E. 372/83 rot. 12; E. 372/84 rot. 7; E. 372/85 rot. 1).

[55] The council apparently considered removing the demesne land associated with Bamborough Castle, along with the manors of Sunderland and Schotton, from the sheriff, and entrusting them to Robert de Crepping, the manorial custodian in the north. But this order was later countermanded, and never took effect: cf. Pipe Roll 22 Henry III (E. 372/82 rot. 4). The sheriff therefore continued to respond for these manors among the profits of the shire.

[56] E. 370/5/76; E. 370/5/74; Pipe Roll 24 Henry III (E. 372/84 rots. 1, 1d).

[57] Originalia Roll 24 Henry III (E. 371/7 m. 3). The manor does not appear on either of the extant *particule*: E. 101/505/14 (21 and 22 Henry III), E. 370/5/41 (22 Henry III).

[58] On the special circumstances attendant to this, see Carpenter, 'Curial Sheriff', 25. From 1233 until 1239, and from 1242 until 1249, Kent's sheriff was the important household official and steward Bertram de Cryoll. When Bertram gave up the shrievalty, Milton was removed from the shire farm.

[59] In Norfolk and Suffolk, for example, the manor of Aylsham was entrusted to the manorial custodian Warner Engayne, but the sheriff continued to farm the manor of Bergholt outside the farm of the shire, and to respond as custodian for Orford.

the 1236 reforms reduced the elasticity of shrieval resources should not therefore be exaggerated. In shires like Norfolk and Suffolk and Yorkshire, where shrieval profits were high, the most important component of the sheriffs' revenues tended to be the farms of royal hundreds (or, in Yorkshire, the farms of the three ridings). These farms made up about two-thirds of the total issues recorded on the *particule* for these shires. The remainder of their revenues was drawn from the amercements of the remaining hundred courts and of course the shire court, sheriff's aid, view of frankpledge, and, in Yorkshire, from the Jews.[60] In shires where the income from the farm of royal hundreds was smaller, the revenues from these other sources was proportionately more important in the composition of the profits.

None of these resources could easily be expanded without directly increasing the burden of shrieval exactions on the countryside. Revenues from frankpledge and from sheriff's aid grew gradually with population, but could be increased in the short term only by extending these levies to persons who previously had not paid them, or else by arbitrarily raising their amounts. Sheriffs did not have the power to put royal hundreds to farm on their own initiative, and it must therefore be doubted whether they could raise the farms on such hundreds without the king's permission.[61] In shires where most of the hundreds were farmed out, the sheriff might thus be even less able to increase the total issues from his shire than would a sheriff who administered these hundreds directly. The presence of powerful lords within a shire might complicate a sheriff's task further, by preventing the sheriff from collecting even his rightful dues and perquisites from the lord's lands and men.[62] This would in turn throw a further burden onto the resources which remained to him unimpeded. But even if sheriffs could have raised the farms on the royal hundreds, this would only have transferred responsibility for extracting the king's increased profits from the sheriff to the farmer of the hundred. A farmer had no obvious

[60] For Norfolk and Suffolk, see E. 101/505/6, E. 370/5/67, E. 370/5/68, E. 370/5/69, E. 370/5/70, E. 370/5/72; for Yorkshire, see E. 370/6/23 m. 1 (mislabelled in the Round Room catalogue as a roll of 43 Henry III; in fact, only mms. 2–5 pertain to that year. Membrane 1 is from the first half of 20 Henry III), E. 370/6/20, E. 370/6/18, E. 370/6/19, E. 370/6/21.

[61] Although it is clear that during the 1250s many sheriffs did in fact let royal hundreds at farm without authorization, this practice was recognized as an abuse. See *Documents of the Baronial Movement of Reform and Rebellion, 1258–1267*, ed. R. F. Treharne and I. J. Sanders (Oxford, 1973), 120–1 ('The Ordinance of the Sheriffs', 1258), and Carpenter, 'Curial Sheriff', 23 and n. 3.

[62] Maddicott, 'Magna Carta and Local Community', 50–1, citing E. 101/505/9.

sources of income which the sheriff himself would not have had were the sheriff to administer the hundred directly. The burden of oppression on the men of the hundred should therefore have remained much the same in either case. The only important difference was that a private farmer expected to make some personal profit out of the arrangement, beyond the farm he collected for the king.[63] In theory at least, a custodial sheriff did not.

This then was the heart of the matter. Henry's new policy with respect to the shire farms attempted to squeeze out the unreported private profits which his sheriffs had previously enjoyed. In many shires, however, the sheriff's capacity actually to increase the shire issues beyond their accustomed levels (i.e., beyond a sum equal to the king's traditional revenues plus the sheriff's customary private profit) was severely restricted by the existence of another set of royal farmers beneath the sheriffs, in whose hands the direct administration of many of the shire's financial resources lay. The king's government never squarely faced this dilemma. Between 1236 and 1240 the custodial system largely avoided it, because the royal council appears to have been content to accept from the shires whatever level of profits the custodial sheriffs succeeded in raising from them. The predictable result was a steady decline in the level of profits from the autumn of 1238 until the autumn of 1240. At Michaelmas of 1240, the council changed course. Having determined the approximate level of the sheriffs' receipts during the preceding four years, it now abandoned the custodial system in the shires, and returned them to the hands of farmers, who were henceforth to answer for a fixed profit each year beyond the shire farms, without allowances.[64]

Reasons for this return to shrieval farmers are not hard to find. Auditing the accounts of the custodial sheriffs was a time-consuming process for the exchequer; the system itself produced irregular receipts for the king from year to year; and it did not provide the king with any leverage by which to increase further the gross receipts from the shires. Furthermore, the gross receipts themselves had declined by more than 15 per cent (about £300) between 1238 and 1240, a decline which reflects either decreasing shrieval efficiency, or increasing

---

[63] There is a useful description of these sub-shrieval officials in Palmer, *County Courts*, 48–55.

[64] Pipe Roll 25 Henry III (E. 372/85), *passim*; Carpenter, 'Curial Sheriff', 21 and n. 3. A list of these new appointments, as these were communicated from the council to the exchequer, is attached to Originalia Roll 25 Henry III (E. 371/8A m. 4 schedule 2).

shrieval peculation through the non-reporting of income. If indeed the custodial sheriffs were not reporting all their income, then even the final argument in favour of the custodial system—that it provided a check on privately motivated shrieval oppression in the countryside— was thus considerably undermined. If custodial sheriffs were in fact continuing to derive a certain private profit from their offices beyond the allowances the king conceded them, then there was no advantage for the king or for county society in continuing with the experiment. The king's council therefore abandoned it.

The profits assigned to the shires in 1240 were set at a cumulative level which corresponded closely to the total of the gross receipts from shire profits in their final year under custodians.[65] In other words, the profits assigned in 1240 drew no more accountable cash from the shires than the custodial system had done in its least efficient year. The difference, of course, was that the king's gross receipts were no longer reduced by shrieval allowances. The king's net revenues from the shires therefore increased by between £400 and £500 per year. It is not clear, however, whether the sheriffs who paid these higher farms after 1240 were able to pass on this increase to the men of the shires through higher charges, or whether the king's additional revenues came out of his sheriffs' own salaries. The situation undoubtedly varied from shire to shire, and was determined not only by the efficiency of the sheriff, but also by the expansibility of his resources, and by the strength of the local opposition he faced. Overall, however, in most shires the profits assigned in 1240 do not appear unreasonable. In Berkshire, Cumberland, Devon, Lancashire, Lincolnshire, Northamptonshire, and Warwickshire and Leicestershire, the new profits were established at levels which corresponded closely to the average net profits, after allowances, taken from these shires during the preceding four years of custodianship. In Nottingham and Derby, Oxfordshire, Shropshire and Staffordshire, Surrey, and Yorkshire, the new profits matched the highest net profits achieved in any single year since 1236—a figure which in Oxfordshire, Surrey, and Shropshire and Staffordshire corresponded almost exactly with their gross receipts in their final year of custody. Even Yorkshire's 200 marks per annum profit, although matched only once under custodians, was nevertheless 100 marks lower than it had been in 1230, before the custodial experiment began.[66]

[65] See the tables in Stacey, 'Crown Finance', 472–83.

[66] This difference probably reflects the removal of the manor of Pickering from the sheriff's hands between 1230 and 1236. In 1229–30, the sheriff held Pickering as part of

Elsewhere, the new profit figures approximately matched the custodial sheriffs' gross receipts from these shires. The only really swingeing increases were in Wiltshire, where the profits jumped from gross receipts of around £45 per annum to a fixed yearly payment of £100,[67] and perhaps in Northumberland, where the huge allowances which the sheriffs had previously received for keeping the shire were eliminated. Receipts from Norfolk and Suffolk showed such wide variations from year to year under custodians that it is hard to determine whether 200 marks per year was a reasonable sum or not for the profits of the shire. It was, however, a sum closely comparable to the net receipts from the two shires in 1238–9, and it was significantly lower than the net receipts in 1237–8. It was therefore probably not unreasonable.

The other consideration which suggests that the 1240 profits were not unreasonable is the number of important curial officials who continued to hold shrievalties thereafter. In 1236, most of the curial sheriffs had been removed from office when the custodial policy was introduced. In 1239, however, with the return of Stephen de Segrave to the king's council, these men returned in force to their shrievalties, where by and large they remained until the end of the following decade.[68] The really decisive exodus of the curial sheriffs from office

the shire's 300 mark increment. He received £31 16s. 5d. in *terris datis* credits for Pickering against the shire farm, and paid in £20 14s. 7d. outside the profits for certain portions of the manor which were held at a fixed farm. His total credit for Pickering was thus £11 1s. 10d. (*Pipe Roll 14 Henry III*, 266–9). Between 1236–8, when Robert de Crepping held the manor as a custodian, it returned £67 8s. 3d. in average net issues, despite fairly heavy expenditures on new stock: cf. Pipe Roll 22 Henry III (E. 372/82 rot. 4). On this basis, the manor of Pickering was worth £78 10s. 1d. (£11 1s. 10d. + £67 8s. 3d.) to the sheriff in 1230. By removing Pickering into the hands of a custodian, and by reducing the shire profits from 300 marks to 200 marks per year, the exchequer thus gained approximately £12 per year.

[67] The new sheriff, Nicholas de Haversham, proved unable to pay these profits, and retired from office at the end of 1245 owing £300 in back profits: cf. Pipe Roll 29 Henry III (E. 372/89 rot. 5). In Jan. 1246, the shire was again placed under a custodian, who responded for £50 8s. 4½d. gross profits for the last three-quarters of 30 Henry III, and for £61 12s. 11d. gross profits for all of 31 Henry III: Pipe Roll 31 Henry III (E. 372/91 rots. 9, 9d). He does not appear to have received any allowance for his expenses.

[68] In 1239, Paulinus Peyvre (steward from 1241) became sheriff of Bedfordshire and Buckinghamshire, Bertram de Cryoll (steward from 1239) became sheriff of Essex and Hertfordshire, the earl of Essex and Hereford took over in Kent, John de Vlecote (baron) took over Norfolk and Suffolk, William de Cantilupe (steward from 1238) became sheriff of Nottingham and Derby, Richard Siward (baron), Paulinus Pevire, and John de Plessy (household banneret) took over Oxfordshire, and Nicholas de Molis (household banneret) became sheriff of Yorkshire. John fitz Geoffrey (steward from 1237) and Herbert fitz Matthew (baron and household banneret) took over Gloucestershire and Somerset and Dorset respectively, at Christmas 1238. Amaury de St Amand, another of the king's household stewards, held Herefordshire continuously from 1234 until 1240,

appears to have occurred in the late 1240s, probably as a result of the additional increments which Henry imposed on the shires after 1248.[69] Until that date, however, members of Henry's household continued to hold important shire offices: Richard de Muntfichet in Essex and Hertfordshire (1242–6), John fitz Geoffrey (1238–46) and Robert Walerand (1246–50) in Gloucestershire, Emery de Sacy (1239–42) and Robert Passelewe (1242–9) in Hampshire, Emery de Cancellis (1240–6) and Walerand Teutonicus (1246–9) in Herefordshire, Bertram de Cryoll (1242–8) in Kent, John l'Estrange (1236–48) in Shropshire and Staffordshire, Hugh de Vivona (1240–9) in Somerset and Dorset, and Henry of Bath (1242–8) in Yorkshire.[70] There seems no question that shrieval office remained attractive to Henry's courtiers for many years after 1236. Their motives for seeking it were probably more political and personal than strictly financial: they did not, in other words, seek shrieval office primarily to profit from the shire revenues. The 1236 reforms, followed by these 1240 increments, squeezed out the bulk of such private profits. What remained to be collected after 1236 simply would not have repaid the attentions of such great men as these. Rather, Henry's courtiers valued shrieval office during the 1240s principally for the other advantages it could confer. Aside from the favours a sheriff might do himself or other local landowners,[71] sheriffs were ideally placed in county society to learn of persons whose estates were encumbered by debts. For money-lenders like Bertram de Cryoll, such knowledge could be invaluable, especially so because Bertram had five sons whom he wished to endow with lands, and a very small patrimony from which to do so.[72] Henry of Bath's financial success is well known, and while the bulk of his wealth probably came from his career as a

when he departed on crusade. The return of these great men to office coincides exactly with the 1238–40 decline in the net yield from shire profits. This is unlikely to have been accidental. For the political context of these changes, see pp. 130–6 below.

[69] For these later increments, see Carpenter, 'Curial Sheriff', 22–3.

[70] PRO Lists and Indexes, vol. 9: *List of Sheriffs for England and Wales*, revised edition (New York, 1963).

[71] For the kinds of local interests a sheriff might wish to protect, see the account of Nicholas de Haversham's career as sheriff of Wiltshire in the biographical appendix to C. A. F. Meekings, ed., *Crown Pleas of the Wiltshire Eyre, 1249*, Wiltshire Archeological Society 16 (1961), 132–40.

[72] Evidence of Cryoll's money-lending emerges incidentally, from the memoranda roll for 22 Henry III (E. 368/12 rot. 10d), and from the records of the 1262 Kent eyre (JI 1/363 m. 13d, m. 31). I owe these eyre references to Dr Paul Hyams. It is likely that money-lending around Henry's court was a major occupation for courtiers, especially for those with contacts or connections with the Jewish exchequer. I hope to develop this point at another time.

royal justice, shrieval office gave him a useful vantage point from which to invest that wealth in land.[73] Indeed, in so far as men like Cryoll, fitz Geoffrey, and Bath sought shrieval office not so much for its revenues as for the other advantages it conferred, they may have been significantly less extortionate sheriffs than the lesser men who began to replace them in the late 1240s, whose only benefits from office came directly from their exploitation of the shire farms.

In the decade or so preceding 1258, almost all of Henry's sheriffs were drawn from the ranks of these lesser men. The record of their increasingly extortionate practices is clear, and can be traced not only in the reform provisions of 1258, but also in the records of the king's exchequer, which illustrate clearly the steadily increasing financial pressure under which these sheriffs operated.[74] During this decade, there can be no doubt that the level of shire profits demanded by the king's council was excessive, and that this was a significant factor encouraging shrieval abuses of power. The effect of these increases was further exaggerated during the 1250s by the emergence of a series of official and unofficial noble liberties, from which the sheriffs were excluded by the power and court influence of these great lords.[75] On the basis of this investigation, however, it must be doubted whether exchequer pressure on the countryside, exerted through the shire profits, should be treated as a continuously developing abuse between 1236 and 1258. There is no evidence to suggest that the custodial sheriffs appointed between 1236 and 1240 were extortionate; indeed, one chronicler who remarked on their appointment considered them a great improvement over the shrieval farmers they replaced.[76] The reintroduction of farmers in 1240 brought a significant increase in the king's net receipts from the shires, but may not have provoked commensurate increases in the sheriffs' gross receipts, particularly in view of the non-pecuniary advantages which shrieval office offered to Henry's curial officials. The profits established in 1240 remained stable until the fall of 1245, when a new series of fairly moderate increases began.[77] It is not really until the late 1240s that these new increments

[73] CM, vol. v, 213–15, 223–4, 240; John R. Maddicott, 'Law and Lordship: Royal Justices as Retainers in Thirteenth- and Fourteenth-Century England' (*Past and Present* Supplement 4, 1978), 13.

[74] Carpenter, 'Curial Sheriff', 21–32; Maddicott, 'Magna Carta and the Local Community', 44–6.

[75] Carpenter, 'Personal Rule', 39–70, esp. 62–70.

[76] CM, vol. iii, 363.

[77] Stacey, 'Crown Finance', 483–92.

began to produce a marked increase in exchequer pressure on the shires; and, significantly, it is only at this date that we find the king's great men abandoning shire office.

The question which remains unanswered is the extent of the private revenue which Henry's sheriffs may have collected beyond the shire farms and profits after 1240. Between 1236 and 1241, the king's reform policies added approximately £1600 to his annual shire revenues, largely by redirecting the private income of the sheriffs prior to 1236 into the royal treasury. If the king's sheriffs continued to collect private revenues during the 1240s at levels comparable to those they had received prior to 1236, then the effect of the 1240 increments upon the level of shrieval oppression in the countryside must have been substantial. For the reasons given above, I am inclined to believe that they did not. That they collected some additional payments beyond the shire farms and assigned profits is almost certain. But it was the king's attempt in the late 1240s to squeeze out even these modest sums through new increments and new men which finally drove the curial officials from the shires, and which gave rise to the abuses which helped propel the 1258 reformers into power. Until that date, Henry's shire profits had not, by and large, been collected at his subjects' cost.

II. *The Exploitation of the Royal Demesne to 1236*

Relative to the revenues from taxation and from justice, the royal demesne played only a minor role even in twelfth-century crown finance.[78] It would be wrong, however, to suggest that the Angevins had no conception of the royal demesne as a separate category of revenue, or that they were indifferent to increasing its issues when opportunity allowed.[79] Bertram Wolffe is surely right to argue that, aside from supporting the king's own family, the primary financial role of the Angevin Crown lands was to provide a fund from which the king's supporters could be rewarded with gifts and grants.[80] Maintaining the political support of the great men of the realm always

---

[78] Bertram P. Wolffe, *The Royal Demesne in English History*, (London, 1971), 30–4. On the financial importance of justice to Henry I, see Judith Green, ' "Praeclarum et Magnificum Antiquitatis Monumentum": the Earliest Surviving Pipe Roll', *BIHR* 55 (1982), 1–17. In some shires, justice contributed more to Henry I's revenues in 1129–30 than either the shire farm or geld: cf. *English Historical Documents*, vol. ii, ed. D. C. Douglas and G. W. Greenaway, 2nd edn. (London, 1981), 611–14.

[79] As does Wolffe, *Royal Demesne*, 17–67. Prior to 1154, there is not enough evidence to pronounce on this matter either way.

[80] Ibid., 34–7.

mattered more to Henry II and Richard I than did the modest increases in revenue they might have achieved by vigorously exploiting their rights as landlords. Patronage and agricultural efficiency, however, were not incompatible objectives. Both kings showed a keen interest in the efficient exploitation of custodies and escheats, despite the political problems which allegations of waste might present, and despite the importance of such windfalls to royal patronage. The eyre justices were probably investigating the stocking and leasing of escheats even before the articles of the 1194 eyre reveal these duties to us.[81] Similarly, the commissioners who compiled the 1185 *Rotuli de Dominabus* made careful inquiries into agricultural conditions on the royal escheats, and it appears that some sort of an inquest 'de dominiis domini regis' was set in motion as part of the 1170 Inquest of Sheriffs.[82] That no consistent or coherent agricultural policy towards the royal demesne emerged under Henry II or Richard reflects their success in raising cash by quicker, less administratively onerous means. It says nothing about the ability of their administrators to conceive of the royal estates as an agricultural entity, nor does it impugn their capacity to exploit these lands if the necessity arose. Nor should it suggest that the royal demesne was conceived of as a financial resource by Henry III in a way fundamentally different from the way it had been considered by his Angevin ancestors.

Elements of the systematic agricultural policy which Henry pursued on the royal demesne between 1236 and 1240 emerged gradually over the preceding forty years. In 1194, King Richard first began to detach individual manors from the shire farms, placing them instead in the hands of the newly reorganized royal escheators, who henceforth answered for their issues as custodians. As we have seen, King John extended this custodial policy to the shires themselves, and in a general way continued the removal of the manors from the undifferentiated shire farms. Very often, however, such removals were still made in perpetual fee-farm. Recipients of these grants must often have paid handsomely for them, but in an inflationary age, such arrangements cost the exchequer much long-term revenue in return for an immediate cash payment. When fee-farms were granted to important supporters, like the grant of Wycombe in Buckinghamshire to Alan Basset in 1204, they might be justified in terms of the political and military support

---

[81] Stubbs, *Select Charters*, 254-5.
[82] *Rotuli de Dominabus et Pueris et Puellis*, ed. J. H. Round, PRS 35 (London, 1913). For the 1170 Inquest of Sheriffs, see Stubbs, *Select Charters*, 177 (cap. 14).

they secured.[83] But grants such as the perpetual fee-farm made to the men of Andover, also in 1204, brought the king nothing beyond immediate cash. Despite the example of the custodian sheriffs, John took no deliberate steps to increase the number of royal manors in custodial hands. Manors not alienated in fee-farm he generally continued to place at farm, sometimes for a term of years, more often at the king's pleasure or for life. The movement away from fee-farms and leases toward the direct exploitation of manorial inland, evident on both lay and ecclesiastical estates in the thirty years after 1184,[84] apparently found no echo on the royal demesne lands until 1236.

This evident royal reluctance to adopt the new trend toward direct demesne management requires some explanation, but in order to do so, it is necessary first to clarify a terminological muddle occasioned by the word 'demesne'. Just as royal officials might refer to manors held directly by the king as 'demesne manors', so too within an individual manor there would often be 'demesne' land—land, that is, which had not been granted out to individuals in heritable tenures, but which could be exploited at the discretion of the manorial bailiff. A bailiff might choose to let this land on short-term leases; he might exploit it directly with the aid of hired labour and whatever customary services the manorial tenants owed; or he might choose to combine the two methods, leasing some of this manorial 'demesne', and directly exploiting other portions of it. Over most of Europe and in most centuries, landlords generally preferred to lease out their 'inland', as I shall henceforth call such manorial demesne. But in England in the two centuries or so after about 1180, landlords generally chose to exploit the inland directly.[85] This system of direct exploitation is commonly known to economic historians as 'demesne farming'. The label is doubly unfortunate, and flatly contradicts medieval usage, which reserved 'farm' as a term for a fixed payment (usually monetary

---

[83] King John granted Wycombe to the Bassets for £20 per year farm and the service of a single knight's fee. Alan Basset then granted the burgesses of Wycombe the farm of their borough for £30 13s. 4d. per year, and retained the demesne land in his own hands. The manor was obviously worth substantially more than the £20 per year the king received from it. Indeed, the burgesses regarded their agreement as so favourable that they later paid Henry III 10 marks to confirm the charter they had executed with Alan Basset: cf. *Charter Rolls 1226–57*, 228–9, and Originalia Roll 21 Henry III (E. 371/4 m. 7, labelled m. 8).

[84] P. D. A. Harvey, 'The Pipe Rolls and the Adoption of Demesne Farming in England', *Ec.H.R.*, 2nd s. 27 (1974), 345–59.

[85] P. D. A. Harvey, *Manorial Records of Cuxham, Oxfordshire circa 1200–1359* (London, 1976), 12–14; Miller and Hatcher, *Medieval England*, 204–13.

by this period) paid by the holder of a manor or tenement to his lord. The 'farmer' might hold in fee-farm, for life, or for a term of years, but the land he held was thus removed from the supply of land available to the bailiff for 'demesne farming', i.e., direct exploitation. There seems no way to eliminate this confusion without abandoning the modern term altogether. In what follows, 'farm' will therefore be restricted to its medieval meaning. What modern historians call 'demesne farming' will instead be called 'direct exploitation (or management) of the manorial inland', or some less cumbersome combination of these words. 'Demesne' will be restricted to its collective meaning in the thirteenth century, as the aggregate of the king's manorial holdings *extra feodum*.

This change-over from a system of fee farms and leases to the direct exploitation of manorial inland seems to have occurred on most of the great English estates between 1180 and about 1220.[86] A few signs of the change can be detected in the 1170s, and it was by no means completed by 1220—but nevertheless, it is the rapidity and the relative thoroughness of the change-over which stands out in the manorial records of the period. Explanations for this shift have been various, the most favoured being inflation and the risks that leasing might create permanent, heritable tenures on inland.[87] Inflation does seem to have been particularly rapid in England during this period, with the price of corn and livestock doubling and perhaps even tripling between 1180 and 1220, and continuing to increase at a more gradual rate until at least mid-century.[88] In such a situation, a long term lease at a fixed farm was clearly a costly proposition for a landlord, and a perpetual fee-farm even more so. Lords were quick to realize this fact, especially with regard to fee-farms; efforts to commute existing fee-farms by repurchase or exchange are a commonplace of thirteenth-century manorial history.[89] Long-term or life leases posed similar difficulties, although at least these farms could be raised when the lease expired.

A system of short-term leases, with frequent increases in the farms at which they were held, would seem to have been a potential solution

---

[86] Harvey, 'Pipe Rolls and Demesne Farming', 345–59; *Cuxham Records*, 13–14.

[87] Harvey, *Cuxham Records*, 13–15; Harvey, 'Inflation 1180–1220', 5–9; Edward Miller, 'Farming of Manors and Direct Management', *Ec.H.R.* 2nd s. 26 (1973), 138–40, and 'England in the 12th and 13th Century: an Economic Contrast?', *Ec.H.R.* 2nd s. 24 (1971), 134–7; Miller and Hatcher, *Medieval England*, 208–11.

[88] See n. 6 above.

[89] Barbara Harvey, *Westminster Abbey and its Estates in the Middle Ages* (Oxford, 1977), 164–7 gives some interesting examples of this process on the Abbey's estates.

to the problem of inflation, and would also have offered lords the advantages of a reliable, fixed income and minimal administrative expenses. It is extremely unlikely that an average inflation rate of about 5 per cent per year (assuming 300 per cent compound inflation over forty years) would have produced noticeable losses to lords who operated on a system of two, three, or even five-year leases, especially when the additional administrative costs of direct seigneurial management are considered. That landlords nevertheless found it advantageous to adopt direct management suggests that inflation was not the only pressure pushing them towards this change. Moreover, although inflation may have been particularly serious in England, it was a European phenomenon; yet only in England did landlords shift on so large a scale toward the direct exploitation of their lands. This too suggests that some peculiarly English phenomenon must also have encouraged this transformation.

A fear that leasing of inland might result in heritable tenures for its holders seems a more promising explanation for the peculiar 'Englishness' of this change. Without the added factor of inflation, heritable tenures might not have posed quite the danger to seigneurial incomes which they did; but when inflation is added to the pervasive effects of the royal action of novel disseisin upon tenures, the two together threatened after 1180 to have a truly devastating effect upon seigneurial control over their lands. The extent to which the legal position of lords versus their free manorial tenants was transformed by the workings of novel disseisin has been brilliantly argued by Professor Milsom.[90] Seisin, suggests Milsom, had originally been a verb in the seigneurial vocabulary; it was something which a lord did to a tenant by entrusting him with lands. The tenant's 'right' in the land, whether he held in fee, for life, or for a term of years, was created and guaranteed by his lord's willingness to warrant the tenant's continued possession of it. Outside that seigneurial warrant, the tenant had no legal 'right' to possession, except in so far as the lord's own court might insist that he act reasonably in his dealings toward his tenants. In such a world, there could be little risk that a lord who granted a series of leases to a tenant, or who was careless about reclaiming simple seisin at the end of the term of a lease, and who instead simply left the holder in possession and renewed the lease, might permanently lose his right to dispose of that land in another way if he chose to dispossess the sitting

---

[90] Milsom, *Legal Framework, passim.*

tenant. A seigneurial *quo warranto* began and ended the matter: Milsom, indeed, describes the action as 'tautologous'.[91] If a lord was no longer willing to warrant his tenant's possession, either because the tenant held only by lease and not by fee, or because the tenant had failed to fulfil the terms of his agreement with the lord, or simply because the lord no longer wished that tenant to hold of him, the tenant was disseised. The tenant did not possess any abstract right of 'seisin' about which legal suit could be brought.

It is highly likely that Henry I reserved the right to intervene in such cases if he desired, and if the disseised tenant had the money and the influence, there is every reason to suspect that the king might have intervened on his behalf.[92] But the new Angevin royal action of novel disseisin suddenly made such intervention accessible to a very great number of people. Only freeholders were protected by the writ; villeins and leaseholders were therefore, by implication at least, excluded from its protection. But no clear legal definitions existed by which any of these groups could be defined.[93] What constituted a freehold tenure? Could a man who paid a yearly farm on manorial inland which his

---

[91] Ibid., 42.

[92] Writs of tolt, by which a case could be removed from a seigneurial court to the shire court, were already common under Henry I, and appear frequently on the only surviving pipe roll for the reign: *Magnum Rotulum Scaccarii, vel rotulum pipae, anno 31 regni Henrici primi*, ed. Joseph Hunter (London, 1833), reissued with corrections by Charles Johnson in 1929. Green points to evidence on this roll that under-tenants were using the royal court to restrain their lord: 'The Earliest Surviving Pipe Roll,' 9, citing *Pipe Roll 31 Henry I*, 62, 68, 85 as examples. The antiquity of the writ pone, by which a case could be transferred from the shire court to the court *coram rege*, is less certain than that of tolt. All surviving exemplars are returnable writs, and Palmer finds no good evidence for their existence before around 1180 (*County Courts*, 148–9). Even if this is so, however, it would be dangerous to conclude, as does Palmer, that Henry I could not therefore transfer cases from shire courts to his own court if he chose. What is at issue is less the legal form of the transfer than Henry I's capacity to effect such a transfer at will, which could have been done with a non-returnable executive writ of the familiar late Anglo-Saxon and Anglo-Norman type. Palmer's discussion of both tolt and pone presumes that they existed as remedies to the biases of local courts, created because 'each higher level of court was less susceptible to bias' (149; cf. also 144). On the contrary, I would suggest that from the king's point of view the great advantage of removing cases to his own court, whether shire or *coram rege*, was that he could then control the outcome of the case. Justice, especially under Henry I, was a critically important form of royal patronage, a fact which is clear from the large sums which magnates were prepared to pay for it on the 1130 pipe roll. Curial impartiality is not a goal Henry I is likely to have thought desirable, and is highly unlikely to have restricted the cases he could bring into his courts if he chose. Cf. Palmer, *County Courts*, 141–50.

[93] In addition to Milsom, *Legal Framework*, see Paul R. Hyams, *Kings, Lords, and Peasants in Medieval England: The Common Law of Villeinage in the Twelfth and Thirteenth Centuries* (Oxford, 1980).

father and grandfather had held before him be disseised from it, simply because a lord claimed that he held by lease and not in fee? The assize protected 'seisin', a noun, an abstract right which could now be pleaded in the king's court, and which might even override a lord's refusal to warrant it. Only if a lord kept careful records of the terms on which he granted entry to his tenants, and then ensured that he had witnesses to these terms and to his actions in enforcing and publicizing them, could he be reasonably confident that long leases would not turn into heritable tenures against his will. Even then, a series of short leases might merge in the minds of jurors into a single extended tenure, which the assize might then guarantee.[94] Great uncertainties were thus introduced into the world of estate management. By 1215 they had produced a transformation in the legal relations of tenant and landlord, a transformation which helped also to effect the remarkable shift from farming to the direct exploitation by lords of their manorial inland which is so noticeable a feature of this same period.

In this context, the delay in moving the royal estates over to the new system is more explicable. Kings were not indifferent to the economically efficient exploitation of their lands, but they did enjoy certain legal and seigneurial advantages not available to other lords. They could, in the first place, bring writs of *quo warranto* which were returnable in their own courts. After the 1180s, every other lord had to bring such actions to the royal court, in practice if not in strict law, or risk having them overturned by a royal novel disseisin.[95] Examples of such proceedings by *quo warranto* against royal manorial tenants are common. The king also had means of compulsion available to him which other lords did not enjoy, or at least enjoyed less confidently. Farming was, after all, an effective and economically efficient means of exploiting the royal demesne so long as the farms were set high enough, and raised often enough, to produce a return commensurate with what the king would enjoy from their direct exploitation through hired and customary labour. And farming also offered the king a steady

---

[94] Notice the results of the well-known case at Cockfield, in which the monks of Bury were adjudged to have disseised an heiress from a heritable holding despite their continuing public efforts to emphasize that the heiress's ancestors had held by lease, and not in fee: *The Chronicle of Jocelin of Brakelond*, ed. H.E. Butler (London, 1949), 58–9, 123–4, 138–9; *CRR*, vol. i, 430; Paul R. Hyams, review of Milsom, *Legal Framework*, in *EHR* 93 (1978), 856–61; and V. H. Galbraith, 'The Death of a Champion (1287)', in *Studies in Medieval History Presented to F. M. Powicke* (Oxford, 1948), 283–95.

[95] Milsom, *Legal Framework*, 47.

income, immune from crop failures, drought, and murrain. So long, therefore, as the king could induce or compel someone (a royal bailiff, a sheriff, or the men of the manor themselves) to take up the farm of a manor at an economic rate, all was well in the royal agricultural world. The king did not need any further 'policy' toward his demesne. His capacity to raise the farms was restricted only by the extent to which the possession of royal demesne manors by farmers at favourable rates was an important type of patronage for great men. And this was a circumstance which affected only a minority of the royal manors.

King John raised the farms of some of the royal manors fairly regularly, but his need for political and military support seems to have prevented him carrying through such a policy on the bulk of the royal demesne. His experiment with custodial sheriffs brought some additional income from the royal demesne into his hands, but ironically did not provide any incentive to the sheriffs to improve the efficiency with which they exploited the demesne manors they held. The fixed increments he charged in certain shires would have been a much more effective inducement to the efficient exploitation of the royal estates which remained in shrieval hands. But one looks in vain during John's reign, punctuated as it was by crises, for signs of a systematic policy to maintain demesne revenues at economically proper levels. Henry III's regency governments did no better. The factional conflicts of the minority placed a premium on the royal demesne as a source of patronage for the supporters of whichever camp held power at court. It was not therefore until 1236 that Henry's new council was free at last to turn its attentions in a thoroughgoing way to improving the agricultural return from the royal demesne lands.

III. *The Reforms of 1236: The Custodes Maneriorum*

Two related questions faced Henry's councillors when they set out to improve the king's demesne revenues in the spring of 1236. The first was primarily administrative: should they continue to place these manors in the hands of farmers, and raise the farms, or should they transfer the manors to custodians, as they chose to do with the shires? The second question was agricultural: should they take steps to ensure the direct exploitation of the manorial inland, or should they let the inland on short-term leases? Decisions on these matters were complicated by the twenty-year period before 1236, during which the farms of many royal manors had been essentially static despite the general agricultural prosperity. The council therefore could not easily judge the potential economic value of these manors to the king. An extent could of course be ordered, but the resulting inquest would tell the council only the present value of the manorial issues; it would not reveal the maximum total issues which might be derived from the manor if it were exploited in the most efficient way. Moreover, the valuations which resulted from extents were not always reliable; manorial bailiffs and the men of the manors themselves had an obvious interest in understating the revenues they could be expected to provide the king, and frequently did so.[96] Under these circumstances, the continued farming of the royal demesne promised more confusion than profit. The council therefore decided to place the royal estates in the hands of custodial keepers.

The decision to entrust the royal demesne to three special *custodes maneriorum* was also closely bound up with the decision to entrust the shires to custodian sheriffs. As we have seen, custodial sheriffs who retained custody of demesne manors had no incentive to ensure the most efficient exploitation of those lands; nor, for that matter, did a series of local bailiffs answering as custodians for the manorial issues outside the shire farms. Maximum returns from the royal demesne could be guaranteed only if the manors were removed from the sheriffs and other local bailiffs, and handed over to royal officials charged explicitly to maximize these profits. On many manors, this would also involve a change from traditional patterns of leasing inland to direct management,[97] which in turn would require significant capital expenditure, at least initially, on new livestock and on the purchase of seed corn and farm implements.[98] That the government was prepared to bear these short-term costs in order to increase its long-term revenues is a sign of the seriousness with which Henry's government approached the task of financial reform during these years. It is also a sign that some force within the government was exercising a consistent and purposeful control over policy.

That force can only have been the king's council. The relationship

---

[96] For an example of the council rejecting an extent as undervalued, see Fine Roll 25 Henry III (C. 60/37 m. 13), printed in *Excerpta e Rotulis Finium*, vol. i, 336 (20 Feb. 1241).

[97] The council seems to have intended this when they initiated the new policy. Most of the writs directed to the manorial keepers in the spring of 1236 referred to the king's 'manors and demesnes', both of which were to be taken in hand and managed for the king's profit. Cf. *CPR 1232–47*, 142, 146, 147, 156.

[98] Restocking the royal manors is mentioned explicitly as one of the goals of the new agricultural policy in *CPR 1232–47*, 147.

between the growing professionalism of seigneurial councils during the thirteenth century and their involvement with estate management has frequently been remarked.[99] It appears now that a similar connection should be drawn between the emergence of the king's own council as a sworn body during these years and its role in administering the royal demesne.[100] In letters patent of 26 May 1236, Henry informed the men of the Peak in Derbyshire that 'by the common counsel of his lieges' he had 'taken into his hands all his manors and demesnes, to stock them and make his profit of them'.[101] So much, perhaps, is commonplace, especially since the purpose of the writ was to seek from the men of the Peak a stock aid for the king. But when the decision was taken a year later to place the forests appurtenent to demesne manors in the hands of the manorial custodians, the role of the council was mentioned again, much more explicitly;[102] and when this order was modified in the following year to restrict the manorial keepers' claims in the forest to pannage, herbage, and honey, the council's responsibility was again asserted, and the message emphasized again by the closing attestation, 'per Willelmum de Ralegh coram rege et consilio'.[103]

The exchequer, by contrast, appear to have played little part in such decisions. The letters patent just quoted, for example, were issued at Tewkesbury on 10 April 1238, during a journey which kept King Henry and his council away from Westminster (and hence from the exchequer) from 6 March until 10 May.[104] The men who made this decision were clearly travelling with the king. Mandates to the manorial keepers between 1236 and 1240 issued exclusively from the chancery, and were often not even recorded on the exchequer memoranda rolls. Indeed, there is not a single original writ which dealt with the exploitation of the royal demesne recorded on the memoranda rolls between 1236 and 1240. The exchequer was of course responsible for

[99] Noël Denholm-Young, *Seignorial Administration in England* (Oxford, 1937); Miller and Hatcher, *Medieval England*, 189–92.
[100] On the 1236 conciliar oath, see pp. 96–8 below.
[101] CPR 1232–47, 147.
[102] 'It has been provided before the king and council that keepers of the king's manors shall have the custody of all parks and demesne woods ...' *CPR 1232–47*, 186–7.
[103] CPR 1232–47, 216. On the significance of this formula, see A.L. Brown, 'The Authorization of Letters under the Great Seal', *BIHR* 37 (1964), 125–56, and A.E. Stamp, 'Some Notes on the Court and Chancery of Henry III', in *Historical Essays in Honour of James Tait*, ed. J.G. Edwards, V.H. Galbraith, and E.F. Jacob (Manchester, 1933), 305–11.
[104] CRR, vol. 16, xlv.

auditing the accounts of the manorial keepers, but it was hampered
even in this by the regular failure of the council to inform it of the
current status of the manors. Accounts for the six months immediately
prior to the mid-year appointment of the manorial keepers in 1236
often remained unheard ten years or more after they should have been
audited, because the exchequer could not discover from the council
who ought to respond for such accounts. So complete was the exchequer's isolation from actual policy-making with regard to the manors
that it was only after the entire custodial experiment had been wound
up in 1240, and the final accounts rendered, that the exchequer took
any independent action to distrain individual bailiffs for their arrears;
and even then the council provided the form for the bailiffs' final
account.[105]

As we have seen, the decision to place the shires under custodial
sheriffs, and the decision to entrust the royal demesne to specially
appointed keepers, were two aspects of a single policy decision. Rec-
ognition of the very minor role played by the exchequer in managing
demesne policy must therefore raise doubts as to whether even the
custodial sheriffs can be said to reflect a distinctive 'exchequer
policy'.[106] Such doubts are confirmed by the records of these shrieval
appointments on the fine rolls, which make clear that although there
was some concern to keep the exchequer informed, the appointments
themselves were made by the council, and were only afterwards communicated to the exchequer.[107] A council draft of the shrieval appointments survives among the miscellanea of the exchequer; it was prepared
at Windsor, and was only later sent to the exchequer to be enrolled.[108]
The terms proposed on this draft were usually more generous to the
sheriffs than were the final versions, a change which probably reflects
consultation with the exchequer. But the policy itself, both in the shires
and on the royal demesne, was clearly initiated and directed by the

[105] The preceding is based on a study of all the memoranda rolls from 1236 until
1242. For the council's role in setting the form of the final account, cf. Memoranda Roll
25 Henry III (E. 368/13 rot. 3); Fine Roll 25 Henry III (C. 60/37 m. 18).

[106] As does Carpenter, 'Curial Sheriff', 3–6, 18, and *passim*.

[107] Notice especially the memorandum attached on the fine roll to the appointment
of William de Lucy to the custody of Warwickshire and Leicestershire, with Kenilworth
Castle: 'Hinc mittendum est ad scaccarium de castro de Kenylleworth' (C. 60/35 m. 10;
compare CPR 1232–47, 143). Similarly in 1240, the newly fixed profits for which the
sheriffs of Yorkshire, and Buckinghamshire and Bedfordshire were to answer were set
'per consilium domini regis'; the exchequer was notified of the amounts by writs, which
were then copied onto the exchequer memoranda roll: cf. E. 368/13 rot. 1d.

[108] As the contemporary heading at the top of the document reveals: E. 163/24/14.

king's council, which continued to supervise it closely over the following four years.

It would be pleasant to report that the king understood and encouraged the policies his council had adopted in his name. In a general way, he probably did, but the evidence we have for his personal role all points the other way. Within a month of the appointment of the three manorial custodians in 1236, Henry appointed his household favourite and royal councillor, Brother Geoffrey the almoner, to the custody of Bromsgrove and Feckenham in Worcestershire, which between them comprised virtually the whole of the king's demesne in that shire. The writ was quickly cancelled, 'because he had it not'; but one would give much to hear the details of the confrontation which must have ensued within the council before the writ was quashed.[109] In the late spring of 1240, soon after the council had decided to end the experiment with manorial custodians and to place the demesne manors instead at farm in the hands of the men of each individual manor, Henry struck again. This time he granted the farm of Basingstoke in Hampshire to the rising royal clerk Walter de Merton on more generous terms and at a lower farm than the council had intended to assign to it.[110] The wording of the king's grant, however, suggests that with respect to the management of his demesne, King Henry between 1236 and 1240 was as much controlled by his council as he was in control of it.

The king commits the manor of Basingstoke with its appurtenances to Walter de Merton, along with two prudent men of that manor whom Walter has associated with himself, to hold for £80 payable to the exchequer for so long as it pleases the king, unless in the meantime the king is counselled to render the aforesaid manor to the men of the same manor, according to the tenor of the royal charter which the same [Walter and his associates] had therein.[111]

[109] *CPR 1232–47*, 147. This grant is doubly puzzling because Brother Geoffrey appears to have been particularly closely involved in the new demesne policy: cf. *Cl.R. 1234–7*, 398; *CPR 1232–47*, 172; *CRR*, vol. 15, no. 1972B.
[110] The grant itself appears only on Originalia Roll 24 Henry III (E. 371/7 m. 5, marked m. 6), but is confirmed by Pipe Roll 25 Henry III (E. 372/85 rot. 7d). Walter de Merton was here charged £90 per year farm for Basingstoke, on a five-year lease. Walter paid £80, and was recorded as owing £10. This debt was later cancelled, however, with the notation 'Set non debet inde summoneri quia consideratum est coram consilio domini regis quod non debet respondere de firma de Basingestok' nisi tantum de £80 sic continetur in originalia et in litteris suis patentibus.' The patent roll for 24 Henry III has not survived.
[111] 'Rex commisit Waltero de Merton manerium de Basingestok' cum pertinenciis una cum duobus probis hominibus de eodem manerio quos idem Walterus se associabit, tenendum pro £80 solvendis ad Scaccarium quamdiu regi placuerit, nisi rex interim

This entry was eventually cancelled in favour of an entry on the originalia roll for the following year, which repeated the grant without the provisional clause 'nisi rex interim ... manerium', and which restricted the lease to five years.[112] By then the king's council had decided that Walter should have the manor at the original £80 farm, as it had been enrolled in the letters patent which the king had given Walter.[113] A year before, the king had not been so sure that he could make the grant stick. His uncertainty tells us much about the relationship between the king and his conciliar administrators during these years.

The first signs of the council's new policy toward the demesne appeared on 21 April 1236, when Walter de Burgo and John de Lexinton were sent to enquire into the state of the royal demesne in Hampshire.[114] Two weeks later, Robert de Crepping, a royal sergeant who had previously served as a royal escheator in the north, was appointed to keep the king's demesne manors in Yorkshire.[115] Both appointments came in the middle of the great purge of sheriffs between 15 April and 12 May, during which custodial sheriffs were introduced into almost all the shires. This coincidence emphasizes yet again the close relationship between the two policies. Lexinton was soon removed from the commission, but on 13 May Walter de Burgo and Warner Engayne were appointed to take in hand all the king's demesne manors (south of the Trent is not specified in the writ, but was clearly understood), with orders to mount the same sort of full-scale inquest which de Burgo and Lexinton had been appointed to make in Hampshire.[116] By August 1236, Robert de Crepping was engaged on the same task in Yorkshire, Northumberland, Cumberland, and Lancashire.[117]

The council apparently intended from the beginning to keep separate

---

consilium habuit reddendi hominibus eiusdem manerii predictum manerium, secundum tenorem carte regis quam ipsi inde h[abuer]u[n]t': Originalia Roll 24 Henry III (E. 371/7 m. 5). Walter de Merton was a local Basingstoke man: cf. *Cl.R.* 1237–42, 131–2, and C. A. F. Meekings, introduction to *Fitznells Cartulary* (Surrey Record Society 26, 1968), lviii–lxxv, reprinted in Meekings's collected papers, *Studies in 13th-Century Justice and Administration* (London, 1981).

[112] Originalia Roll 25 Henry III (E. 371/8A m. 4).
[113] See n. 110 above.
[114] *CPR 1232–47*, 142.
[115] Ibid., 145.
[116] Ibid., 146. If Lexinton and de Burgo ever began their inquiry, it certainly could not have proceeded very far.
[117] Ibid., 156.

the administration of the demesne north and south of the Trent; but it is not clear, at least from the chancery enrolments, just how extensive the new demesne policy was initially intended to be within each area. Walter de Burgo took possession of manors in Berkshire, Essex, Hertfordshire, Middlesex, and Worcester, and of a few manors in Hampshire and Northamptonshire, in May 1236. He took over the remaining manors in Hampshire and Northamptonshire at Michaelmas 1236, along with all the Wiltshire manors except Corsham, which the king's household steward Ralph fitz Nicholas managed to retain until July 1237.[118] The reappointment of de Burgo and Engayne in January 1237 was accompanied by a mandate to the sheriff of Somerset and Dorset to hand over all the manors in those shires to the two keepers.[119] It is not clear which manors the council had in mind. Somerton had been taken over by de Burgo on 1 August 1236, Bridport and Dorchester at Michaelmas, but Henry fitz Nicholas (the brother of Ralph fitz Nicholas) retained Fordington until early 1238 when he died. In Herefordshire, meanwhile, the demesne manors were not removed from the shire farm to the keepers until Michaelmas 1237, when de Burgo also took over the demesne manors in Gloucestershire.[120] The sheriff of Gloucestershire had previously responded for these as a custodian.[121]

The new regime took hold equally slowly in the north. Although Crepping was appointed keeper of the Yorkshire manors in May 1236, he did not take possession of them until Michaelmas.[122] A separate keeper was initially appointed to act in Cumberland and Northumberland, and did indeed respond for the demesne in Cumberland up to Michaelmas 1236, when Crepping took over his duties in that shire.[123] The council's initial decision to include Northumberland in the scheme was countermanded, and the demesne there remained in the hands of the sheriff.[124] Lancashire, meanwhile, was added to

---

[118] These dates are all derived from de Burgo's enrolled exchequer accounts on Pipe Roll 22 Henry III (E. 372/82 rots. 1–3d).

[119] CPR 1232–47, 173.

[120] Pipe Roll 22 Henry III (E. 372/82 rots. 1–3d).

[121] Cf. Pipe Rolls 20 and 21 Henry III (E. 372/80 rot. 6; E. 372/81 rot. 7d).

[122] Pipe Roll 22 Henry III (E. 372/82 rot. 4).

[123] CPR 1232–47, 148; Pipe Roll 20 Henry III (E. 372/80 rot. 14d).

[124] CPR 1232–47, 156, 174, mention Northumberland as one of the shires in which Crepping was to have custody of the royal demesne. But in his account on Pipe Roll 22 Henry III (E. 372/82 rot. 4), all listings for manors in Northumberland are cancelled, with a notation: 'quia Vic' Norhumb' respondet in Norhumb' sic continetur in rotul' de particulis proficui quam liberavit in thesauro.'

Crepping's circuit by Michaelmas 1236, although no chancery writ survives to record the appointment.[125]

These alterations and adaptations, north and south, in part reflect new information coming into the council from the inquests it ordered in the spring and summer of 1236. Primarily, however, they reflect conciliar caution in introducing the new policy. The need for such caution was brought home to the council by the political uproar which de Burgo's initial demesne resumptions produced. Taking literally the council's command 'to take in hand all the king's manors and demesnes,' de Burgo disseised at least a dozen English magnates from royal estates which they held by royal charter. So direct an attack on the security of seisin produced an immediate political outcry, which the council quickly heeded. The magnates were restored to their estates, and de Burgo admonished to restrict his attentions to estates for which no charter right could be alleged.[126] In extending the custodial scheme thereafter, the council proceeded more circumspectly. It was, after all, less than two years since an attempt to redistribute a few royal manors had brought down the regime of the bishop of Winchester.

The council's approach to demesne management, however, remained thoroughgoing and radical. Characteristically, the reforms began with an exhaustive inquest into the state of the royal demesne. The precise articles of the inquest are now lost, but its concerns are clear enough from de Burgo's and Engayne's commission.

The king has appointed the said Walter and Warner to take into his hands all his manors and demesnes, with their parks, woods and other appurtenances, and to enquire how much they are worth yearly in demesnes, rents, services, villeinages, and other issues, and touching lands alienated, and to do other things enjoined upon them...[127]

Some idea of the specificity of the information sought can also be gained from the extant return to the inquest the council launched in the summer of 1240, when it wound up the experiment with manorial custodians in order to return the manors to local men at farm.[128] The 1240 commissioners took a thorough inventory of all the stock on the

---

[125] Pipe Roll 22 Henry III (E. 372/82 rot. 4).
[126] For a more detailed discussion of these threats to seisin and their political consequences, see Ch. 3.
[127] CPR 1232–47, 156.
[128] *Book of Fees*, vol. i, 620–4; *Cl.R.* 1237–42, 220.

manor, and of all the crops both standing and in granaries. They recorded the fixed rents on the manor, the value (and probably the nature) of any customs owed, and the annual value of any manorial markets, forests, or courts. They also inventoried the manorial inland, recording its value if leased and also the value of all pastureland, both without stock and if fully stocked. It was on the basis of such information as this that de Burgo decided, in 1236, how best 'to make the king's profit of the said manors and demesnes ...'[129] on each of the manors he toured.

The agricultural policies pursued by the king's manorial custodians need only detain us briefly here.[130] In the north, Robert de Crepping's accounts survive complete on the pipe rolls,[131] although the form in which they were enrolled makes it difficult to analyse the agricultural policies he pursued. The exchequer clerks treated him as a custodian of the traditional sort, answering for a set farm for each manor in his custody, and then answering separately for all issues beyond that farm, regardless of whether Crepping exploited the manorial inland directly, or leased it out. For the most part, however, Crepping seems to have brought few changes to the agricultural management of these estates. In Lancaster and Cumberland, he raised some farms, and added stock to a few manors, but continued to lease out the inland on most of the manors in his custody. Only at Riggeby (Lancs.) did Crepping manage the manorial inland directly. Riggeby, however, had been held until 1240 by a royal clerk in free alms. When Crepping recovered it upon the clerk's death, he managed it directly until Michaelmas 1242, probably to determine its real value. Thereafter, he responded for the estate at a revised fixed farm, and leased out the inland, in keeping with practice on the other Lancashire estates.

In Yorkshire, Crepping managed the inland directly at Pickering, and after overcoming the resistance of the chief justice of the northern forest, assarted 200 acres of new inland at Easingwold, which he then

---

[129] *CPR 1232–47*, 142.

[130] These are described in detail in Robert C. Stacey, 'Agricultural Investment and the Management of the Royal Demesne Manors, 1236–40', *Journal of Economic History*, 46 (1986), 919–34.

[131] Crepping responded every two years, on the foreign roll attached to the pipe roll, for the manors in his possession: cf. Pipe Roll 22 Henry III (E. 372/82 rot. 4); Pipe Roll 24 Henry III (E. 372/84 rot. 2d); *Pipe Roll 26 Henry III*, ed. H. L. Cannon (New Haven, 1918), 116–20; Pipe Roll 28 Henry III (E. 372/88 rot. 12); Pipe Roll 30 Henry III (E. 372/90 rot. 9d); Pipe Roll 31 Henry III (E. 372/91 rots. 14, 14d). Unless otherwise noted, all information on Crepping's policies as a custodian is derived from these accounts.

leased out for 10 marks per year.[132] But here as elsewhere, Crepping's most dramatic improvements derived from the profits of stock management. At Wirral, Lonsdale, and Amounderness in Lancashire, Crepping doubled the gross issues from the forest and its pastureland between 1237 and 1245, with the increase deriving entirely from the management of stock. Some of this new stock Crepping purchased, but most of it came from the lands of the vacant bishopric of Durham.[133] At Pickering, Crepping purchased 18 oxen and 360 ewes with lambs, and received an additional 791 sheep from Durham, some of which he later transferred to Easingwold.[134] Sixty more cows with 54 calves were added at Pickering between 1238 and 1240,[135] but thereafter Crepping purchased new stock at a much reduced rate, and probably only to replace ageing animals. Between 1236 and 1238, Crepping raised the average annual value of Pickering by about 25 per cent, from around £88 to around £112 per year, although the form of his account makes it impossible to determine how much of this increase derived from his direct management of the arable inland, and how much from the increased value of the stock. Thereafter, however, the value of the manor remained essentially constant, despite the return of the manor to shrieval custody in 1242.

The financial success of the custodial experiment in the north was thus fairly modest. Removal of Easingwold and Falsgrave (Yorks.) from farmers produced markedly higher returns from these two manors without any major changes in agricultural practice. Acquisition of new stock, much of it obtained without cost to the king, brought improved profits at Wirral, Lonsdale, and Amounderness, and supplemented the value of Easingwold. New stock and direct exploitation of the manorial inland added perhaps £25 per year to the value of Pickering, and helped to establish an economic farm at Riggeby. Elsewhere, Crepping had little impact. After deductions for his own yearly fee, his appointment added only about £125 to £150 per year

---

[132] Pipe Roll 22 Henry III (E. 372/82 rot. 4); *Pipe Roll 14 Henry III*, 35; *CRR*, vol. 15, no. 1919; *CLR 1226–40*, 245; *Cl.R. 1234–7*, 392; *Cl.R. 1237–42*, 40; Originalia Roll 21 Henry III (E. 371/4 m. 2, marked m. 3).

[133] Crepping purchased 45 head of cattle, but brought in 254 head from the Durham vacancy: Pipe Roll 22 Henry III (E. 372/82 rot. 4); *Cl.R. 1234–7*, 444, 449, 456; *Cl.R. 1237–42*, 20.

[134] Pipe Roll 22 Henry III (E. 372/82 rot. 4). The Yorkshire manors also profited from a stock aid granted to the king by the Cistercians in the spring of 1236, apparently in lieu of a cash contribution toward the aid to marry the king's sister Isabella: cf. *CPR 1232–47*, 150.

[135] Pipe Roll 24 Henry III (E. 372/84 rot. 2d).

to the king's revenues, an increase of perhaps one-third on the value
of these manors to the king in 1236.

In the south, although Walter de Burgo and Warner Engayne were
appointed jointly as custodians,[136] Engayne in fact held only five
manors, four of which the king had alienated by the middle of 1238.[137]
Walter de Burgo was clearly the expert in estate management, and it
was he who supervised the remaining forty or so southern manors, on
which the great bulk of the king's arable inland was concentrated. In
exploiting these manors, de Burgo was specifically encouraged by the
council to begin direct management of the manorial inland, to revoke
demesne leases where necessary, and to increase the amount of stock
on the manors.[138] Such policies were expensive; but despite the stringent
financial circumstances of 1236 and early 1237,[139] the council was
clearly prepared to bear such short-term investment expenses in order
to increase the long-term return from the king's estates. During the
first two years of his custody, de Burgo spent large sums on the
purchase of new seed corn, on new draught animals and ploughs, and
on marling and smother crops to condition the soil.[140] He also invested
heavily in new stock, renewing the sheep flocks with younger animals,
and introducing new dairy herds on several estates. De Burgo was also
active in the meat market, buying pigs and steers in the spring, fattening
them over the summer, and selling them in the autumn, at an average
profit of about 33 per cent.

De Burgo's agricultural methods were highly capital intensive,
especially on the twenty-five manors on which he managed the manorial inland directly. During his first full year of custody, de Burgo
reinvested almost 50 per cent of the gross issues from these manors in
new stock, seed, and other improvements. Although investment levels
dropped during his second year to less than 20 per cent of total issues,
de Burgo still averaged better than 30 per cent annual reinvestment on
these twenty-five manors during his first two years of custody, a figure
four to five times the investment level on most medieval estates.[141]

---

[136] *CPR 1232–47*, 146.

[137] Torksey (Lincs.), Lothingland (Suffolk), Mansfield and Oswaldsbeck (Notts.), and
Aylsham (Norfolk): cf. *Cl.R. 1237–42*, 12, 60; *CPR 1232–47*, 206; Pipe Roll 28 Henry
III (E. 372/88 rot. 4).

[138] *CPR 1232–47*, 142, 146, 147, 156.

[139] See pp. 98–110 below.

[140] Records for the first two and a half years of de Burgo's custody survive as a foreign
roll attached to Pipe Roll 22 Henry III (E. 372/82 rots. 1–3d). Unless otherwise noted,
all information on de Burgo's agricultural policies is derived from these accounts.

[141] Stacey, 'Agricultural Investment', *passim*; M. M. Postan, 'Investment in Medieval

Such policies were a marked departure from traditional approaches to managing the royal demesne, and although the council was prepared to back de Burgo financially, even to the point of loaning him money for investment purposes, it intended to monitor carefully the success of this expensive custodial experiment. Both the extraordinary detail and the overall structure of de Burgo's pipe roll accounts bear witness to the council's close attention to demesne policy during these years. In contrast to Crepping's accounts, which grouped receipts from all the manors together at the front of the account, and expenses from all the manors together at the end of the account, the exchequer made a deliberate effort in recording de Burgo's accounts to keep the direct agricultural issues and expenses for each manor together on the rolls. This enabled the exchequer to strike a yearly balance for each manor, and thus to measure the relative success of the custodial experiment from year to year. De Burgo's accounts were far more elaborate and time-consuming for the exchequer to prepare, but they were also far more reliable tests of custodial efficiency. The willingness of the exchequer to devote so much official time to compiling these accounts is a good indication of the importance which the council attached to the new demesne policy.

By the autumn of 1238, profits from grain sales on de Burgo's manors had increased dramatically over their pre-1236 levels, and although stock profits were still largely eaten up in the purchase of new animals, the herds themselves were now of far better quality than they had been when de Burgo took over.[142] Profits from this improvement would emerge in subsequent years. Records from the final two years of de Burgo's custody have not survived, and so we cannot follow in detail the results of all his innovations. But already by 1238 de Burgo had raised the net issues on most of his manors by almost 50 per cent over their pre-1236 levels. He had accomplished this partly through grain sales, but primarily by increasing the returns from customary rents and renders, and from the judicial pleas and perquisites of the manorial courts. De Burgo's accounts do not usually allow us to say how precisely he accomplished such increases. But on the whole, it does not appear that they were purchased at the cost of vastly increased oppression of the manorial tenants. Occasionally one

Agriculture', *Journal of Economic History* 27 (1967), 576–87; M. Mate, 'Profit and Productivity on the Estates of Isabella de Forz (1260–92)', *Ec.H.R.* 2nd s. 33 (1980), 326–34.

[142] See Tables 2.1 and 2.2.

TABLE 2.1 *Grain sales and purchases 1236–8*

	1236–7		1237–8	
	Issues from corn sales	Expenses from corn purchases	Issues from corn sales	Expenses from corn purchases
Bray	£ 28 2s. 4½d.	£ 12s. 7½d.	£ 36 8s. 8½d.	£ 5 10s. 4d.
Cookham	£ 20 15s. 10d.	£ 6 4s. 4d.	£ 31 19s. 8d.	£ 13s. 4d.
Windsor	£ 17s. 3d.	£ 12 4s. 9d.	£ 29 16s. 4d.	£ 2 1s. 6d.
Brill	£ 3 13s. 0d.	—	£ 9 0s. 1d.	£ 2 17s. 8½d.
Essendon and Bayford	£ 13 16s. 6d.	£ 4 8s. 0d.	£ 14 10s. 6d.	—
Hatfield	£100 11s. 11d.	£ 39 6s. 8d.	£102 12s. 8½d.	—
Newport	£ 22 1s. 3d.	£ 3 9s. 8½d.	£ 30 0s. 0d.	£ 1 4s. 6d.
Writtle	£ 99 5s. 5d.	£ 23 5s. 0d.	£111 3s. 3d.	—
Ospringe[a]	£ 13 0s. 2½d.	£ 1 12s. 3½d.	£ 29 6s. 11d.	£18 8s. 3½d.
Brigstock	£ 8 3s. 1d.	£ 2 12s. 4½d.	£ 32 4s. 5d.	£ 2 7s. 9d.
Finedon	£ 17 0s. 0d.	£ 13 1s. 5½d.	£ 31 0s. 0d.	£ 8 15s. 10d.
Silverstone	£ 7s. 6d.	£ 2 5s. 4½d.	£ 13s. 8d.	£ 3 0s. 10½d.
Somerton	£ 9 0s. 0d.	£ 7 1s. 4½d.	£ 17 1s. 2d.	£ 9 2s. 6d.
Rowde	—	£ 4 8s. 8½d.	£ 27 16s. 5½d.	£ 6 5s. 4d.
Melksham	£ 22 17s. 3½d.	£ 10s. 11½d.	£ 21 1s. 4½d.	—
Feckenham	£ 2 5s. 0d.	£ 24 10s. 9½d.	£ 39 0s. 0d.	£14 11s. 8d.
Kempton	£ 6 5s. 5d.	£ 3s. 10d.	£ 19 0s. 11d.	—
Total	£368 2s. 1½d.	£145 18s. 3d.	£582 16s. 2d.	£74 19s. 7½d.

[a] The year 1237–8 was the first year of custody; de Burgo held Ospringe from 2 February 1237. Otherwise, all these manors were held for two complete years by de Burgo. Manors not held for two years are omitted from this table.

does find evidence of such oppression. At Feckenham (Worcs.), de Burgo increased work services beyond their customary bounds; he demanded one-half of the issues from lands leased in champerty, instead of the customary one-third; he amerced men too heavily in the manorial court for judicial offences; and he disseised five poor men of a meadow, which he claimed as alienated demesne. In 1238, the royal council ordered a stop to all these practices, and the reseisin of the aggrieved meadow owners.[143] At Bromsgrove (Worcs.), de Burgo raised rents on the manor from 10s. 8d. to 13s. 4d. per virgate,[144] he collected a £16 aid to stock the manor which in fact went straight to the king, and in 1238 he levied fines *de terris retinendis* which produced about

[143] Cl.R. 1237–42, 142.
[144] CPR 1232–47, 181.

TABLE 2.2 *Stock rearing 1236–8*

	1236–7		1237–8	
	Issues	Expenses	Issues	Expenses
Bray	£ 7 19s. 4d.	£ 12 19s. 3½d.	£ 11 16s. 8½d.	£ 11 9s. 2d.
Cookham	£ 5 17s. 6d.	£ 6 12s. 7d.	£ 7 4s. 0½d.	£ 7 7s. 7d.
Windsor	£ 2 15s. 4d.	£ 2 11s. 6½d.	£ 10s. 10d.	£ 8s. 4d.
Brill	£ 6 15s. 9d.	£ 20 3s. 1d.	£ 7 11s. 8d.	—
Essendon and Bayford	£ 7 10s. 8½d.	£ 21 14s. 5d.	£ 27 13s. 7d.	£ 25 7s. 8d.
Hatfield	£ 8 11s. 6d.	£ 40 8s. 4d.	£ 31 8s. 0½d.	£ 10 2s. 9d.
Newport	£ 4 16s. 3d.	£ 16 0s. 7½d.	£ 3 13s. 1d.	—
Writtle	£ 17 14s. 8d.	£ 62 15s. 5d.	£ 39 12s. 6½d.	£ 5 12s. 8d.
Ospringe	£ 3 10s. 4d.	£ 2 14s. 7½d.	£ 2 5s. 6d.	£ 10 9s. 7½d.
Brigstock	£ 6 17s. 1d.	£ 18 7s. 3d.	£ 43 5s. 3½d.	£ 48 17s. 1d.
Finedon	£ 6 0s. 0d.	£ 16 9s. 2d.	£ 6 13s. 8d.	£ 3 14s. 1d.
Silverstone	£ 11 3s. 0d.	£ 20 0s. 0d.	£ 23 4s. 11½d.	£ 21 4s. 11d.
Somerton	£ 9 19s. 0d.	£ 30 14s. 0d.	£ 12 17s. 6d.	£ 19s. 9d.
Rowde	—	£ 2 15s. 0d.	£ 2s. 4d.	—
Melksham	£ 66 1s. 0d.	£ 98 0s. 5½d.	£ 52 16s. 11d.	£ 40 5s. 10d.
Feckenham	£ 7 10s. 10d.	£ 12 18s. 4d.	£ 16 13s. 10d.	£ 9 0s. 9d.
Kempton	£ 6 13s. 1½d.	£ 12 16s. 3d.	£ 3 10s. 6d.	—
	£179 15s. 5d.	£398 0s. 4½d.	£291 0s. 11d.	£195 0s. 2½d.

One-year accounts

Barton Gloucester			£ 10 13s. 4d.	£ 7 11s. 10½d.
Rodley			£ 8 16s. 6d.	£ 10s. 3d.
Slaughter			£ 7 17s. 0½d.	£ 23 11s. 3½d.
Lugwardine			£ 1 11s. 5d.	£ 18s. 2d.
Marden			£ 1 14s. 3½d.	£ 14s. 0d.
Fordington			£ 3 16s. 11d.	£ 20s. 0d.
Corsham			£ 10 12s. 0d.	—
			£ 45 1s. 6d.	£ 34 5s. 7d.
Total	£179 15s. 5d.	£398 0s. 4½d.	£336 2s. 5d.	£229 5s. 9½d.
Two-year total Issues		£515 17s. 10d.		
Expenses		£627 6s. 2d.		

£30. He also arrented a number of assarts.[145] The combined effect of these exactions and reclamations raised the gross issues of Bromsgrove from £58 in 1236 to £144 in 1238, without any direct cultivation of the manorial inland, which remained entirely on leaseholds.

[145] *Cl.R.* 1234–7, 398.

In general, however, instances of extortion, peculation, or fraud by de Burgo or his local manorial bailiffs are surprisingly hard to discover. When the council dismissed de Burgo in the spring of 1240, it sent teams of royal officials to inquire into the state of all the manors he had held in custody. The only complete return which survives from this series of inquests comes from Ospringe in Kent.[146] As was usual when the government sent out inquisitors to solicit complaints, complaints were found, but at Ospringe the local jurors declared them all to be groundless, and vindicated the conduct of de Burgo's bailiffs. The jurors were not, in this case, under any evident compulsion to render so favourable a verdict. Another set of complaints, alleging the fraudulent substitution of poor-quality beasts for the good ones which de Burgo had left on the Wiltshire manors, was also found to be groundless.[147] Some abuses there certainly were. There is no doubt that de Burgo disseised a number of manorial tenants without judgement, particularly at Alton in Hampshire.[148] In another case, he took 8 marks from an individual *ad opus regis*, which the king later ordered him to repay, but which the king allowed him to deduct against his account.[149] However irregular, the payment did at least go to the king, and not into the pockets of his bailiff. But for a man who handled more than £10,000 in gross receipts during his four years in office, the sum total of such incidents is remarkably small, and speaks well for the quality of de Burgo's administration.

All this makes even more surprising the council's decision in the spring of 1240 to wind up the custodial experiment in the south, and to return the royal demesne at fixed farms to the men of the manors themselves. Contrary to Hoyt's opinion, that 'the *custodes* appointed in 1236 merely piled up debts at the Exchequer',[150] the custodial experiment had in fact been a resounding financial success. By the spring of 1240, de Burgo had produced a permanent increase in the king's demesne revenues of between £600 and £700 per year, an increase of approximately 60 per cent on pre-1236 levels, exclusive of wool issues, the proceeds from which are not recorded on these

[146] *Book of Fees*, vol. i, 620–3.
[147] Fine Roll 26 Henry III (C. 60/38 m. 12).
[148] *Cl.R. 1237–42*, 142; *CRR*, vol. 16, no. 1428; and for the Alton case, *CRR*, vol. 15, no. 2059, 2075; *CRR*, vol. 16, nos. 43, 84, 117D, 125, 149A; *Cl.R. 1234–7*, 433, 482, 529; *Cl.R. 1237–42*, 82, 90; *Extracta e Rotulis Finium*, vol. i, 325–6.
[149] *Cl.R. 1237–42*, 264.
[150] Hoyt, *Royal Demesne*, 160.

TABLE 2.3 *Increased demesne revenues 1236–41*

Manor	Value in 1236 per year	Value in 1241 per year	Increase (decrease)	Terms of 1241 lease
Bray and Cookham	£ 126 0s. 0d.	£ 160 0s. 0d.	£ 34 0s. 0d.	stock lease
Windsor	£ 26 0s. 0d.	£ 40 0s. 0d.	£ 14 0s. 0d.	
Brill	£ 23 0s. 0d.	£ 38 0s. 0d.	£ 15 0s. 0d.	stock lease
Essendon and Bayford	£ 20 0s. 0d.	£ 40 0s. 0d.	£ 20 0s. 0d.	stock lease
Newport	£ 41 3s. 4d.	£ 40 0s. 0d.	(£ 1 3s. 4d.)	stock lease
Barton Gloucester	£ 19 0s. 0d.	£ 46 0s. 0d.	£ 27 0s. 0d.	stock lease
Dymock	£ 33 6s. 8d.	£ 50 0s. 0d.	£ 16 13s. 4d.	
Minsterworth	£ 17 0s. 0d.	£ 28 0s. 0d.	£ 11 0s. 0d.	
Newnham	£ 10 0s. 0d.	£ 10 0s. 0d.	—	
Rodley	£ 20 0s. 0d.	£ 42 0s. 0d.	£ 22 0s. 0d.	stock lease
Slaughter	£ 20 0s. 0d.	£ 40 0s. 0d.	£ 20 0s. 0d.	stock lease
Winchcombe	£ 50 0s. 0d.	£ 50 0s. 0d.	—	
Alton	£ 85 0s. 0d.	£ 90 0s. 0d.	£ 5 0s. 0d.	
Andover	£ 104 0s. 0d.	£ 104 0s. 0d.	—	
Basingstoke	£ 72 12s. 0d.	£ 80 0s. 0d.	£ 7 8s. 0d.	
Acornbury	—	£ 8 0s. 0d.	£ 8 0s. 0d.	
Dilwyn	—	£ 40 0s. 0d.	£ 40 0s. 0d.	
Lugwardine	£ 15 0s. 0d.	£ 42 0s. 0d.	£ 27 0s. 0d.	
Marden	£ 22 4s. 0d.	£ 51 0s. 0d.	£ 28 16s. 0d.	
Ospringe	?	£ 55 0s. 0d.	?	stock lease
Kempton	?	?	?	
Abthorpe	£ 24 0s. 0d.	£ 37 0s. 0d.	£ 13 0s. 0d.	
Brigstock	£ 18 0s. 0d.	£ 40 0s. 0d.	£ 22 0s. 0d.	
Geddington	£ 30 0s. 0d.	£ 46 0s. 0d.	£ 16 0s. 0d.	
Finedon	£ 24 0s. 0d.	£ 60 0s. 0d.	£ 36 0s. 0d.	stock lease
King's Cliffe	£ 40 0s. 0d.	£ 60 0s. 0d.	£ 20 0s. 0d.	
Silverstone	£ 12 0s. 0d.	£ 26 0s. 0d.	£ 14 0s. 0d.[a]	stock lease
Thorpe	£ 47 17s. 0d.	£ 60 0s. 0d.	£ 12 3s. 0d.	
Bridport	£ 10 10s. 0d.	£ 14 0s. 0d.	£ 3 10s. 0d.	
Dorchester	£ 12 12s. 0d.	£ 16 0s. 0d.	£ 3 8s. 0d.	
Fordington	£ 32 0s. 0d.	£ 45 0s. 0d.	£ 13 0s. 0d.	
Somerton	—	£ 60 0s. 0d.	£ 60 0s. 0d.	
Corsham	—	£ 60 0s. 0d.	£ 60 0s. 0d.	stock lease
Rowde	£ 25 0s. 0d.	£ 42 0s. 0d.	£ 17 0s. 0d.	stock lease
Devizes	—	£ 46 12s. 4d.– £ 33 6s. 8d. fee	£ 13 5s. 4d.	stock lease
Melksham	£ 50 8s. 0d.	£ 80 0s. 0d.	£ 29 12s. 0d.	stock lease
Feckenham	£ 20 0s. 0d.	£ 40 0s. 0d.	£ 20 0s. 0d.	stock lease
Total	£1,050 13s. 0d.	£1,753 5s. 4d.	£647 12s. 4d.	

Note: Manors alienated by the king between 1236 and 1241 are excluded from this table.

[a] By the end of their five-year lease, the men of Silverstone were £97 10s. in arrears on their farm. They still owed this amount in 1248.

accounts.[151] Moreover, the stock on these manors was probably more numerous, and certainly of higher quality, than when de Burgo took over as custodian. Nor had he fallen behind in his payments to the exchequer. De Burgo cleared his first account at Michaelmas 1238 owing less than £40 on total receipts of more than £5300.[152] His next account was not due until Michaelmas 1240. When de Burgo did account for this final term, he cleared his account owing only about £270, all of which was in turn owed to him by his own manorial bailiffs.[153] It therefore seems unlikely that mounting debts could have brought the council to its decision.

Administratively, the decision can at least be justified, albeit not entirely explained. Having determined the maximum annual value of these manors, the council may have been reluctant to continue taking up valuable exchequer time with the lengthy audit which de Burgo's accounts inevitably required. It was far simpler to let the estates on short-term leases which would reflect their increased value under de Burgo's care. This was what the council now set out to do. Teams of royal officials were appointed in July 1240 to view de Burgo's manors, value their crops and stock, and report their findings to the council, in preparation for handing them over to the men of the manors on five-year leases.[154] The council's new approach to the royal demesne was set out in September 1240 in a writ on the originalia roll:

Because it has been provided by the royal council that all the royal demesne shall henceforth be handed over at farm to the men of each manor, the bailiffs of Somerton are commanded to convoke the men of the aforesaid manor and to hand over that manor to the aforesaid men along with fallowland, hayfields, ploughs and all the other stock which the king has in the same manor, all of

---

[151] See Table 2.3. De Burgo's wool clip may have been marketed separately, in keeping with practice on many large English estates: cf. Edmund King, *Peterborough Abbey* (Cambridge, 1973), 158–9; Miller and Hatcher, *Medieval England*, 226.

[152] Pipe Roll 22 Henry III (E. 372/82 rots. 1–1d).

[153] Memoranda Roll 25 Henry III (E. 368/13 rot. 12 and *passim*) is the only record to reflect de Burgo's efforts to clear his account. This debt was never transferred to the pipe rolls, which may suggest that de Burgo compounded for it as part of the 400 mark fine he made with the king in May 1242 to be quit of all charges and trespasses stemming from his time as keeper of the royal demesne: *CLR 1240–5*, 133. The debt de Burgo owed from his Michaelmas 1238 account (£38 7s. 8d.) was not transferred to the pipe rolls until 1261: cf. Pipe Roll 45 Henry III (E. 372/105 rot. 11).

[154] *CLR 1226–40*, 482–3; Fine Roll 25 Henry III (C. 60/37 m. 16). In most shires, these same officials were also charged to inquire into Jewish chattels, preparatory to the assessment of the 20,000 mark tallage of 1241–2: cf. pp. 146–8 below. Knowledge of this impending tax, and of the extra burdens it would place on the exchequer, may also have encouraged the council to end the custodial experiment when it did.

which stock shall be appraised by the oath of prudent and law-worthy men before it is demised to the aforesaid men; and the bailiffs shall certify its value to the king later, through those whom the king shall have sent to those parts in order to certify to the aforesaid men at what price the king grants them to hold the aforesaid manor and stock at farm, saving to the king his grain which he caused to be sown in the aforesaid manor this year, anno 24, which the bailiffs shall keep in custody for the king's use.

In the same manner were written the bailiffs of Essendon and Bayford, Feckenham, Newport, Marden, Acornbury, Lugwardine, Abthorp, Geddington, Finedon, King's Cliffe, Brill, Brigstock, Thorp, and Fordington.[155]

There was, therefore, a distinct element of compulsion in these new leases. There is no reason to think that the council consulted any local men to determine whether or not they wished to hold their manor at farm. The council simply ordered them to do so. It is also clear that these itinerant royal officials arrived on the manors with a firm idea as to the farm at which they intended to lease it, before they had viewed a single lamb or surveyed a single virgate of land. With only two exceptions, the farms assigned in 1240 reflected closely the level of net issues which Walter de Burgo had taken from the manors after the 'start-up' costs of initial stock and seed purchases had been met.[156] These new farms appear to have been agreed in council before the royal officials ever set out on their inquests.

Some negotiation did, of course, occur. The men of Ospringe, for example, tried hard to convince the royal inquisitors that the crops they saw standing in the fields were at least a sixth more valuable than usual, and that their farm should be set accordingly. But their plea fell on deaf ears. The farm of Ospringe was one of the more difficult farms imposed.[157] A more promising subject for negotiation than the farm of the manor was the fate of the stock. The council intended for most of the new leases to include the stock which de Burgo had left on the manors, but in individual cases the itinerant royal officials retained the

---

[155] Originalia Roll 24 Henry III (E. 371/7 m. 4, marked m. 5); Latin version in Hoyt, *Royal Demesne*, 160–1 n. 83.

[156] Slaughter (Gloucs.) and Silverstone (Northants.) were both set particularly high farms relative to de Burgo's receipts from these manors: cf. the tables in Stacey, 'Crown Finance', app. II. At Silverstone, the men found themselves unable to meet this new farm, and by the end of 1245, when their lease expired, they owed £97 10s. arrears on a yearly farm of £26: Pipe Roll 31 Henry III (E. 372/91 rot. 13d). They did however, manage to pay the farm in full between 1245 and 1248: Pipe Roll 32 Henry III (E. 372/92 rot. 8d).

[157] *Book of Fees*, vol. i, 620–3. In 1237 and 1238, de Burgo's net receipts from Ospringe were less than £30. In 1240, the manor was farmed for £55 per year.

stock on a manor for the king.[158] On a few estates, some of the animals which de Burgo had introduced onto the manors may have been sold off before the manor and its remaining stock were transferred to the new lessees.[159] And in some cases, the manors were let not to their local men, but rather to a royal household official, or to a favoured abbey.[160] Predominantly, however, the new farms were set in accordance with the council's instructions. The men of the manors were awarded five-year leases, which included the chattels and stock attached to the manor when Walter de Burgo resigned their custody in the spring of 1240.

IV. Conclusion

Four years of consistent, purposeful conciliar policy towards the shire farms and the royal demesne had produced an additional £2000 per year in clear profits for the king by the autumn of 1240.[161] This represented an increase of almost 10 per cent in the king's average

---

[158] At Fordington (Wilts.) and Somerton (Som.), it is clear that the king retained the manorial stock in his own hands: cf. Originalia Roll 25 Henry III (E. 371/8A m. 4); Fine Roll 25 Henry III (C. 60/37 mms. 18, 16). Although the stock record on Originalia Roll 25 Henry III (E. 371/8A m. 4) states that there was no stock at Brigstock (Northants.), the grant of the manor to its men on Originalia Roll 24 Henry III (E. 371/7 m. 5, marked m. 6) ordered the stock retained for the king, and commands Walter de Tywe, the bailiff of Woodstock, to take custody of it: cf. also *CLR 1226–40*, 498; *CLR 1240–5*, 76. The stock was apparently removed from the manor between 11 Oct. 1240 (the date of the grant) and the date of the inquest whose results are recorded on E. 371/8A m. 4, a valuable clue to the date of the latter document. References on E. 371/8A that there was no stock on a manor do not, therefore, necessarily reflect a long-standing state of affairs. The king evidently disposed of some stock before handing the manors over to their men.

[159] This appears to have happened at Silverstone (Northants.), a fact which may help to explain the difficulty the men of Silverstone had in meeting their farm: cf. Fine Roll 25 Henry III (C. 60/37 mms. 18, 17); Pipe Roll 22 Henry III (E. 372/82 rot. 3); Originalia Roll 25 Henry III (E. 371/8A m. 4).

[160] Barton Gloucester went to the abbot of St Peter's, Gloucester, on a five-year lease; Winchcombe to its abbot on a ten-year lease, starting at Michaelmas 1239; Basingstoke to Walter de Merton, at a somewhat reduced farm (see note 110 above); Acornbury to its nuns; and Devizes and Rowde to John de Plessy, whose name was substituted on the fine roll in place of the local men: Fine Roll 25 Henry III (C. 60/37 m. 17). De Plessy's 50 mark annual fee as constable of Devizes Castle was deducted from its farm. Cheltenham went to Peter d'Aigueblanche, the newly elected bishop of Hereford, at Michaelmas 1240, at a farm slightly higher than the men of Cheltenham had been paying for it (£70 as against £64). Corsham was granted freely to Richard Earl of Cornwall at Michaelmas 1241.

[161] Approximately £1200 per year from increased shire profits, £600 to £700 per year from the manors in de Burgo's custody (see Table 2.3), and £100 to £150 per year from the manors in the custody of Robert de Crepping.

annual cash revenues,[162] an achievement which confirmed the wisdom of the long-term view the council took between 1236 and 1239 in managing these royal resources. None the less, there are signs from 1239 on that conciliar support for the reforms was flagging. The return of the curial sheriffs to the shires was the most obvious example of this change, but the 1240 leases of royal demesne manors to household men like John de Plessy, Walter de Merton, and Peter d'Aigueblanche are another indication of the new, less daring spirit at work in the council. The peculiar timing of Walter de Burgo's dismissal as manorial custodian is another suggestion of the change. De Burgo was dismissed at Pentecost, right in the middle of the growing season, for reasons which remain obscure. Although offences were apparently alleged against him,[163] the fact that we cannot now trace them suggests that they did not play a major role in bringing the custodial experiment to an end. Rather, de Burgo's dismissal reflects a more fundamental shift in the council's approach to royal finance, away from the politically delicate and administratively demanding reforms of 1236–9, towards a financial strategy which required fewer restrictions on royal patronage and which relied less directly on the consent of the magnates for the king's policies. In the chapters which follow, we shall examine first the circumstances and then the consequences of this shift, for the realm and for the king's overseas ambitions.

[162] See pp. 206–10 below.

[163] In 1242, de Burgo fined with the king for 400 marks to be quit of all trespasses and complaints concerning his tenure as the king's manorial custodian: *CLR 1240–5*, 133. Such fines are not, however, good evidence of guilt. They were a useful form of insurance for any departing royal bailiff, and while de Burgo's fine was high, at the time he paid only 50 marks on it. Because the fine was never enrolled on the pipe rolls, we cannot determine whether he paid any further sums against it. It is also possible that the fine included his £270 outstanding debt at the exchequer, a supposition which would explain why this debt was never enrolled on the pipe rolls (see n. 153 above). If so, de Burgo paid nothing at all for protection against any future claims against him.

3

Conciliar Personnel and Policy
1236–1239

THE identity of the men who directed royal policy in the six months preceding the king's wedding to Eleanor of Provence in January 1236 is obscure. The archbishop of Canterbury had played a central role in resolving the conflicts which had brought about the fall of the des Roches regime in 1234, but the pattern of his attestations at court during 1235 suggests that he was not a constant attender upon the king.[1] The archbishop of York was even less frequently at court; although he did witness several charters between August and December 1235, these were his sole recorded appearances there between mid-1233 and mid-1236. The bishops of Ely and Hereford may have played a role in negotiating the king's marriage—they were both at court during the summer of 1235, when the marriage to Eleanor was first discussed, and they escorted the lady to England[2]—but Hereford at least played little role otherwise at court. The bishop of Ely had been an ally of de Burgh, as had Jocelin of Wells, the aged bishop of Bath. Both men were frequently at court; in the anti-Poitevin atmosphere of 1235,[3] they were probably influential figures. The most powerful bishops around the king, however, were his two great officers: the treasurer, Bishop Walter of Carlisle, and the chancellor, Ralph de Nevill, bishop of Chichester.

Among the earls, Richard of Cornwall and John of Lincoln were the dominant figures, although William Earl Warenne and Humphrey de Bohun, earl of Hereford, were also frequent witnesses to the king's charters. Gilbert Marshal, earl of Pembroke, was frequently at court, but may not have been entirely trusted by the king. The dust had not

---

[1] Unless otherwise noted, all references to an individual's presence at court and to the frequency of his charter attestations are based on C. A. F. Meekings' unpublished notebooks of 'Charter Roll Witnesses', available on request in the PRO through Dr David Crook, who kindly made them available to me.

[2] *CM*, vol. iii, 335.

[3] On the anti-Poitevin atmosphere at court in 1235, see *Royal Letters*, vol. i, 467–9.

yet settled from the king's war with Gilbert's brother Richard Marshal in 1233–4. Although Gilbert Basset had returned with Gilbert Marshal to court, their ally Richard Siward was still in exile in Scotland, driven there by the continuing enmity between himself and Richard of Cornwall.[4] The Marches of Wales remained unsettled from the war, a number of men disseised from their holdings during the hostilities had still not recovered their lands, and gangs of pirates and malefactors continued to roam the land.[5] Gilbert Marshal's final peace with the king was apparently not sealed until April 1236, when a formal charter of concord was enrolled on the close rolls.[6] Even then the peace did not last.[7] The Marshal's consent to policy in 1235 was essential, but his influence on its formation must be doubted. Among the remaining earls, Derby was a virtual invalid from gout,[8] and Norfolk, Aumâle, and Oxford were rarely at court. Simon de Montfort, not yet invested with the earldom of Leicester, and William Longsword, claimant to the earldom of Salisbury, were much more important figures in the king's counsels, but both these men were apparently away from court between August 1235 and January 1236. De Montfort especially was a rising man, but his movements between 1232 and 1236 are shadowy.[9] It is not until 1237 that he emerges clearly in the front rank of the king's councillors.[10]

Charter attestations are not an invariably accurate guide to influence at court. A man might be always present, but still rarely listened to.[11]

---

[4] *CM*, vol. iii, 363; Annals of Osney and Chronicle of Thomas Wykes, *AM*, vol. iv, 80–2; *CPR 1232–47*, 158, *Cl.R 1234–7*, 363, 364, 366, 367.

[5] For continuing problems arising from the 1233–4 disseisins, cf. *Cl.R 1234–7*, 350, 375; for the king's campaigns during July and August 1236 against criminal gangs in the forests, see ibid., 362–3, 295; *CPR 1232–47*, 164–5. On the pirates of Lundy Island and their connections to the 1233–4 war, see Powicke, *Henry III*, 740–59, adapted from 'The Murder of Henry Clement and the Pirates of Lundy Island', *History* 25 (1941) 285–310, and reprinted with some changes in *Ways of Medieval Life and Thought: Essays and Addresses by F. M. Powicke* (London, 1949), 38–68.

[6] *Cl.R 1234–7*, 350.

[7] Gilbert Marshall was excluded from the Christmas court in 1238, and again in January 1240, when the king brought charges against him: cf. *CM*, vol. iii, 522–4; vol. iv, 3–4.

[8] Noël Denholm-Young, 'The "Paper Constitution" Attributed to 1244', *EHR* 58 (1943), reprinted in his *Collected Papers* (Cardiff, 1969), 147.

[9] Charles Bémont, *Simon de Montfort, Earl of Leicester*, trans. E. F. Jacob (Oxford, 1930), 51.

[10] *CM*, vol. iii, 412.

[11] Geoffrey Despenser may be an example of such a man at Henry's court. In frequency of attestations between 1233 and 1243 he ranks with the stewards, but his influence at court is elsewhere hard to trace. For rare examples of his influence, see *CPR 1232–47*, 96, and p. 145 n. 64 below.

They are, however, a better guide to influence at Henry III's court than for some other kings. Henry was a changeable man, whose views tended to be shaped by the people he had around him at the time—a portrait which emerges not only from the pages of Matthew Paris, but also from the pattern of royal grants between 1227 and 1236.[12] And for constancy of influence, none of the bishops could match the position at court of the king's household stewards, Ralph fitz Nicholas, Godfrey de Craucombe, John fitz Philip, and Amaury de St Amand. Along with William de Ralegh, the chief justice *coram rege*, these men were the backbone of the king's court. They were the most frequent witnesses to his charters (matched only by Walter bishop of Carlisle in the period 1232–43, and roughly double that of their other nearest competitors), and they authorized by far the largest number of attested chancery writs.[13] With rare exceptions, at least two of the stewards attended the king at all times; during the last six months of 1235 it appears that fitz Nicholas, Craucombe, and St Amand were all at court. John fitz Philip was overseas, involved in the negotiations for the king's marriage.[14]

Ralph fitz Nicholas was the senior member of this group, and appears to have been the dominant figure. St Amand had only been appointed a steward in 1233, and was still relatively new to the cut and thrust of court politics. Craucombe was an old hand, but appears to have been a somewhat retiring figure, anxious to protect his modest gains from royal service, and prepared to serve under any regime that would have him. He had served the Poitevins as faithfully as he had served de Burgh. When finally he did fall, in 1233, his period in exile was brief.[15] Ralph fitz Nicholas was a very different man. His rewards from royal service had been richer, and he had suffered more than any of the other stewards from the regime of the bishop of Winchester. It is a reasonable guess that he did not intend to suffer in such manner again. The expulsion of Peter des Riveaux and Stephen de Segrave as outlaws on 2 January 1236 probably represents the high-water mark of fitz Nicholas's influence at court.[16]

[12] As David Carpenter has shown in 'Sheriffs of Oxfordshire', 214–74.

[13] For attestations of chancery writs, see the tables compiled by Meekings in *CRR*, vol. 15, lxi–lxiv.

[14] *CPR 1232–47*, 121–2; *Cl.R. 1234–7*, 220; *CRR*, vol. 15, lxiii; *Foedera*, vol. i, pt. 1 (1816), 219–20.

[15] Craucombe was finally ousted by the Poitevins in May 1233, but he was back at court by Mar. 1234. The best discussion of his career is in Carpenter, 'Sheriffs of Oxfordshire', 214–74.

[16] *Cl.R. 1234–7*, 332. It is not known whether this order was ever enforced. Its cancellation, noted on the close roll, probably dates from June 1236 when des Riveaux,

That influence was not to last. The king's marriage brought to England the queen's uncle, William of Savoy, bishop-elect of Valence, and with his arrival, a new chapter opens in the history of the king's council. William established himself at court with astonishing speed. He had ousted fitz Nicholas by 29 March, when Ralph was granted peace to come and speak with the king.[17] By the middle of April, it is clear that a new guiding intelligence had taken hold of the council; by the end of April, this fact appears to have been evident to the country as well.[18]

The emergence of this newly sworn royal council was noted by the Dunstable annalist in a retrospective account which he placed as the first entry *sub anno* 1237.

In the year of grace 1237, the elect of Valence, uncle of our queen, came to England, and was made principal counsellor of the king, with eleven others, who swore on holy objects that they would offer faithful counsel to the king. And the king swore similarly that he would obey their counsels; but we think neither party free from perjury.[19]

Henry did indeed require an oath of his councillors in 1237, when three new men were added to that body; but it is clear both from Matthew Paris's account of the 1237 oath and from the attesting formulae of several chancery writs which issued from Windsor in mid-April 1236 that the initial conciliar oath must date from 1236.[20] Of the king's oath to obey the council we need take little note,[21] although the

Segrave, and Robert Passelewe were received back into favour by the king: cf. *CM*, vol. iii, 368. On 1 Aug. 1236, Segrave was commissioned to take an assize: cf. Meekings in *CRR*, vol. 15, xxxii.

[17] *Cl.R.* 1234–7, 347; *CRR*, vol. 15, xxxviii.

[18] Denholm-Young, 'Paper Constitution', 141–6; Carpenter, 'Curial Sheriff', 16–18. The major chronicle references are *CM*, vol. iii, 362–4; Annals of Tewkesbury, *AM*, vol. i, 102; and Annals of Dunstable, *AM*, vol. iii, 145–6.

[19] 'Anno gratiae MCCXXXVII venit electus Valenciae, avunculus reginae nostrae, in Angliam; et factus est consiliarius regis principalis, cum aliis undecim, qui super sacrosancta juraverunt, quod fidele consilium regi praestarent. Et ipse similiter juravit quod eorum consiliis obediret; sed neutram partem credimus immunem a perjurio.' Annals of Dunstable, *AM*, vol. iii, 145–6. For the text of a similar oath taken by Henry's councillors in 1257, see the Annals of Burton, *AM*, vol. i, 395–7.

[20] *CM*, vol. iii, 383; Denholm-Young, 'Paper Constitution', 141–5.

[21] Such is the clear meaning of the passage, despite the grammatical infelicity of 'ipse' noted by Denholm-Young, 'Paper Constitution', 143–4; Henry had expressed similar such sentiments in Aug. 1235 in accepting the marital advice of his council, 'cui fidem adhibere tenemur': *Foedera*, I, i (1816), 218. Matthew Paris claims that Henry made another such promise in 1238, in the aftermath of Richard of Cornwall's rebellion: see below, p.120 and n. 150. There is no such language in the 1257 council oath: cf. Annals of Burton, *AM*, vol. i, 395–7. There is an obvious precedent for such self-restricting

language of the chancery writs which issued on and after 12 April does show a new emphasis on the king and council acting in concert to establish policy.[22] The most telling signs of the new council's influence, however, are the radical changes in the administration of the shire farms and of the royal demesne which were introduced at Windsor and continued at Westminster between 15 April and 13 May 1236,[23] and the series of informational inquests which the council began almost immediately. On 15 April, only a few days after the probable date of the conciliar oath at Windsor, the king sent word to his treasurer that he would soon be travelling from Windsor to Westminster by way of Reading. In addition to sending the king £100 at Reading for his expenses, Henry ordered the treasurer to report to him the total amount of his receipts at the exchequer since the start of the fiscal year.[24] The king was travelling to Westminster to meet his barons, but since he did not intend to ask an aid from them, this financial information was probably for the use of the council rather than for the forthcoming parliament. The new council was apparently taking stock of the king's financial position.[25] This effort continued into May, when the council initiated two new inquests, one to ascertain the value of the royal demesne lands, the other to compile a massive survey of all the knights' fees in England.[26] The scale of these manorial surveys has already been discussed in Chapter two. The very patchy survival of the returns from the inquest into fees makes it difficult to judge its success, but in its intended scope it appears to have been comparable to the *Cartae Baronum* inquests launched by Henry II in 1166. Both the manorial inquest and the inquest into fees were major undertakings,

---

royal oaths in Magna Carta, and so it is not impossible that Henry did swear formally in 1236 to follow the council's advice, and to support its decisions. But these oaths were never effective for long, as the 1258 reformers were to discover. They lasted as long as the king wished to abide by them.

[22] *Cl.R.* 1234–7, 348–9 (12 Apr.): 'De consilio nostro providimus quod ... '; Fine Roll 20 Henry III (C. 60/35 m. 10: 14 Apr. to 4 May): 'et sciendum quod totum consilium domini Regis testatur quod ...; *Cl.R.* 1234–7, 351–2 (22 Apr.): 'prout consilio nostro videbatur ... nobis aut alicui de consilio nostro id non poteritis aliquatenus imputare ...'; and, on a writ pardoning Henry de Trublevill £300 in prests, an attestation following the dating clause 'Per ipsum regem coram consilio suo' on ibid., 259–60 (24 Apr.).

[23] *CPR* 1232–47, 141–6; and see Ch. 2 above.

[24] *Cl.R.* 1234–7, 258. Notice the necessity of correcting anno 20 in the writ to anno 19.

[25] This request was repeated on 30 May, when Henry asked to know his receipts up to 26 May 1236: *Cl.R.* 1234–7, 271.

[26] *CPR* 1232–47, 146; *Book of Fees*, vol. i, 574–601.

carried out with remarkable speed and apparent efficiency, in an atmosphere of distinct financial crisis.

This crisis was provoked partly by the cost of the king's own marriage, but primarily by that of his sister Isabella to Emperor Frederick II of Germany. Henry had promised his sister a dowry of 30,000 marks, half to be paid by Easter 1236, the other half to be paid in two further instalments, 5,000 marks at Michaelmas 1236, and the remaining 10,000 marks the following Easter.[27] To provide this sum, the king had been granted an aid of 2 marks per fee on all the knights' fees in England, both de veteri and de novo.[28] The first instalment of this aid was due in November 1235, delayed from Michaelmas, and apparently did not come up to expectations.[29] In writs to his sheriffs on 28 February 1236, Henry ordered them to bring all the arrears from the first term's payments with them to Westminster when they came at Easter to deliver the second and final term's payments.[30] Only partial records of the receipts from this aid survive, but it cannot have raised more than 12,000 marks, and probably raised far less.[31] The king's government suspected fraud, which it hoped to uncover through the returns to the inquest into knights' fees it ordered in May. But even this reduced amount could not be devoted entirely to Isabella's dowry. Henry was already directing payment of the second term receipts into the wardrobe during February and March to defray his own household expenses.[32] By July 1236, only 15,000 marks of the dowry had been

[27] Terms of the dowry are given in the matrimonial contract sealed on 22 February 1235: *Foedera*, vol. i, pt. 1 (1816), 223–4.

[28] Mitchell attached no importance to these terms, believing that they were 'probably not used in the technical sense employed under Henry II': *Studies*, 211 n. 158. This may not be correct. In 1210, King John began a renewed attempt to charge his tenants-in-chief scutage on all their fees, *de veteri* and *de novo*, instead of abiding by the compromise assessments which had been worked out under Henry II after 1166; the assessment of Earl Roger Bigod with $125\frac{1}{4}$ fees *de veteri* plus an additional $37\frac{1}{2}$ fees *de novo* on *Pipe Roll 13 John*, 4, is an example of this new policy at work. For the scutage of 1217, Earl Roger was again assessed at this new, increased number of fees: *Pipe Roll 2 Henry III*, 25; *Pipe Roll 3 Henry III*, 50. Walter de Wahull had a similar experience: cf. Ivor J. Sanders, *English Baronies: A Study of their Origin and Descent, 1086–1327* (Oxford, 1960), 69 n. 2. The matter needs further investigation, but it seems possible that *de veteri* and *de novo* did retain a precise meaning during Henry III's reign, and that in some cases at least, they do indeed refer back to the 1166 *Cartae Baronum* returns.

[29] The Nov. due date is given in Fine Roll 20 Henry III (C. 60/35 m. 14); the Michaelmas due date in *Cl.R. 1234–7*, 189. See also Mitchell, *Studies*, 211.

[30] Fine Roll 20 Henry III (C. 60/35 m. 13).

[31] There were only about 6000 knights' fees total in England during the 1230s, including the many partial fees. The returns which survive from the aid are printed in *Book of Fees*, vol. i, 405–573.

[32] Fine Roll 20 Henry III (C. 60/35 m. 13); wardrobe account (E. 372/80 rot. 2d).

paid,[33] and the entire proceeds of the aid had already been collected. The final instalment of a 10,000 mark tallage on the Jews, due at Michaelmas 1236, would go some way toward making up the remainder; but if the Jews had been keeping up on their payments, only about 1,500 marks remained to be collected from this tax.[34] A new forest eyre, launched on 14 March, promised quick financial gains to the exchequer, as did the third and final stage of the general eyre, initiated on 12 April.[35] Nevertheless, it was evident in the spring of 1236 that payment of the remaining dowry would require truly extraordinary financial efforts. The reorganization of the council around William of Savoy was Henry's response to the spectre of impending financial collapse.

These 1236 changes in conciliar personnel and policy apparently provoked almost immediate baronial concern. But it is very hard to know what to make of Matthew Paris's famous account of the king's meeting with his magnates in late April.[36] Most of the changes which Paris ascribed to this parliament—the dismissal of the sheriffs, the removal of Ralph fitz Nicholas from the household—had already been carried through before the gathering met. The magnates were presented with a *fait accompli*, and this fact alone may explain part of the tension evident between the parties. But despite the attention which events since 1232 had focused on the people around the king, it is unlikely that the personnel changes alone, or the mere swearing of the council, newly reorganized around the elect of Valence, could have set off the kind of opposition which Paris describes. Indeed, the April oaths brought surprisingly few changes in the identity of the king's councillors. Ralph fitz Nicholas was the only immediate casualty; otherwise, the men who had dominated the council during 1235—Ralegh,

---

[33] See the letter from the emperor dated 24 July [1236] acknowledging receipt of this amount, enrolled on Memoranda Roll 21 Henry III (E. 159/15 m. 24d). This letter was probably in response to Henry's request for such a receipt on 30 June 1236: *Foedera*, vol. i, pt. 1 (1816), 228.

[34] *CPR 1232–47*, 12–13. There is clearly something wrong with the regnal years given in this writ; for discussion, see p. 144.

[35] *Cl.R. 1234–7*, 344, 348–9.

[36] *CM*, vol. iii, 362–4. Paris claims that when Henry arrived in London for this council, he tried to hold it in the Tower of London, where he was then staying, rather than in its traditional location at Westminster, near the royal palace. The magnates, however, feared to come to Henry at the Tower, and the king was eventually forced to return to Westminster. Henry may have been planning to stay at the Tower from at least 14 Apr.: see the order issued on that date from the king at Windsor to the constable of the Tower to construct meal tables 'ad magnum deisium [dias?] regis in magna aula ibidem' (*Cl.R. 1234–7*, 257).

Lincoln, Craucombe, St Amand, the bishop of Carlisle—continued as the dominant figures during 1236. Simon de Montfort returned to the court for the king's wedding, after a brief absence during the latter half of 1235, but his real rise to prominence seems to have come in 1237, while William of Savoy was absent from England.[37] Master Simon the Norman was another rising man in the king's service, who may have been included in the conciliar oath of April 1236, but his rise owed nothing to the favour of William de Savoy.[38] Richard of Cornwall may have been away from court during April (there is no evidence either way), but there is no sign that he was unwelcome there, and Paris says nothing about his involvement with the opposition at the April parliament.[39] There is, moreover, no evidence at all to support Matthew Paris's assertion that King Henry tried at this time to remove the Great Seal from the custody of the chancellor, Ralph de Nevill.[40] Paris wrote this entire section of his chronicle at some date after 1245,[41] and it appears that in this case, he was reading back the events of 1238 into the circumstances of 1236.

The opposition, such as it was, must have been sparked by policies; but which policies is unclear. The shrieval changes might seem a likely candidate, but Matthew Paris at least greeted these enthusiastically, and if Dr Carpenter is correct, so too did county society.[42] The king's new policy towards the royal demesne is a more likely source of friction between king and magnates, but this policy was still in the planning stages. Engayne and de Burgo's inquests and resumptions did not begin until at least 13 May.[43] Paris ascribed the opposition largely to the magnates' hostility toward William of Savoy, whom he detested.[44]

---

[37] *CM*, vol. iii, 412. Compare Meekings, *CRR*, vol. 15, xxxv n. 5, and see below, p. 115.

[38] Simon was at court intermittently during Feb. and Mar. 1236, while engaged with John Gumbaud in settling a town–gown riot in Oxford: cf. *CPR 1232–47*, 163; *Cl.R. 1234–7*, 343. In May 1236, he travelled to Rome with Peter Saracen to request that a papal legate be sent to England: *CPR 1232–47*, 147. See also Powicke, *Henry III*, 776–7.

[39] Matthew's silence on this point is significant because Richard of Cornwall was among his most regular and important sources of information: cf. Denholm-Young, *Richard of Cornwall*, 36 and *passim*.

[40] *CM*, vol. iii, 364.

[41] Richard Vaughan, *Matthew Paris* (Cambridge, 1979), 49–61, esp. 59–60.

[42] *CM*, vol. iii, 363; Carpenter, 'Curial Sheriff', 20 and *passim*.

[43] *CPR 1232–47*, 146.

[44] *CM*, vol. iii, 362. Several other chronicles, for example the Annals of Tewkesbury, *AM*, vol. i, 102, attribute these policy changes to William of Savoy, but none mention specifically the April parliament.

This is certainly possible, but again may be a largely retrospective view. The most likely inference from all this is that, with the changes at Windsor only two weeks old, rumours at the April parliament were rife. No one knew what the king and his new council planned to do, and Henry's abortive retreat into the Tower of London during the parliament suggests that he was not forthcoming about his plans. Something was up, but by the end of April 1236, Henry's nobles knew little more than that.

By 8 June, however, when king and magnates met again, at Winchester, the designs of the king's government were becoming clear, and were causing alarm.[45] The king's new demesne policy was apparently at the heart of the difficulties. As noted above, uncertainty about the intended scope of this policy continued for at least a year after it was first introduced in May 1236.[46] Engayne and de Burgo, however, interpreted their commission 'to take into the king's hands all his manors and demesnes ... '.[47] in the widest possible sense, and immediately launched a full-scale resumption of royal demesne manors, including life grants warranted by charter. If this had ever been the intention of the council, that body quickly backed away from it. On 29 May, shortly before the June meeting with his nobles, Henry issued clarifying instructions to Engayne and de Burgo.

Because it was not the king's intention when he ordered Warner Engayne and Walter de Burgo to seize into the king's hand the king's manor and demesnes, that they seize any manor into the king's hand of which anyone is enfeoffed by his or by his royal predecessor's charter, they are commanded not to intrude themselves in any way into the manor of Aylesbury which the aforesaid John fitz Geoffrey holds by the enfeoffment of the lord King John, father of this king, nor into the other manors and demesnes which are held from the king by his or his predecessors' charter, nor shall they impede the same John from disposing of all things as he previously disposed of them before the seisin which they created by the aforesaid occasion.[48]

[45] *CM*, vol. iii, 368.
[46] See above, pp. 78–80.
[47] *CPR 1232–47*, 146.
[48] *Cl.R. 1234–7*, 357, my translation. The significance of this writ for the events of Jan. and Feb. 1237 (on which see below, pp. 112–15) have been somewhat obscured by a scribal error, which in the margin of the enrolment recorded this writ as being in favour of *Galfrido filio Johannis*. There is no doubt, however, that the man in question is John fitz Geoffrey.

On the following day a similar admonition was sent to Robert de Crepping, then engaged upon his own inquest in Yorkshire.[49] The matter did not, however, end with these orders. The stream of writs which flowed from chancery between June and November 1236 ordering the reseisin of tenants expelled by the king's bailiffs gives a clear picture of the scale of these resumptions of royal demesne.

What is most remarkable about the list in Table 3.1 is the number of great men whose manors had been revoked into the king's hands, often in defiance of the prescriptive rights of a royal charter.[50] That great men should have succeeded far more frequently than lesser men in reversing such losses goes without saying. What is remarkable is that Engayne and de Burgo should have dared to effect such disseisins in the first place. Such daring suggests a council confident of its ability to control opposition in pursuing its policies. It suggests, too, a council very sure that it enjoyed the unqualified support of the king.

The autumn of 1236 saw the new council at the peak of its efforts to revamp and reorganize the king's financial affairs. A new emphasis on the accountability of royal bailiffs for their offices is evident throughout the administration, and became one of the keynotes in conciliar policy between 1236 and 1239. Pursuant to a decision made by the king in the exchequer, that body was busy summoning and enrolling all the back debts owed to the king from the fifteenth of 1225, the sixteenth of 1226, the fortieth of 1232, the carucage of 1220, and from the reign of King John.[51] A thorough audit of these accounts was also underway, in the case of the fortieth for the first time since the tax itself had been collected.[52] In October 1236, the council summoned the treasurer and chamberlains of the exchequer before it at Kempton, to audit their accounts.[53] And in the following year, the exchequer itself imposed strict new requirements on the auditing of

[49] Cl.R. 1234–7, 357.

[50] John fitz Geoffrey was the son of Geoffrey fitz Peter, and a former royal sheriff of Yorkshire; Henry de Hauvill was a former royal falconer who held several demesne manors; Osbert Giffard was a former royal steward under John, as was William de Cantilupe; Thomas de Gorges, Walter de Godarvill, Engelard de Cigogné, and Nicholas de Molis were all members or former members of the king's military household, with Godarvill an important baron besides; Robert de Blakeford was a leading shire knight in Somerset and Dorset; and Robert de Courtenay was a member of the most important baronial family in the south-west.

[51] Memoranda Roll 21 Henry III (E. 159/15 m. 17d: 26 Nov. 1236).

[52] Memoranda Roll 22 Henry III (E. 368/12 m. 5d); Cl.R. 1234–7, 394–5; Foreign Accounts, Henry III, vii, 63–73.

[53] Cl.R. 1234–7, 380.

TABLE 3.1   *Disseisins by the king's bailiffs, 1236*

Tenant	Manor	Date
John fitz Geoffrey	Aylesbury, Bucks. (charter)	29 May
Prior of Hatfield	Hatfield, Essex (lease at farm)	4 June
Henry de Hauvill	Brigstock, Northants[a]	11 June
Osbert Giffard	Gillingham, Dorset (3 virgates-charter)	23 June
William de Cantilupe	Calne, Dorset	24 July
Thomas de Gorges	Powerstock, Dorset (charter)	2 Aug.
Walter de Godarvill	Chippenham, Wilts. (charter)	4 Aug.
Engelard de Cigogné	Windsor, Berks purpresture[b]	6 Aug.
Nicholas de Molis	Diptford and Kerswell, Devon	13 Aug.
Roger la Zouche	King's Nympton and Black Torrington, Devon	23 Aug.
John Wascelin	Carleton-in-Lindrick, Notts. (life grant by charter)	2 Sept.
Roger, William de Leya	Cookham, Berks. 2 mills	24 Sept.
Robert Stoffin	Oddhouse, Hull, Owthorpe, Notts (charter)	28 Sept.
Abbot of Cleve	Brompton Regis, Som.[c]	8 Oct.
Robert de Blakeford	Braunton, Devon (charter)	16 Oct.
Robert de Courtenay	Shebbear, Devon (charter)	28 Nov.

Note: Blank spaces beneath the name of a manor indicate that the nature of the warrant claimed by the disseised tenant is unspecified. The date given is the date on which their reseisin was ordered, not the date on which they were disseised. For the texts of these orders, see, in order, *Cl.R.* 1234–7, 357, 272, 275, 281, 293, 296, 297, 298, 302, 306, 310, 315, 317, 321, 323, 398.
[a] Henry de Hauvill did not in fact recover the manor, despite this order: cf. Pipe Roll 22 Henry III (E. 372/82, rots, 1–3d.)
[b] Engelard was granted the crops he had sown on this land, but did not recover the purpresture itself.
[c] Misidentified in the index to *Close Rolls 1234–7* as Braunton, Devon.

accounts for royal works, insisting on itemized accounting of expenditures in place of the old general oath from the overseer, supported by the view and testimony of two lawful men.[54]

[54] Ibid., 482; Memoranda Roll 22 Henry III (E. 368/12 m. 2d). It is uncertain whether this order was ever widely enforced. Engelard de Cigogné, however, was clearly

The exchequer clerks, meanwhile, were searching through the ancient rolls of their department for customary payments which might have escaped their recent attentions. In December 1236 they discovered from a roll of 6 Henry that the knights of the honour of Leicester had then been paying annually to the king £55 in sheriff's aid, which they no longer paid.[55] A few months later, they discovered through an inquisition conducted by William de Ralegh that the manor of Somerton had paid £42 blanch per year toward the county farm under Henry II.[56] Currently, Somerton contributed only £2. 10s. per year *numero* to the shire farm of Somerset.[57] A second inquest was ordered to determine the manorial appendages of Somerton which had contributed towards this £42 total, in case some of these outlying areas were escaping their obligations to the exchequer.[58] The council even attempted to breathe new life into the enforcement of the ancient Anglo-Saxon obligations to bridge-building, and renewed Henry II's prohibition against hawking along the king's riverbanks, with amercements for offenders. These orders were sent to all sheriffs for public proclamation, and, in the case of the bridge-building obligations at least, were apparently enforced.[59]

The use of such public proclamations points also to the marked stress which the new council placed on legal matters, both great and small. The guiding spirit behind these reforms is clearly William de Ralegh, in these years the only professional justice to sit regularly in the court *coram rege*.[60] Ralegh came to the king's court by transfer from the Bench in May 1234, and continued there as chief justice until early in 1239. It is not, therefore, surprising that the legal reforms carried through between January 1236 and February 1237 should bear

concerned enough about its provisions to secure an exemption from them. The 'per visum et testimonium' formula continues to appear on the pipe roll enrolments of such accounts, but the formula tells us nothing about the way in which the account itself was rendered at the exchequer. The pipe roll records only the sum finally allowed to the supervisor of the works for the expenses, not the method by which this sum was determined.

[55] Memoranda Roll 21 Henry III (E. 159/15 m. 18). I can find no such reference on the pipe roll for 6 Henry II.

[56] Memoranda Roll 21 Henry III (E. 159/15 m. 24).

[57] Pipe Roll 20 Henry III (E. 372/80 rot. 16).

[58] Memoranda Roll 21 Henry III (E. 159/15 m. 24).

[59] *Cl.R.* 1234–7, 378; for evidence of the enforcement of the bridge-building obligation, see ibid., 394. These orders were repeated in 1240 (*CLR* 1226–40, 443; *Cl.R.* 1237–42, 244–5) and again in 1241 (*Cl.R.* 1237–42, 363).

[60] On the court *coram rege*, see Meekings, *CRR*, vol. 15, xxi–xxxix.

distinct similarities to those enacted in the autumn of 1234, when the trail of legal reform really begins.[61] In no other sphere are the links between the policies pursued by the king's new council and those pursued in the previous two years so strong as in the realm of law. But even here, the pace of change quickened noticeably in 1236, although the change really dates not from April but from January, when the magnates who had assembled for the king's wedding approved the Statute of Merton. We do not know that Ralegh was the principal author of this statute, but it is likely that he was.[62] We know from Grosseteste's appeals to him that he played a key role in the related discussions about the common law of bastardy, which the magnates assembled at Merton refused to bring into accord with Roman and canon law on this subject.[63] We know too that Ralegh was responsible for introducing important new clauses into the texts of assize commissions in February 1236, and that he was behind the April 1236 order to the Bench to transfer *coram rege* all cases which might turn on dubious points of law.[64] As the king's chief legal advisor, we must suspect him also of playing the most important role in the conflict which erupted soon afterwards with Grosseteste over the scope of the king's writs of prohibition, when directed against clerics attempting to plead in courts Christian.[65] The council's consistent concern during 1236 to bring Irish law into accord with English legal practice may also reflect Ralegh's own personal interest in and connections with Ireland.[66] And in the legal changes which

---

[61] For some of these 1234 reforms, see *Cl.R. 1231–4*, 587–9, 592, 598, discussed by Powicke, *Henry III*, 147–8.

[62] Ralegh certainly drafted Merton cap. 4, restricting the right of common: cf. Thorne, *Bracton*, vol. iii, 179.

[63] *Roberti Grosseteste Epistolae*, ed. H. R. Luard (Rolls Series, London, 1861), hereafter Grosseteste, *Epistolae*, 76–97; *BNB*, vol. i, 107. There are discussions of this famous controversy in Powicke, *Henry III*, 150–2; Thorne, *Bracton*, vol. iii, xv–xvii; C. H. Lawrence, *St Edmund of Abingdon* (Oxford, 1960), 158–60; and in *Councils and Synods, with Other Documents Relating to the English Church, Volume II*, ed. F. M. Powicke and C. R. Cheney (Oxford, 1964), 198–9.

[64] On the assize commissions, see Meekings, *CRR*, vol. 15, xxxiv–xxxv; for other writs invented by Ralegh, see Thorne, *Bracton*, vol. iii, xxxi–xxxii. On the order to the Bench in April 1236, see *Cl.R. 1234–7*, 348; Meekings, *CRR*, vol. 15, xix–xx; C.A. F. Meekings, 'Adam fitz William (d. 1238)', *BIHR* 34 (1961), 11–12, reprinted in *Studies in 13th-Century Justice and Administration*.

[65] *Cl.R. 1234–7*, 360. Note Ralegh's explicit role in a very similar case during 1237: ibid., 528; *CPR 1232–47*, 200. See also Grosseteste, *Epistolae*, 63–5, 76–97.

[66] *Cl.R. 1234–7*, 353–5 (May 1236); *CPR 1232–47*, 153 (July 1236); *Cl.R. 1234–7*, 375–6 (Aug. 1236); *CPR 1232–47*, 176–7 (Mar. 1237). Ralegh now appears as the most likely author of the treatise we know as *Bracton*, although the work was later revised

accompanied the reconfirmation of Magna Carta in January and February 1237, we again find William de Ralegh in the lead, as he appears to have been in almost all matters connected with this parliament.[67] After a lengthy debate among the assembled magnates, some of whom alleged that it violated the terms of Magna Carta clause 34, Ralegh's new writ of cosinage was approved, extending the degrees of familial relationship within which a plantiff might successfully bring a writ of *mort d'ancestor*.[68] Closely related to this extension was the decision at this same parliament to move forward in time the limits on the royal possessory assizes.[69] Here too we should probably see Ralegh's hand.

This new emphasis upon legal enforcement and strict administrative accountability produced a noticeable change in the tenor of the king's administration. Nowhere was this more clearly the case than in the administration of the king's wines. 1236 began with serious shortages of both red and white wines all over England. These shortages became so acute as to force the king in January 1236 to suspend until Easter the fixed retail prices set by the assize of wines.[70] Not surprisingly, Eastertide brought no new supplies of wine to England. The king therefore made no attempt to reimpose the assize until November 1236, when the first fruits of the new Gascon wine crop began arriving in England.[71] Meanwhile, the high prices which merchants could now get for their wines made them even more reluctant than usual to have their wines seized by the king's purveyors for purchase at the preferential price of 20s. per tun paid by the king.[72] Even when wine was plentiful a merchant could usually get 40s. a tun for wines.[73] In

extensively: cf. Thorne, *Bracton*, vol. iii, xiii–lii. On Ralegh's Irish connection and the possible relationship of *Bracton* with Irish law, see Paul A. Brand, 'Ireland and the Literature of the Early Common Law', *The Irish Jurist* n.s. 16 (1981), 95–113, esp. 97, 112–13.

[67] Ralegh was the king's spokesman in this parliament (*CM*, vol. iii, 380) and also at the 1237 legatine council (*Councils and Synods II*, 242–3).

[68] On the writ of cosinage, see *BNB*, no. 1215; Thorne, *Bracton*, vol. iii, 318–19; Meekings in *CRR*, vol. 15, lvii n. 1; Denholm-Young, 'Paper Constitution', 154 and n. 1; Frederick W. Maitland, *Collected Papers*, ed. H. A. L. Fisher (3 vols., Cambridge, 1911), vol. ii, 146–9; and Clanchy, 'Magna Carta, Clause 34', 542–8, esp. 545.

[69] *Cl.R. 1234–7*, 520–1.

[70] Ibid., 333, cf. also 326–7.

[71] Ibid., 386, 512–3.

[72] *CPR 1232–47*, 148; *CLR 1226–40*, 273.

[73] Angevin wines tended to be cheaper than Gascon wines. In June 1237, the king was paying 42s. per tun for Angevin wines in London (*CLR 1226–40*, 273); in Nov. 1237 he paid 53s. 4d. per tun for Gascon wines at Bristol (Memoranda Roll 22 Henry III: E. 368/12 m. 9). For other examples of wine prices, see *CLR 1226–40*, 282–5, and *passim*.

times of shortage, bulk prices might even double, especially with the suspension of the assize. To fulfil his allowed quota of prise purchases, the king was therefore compelled to order a number of forced sales of wine during late 1235 and 1236, in several cases ordering city bailiffs to detain a wine merchant and all his stock until the king's purveyors could arrive in the port to make their purchases.[74] Whether the king made any deliberate profit by reselling such prise wine at market rates is not known; that his purchasing agents may have been doing so is implied by the statute of February 1237 which regulated purveyance, but cannot now be proved.[75] However, there was certainly no control exercised by the king's chamberlain of wines to prevent his local agents from thus exploiting their positions. This fact became clear when, in November 1236, the unfortunate chamberlain was summoned before the exchequer barons to present his accounts.

A day was given to John de Colemere on the Saturday next after the feast of St. Martin to render his account to the lord king for the king's wines purchased from the time since he first took office, and for the money which he had received in order to buy these wines, and also to render his account for the issues of the king's chamber of London and Sandwich and Southampton from the time when the lord king committed to him the custody of this chamber. And the same John came before the barons of the exchequer and said that he could not render account either for the aforesaid wines purchased nor for the money which he had received in order to buy the wines, because when he first took up the office of wines at the king's command he had not understood that he ought to render an account for them ('non intellexit quod inde compotum reddere debet'), nor was he told that he should render an account, nor was a form of account given him, as he says, and so in no way can he render an account concerning the money or the wines, as he says.

Concerning the account of the chamber, he says that he cannot render it nor did he wish to burden himself concerning the issues of the chamber ('de compoto camerarius dixit quod illud reddere non potuit nec voluit se de exitibus camerarius onerare') because according to the assizes of the exchequer he could not show a warrant through which he could exonerate himself; but in the king's wardrobe he would freely respond concerning the issues of the same chamber through its rolls.

And since he was a bailiff of the lord king and he received and expended money for which he could not render an account, nor wished to burden

---

[74] The clearest examples are from Nov. and Dec. 1235: cf. *Cl.R.* 1234–7, 203, 206, 214, 219(2); for 1236, see ibid., 225, 227, 234, 252, 259, 268.

[75] See the text of the statute in *Cl.R.* 1234–7, 522, or in the Annals of Burton, *AM*, vol. i, 253.

himself, as previously stated, it is determined by the barons of the exchequer in the presence of the bishop of Carlisle and the justice(s) of the Bench that according to the assizes of the exchequer he should be bodily arrested. But because he is a cleric they will permit him to go to the lord king; therefore he shall swear an oath that immediately he will present himself before the lord king and seek the king's grace *pro posse sua*.[76]

After such a performance, it is not surprising that on the same day, two new chamberlains of the king's wines were appointed at the exchequer to replace John de Colemere. Before the exchequer barons, and in the presence of the bishop of Carlisle and the King's Bench justice Robert de Lexinton, the new chamberlains swore 'that they would faithfully keep the lord king's chamber of wines of London and Sandwich in the form in which it was given them and would faithfully respond for it'.[77] This oath was enrolled on the memoranda roll of the exchequer, just to make sure there would be no such repetition of their experience with John de Colemere. The days of such free and easy accounting were over.

The exchequer's attempt to audit Colemere's accounts coincided with the council's first concerted attempt to reimpose the assize of wines. On 28 November, the assize was reproclaimed in London, along with an additional provision forbidding Londoners to impede any merchants coming by land or sea from selling wine in London.[78] This may suggest an effort by some London wine merchants to protect the high value of wines stocked during the shortage from the competition of the new wine pressing. The assize was not proclaimed throughout the country, however, until 7 February 1237, when the proclamation was coupled with a new statute which for the first time regulated the conduct of the king's purveyors.[79] All the king's purchasing agents were hereafter to receive letters specifying exactly how much of each

[76] Memoranda Roll 20 Henry III (E. 159/15 m. 16d). London, Sandwich, and Southampton were the three principal ports for prise purchases of wines. The king's chamber, referred to here, was the administrative office and storage facility for the royal wines at these places. The chamber was sometimes in the hands of a single keeper, as with John de Colemere here, and sometimes divided by location between two or more keepers. One will therefore find references also to the king's chamber of London, separate from the other ports.

[77] ' … quod fideliter custodient camerarium domini Regis de vinis suis de London' et Sandwic' in forma in qua eam eis tradidit et fideliter inde respondebunt'. Memoranda Roll 21 Henry III (E. 159/15 m. 16d).

[78] *Cl.R. 1234–7*, 512.

[79] Ibid., 522–3. London again got an extra provision, ordering its citizens not to impede merchants coming to London to sell wines.

item they were authorized to purchase; henceforth they were forbidden to buy more than the amounts specified in the warranting writs they carried. The king, furthermore, promised not to take more 'for his use than he himself had need of'.[80] As the first known attempt by an English king to regulate by statute the conduct of purveyance, this writ is of some interest. It was prompted in part by the peculiar tensions which the 1236 wine shortage had created in the wine markets, a connection emphasized by its association with the new assize of wines on the close roll. But it was also apparently one of the concessions which the king and his council were willing to make in order to secure from the magnates in parliament a grant of a thirtieth on moveables. The relationship between the redress of grievances associated with purveyance, and the willingness of a parliament to grant supply, can be dated from at least 1237.[81] It was, needless to say, an idea with a future.

All of this administrative activity was being carried on amidst the most acute financial difficulties. Another 5,000 mark instalment on Isabella's dowry was due to be paid at the end of September 1236; on 1 September, Henry ordered a complete stop on the exchequer's payment of all regular writs of liberate. Only writs with a special counterseal were to be honoured, presumably until the emperor had been paid.[82] This order was still in force at the end of October, and may have continued into November.[83] Despite these measures, it was not until 8 December that the king could gather the 5,000 marks to send to the emperor.[84] The remainder of the debt, 10,000 marks, was due at Easter 1237, and promised to be even harder to collect than previous instalments.[85] Without some extraordinary aid, Henry's hand-to-mouth financial existence might be prolonged for years. Worse, the delays in paying the dowry threatened also to neutralize the diplomatic

---

[80] 'ad opus domini regis quam ipse dominus rex necesse habuerit': *Cl.R.* 1234–7, 522; Annals of Burton, *AM*, vol. i, 253.

[81] Compare Gerald Harriss, *King, Parliament and Public Finance in Medieval England to 1369* (Oxford, 1975), 57–8, who points to complaints about purveyance in 1258, but who finds a link between purveyance and supply only from the 1290s. See also the discussion by W. S. Thomson in *A Lincolnshire Assize Roll for 1298* (Lincoln Record Society 36, 1944), lxvi–lxxix.

[82] *Cl.R.* 1234–7, 310. Although this condition was not explicitly stated in the 1236 order, it was noted in a similar stop ordered in Apr. 1237: *CLR 1226–40*, 264–5.

[83] *CLR 1226–40*, 241.

[84] Ibid., 248.

[85] Ibid., 264–5, 275. Henry's request to the emperor to extend the terms on the debt to Michaelmas 1237 apparently fell on deaf ears: *Foedera* (1816), vol. i, pt. 1, 228, dated 30 June 1236.

advantages of the marriage, which ought to have been considerable.[86] This situation could not be allowed to continue. By the middle of October 1236, the king's council had decided to summon the magnates to Westminster in January 1237 to request from them a thirtieth on moveables for the financially beleaguered king.[87]

Between October and January, the council turned its attentions to the forests, the last remaining source of immediate royal revenue. Characteristically, however, the council did not simply order that the king's timber be sold. It first commissioned Richard de Muntfichet, the newly appointed chief justice of the forests,[88] to make an inquest into their economic potential, paying attention not only to the profits which might be realized from the sale of timber and underbrush, but also noting where and to what extent the king's demesnes could be enlarged by assarting.[89] The terms of this inquest reflect several months of increasingly close attention by the council to the efficient exploitation of the king's forest resources.[90] What emerged during the autumn of 1236 was a decision to extend the resumptions policy from the royal demesne manors to the king's woods, and to entrust the administration of all parks and woods attached to demesne manors to the newly appointed manorial custodians: Robert de Crepping in the north, and Warner Engayne and Walter de Burgo in the south.[91]

The close connection between the policies which the council was now pursuing with respect to the forests and those affecting the royal demesne manors is evident from the patent roll enrolment of Engayne's and de Burgo's forest appointment on 12 January 1237. Three separate commissions were enrolled to them on that day.

Appointment of Walter de Burgo and Warner Engayne to take into the king's hands all his manors and demesnes, with mandate to sheriffs to cause them to have full seisin of the same.

Appointment, during pleasure, of the same Walter and Warner to the

---

[86] See Ch. 5.

[87] Meekings in *CRR*, vol. 15, lvi n.5.

[88] *CPR 1232–47*, 167: 11 Nov. 1236.

[89] *Cl.R. 1234–7*, 519: 12 Jan. 1237.

[90] A forest eyre had been underway since Mar. 1236: *Cl.R. 1234–7*, 344.

[91] Crepping was appointed custodian of the king's demesne woods in Cumberland, Northumberland, Lancashire, and Yorkshire in Oct. or Nov. 1236: *CPR 1232–47*, 160, 166. He was reappointed on 27 Jan. 1237: ibid., 173. Engayne and de Burgo were not appointed officially to the custody of the southern demesne forests until 12 Jan. 1237 (ibid., 173), but these woods appear to have been in their hands since Aug. 1236: ibid., 156.

custody of the king's demesne woods and parks pertaining to his demesnes within forests and without, to answer for the vert and venison thereof before the chief justice of the forest, and to the king for the other issues: directed to verderers, foresters and agisters of counties wherein the same are.

Mandate to the said Walter and Warner to take into the king's hands all lands given, sold, or otherwise alienated out of the king's demesnes which are in the king's custody, in whosoever hands they may be, and to keep them safe until further order.[92]

We have already seen the opposition which the 1236 revocations of royal demesne grants had created in the countryside. Writs ordering the reseisin of one magnate or another continued to issue from the chancery throughout 1236 and into 1237.[93] This blanket reappointment threatened further such disseisins from demesne manors, and threatened in addition to produce a similar round of disseisins from demesne forests.[94] Previously, the administration of demesne woods had lain in the hands of the local royal foresters, many of whom held their positions heritably as foresters in fee.[95] By this new order, such men were now entirely displaced, and a large chunk of the forest land of England was removed from the supervision of the chief forest officials. The third commission was perhaps the most inflammatory of all. It threatened with disseisin every tenant in England holding land from the king's demesne who had demised or alienated some portion of his holding, whether or not he had a prescriptive right to do so guaranteed to him by a royal charter. All the recipients of such alienated lands were of course also threatened with disseisin.

Fears that the council planned a new and even more sweeping round of disseisins were further intensified by yet another council-directed inquisition. On 15 December 1236, the exchequer ordered the sheriffs to launch an inquest into all the lands which had been held in England by Normans, Bretons, and other foreigners in the time of King John and of the present king. It wished to know which lands these were, how much they were worth, who presently held them, and by whose grant. This information was to be returned to the exchequer by 2

[92] Ibid., 173.

[93] For writs issuing in 1236, see Table 3.1. For the 1237 writs, see *Cl.R.* 1234–7, 419, 432, 506 (which went not to a magnate, but to the men of Cheltenham, Gloucs.).

[94] Ibid., 412, 414, 522.

[95] On forest administration, see Young, *Royal Forests*. There is also a great deal of information in Cyril E. Hart, *Royal Forest: a History of Dean's Woods as Producers of Timber* (Oxford, 1966).

February 1237.[96] To the magnates, this inquest was especially alarming because *terre Normannorum* was held explicitly *de ballio regis*, making it therefore legally revocable at the king's will. At best, a magnate could claim only a life interest in such property. Legally, these lands could never be handed down from father to son by any kind of heritable right. They therefore lay outside the normal bounds of law and custom which protected almost all other freehold tenures from the king's *arbitrium*.

It was in the apprehensive atmosphere created by these apparent threats to the security of seisin that the magnates met at Westminster to consider the king's request for a thirtieth on moveables. The session, summoned initially to meet on 13 January, did not in fact get under way until 22 January.[97] William de Ralegh presented the council's plea for the grant. He laid the blame for the parlous state of the king's finances partly on the inadequate administrative practices of previous royal officials, who had rendered the king an incorrect account of his funds, and partly on the expenses of the king's marriage and of Isabella's dowry. And he promised the gathering that the proceeds from the proposed grant would be kept for the 'necessary uses of the kingdom' ('usus regni necessarios'), and would be expended at the discretion of any representatives whom the assembled magnates might wish to select.

The magnates drove a harder bargain than that. In return for permission to levy the thirtieth, they secured a package of concessions and changes in the king's government which is unparalleled before the 1290s. Their most important victory was the reconfirmation by the king of Magna Carta. It has sometimes been argued that this reconfirmation was necessary because there was serious doubt in 1237 whether the king considered himself bound by a charter which had previously been issued and confirmed only during his minority.[98] This seems to me to mistake the point at issue between king and magnates in 1237. Henry had stated clearly and explicitly in 1234 that he accepted

[96] Memoranda Roll 21 Henry III (E. 159/15 m. 18d); cf. *Book of Fees*, vol. i, 611–19.

[97] For the date of this gathering, see Meekings, *CRR*, vol. 15, lvi and n. 5. Unless otherwise noted, description of the events of this parliament is from *CM*, vol. iii, 380–4.

[98] Holt, *Magna Carta*, 282–3. It is hard to be sure what Powicke thought on the matter: cf. *Henry III*, 154; *The Thirteenth Century* (Oxford, 1962), 75. The *non obstante* clause noted by Holt in support of his interpretation may in fact imply the opposite of what Holt suggests, i.e., that Henry reconfirmed the charters in 1237 notwithstanding the fact that they were already valid by virtue of the grant made in 1225. See also *Charter Rolls 1226–57*, 225–6.

Magna Carta as law, and that he intended to abide by it. Indeed, his interpretations of the Charter in that year were, if anything, over-scrupulous.[99] Conciliar policy during 1236 had, however, seriously threatened the security of certain kinds of tenures which the magnates believed should be protected by the due process clauses of the Charter. Fee-farm tenants holding royal demesne manors by charter, and for-esters holding heritable offices in fee, had each been treated by the king's bailiffs as if they were mere tenants at will, who could be disseised from their holdings at the king's command. In reversing these disseisins, the magnates insisted that in future the king proceed against such persons only in accordance with the law of the land. In the order which restored the hereditary foresters to their offices, this requirement was made explicit.

Concerning foresters who are enfeoffed by charters and who were disseised by the bailiffs of the lord king, it is provided that they shall have their seisin back in the same state in which they previously held it; and later, if the lord king pleases, they may be summoned to show their warrants, and brought to trial according to the law of the land.[100]

Magna Carta meant two things to the magnates of England after 1225: security of tenures and protection for the liberties of the church. Whenever we find the Charters being confirmed or re-proclaimed under Henry III, we may be confident that one at least of these two fundamental principles was thought to be in danger.[101] The Charters had a very specific meaning during Henry's reign, on which king and magnates basically agreed. Their reconfirmation was never merely a demand for a royal token of good faith.[102]

Reconfirmation of Magna Carta was, however, only one part of the settlement reached between the king and his magnates. In addition, the *terre Normannorum* inquests were left in unofficial abeyance.[103] Although we have no record of any discussion of this matter at the

---

[99] *Cl.R.* 1231–4, 551, 588–9, 592–3. For discussion see Holt, *Magna Carta*, 283–4; Powicke, *Henry III*, 147–8.

[100] *Cl.R.* 1234–7, 522: 6 Feb. 1237, my translation.

[101] For episcopal liberties and Magna Carta, see pp. 136–9.

[102] Compare Holt, *Magna Carta*, 284–5; McKechnie, *Magna Carta*, 158; and now Maddicott, 'Magna Carta and the Local Community', *passim*.

[103] The surviving returns from this inquest are few: cf. *Book of Fees*, vol. i, 611–19. On the other hand, there are fragmentary returns from fifteen different counties, which suggests that the returns themselves may once have been quite extensive. That nothing was done with them was therefore more likely the result of a conciliar decision than of the insufficiency of the inquests themselves.

parliament, the king's government took no further action on this front again until 1244.[104] Meanwhile, Engayne's and de Burgo's commission to reclaim all alienations from demesne lands was 'revoked and broken into pieces'. When it was reissued on 10 February, at the conclusion of this extended gathering, Eugayne's and de Burgo's attentions were restricted to alienations by villeins. Free men were explicitly exempted from the terms of their revised commission.[105] Custody of the demesne forests was returned to the hereditary foresters, under the supervision of the chief justices of the forest. The manorial custodians were now restricted to taking nuts, honey, pannage, and herbage from the forest, and even these they could take only under the supervision of the appropriate forest officials.[106] Complaints against the king's purchasing agents were met by the new statute on purveyance, and by the reimposition of the assize of wines.[107]

The session also carried through a number of personnel changes in the membership of the king's council. Godfrey de Craucombe became the scapegoat for the council's sins. He lost his stewardship and was removed from the council.[108] His replacement, John fitz Geoffrey, had been the first magnate disseised by Engayne's and de Burgo's inquests.[109] In no sense, however, was he a man hostile to the court. He had long-standing family connections with royal administration, and had served for several years himself as sheriff of Yorkshire and as a royal forester.[110] In contrast to most of the stewards, he had not had previous experience in the king's military household. He was, however, eager to make up for lost time, and quickly became one of Henry's most trusted servants.[111] Much the same can be said about the two other baronial nominees to the council. The Earl Warenne had been strangely absent from court between April and December 1236. He was therefore not implicated in any of the council's objectionable

---

[104] See pp. 250–1.

[105] *CPR 1232–47*, 173, 175; and see pp. 110–111.

[106] *Cl.R. 1234–7*, 521–2. This order was repeated in Apr. 1238: *CPR 1232–47*, 216.

[107] Contra Meekings, *CRR*, vol. 15, lvii n. 1, the reissued assize did not alter the prices at which wine was sold. Meekings may have been misled by the wording of *CPR 1232–47*, 148.

[108] Meekings, *CRR*, vol. 15, xxxviii–xxxix.

[109] *Cl.R. 1234–7*, 357; and above, pp. 101–3.

[110] His father was Geoffrey fitz Peter, justiciar to King John, and a candidate for the authorship of *Glanvill*. For his career before 1237, cf. *CPR 1232–47*, 52; *Cl.R. 1234–7*, 6, 12, 33, 141, 153.

[111] *CM*, vol. iii, 417; Meekings, *CRR*, vol. 15, xxxvi; and below, p. 123, for John fitz Geoffrey's role in the crisis of 1238.

policies. But he had been frequently at court before that date, and he became a regular attender on the king thereafter.[112] He too must be considered a 'king's man'. William de Ferrers, the son of the earl of Derby, suffered like his father from gout.[113] He attested a number of royal charters throughout this period, but there are few other signs that he wielded much power around the court. He too had been a victim of the resumptions of royal demesne manors, losing Bolsover in Derbyshire to Warner Engayne.[114] But unlike John fitz Geoffrey, he did not succeed in recovering the manor, despite his elevation to the council.

William of Savoy may also have been a casualty of this parliament, albeit a temporary one. In late February 1237 he left England, for reasons which remain unexplained, appointing an attorney to administer his English lands until September.[115] Although he had returned to England by the end of April, he did not resume his regular attendance at court until August.[116] In his absence, the earl of Lincoln, Simon de Montfort, and Brother Geoffrey the king's almoner strengthened their grip on the court.[117]

The basic policies of the council, however, did not change, despite the concessions made to the January parliament, and despite the absence of the elect of Valence, its titular head, during much of 1237. The custodial experiment in the shires and on the royal demesne manors continued unchecked; the exchequer continued to enrol and collect its back debts, to audit its accounts, and to enforce an ever stricter control over the king's officials; and the stream of legal innovations and inquests went on without interruption. There is an essential unity to conciliar policy with respect to all these matters from April 1236 until at least the end of 1238. Real change in these matters begins to come only in 1239, when William de Ralegh departed from the council to become bishop of Norwich and Stephen de Segrave took over from Ralegh as the king's chief minister.[118] These coincidences are probably not accidental. William of Savoy brought to the council an ability to persuade the king to go along with the new policies, but

---

[112] He was with the king, for example, in 1238 when the papal legate Otto arrived at court after his flight from the attack on him at Osney Abbey (*CM*, vol. iii, 483); and he rewarded the messenger who brought him news of the birth of Henry's son Edward in 1239 with a fee of £10 per year for life (*CLR 1240–5*, 292).

[113] Denholm-Young, 'Paper Constitution', 147.

[114] *CLR 1226–40*, 269.

[115] *CM*, vol. iii, 387–8; *CPR 1232–47*, 176.

[116] Meekings, 'Charter Roll Witnesses, 1227–1243'.

[117] *CM*, vol. iii, 412; Meekings, *CRR*, vol. 15, xxxv and n. 5.

[118] See below, pp. 132–6.

it seems unlikely that a man who had been in England barely three months could possibly have learned enough about English administration and English local conditions to design so thoroughgoing a programme of financial reform as the council set underway in April 1236.[119] Credit for this programme must surely to go Ralegh.[120] The blame for it may well have attached to William of Savoy.[121] If so, this was not the least of William de Ralegh's accomplishments during these years.

The council had asked for a great deal during 1236 and early 1237. Consequently it had a great many counters with which to bargain in the January parliament. Ralegh and his colleagues were able to give ground on such matters as purveyance and the forests, without critically undermining their overarching financial strategy. In return for these concessions, they gained for the king a much more significant addition to his treasury than either purveyance or the forests could have provided him. And the reconfirmation of the charters cost the king nothing at all. In thus securing the thirtieth on moveables without giving way on either shire or demesne policy, the council could claim a real measure of success from the January parliament.

Assessment of the thirtieth was deferred until September, when the autumn crops would swell the assessments.[122] Collections were to be made in two instalments, the first due on 1 December 1237, the second due at the end of May 1238.[123] At the suggestion of the council, and in view of the proclaimed poverty of the king's people, payment of the second instalment was later divided into two parts, with half of the instalment due in May, and the other half due at Michaelmas 1238.[124] Exemptions were limited to the Hospitallers, the Templars, the Pre-

---

[119] Compare Carpenter, 'Curial Sheriff', 16–19, who recognizes this difficulty, but suggests that Savoy was advised by the exchequer. Powicke, *Henry III*, 153, and Denholm-Young, 'Paper Constitution', *passim* seem not to have considered this problem in ascribing responsibility for the reforms to William of Savoy.

[120] For additional references to Ralegh's personal responsibility for aspects of the reform programme, see Memoranda Roll 20 Henry III (E. 159/15 mms. 15, 18d, 19d); *CRR*, vol. 15, xxxvi, lvii n. 1; *CRR*, vol. 16, no. 14.

[121] *CM*, vol. iii, 362, 387–8; Annals of Tewkesbury, *AM*, vol. i, 102; Annals of Dunstable, *AM*, vol. iii, 145–6.

[122] *Cl.R.* 1234–7, 545; cf. Sydney Knox Mitchell, *Taxation in Medieval England* (New Haven, 1951), 150–2.

[123] *Cl.R.* 1234–7, 543–5. For the mechanics of the assessment and collection of this aid, see Mitchell, *Studies*, 214–21, and *Taxation*, 42–7.

[124] *Cl.R.* 1237–42, 130. This decision was probably influenced by the unrest brought about by the revolt of Richard of Cornwall early in 1238, on which see pp. 118–24.

monstratensians and the Cistercians.[125] The royal demesne was also exempt, but paid a tallage in the following year.[126]

Ultimately, deferring the tax to the autumn was to the king's advantage, but it did mean that the final 10,000 marks of Isabella's dowry had to be found from some other source. The emperor's envoys arrived in England at the end of April, to collect the money which was due at Easter.[127] Henry immediately ordered yet another stop on the exchequer, to last until the emperor had been paid.[128] The men around the court were getting to be experienced hands at this sort of thing, however, and so the order had little effect on the payment of their own fees and expenses. Most were careful to secure liberate writs which included a *non obstante* clause dispensing with the stop on the exchequer.[129] In part for this reason, payment of the final instalment proved an even more tedious business than usual. The emperor's envoys waited in London from the end of April until 17 June, when a writ of liberate for 10,000 marks was finally issued to them.[130] However, securing a writ and securing payment on that writ were two very different matters. On 28 June, letters patent were issued to the treasurer of the Temple in London to pay the envoys their money.[131] Still they waited. But somehow the money was found. On 12 July, the envoys left England, apparently with the full sum due to the emperor.[132] No further mention of arrears owing on the dowry occurs in the rolls.

The last six months of 1237 saw steady progress toward financial stability at Westminster. Although Henry imposed a temporary stop on the exchequer around 11 September, this probably lasted only until Michaelmas, when the new term's receipts began to flow into the treasury.[133] Michaelmas receipts were further swelled by the proceeds of a 3,000 mark tallage on the Jews, imposed in April 1237,[134] and by the revenues from the council's experiment with custodial sheriffs and

---

[125] *Cl.R. 1234–7*, 566–7. Hospitals were also exempt: *Cl.R. 1237–42*, 2, 8.

[126] *Cl.R. 1237–42*, 16, 37, 64, 115, and cf. Mitchell, *Studies*, 216.

[127] *CLR 1226–40*, 264: 26 Apr., the bailiffs of Dover are to find them a ship; ibid., 264–5: 28 Apr., a stop on the exchequer; ibid., 265: 30 Apr., a grant to one of the envoys.

[128] Ibid., 264–5.

[129] Cf. Ibid., 264–70, *passim*.

[130] Ibid., 275.

[131] *CPR 1232–47*, 188.

[132] *CLR 1226–40*, 278, 288; Memoranda Roll 21 Henry III (E. 159/15 m. 24d).

[133] *CLR 1226–40*, 292.

[134] This tallage was supposed to be paid within a month from Apr. (*CPR 1232–47*, 178), but payments were still coming in early in 1238: cf. *Cl.R. 1237–42*, 31. For more discussion of this tallage, and of the significance of Jewish taxation to Henry's finances, see Ch. 4.

manorial custodians, which had just completed its first full year. Between the end of September and the middle of January 1238, the king apparently paid his bills from current receipts, without being forced to borrow on the thirtieth. In mid-December, Henry issued orders to transfer the first instalment of the aid from the shire depositories in which it had been held to three central treasuries, at Bristol, Nottingham, and London.[135] All signs were that the king might indeed be able to hold to his promise to keep these funds as a reserve, which might form the nucleus of a war chest to recover his lost French territories.

Upon this apparent calm, the revolt of Richard of Cornwall in January 1238 broke like a sudden storm. The immediate cause of this rebellion was Henry's apparently impulsive decision to marry their sister Eleanor, the widow of William Marshal the younger, to Simon de Montfort, the *parvenu* claimant to the earldom of Leicester.[136] There may also have been resentment at the forthcoming marriage of Richard de Clare, minor heir to the earldom of Gloucester, to the daughter and heir of the earl of Lincoln.[137] Richard de Clare had been married, apparently secretly, to the daughter of Hubert de Burgh while he was in de Burgh's custody, but the marriage had been overridden, and in November 1237 the unfortunate lady had died.[138] Already in October 1237, an agreement had been reached that if by January 1238 Henry could not contract a marriage for Richard with one of the daughters of the count of La Marche, the youth should marry the daughter of the earl of Lincoln.[139] Richard of Cornwall was the boy's stepfather; although he is recorded as one of the councillors approving this arrangement with Lincoln, he may not in fact have been very happy about uniting these two powerful earldoms.[140] As brother-in-law to the king's sister, and uncle of Richard de Clare, Gilbert Earl

---

[135] CLR 1226–40, 302–3. Devizes also acted as a provincial treasury for the thirtieth, as well as being the depository for Wiltshire, but it is not clear just when it began to fulfil the former role: cf. Cl.R. 1237–42, 118; CLR 1226–40, 318, 468, 482; CLR 1240–5, 107, 116; CLR 1232–47, 213, 274.

[136] CPR 1232–47, 209; CM, vol. iii, 475–80; Annals of Tewkesbury, AM, vol. i, 106.

[137] This marriage had been arranged in Oct. 1237, and was to take place at any date after 13 Jan. 1238; it was officially solemnized on 26 Jan.: cf. CPR 1232–47, 199–200, 208. The revolt had begun by 21 Jan.: cf. Denholm-Young, Richard of Cornwall, 35.

[138] Powicke, Henry III, 760–8, reprinted from EHR 56 (1941), 539–48.

[139] CPR 1232–47, 199–200. Lincoln paid 5000 marks for this privilege, of which the king pardoned him 2000 marks. For Henry's efforts to win the support of the count of La Marche during these years, see Ch. 5.

[140] CPR 1232–47, 199–200; CM, vol. iii, 476; Denholm-Young, Richard of Cornwall, 34.

Marshal had an equal claim to feel that the family honour had been affronted by Eleanor's marriage. Moreover, he was probably not even consulted about the marriage of Richard de Clare, having been away from court since February 1237. He cannot have been indifferent to a match which would affect so decisively the balance of power in the Welsh Marches. Cornwall and Gilbert Marshal formed the backbone of this revolt.[141]

The aims of the revolt are unclear. We have only two chronicle accounts, which are at least independent of one another, although neither is an untainted contemporary record. The Annals of Tewkesbury described the events as follows:

> The sister of the king of England, once the wife of the young Marshal, married Simon de Montfort, whereupon the earl of Cornwall was moved to anger. . . . The daughter of the earl of Lincoln married Richard de Clare, around the Purification of the Blessed Virgin. Dissension was heard of between the king of England and his brother Richard earl of Cornwall and many other magnates, on account of the marriage of the countess of Pembroke to Simon de Montfort, and because they wished to remove the king's council, which was not useful to the kingdom, and foreigners.[142]

If the final clause is contemporary, and not an addition made by the copyist around 1253, then we may infer from this account that Cornwall and the Marshal were concerned not just about the marriages, but also about control over the royal council which had arranged them. Lincoln and de Montfort were clearly the dominant lay magnates on the council during the latter half of 1237;[143] these marriages threatened to make their positions impregnable. The ref-

---

[141] Earl Richard had married Isabella, the widow of Gilbert earl of Gloucester, in 1231. She was a daughter of the elder William Marshal, and thus sister to Gilbert Marshal, earl of Pembroke. Earl Richard and Gilbert Marshal were thus brothers-in-law through two separate marriages. The only other earl whose involvement can be proved in this revolt is Winchester: cf. *CPR 1232–47*, 208. He was almost never at court, either before or after the revolt, and his reasons for joining it are unknown.

[142] 'Soror regis Angliae, uxor quondam junioris Mariscalli, nupsit Symoni de Monteforti, unde comes Cornubiae in iram commotus est . . . Filia comitis Lincolniae nupsit Ricardo de Clare, circa Purificationem beatae Virginis. Orta est dissentio inter regem Angliae et fratrem suum Ricardum comitem Cornubiae et plures alios magnates, tum propter desponsationem comitissae Penbroc Symoni de Monteforti, tum quia voluerunt amovere concilium regis non utile regno et alienigenas.' *AM*, vol. i, 106. On the composition of the Tewkesbury annals, see Lawrence, *St Edmund*, 173–5; Antonia Gransden, *Historical Writing in England, 550–1307* (London, 1974), 405 n. 13; and now David Carpenter, 'What Happened in 1258?', *War and Government in the Middle Ages: Essays in Honour of J. O. Prestwich* (Cambridge, 1984), 111 n. 22.

[143] *CM*, vol. iii, 412, 475–6; Meekings, *CRR*, vol. 15, xxxv n. 5.

erence to removing foreigners from the realm is more problematic, however, and must raise suspicions that this clause owes more to the events of the late 1240s and 1250s than it does to the aims of the rebels in 1238. At this time, the only foreigners in positions of power at court were William of Savoy, who had returned to court full-time in August 1237, and Master Simon de Steiland.[144] De Montfort, too, might have been considered a foreigner, but the fact that Matthew Paris described him as English casts doubt on such an identification.[145] None the less, an attempt to get rid of William of Savoy is not unlikely. He had by now accumulated substantial property in England, including the honour of Richmond,[146] and his hold over the king was common knowledge. The only other foreigner around the court was the papal legate, who had arrived in England in July 1237. His reform synod of November 1237 evidently caused great unrest among some magnates, who were even thought to be plotting against his life because of the provisions he intended to announce against the presentation of illegitimate noble children to church livings. But these provisions were withdrawn at the last minute, and the legate does not figure explicitly in any of the complaints associated with the 1238 revolt.[147]

All in all, the Tewkesbury account does not give us much to go on, and certainly cannot support the burden of importance which historians have placed on this revolt.[148] Everything hinges on what we make of Matthew Paris's account of this crisis. Matthew portrayed the revolt as a rising of all England against the king.[149] Henry, supported only by the legate and by Hubert de Burgh (!), retreated in confusion to the Tower of London, and finally yielded to the demands of his opponents. A written agreement was executed and sealed by all, in which 'the king submitted himself to the management of some of the more influential parties, and swore to abide by their decision'.[150]

---

[144] On Master Simon, also known as Master Simon the Norman, see the study by Powicke, *Henry III*, 772–83.

[145] *CM*, vol. iii, 412.

[146] *Cl.R.* 1234–7, 310–11.

[147] *CM*, vol. iii, 418–19. See also Dorothy Williamson, 'Some Aspects of the Legation of Cardinal Otto', *EHR* 64 (1949), 145–73, esp. 164 and n. 4.

[148] William Stubbs, *The Constitutional History of England*, 3rd edn. (Oxford, 1887), vol. ii, 56–7; Powicke, *Henry III*, 290–3; Powicke, *Thirteenth Century*, 75–9; Denholm-Young, 'Paper Constitution', *passim*; C. R. Cheney, 'The "Paper Constitution" Preserved by Matthew Paris', *EHR* 65 (1950), 213–21, esp. 220.

[149] *CM*, vol. iii, 475–9.

[150] The English translation is by J. A. Giles, *Matthew Paris's English History*, 3 vols. (London, 1852–4), vol. i, 123. For the passage in Latin, see *CM*, vol. iii, 478.

But at the last minute, de Montfort and Lincoln humbled themselves to Earl Richard, and the scheme of reform came to nothing.

On this basis, historians have sought to explain the tensions and offences which could have produced so massive a revolt. For the most part, they have fixed their attentions on the administration of the thirtieth on moveables. By accepting the historical truth of the assertion which Matthew Paris puts in the mouths of the barons in 1242, that 'the king, of his own free will, and by the advice of the barons, promised them [in 1237] that the whole of the money arising from the said thirtieth part, should be placed in safe custody in his royal castles, under the charge of four nobles of England, namely Earl Warenne, and others, at whose discretion, and by whose advice, the same should be expended',[151] they have interpreted the king's promise in late November to spend the thirtieth only with the advice of the legate[152] and his mid-December decision to transfer the funds from the shire depositories to three provincial treasuries[153] as manifest breaches of good faith.[154] And by linking the revolt of 1238 with criticisms which Matthew Paris puts into the mouth of Richard of Cornwall *sub anno* 1237—that Henry wasted his money by distributing it 'amongst those who were plotting against him and his dominions'; that the king had had many escheats and episcopal vacancies, yet his treasury had shown no profit; and finally, that the king was overly dependent on the legate—the myth has grown up that Henry entirely frittered away the thirtieth.

This he afterwards ordered to be collected and estimated, not at the royal valuation, but according to the common value, and not to be placed in convents and castles, as he had been pre-arranged and determined on, nor to be expended at the discretion of nobles; but without taking the advice of any one of the natural subjects of his kingdom, he gave it to foreigners to be carried abroad, and he became like a man bewitched, as if he had no sense.[155]

---

[151] Giles, *Matthew Paris*, vol. i, 401; cf. *CM*, vol. iv, 186.

[152] *CPR 1232–47*, 205.

[153] *Cl.R. 1237–42*, 116–17; *CLR 1226–40*, 302–3.

[154] Denholm-Young, *Richard of Cornwall*, 33; Denholm-Young, 'Paper Constitution', 148; Reginald F. Treharne, *The Baronial Plan of Reform, 1258–1263* (Manchester, 1971), 52. Mitchell, *Studies*, 218–19, is more cautious.

[155] Giles, *Matthew Paris*, vol. i, 67–8; *CM*, vol. iii, 411. For the myth, see, for example, Powicke, *Henry III*, 303.

The final extension of this tissue of inferences and conjecture has been the attempt to redate the radical proposals of the 'Paper Constitution' from 1244 to 1238.[156] The four baronial conservators of liberties mentioned in that document have therefore been identified with the three new appointees to the king's council in 1237, who are thus transformed into the baronial spokesmen whose advice was allegedly ignored in the expenditure of the thirtieth. A search for the fourth conservator of liberties has found a promising candidate in Ralph de Nevill, the chancellor, from whom Henry withdrew the Seal in the summer of 1238 on his postulation to the bishopric of Winchester.[157]

One can never merely dismiss Matthew Paris. Even when he is writing years after the events he describes, as he was in this case about the events of 1238, his information is often extraordinarily accurate.[158] In this case, however, Matthew's account of the crisis of 1238 is so entirely coloured by his knowledge of the events and complaints of 1242 and afterwards that his interpretation cannot be used without the greatest caution. And without a firm base in Matthew Paris, the elaborate arguments and inferences which have been built upon his account cannot stand. Local depositories were standard features in the collection of an aid,[159] but they were unsafe and administratively inefficient as long-term repositories for the king's treasure. They were always emptied soon after the local collections were completed, whereupon the money would be transferred to more central locations. Such was surely the intention with respect to the thirtieth also. If there is any truth at all in Matthew Paris's claim that 'the money ... when collected, was to be placed in some convent, sacred house, or castle, so that if the king should endeavour to retract his promises, the property of each should be restored to him',[160] it was probably as a

---

[156] Denholm-Young, 'Paper Constitution', *passim*. His arguments for re-dating this document to 1238 were accepted by Powicke in *Henry III*, 290–3, with reservations; further reservations were added in *Thirteenth Century*, 75–9, after reading the criticisms of Denholm-Young by Cheney, 'Paper Constitution', *passim*, and by Bertie Wilkinson, *The Constitutional History of England, 1216–1399*, 3 vols. (New York, 1948–58), vol. i, 117–130.

[157] Denholm-Young, 'Paper Constitution', 146.

[158] Matthew's report *sub anno* 1237 (CM, vol. iii, 413) that Henry sent a gift of 1000 marks to his father-in-law, the count of Provence, is corroborated by the very secretive and rather vague order confirming the payment of such a sum by Brother Geoffrey the almoner 'for the expedition of the king's affairs', in the presence of an unusual number of the king's councillors: *CLR* 1226–40, 299, confirmed by the wardrobe account for the period from 28 Oct. 1237 to 6 Feb. 1238 (E. 372/81 rot. 13).

[159] Mitchell, *Taxation*, 96–108.

[160] Giles, *Matthew Paris*, vol. i, 45–6; CM, vol. iii, 383.

guarantee that the king would indeed reconfirm the Charters, and cause them to be read in every shire. Matthew does record Ralegh's 1237 offer to expend the thirtieth under the supervision of nobles elected for this purpose, but he says nothing about the magnates accepting this offer.[161] Furthermore, there is no evidence at all that the three new appointees to the council in 1237—fitz Geoffrey, Warenne, and William de Ferrers—ever conceived of their role in this light. So far as we know, none of them joined Earl Richard's revolt; on the contrary, John fitz Geoffrey was one of the king's most trusted supporters in the negotiations leading up to a settlement.[162] And finally, there is no evidence that Henry had spent a penny from the thirtieth on anything whatsoever until after the revolt began. And even then, his loan of £1000 from the thirtieth to Brother Thierry of Nussa, head of the English Hospitallers and a great friend of Richard of Cornwall, for use in the Holy Land, looks very much like a preliminary attempt to placate Earl Richard.[163] Indeed, what seems finally to have brought Earl Richard around to the king's side in this affair was a 6000 mark bribe paid to him out of the proceeds of the thirtieth.[164] This sum was sent to Paris for his use, and was undoubtedly intended to assist his crusade, which he had been planning since mid-1236. A similar bribe, of 3000 marks from the Jews, had purchased Richard's support a year earlier, just before the meeting of the January 1237 parliament.[165] 'Richard never quarrelled with his brother without coming away a richer man.'[166] If anyone deserves the blame for frittering away the thirtieth on foreigners, it is as much Richard of Cornwall as the king.

Thus purged of its post-1240 accretions, the revolt of 1238 emerges as much less a constitutionally motivated rebellion than a personal and conciliar one. This is evident not only in the nature of the grievances which produced it, but also in the personal reconciliations which brought it to a close. The governmental concessions which Matthew Paris claims were agreed came to naught, because Richard of Cornwall gained what he had been seeking without them. The rebellion brought the dominance of Lincoln and de Montfort on the council to an end. Although Lincoln continued as a member of the king's inner circle, he is never again referred to as a leading figure. After a long illness, he

---

[161] CM, vol. iii, 380–1.
[162] CPR 1232–47, 208.
[163] Ibid., 209; Wardrobe account (E. 372/81 rot. 13).
[164] CPR 1232–47, 222; CM, vol. iii, 476; Denholm-Young, *Richard of Cornwall*, 36–7.
[165] CPR 1232–47, 173. This too was intended to forward the crusade.
[166] Denholm-Young, 'Paper Constitution', 150.

died in June 1240. Simon de Montfort left England altogether in late March 1238, to seek papal confirmation for his marriage at Rome.[167] He did not return to England until October. In late November, his wife bore him a son at Kenilworth, for whom King Henry acted as godfather,[168] and in February 1239, he was formally invested as earl of Leicester. But de Montfort seems never to have recovered the influence that he lost as a result of the rebellion of Richard of Cornwall, and in August 1239 he was driven from the court again, this time by the wrath of the king. Relations between the king and his brother-in-law were never again untroubled.[169] William of Savoy, meanwhile, left England in May 1238, and died abroad.[170] If I am right in connecting his final departure with the rebellion by Cornwall, then it may well be that Henry's over-zealous efforts in 1238 and 1239 to have William elected bishop of Winchester reflected the king's awareness that he could not safely bring William back to England simply as a councillor. Ralegh continued in charge of the royal administration, but on policy matters, Richard of Cornwall now reigned supreme in his brother's counsels.[171]

The baleful effects of Cornwall's influence on royal administration quickly became apparent. Ever since Ralegh had joined the court *coram rege*, the justices had demonstrated a notable concern to investigate and

---

[167] *CPR 1232–47*, 214; *CM*, vol. iii, 479–80; Bémont, ed. Jacobs, *Simon de Montfort*, 56–8.

[168] The date of Henry de Montfort's birth is usually cited as 28 Nov., on the basis of Matthew Paris's comment that he was born 'in Adventu Domini' (*CM*, vol. iii, 518). In fact, the date should be a few days earlier, perhaps 26 Nov. On that day, King Henry departed from Woodstock, where he had been staying, and arrived in Kenilworth by nightfall, a very rapid trip. He left Kenilworth on 28 Nov., and travelled by more leisurely stages back to Woodstock. This information is drawn from the unpublished almoner's roll for 23 Henry III (C. 47/3/44); the published itinerary in *CRR*, vol. 16, xlv requires correction at this point. King Henry was thus present at the baptism of his godson, and gave his personal permission for the child to be named Henry. The incident gives a small glimpse of the warm relations which existed at this time between the king and his brother-in-law.

[169] Bémont, ed. Jacobs, *Simon de Montfort*, 56–64.

[170] *CM*, vol. iii, 486, 491, confirmed by *CPR 1232–47*, 221; *Cl.R. 1237–42*, 68; *CLR 1226–40*, 359, 365, 400. William went to assist the imperial armies in Italy. See also Powicke, *Henry III*, 187–8.

[171] Gilbert Marshal, earl of Pembroke, gained absolutely nothing from the revolt; indeed, the outright hostility expressed by the king towards him at Christmas 1238 (*CM*, vol. iii, 523–4) and again in Jan. 1240 (*CM*, vol. iv, 3–4) suggests rather that he had lost whatever small trust the king might previously have reposed in him. Gilbert Marshal and the king were not reconciled until shortly before Richard of Cornwall set off on his crusade. Even then, the price of Richard's mediation may have been Gilbert's oath to join the crusade: cf. *CM*, vol. iv, 56.

recover usurped royal rights.[172] Walter de Burgo continued such efforts throughout 1236 and 1237, bringing a number of *quo warranto* cases personally before the court. Early in 1238, however, the council decided to broaden these efforts, and in the Devon eyre circuit of that year, instructed the justices to challenge every lord of a private hundred to show the warrant by which he held it.[173] Hundreds were particularly important in Devon, a large county whose deep valleys made central administration slow and difficult; and as a local Devon man, it is likely that Ralegh's local knowledge lay behind the decision to mount such challenges first in Devon. If so, the failure of the scheme is all the more significant; for in the end, not a single hundredal holder lost his rights, or even found it necessary to have them confirmed by royal charter. Although the inquests themselves were carried out, and the results communicated to the council,[174] they were not followed up by any further action. Like the *terre Normannorum* inquests of the previous year, they remained a dead letter. Ralegh's departure from the council in early 1239 presumably had something to do with this, but much more important may have been the opposition of Richard of Cornwall, who held one of these Devon hundreds personally, and who was the patron, guardian, and father-in-law of the young Earl Baldwin III of Devon, who held no less than six. Baldwin's interest in these hundreds is clear; among his first known actions after coming of age in late 1238 was to file suit in King's Bench to enforce suit of court to one of them.[175] Earl Richard's role in protecting his own and his ward's interests in these Devon hundreds can only be inferred, but it is certainly consistent with his other activities on the council during 1238 and 1239, which are better documented.

The extent of Cornwall's dominance is clearly reflected in the expenditure of the thirtieth. Richard's overriding concern during 1238 was

---

[172] During 1234 and 1235, Ralegh and his colleagues launched several *quo warranto* campaigns to recover alienations on individual royal manors. At Havering in Essex, for example, at least twenty royal tenants were summoned *coram rege* to answer for their holdings during these years: cf. *CRR*, vol. 15, nos. 1027, 1083, 1145, 1156, 1191, 1241, 1350. In 1235 and 1236, these campaigns were extended to Wiltshire, Worcestershire, Hampshire, and Surrey: cf. *CRR*, vol. 15, nos. 1885, 1892, 1952, 1963, 1971, 1972B, 1993; *CRR*, vol. 16, nos. 2, 3, 19, 20, 34, 35, 77, 84, 87, 117D, 117G, 124, 125, 129, 132, 149A.
[173] For what follows, see H. R. T. Summerson's introduction to his edition of the *Crown Pleas of the Devon Eyre of 1238* (Devon and Cornwall Record Society, n. s. 28, 1985), xxiii–xxvii. I am indebted to Dr Summerson for making available to me the results of his research.
[174] The surviving records are printed in *Book of Fees*, vol. ii, 1367–72.
[175] *CRR*, vol. 16, nos. 1023, 1035, called to my attention by Dr Summerson.

with the crusade he had been planning since the middle of 1236.[176] Of the approximately 17,000 marks from the thirtieth which we know to have been spent between February and August 1238, almost half went directly to the preparations for Richard's crusade.[177] In addition to these sums, Henry also agreed to support a force of 100 knights to fight in the service of the Emperor Frederick in the siege of Brescia, which was underway during the summer of 1238.[178] This force cost the king an additional 8000 marks, which apparently came out of general revenues.[179] Henry certainly hoped that Frederick would become a useful ally in any war against the king of France, and to this extent, Henry had an interest in his brother-in-law's success in Italy. But Richard of Cornwall's interests in that campaign were much more direct. In late March or early April 1238, Richard had received a letter from the emperor, urging him to defer his crusade until the summer of 1239, when the truce with the sultan would expire, and Frederick might be able to lend more assistance to the crusaders.[180] Earl Richard knew full well that so long as Frederick was occupied in Italy, he could not join the crusade. A victory over the Italian city-states, however, might free the emperor to devote his attentions to the Holy Land. In this respect, Henry's military assistance to Frederick is yet another example of his subservience in these months to Earl Richard's interests in the crusade. Between February and May, Henry spent over 16,000 marks in support of this cause, almost half the recorded total of the king's receipts from the thirtieth on moveables.[181]

Beyond the sums he spent on the crusade, Henry directed an additional 6200 marks from the thirtieth into his wardrobe during 1238.[182] Of this sum, however, 3400 marks went in loans to the men

---

[176] Denholm-Young, *Richard of Cornwall*, 32–3, 38–9.

[177] 1500 marks to the Hospitallers on 3 Feb. (CPR 1232–47, 209); 750 marks to the Latin emperor of Constantinople on 29 Apr. to 1 May (CPR 1232–47, 217; CLR 1226–40, 326–7), whose cause Richard also supported with a gift (CM, vol. iii, 481, 486); and 6000 marks to Richard himself on 28/30 May (CPR 1232–47, 222).

[178] CM, vol. iii, 485–6, 491.

[179] CPR 1232–47, 221. It is possible that the real cost of the expedition was at least 1000 marks more than this: cf. CLR 1226–40, 365.

[180] CM, vol. iii, 471–2.

[181] *Red Book*, vol. iii, 1064 records total receipts from the tax as 33,811 marks 2s 1d.

[182] Wardrobe account from 6 Feb. 1238 to 3 Feb. 1240 (E. 372/83 rot. 7). The largest of these sums, 3000 marks paid to Brother Geoffrey the almoner from the thirtieth in the Tower, is not precisely datable; but since all other payments listed here date from 1238, this one probably does also. The 2000 marks authorized to Brother Geoffrey by CPR 1232–47, 211, appear never to have been paid. Thomas of Newark received 3000 marks for the same purpose a few days later: CPR 1232–47, 212; CLR 1226–40, 317.

around Henry's court, the bulk of these loans being carried overseas: 2350 marks to Simon de Montfort, travelling to Rome to regularize his marriage, and 417 marks to William of Savoy, on his way to Brescia.[183] Both debts were eventually pardoned by the king.[184] In March, another 2265 marks went to the king's wardrobe clerk, Thomas de Newark, to pay the arrears owing on their yearly fees to Henry's Gascon and Poitevin retainers.[185] Payment of these fees amounted to at least 2500 marks per year, and had fallen seriously into arrears while the king struggled to pay Isabella's dowry.[186] Another 1000 marks went with Walter de Cantilupe, bishop-elect of Worcester, to Rome as a loan to defray his expenses in securing his confirmation to the bishopric.[187] Between 6 February 1238 and 3 February 1240, after which the wardrobe accounts fail us, only about 3000 marks from the thirtieth passed through the wardrobe to pay the king's household expenses.[188] An additional 1200 marks from the tax may have passed through the wardrobe during 1240.[189] Even if we include this additional 1200 mark sum, however, this represents an average annual expenditure from the thirtieth on household expenses between the autumn of 1237 and 1241 of no more than 1000 marks per year. Whatever else one may say about his faults, the king's alleged domestic extravagance played a relatively minor role in the 'wasting' of the thirtieth. Earl Richard of Cornwall deserves a far larger share of the blame.

Loss of the patent rolls for 23 and 24 Henry III deprives us of any accurate knowledge of expenditures from the thirtieth between October 1238 and October 1240, except for the sums which passed through the king's wardrobe. It appears, however, that by August

---

[183] *CLR 1226–40*, 410; E. 372/83 rot. 7.

[184] Savoy's debts were all pardoned on his death in Nov. 1239; de Montfort's debts were pardoned in 1243 (Pipe Roll 27 Henry III: E. 372/87 rot. 14).

[185] *CLR 1226–40*, 317; *CPR 1232–47*, 212. Although these writs authorized the issue of 3000 marks, they directed the expenditure of only 2265 marks. The £475. 6s. 10d. paid by Thomas into the wardrobe at Newark (E. 372/83 rot. 7) is probably the remainder of the 3000 marks he received in Mar.

[186] See pp. 182–3 below.

[187] The sources differ on the amount of this prest. *CPR 1232–47*, 213 and *CLR 1226–40*, 318, 482, agree that the bishop-elect took 675 marks from the thirtieth at Devizes. But according to the Fine Roll for 23 Henry III (C. 60/36 m. 9), he took 1000 marks prest from the thirtieth plus 200 marks prest from the exchequer. The pipe roll record of this loan confirms the 1000 mark + 200 mark figure: cf. Pipe Roll 24 Henry III (E. 372/84 rot. 7), as does *CPR 1232–47*, 235.

[188] Wardrobe account (E. 372/83 rot. 7). An additional 650 marks authorized by chancery writs (*CLR 1226–40*, 343; *CPR 1232–47*, 230, 231) were apparently never paid.

[189] *CLR 1226–40*, 459.

1241, only about 9300 marks remained to the king from the aid,[190] with perhaps an additional 250 marks still owing in arrears.[191] If the Red Book is correct in recording that the thirtieth produced a total of 33,811 marks 2s 1d., then we may conclude that between October 1238 and October 1240, the king spent approximately 4000 marks more from the thirtieth, the expenditure of which is unrecorded on any surviving record.[192] A rough balance sheet of expenditures from the thirtieth would thus show approximately 8250 marks in direct crusade costs, 4400 marks in prests, mostly to de Montfort and Walter Cantilupe, 4000 marks in household expenses, 1450 marks in collection costs and arrears, 11,750 marks on foreign affairs (fees to Gascon and Poitevin retainers, the 1241 Welsh war, and the 1242 expedition to Poitou), and 4000 marks in unrecorded expenditures, not including the 8000 or 9000 marks the king sent to Brescia. In one way or another, Earl Richard's revolt thus cost the king almost 20,000 marks in recorded expenditures during 1238 alone: 8250 marks to the Holy Land, 2350 marks to de Montfort, and 8000–9000 marks to Brescia.

Henry seems to have accepted the financial costs of the 1238 revolt with equanimity. And indeed, it can be observed in favour of the bargain that, in return for this sum, Henry guaranteed his brother's loyalty for the remainder of the reign.[193] Never again did Richard of Cornwall line up with any rebel against the king. But Henry was not prepared to acquiesce so quietly in the loss of his favourite councillor, William of Savoy. The death of Peter des Roches on 9 June 1238

---

[190] This sum is derived from the following transfers: 24 Aug. 1241, £2,744.3s., the entirety of the treasure at Nottingham, is transferred to the wardrobe (*CPR 1232–47*, 257); 1–15 Mar. 1242, £453. 10s. is carried from Lincolnshire to the New Temple, London, where it is delivered to Bartholomew Peche and John de Colemere (*Cl.R. 1237–42*, 401, 408, 409; *CPR 1232–47*, 275, 277, 278; *CLR 1240–5*, 114); 12 Mar. 1242, £522. 10s. is carried from Devizes to Winchester, where it is delivered to Nicholas de Bolevill (*CLR 1240–5*, 107, 116; *CPR 1232–47*, 274, 277, 347); 5–9 Mar. 1242, £1638 is delivered from the Bristol treasury to Nicholas de Bolevill at Winchester (*Cl.R. 1237–42*, 392; *CLR 1240–5*, 107; *CPR 1232–47*, 284); Apr. 1242, 1247 marks 2s. 10½d. of the thirtieth in the Tower is sent to the king on his way to Gascony (*CPR 1232–47*, 281).

[191] Total arrears on Pipe Rolls 26–28 Henry III (E. 372/86–88) amount to £172. 0s. 3½d.

[192] This figure is derived by subtracting from the 34,000 mark total receipts 18,000 marks spent prior to Dec. 1238; 1200 marks, approximately, in collection costs; and 1400 marks paid out during Apr. and May 1240 for the king's affairs by writs of liberate (*CLR 1226–40*, 459, 468, 482); and the 9300 marks which remained in the king's treasury as of Aug. 1241. I have not reckoned in here the approximately 250 marks in arrears which had not been collected by 1242.

[193] Denholm-Young, *Richard of Cornwall*, 37, makes this point, but records the cost as only 6000 marks.

presented the king with an ideal opportunity to bring William back to England as the new bishop of Winchester. Henry wasted no time in communicating his desires to the chapter of Winchester. The king argued his case personally throughout the month of August in an unseemly display of coercion which only increased the reluctance of the monks to vote for this 'man of blood'.[194] When the beleaguered monks suggested as their preferred candidate William de Ralegh, Henry reportedly exploded in anger, remarking that Ralegh had killed more men with his tongue than William of Savoy had killed with a sword. Ralegh did not at this time press his candidacy—he probably understood how much the king wanted the elect of Valence back in England—but he never forgot the insult. Ralph de Nevill, however, was not so cautious. When Nevill accepted election from the monks, Henry stripped him of the custody of the Great Seal (although not of its emoluments), and appealed to Rome against the election.[195] The appeal was his third in as many years. By the end of 1238, the bishoprics of Winchester, Durham, and Norwich were all vacant as a result of royal objections to monastic elections,[196] and Coventry had just fallen into the king's hands on the death of its bishop.

It is very hard to be sure who was directing the king's policy toward the Church during these years. Master Simon the Norman was the king's favourite agent in prosecuting his appeals, but he spent so much time at Rome between 1236 and 1238 that it seems unlikely he could have played much part in actually formulating the policies he executed.[197] In 1238, the king himself was clearly the moving force behind the campaign for William of Savoy at Winchester. In encouraging the Norwich and Durham appeals, however, Ralegh may well have played a role. That the king should now turn this policy against Ralegh at Winchester is not merely ironic. It also says much about the lack of personal loyalty towards faithful servants which characterized every Angevin except King Richard, and which Henry III shared in full measure with his ancestors.

---

[194] *CM*, vol. iii, 493–4. Henry did indeed spend the entirety of Aug. in or around Winchester: cf. Meekings, *CRR*, vol. 16, xx, xlv. For William's martial background, see the account of his career in Eugene L. Cox, *The Eagles of Savoy* (Princeton, 1974).

[195] *CM*, vol. iii, 494–5; *CPR 1232–47*, 232; *Cl.R. 1237–42*, 95; Meekings, *CRR*, vol. 16, xx–xxi.

[196] Powicke, *Henry III*, 778.

[197] Compare Powicke, *Henry III*, 295, who sees Master Simon as Henry's 'chief counsellor in ecclesiastical affairs' between 1237 and 1240. Powicke may be right, but the evidence seems to me insufficient.

The effect of the king's efforts to return William of Savoy to his council was thus to drop William de Ralegh from it. As bishop of Winchester, it is possible that Ralegh, like Peter des Roches before him, might have continued to play an active role in advising the king, even though he could not have continued as chief justice *coram rege*. But after the king's rebuff in 1238 over Winchester, Ralegh seems to have given up any intentions of remaining in the king's private counsels. The recall of Stephen de Segrave to the council in early February 1239 signalled Ralegh's intention to leave it.[198] In late February, he was elected bishop of Coventry and Lichfield; in April, he accepted election to the see of Norwich, 'for he preferred to remain in England with the English, rather than in Wales with the untamed Welsh'.[199] He left the court soon after.[200] His relations with Henry were not yet hostile—that would come only with Ralegh's second candidacy at Winchester, in mid-1240—and in June 1239, Ralegh was one of the bishops and courtiers who assisted at the baptism of the infant Prince Edward.[201] But his resignation from the king's business seems to have come in April, a date suggested also by Henry's apparent panic over the prospect of meeting the magnates at the April 1239 parliament.[202] With Ralegh and Savoy both gone, he had no one left to manage the parliament. His attempt at that parliament to recall Ralph de Nevill as chancellor has all the bumbling hallmarks of Henry's own inspirations; it was brusquely rebuffed by Nevill himself.[203]

The departure of William de Ralegh from the council brought the active period of reform to an end; the death of William of Savoy at Viterbo in November 1239 confirmed it. During the preceding three years, Ralegh and Savoy had combined close attention to the king's administration with a wide-ranging attempt to reclaim and intensify the exploitation of the king's rights. Their efforts had affected a very broad cross-section of the realm, but had not rested over-heavily on any single royal resource or on any single group of subjects. The royal demesne, the shires, the Jews, the forests—all had played a role in the council's schemes. Nor had the magnates of the realm been immune from the king's financial pressure. The removal of the curial sheriffs

---

[198] On the recall of Segrave, see *CM*, vol. iii, 524; Meekings, *CRR*, vol. 16, xxi–xxii.
[199] Giles, *Matthew Paris*, vol. i, 166; *CM*, vol. iii, 525, 531–2.
[200] *CRR*, vol. 16, xx–xxi.
[201] *CM*, vol. iii, 539–40.
[202] Ibid., 526.
[203] Ibid., 530.

from the shires, Walter de Burgo's disseisins and revocations of alienated demesne, the *terre Normannorum* inquests, and the *quo warranto*
challenges to private franchise holders had all provoked anxiety and
alarm among the magnates, who were among their principal victims.
And like the rest of the realm, the magnates too had contributed
towards the thirtieth on moveables, the centre-piece of Ralegh's plans
to stabilize the king's finances.

The dangers of such an aggressive royal policy are clear, not least
in the complaints of the 1237 parliament. But here as elsewhere between
1236 and 1239, these dangers were mitigated by the large number of
important magnates who sat on the king's council, and by Ralegh's
willingness to bargain concessions to the realm against a grant of
supply for the king. It is a mark of the conceptual soundness of
Ralegh's approach to financial reform that when rebellion finally came,
it was prompted by the essentially private concerns of Richard of
Cornwall and Gilbert Marshal, and not by any widespread sense of
baronial grievance over policy. Financially, the 1236–9 reforms were
an unqualified success, adding at least £2000 per year to the king's
regular revenues, and producing a reserve fund of around £23,000
which might have formed the nucleus of a war chest to recover the
lost French territories. The success of Ralegh's schemes, however, had
required a combination of administrative expertise and political skill
in managing the magnates in parliament which neither the king nor
his courtiers after 1239 possessed. With Ralegh gone, the abandonment of these reforms followed quickly. In their place, a new type of
council and a new approach to Crown finance began to take shape
at Westminster, which was to have lasting consequences for the
history of Henry's reign. These are the subjects we shall examine in
Chapter 4.

4

The King, the Council, and the Jews
1239–1242

RALEGH'S replacement on the council and on the court *coram rege* was Stephen de Segrave, a cautious survivor of the pre-1236 factional conflicts at court, whom Matthew Paris described as the king's chief councillor from 1239 until his death in 1241.[1] 'Vir flexibilis', as Roger of Wendover called him,[2] Segrave was a veteran of the de Burgh regime, who became justiciar under the Poitevins between 1232 and 1234. Although received back into the king's grace along with Peter des Riveaux in June 1236, his career did not really resume again until June 1237, when he was appointed justiciar of Cheshire.[3] He had not been involved in the reforms of 1236–9, and under his leadership, the council quickly abandoned them. In the autumn of 1239, the council returned a large number of curial sheriffs to the shires; during 1240, it returned both the shires and the royal demesne manors to the hands of farmers, thus bringing to an end the four-year experiment with custodial keepers. The new council also showed itself to be much less strict in enforcing administrative accountability upon the king's bailiffs than the 1236–9 council had been. The impact on the king's finances of this newly relaxed administrative atmosphere is apparent in the 15 per cent drop in shire revenues between 1239 and 1240, during the final year of the custodial experiment. This result may in turn have contributed to the council's decision in the spring of 1240 to return the shires to farmers, who henceforward responded for a fixed yearly profit, without allowances.

Emery de Sacy, in 1239 the newly appointed curial sheriff of Hampshire, exemplifies the effects of the new council's more relaxed approach to administering the king's finances. When called before the exchequer barons in October 1240 to present his accounts for his first

---

[1] *CM*, vol. iii, 545; vol. iv, 169.
[2] *CM*, vol. iii, 240.
[3] *CPR 1232–47*, 188; *Cl.R. 1234–7*, 538–9.

year in office, Emery declared that he could not account for the shire, because he had not received the exchequer summonses necessary to collect his debts. The barons checked their rolls, discovered that the proper summonses had been handed over to Roger the usher for delivery to Emery, and called in their usher to explain his failure. Roger swore that he had delivered all the summonses, some of them directly to Emery in the king's chamber, in the presence of Arnold de Bosco and John de Gray, and the rest to the clerk of the seneschal of St Swithin's Winchester, to be delivered to Emery in Hampshire. Arnold and John both swore that they had witnessed Roger deliver the summonses to Emery *in camera regis*; faced with this evidence, Emery conceded that he had lied. Further investigation would be necessary to determine what had happened to the summonses sent to St Swithin's, but in the meantime, de Sacy could not account.[4] For this transgression, he was fined only 10 marks.[5] He remained sheriff of Hampshire until 1242, when he resigned to accompany the king to Poitou.

A similarly relaxed attitude towards administrative accountability is also evident in the king's household after 1239. Before 1235, wardrobe accounts had rarely been rendered to the exchequer,[6] but in that year, the council first began to insist on an annual audit of the wardrobe accounts. Master Walter de Kirkham rendered the first of these accounts, for the period from 17 May 1234 to 2 May 1235, and again from 3 May 1235 to 27 October 1236.[7] His successor as keeper of the wardrobe, Brother Geoffrey the almoner, accounted from 28 October 1236 to 27 October 1237, and then from 28 October 1237 to 6 February 1238,[8] a change perhaps prompted by the exchequer's desire to lessen its work-load during October and November, when press of work was always greatest. Brother Geoffrey then accounted for the two years between 6 February 1238 and 3 February 1240 in an account which broke with the tradition of yearly audits, but which preserved the tradition begun in 1235 of requiring the keeper not only to account

---

[4] Memoranda Roll 24 Henry III (E. 159/18 rot. 11).

[5] Pipe Roll 24 Henry III (E. 372/84 rot. 6d).

[6] The first true wardrobe account for Henry III's reign covers the period 1224–7, and is printed in *Foreign Accounts Henry III*, 50–4. It should be noted, however, that the account presented by the executors of William the Marshal for the period 1217–19, reprinted ibid., 32–7, is very similar to a wardrobe account. No accounts at all are known to exist between 1219–24 and 1227–34.

[7] Pipe Roll 19 Henry III (E. 372/79 rot. 11d); Pipe Roll 20 Henry III (E. 372/80 rot. 2d).

[8] Pipe Roll 21 Henry III (E. 372/81 rots. 13, 13d).

for the cash receipts and expenditures of the wardrobe, but also to inventory the royal closet, reporting and recording all transactions involving cloth, robes, or jewels.[9] Thereafter, however, policy changed. Geoffrey's successor, Peter d'Aigueblanche, never accounted at all for the period from 4 February 1240 to 27 October 1241, having been exempted from all account by the king in December 1240.[10] From October 1241, when Peter Chaceporc took over custody of the wardrobe, the accounts were once again audited and enrolled on the pipe rolls, but they were no longer rendered yearly, and never again matched the detail of the 1235–40 accounts, being now reduced to a record of cash receipts and expenditures only.[11] One can only conclude that, as with the custodial accounts of the shires and demesne, after 1239 the king and his council found such detailed reporting unnecessary and therefore dispensed with it. The time saved for the exchequer was no doubt considerable; but such savings were accompanied by an appreciable loss of control by the council over the details of the king's financial administration.

Given the chronological coincidences, it is tempting to ascribe this new administrative approach to Segrave's renewed influence on the council. But beyond circumstantial plausibility, there is little to link Segrave personally with these policy changes. Segrave was clearly the man who set the level of the fixed profits assigned to the sheriffs in 1240,[12] and on that basis we might suspect him to have been the moving force behind the decision to wind up the custodial experiment in the shires, and perhaps on the royal demesne as well. But aside from these few references, there is no other evidence which ties him directly to these decisions, except his controlling influence over the council which took them.[13] Matthew Paris's related claim, that during these years Segrave 'managed almost all the affairs of the kingdom at his will, but

[9] Pipe Roll 23 Henry III (E. 372/83 rot. 7).

[10] *CPR 1232–47*, 240.

[11] Chaceporc responded for the period from 28 Oct. 1241 to 24 June 1245 on Pipe Roll 28 Henry III (E. 372/88 rot. 14) and for the period from 24 June 1245 to 17 Feb. 1252 on Pipe Roll 35 Henry III (E. 372/95 rot. 7). The account by his executors for his months of custody from 18 Feb. 1252 to 27 Oct. 1252 is found only on the Chancellors' Roll for 36 Henry III (E. 352/45 rot. 20).

[12] Memoranda Roll 25 Henry III (E. 368/13 rots. 1d, 4); and see also Mills, 'Reforms . . . 1232–42', 125.

[13] His predominance on the council, however, is clear: cf. Meekings, *CRR*, vol. 16, xxi; *CM*, vol. iii, 524, 545; *AM*, vol. iii, 150; *Liber de Antiquis Legibus*, ed. Thomas Stapleton (Camden Society, 1846), 237–8.

always more in his own interest than in the commonwealth's',[14] finds some confirmation in the number of gifts and grants he collected from the king during these years,[15] but does not connect him to any specific policy initiatives. As chief justice, the only legal innovation which can be traced to him is the introduction of chirographs into the regular procedure of the court *coram rege*.[16] As a councillor, apart from setting the shire profits, the only other action with which he personally can be linked is the proclamation of 12 July 1240 which expelled all ultramontane merchants from England for having lent at usury.[17] And this order too, despite its sweeping language, proved in practice to be a characteristically hesitant example of Segrave's approach to policy-making. Although the order included all foreign merchants who had lent usuriously, it appears to have been prompted by the arrest of some Sienese merchants for money-lending in August 1239, and may always have been aimed primarily at the Sienese.[18] On 13 July, only a day after Segrave's initial order had been enrolled at the exchequer, a close roll writ allowed Roman, Bolognese, and Florentine merchants to remain in the kingdom until 11 November; and on 17 November, even the Sienese merchants were given licence to renew their old debts by new contracts, and to remain in the kingdom to collect them, provided that they did not make any new usurious loans, notwithstanding the king's former mandate expelling them.[19] Matthew Paris suspected bribery;[20] if so, it was the only profit the king derived from the entire episode. Italian money-lending continued unchecked in England, as it did across the rest of Europe, and Henry took no further action against it until 1244. From the attempt to expel the Italian merchants, the king gained nothing but a reputation for malleability under pressure.

Although Segrave was the king's chief councillor from 1239 until 1241, his personal influence over conciliar policy remains shadowy.

---

[14] 'omnia fere regni negotia pro libitu disposuit, sed semper plus sui amicus, quam reipublicae': *CM*, vol. iv, 169.

[15] *CLR 1226–40*, 445, 481; *CLR 1240–5*, 43; *Cl.R. 1237–42*, 150, 177, 205; and earlier, *Cl.R. 1237–42*, 55, 77. Although not outrageous, these rewards were much greater than those Ralegh received.

[16] Meekings, *CRR*, vol. 16, xx.

[17] Memoranda Roll 24 Henry III (E. 159/18 rot. 19d), modifying the order on *Cl.R. 1237–42*, 239, which may have been a draft, as it was never enrolled at the exchequer.

[18] *CLR 1226–40*, 411; note the pardon of one of these merchants on 8 Dec. 1239 in *Cl.R. 1237–42*, 160. Matthew Paris reports this expulsion specifically with reference to the Sienese: *CM*, vol. iv, 8.

[19] *Cl.R. 1237–42*, 239; *CPR 1232–47*, 239.

[20] *CM*, vol. iv, 8.

But whatever the extent of his individual influence, it is clear at least that the council under Segrave did not exercise the same purposeful control over Crown financial policy after 1239 which the 1236–9 council had done. The reforms set in motion in 1236 represented a coherent and consistent attempt to enhance Crown revenues, and they were pursued and implemented over three years despite signs that the king himself only partially understood the strategy behind them.[21] Henry was not a lazy king, but between 1236 and 1238 he appears to have been content to leave the administration of his financial affairs largely in the hands of his council. By the secret marriage of his sister, however, Henry sparked a rebellion in 1238 which only he could resolve; and thereafter, his personal influence over administrative and fiscal policy becomes steadily more apparent. Some sign of the king's irritation with the tight accounting requirements of the 1236–9 council may be reflected in the numerous small sums paid to the king during 1240 and 1241 'to do with as he wishes'.[22] With respect to the custodial experiment too, the king's own will and the importance of his favour are apparent in the 1239–40 appointments of the household knight John de Plessy as farmer of Devizes and Rowde, and of the household clerks Walter de Merton and Peter d'Aigueblanche to farm Basingstoke and Cheltenham respectively.[23] The signs of his disfavour also become more evident and more central to the conduct of government after 1238. The sudden dismissal and persecution of the household clerk Ranulf Brito was of relatively little political consequence all in all, although it does not reflect well on the king's loyalty to his servants.[24] But the same cannot be said of the treason charges which Henry renewed against Hubert de Burgh in July 1239, and against Gilbert Marshal in the spring of 1240.[25] In the end, both trials were compromised, but they were ugly reminders of the kinds of personal vendetta which had been so noticeably absent from Henry's government between 1236 and 1239. As such, they recalled memories of the factional strife of the early 1230s which could benefit no one, least of all the king.

The council did no better in directing royal policy towards the Church during these years. A papal legate had been resident in England

---

[21] See pp. 77–8 above.
[22] For examples, see *CLR 1226–40*, 489; *CLR 1240–5*, 3, 6, 80, 89.
[23] See p. 91 and n. 160.
[24] *CM*, vol. iii, 543–5.
[25] *CM*, vol. iii, 618–20; vol. iv, 3–4; vol. vi, 63–74.

since 1237, and by 1239 his presence was beginning to produce serious frictions. The king's attachment to him, however, remained undiminished. The archbishop of Canterbury had had a series of excommunications reversed by the legate, and had already journeyed once to Rome to plead, unsuccessfully, for the legate's recall.[26] Resentment against papal provisions of foreigners into benefices, the rights of presentation to which belonged to English magnates, produced in August 1239 a formal appeal by the magnates against these provisions. Henry joined in the appeal, which succeeded in forcing a temporary retreat by the papacy, but the king himself gained little credit from its success. It was simply too evident that he had been forced into the appeal by his magnates, and especially by Richard of Cornwall, whose supporter, Robert de Tweng, had initiated the original complaint which precipitated the magnates' protests.[27] Meanwhile, the financial pressure of the legate's procurations and of the various papal taxes imposed on the English clergy in 1239 and 1240 to support the papal war against the emperor were also fertile grounds for complaint,[28] not least because this war against the king's own brother-in-law was being carried on in such manifest and public contempt of the military needs of the Holy Land.

Moreover, the anger generated by such offences and affronts was increasingly coming to focus on Henry himself after 1238, yet another by-product of the king's very personal identification with his government's policies after Ralegh's departure. Henry himself had invited the legate to England, and Henry remained the legate's principal supporter, emphasizing the personal connection between them by robing Otto as a member of his private household at the Pentecost

[26] Such at least is Matthew Paris's claim as to the purpose of the archbishop's journey: *CM*, vol. iii, 470, 480. As Lawrence has shown (*St Edmund*, 162–8), this was certainly not the only reason for the trip; but that there was hostility between the archbishop and the legate seems overwhelmingly probable, notwithstanding Paris's obvious bias against Cardinal Otto. Archbishop Edmund was the heir to a long Canterbury tradition of opposition to papal legates, and although he was undoubtedly willing to work with the legate when his own interests dictated, Edmund cannot have been happy with the legatine threat to his primacy in England. Compare Lawrence, *St Edmund*, 162–4, who finds no hostility between legate and archbishop. For Edmund's excommunications, overturned by the legate on appeal, see *Cl.R. 1237–42*, 93–4, 154.

[27] *CM*, vol. iii, 609–14. Tweng had also been involved in the 1232 anti-Italian riots which helped bring down Hubert de Burgh's government: cf. Carpenter, 'Fall of Hubert de Burgh', 11–13. In 1240, Tweng accompanied Richard on his crusade, and acted as his ambassador to the emperor: *CM*, vol. iv, 47.

[28] William E. Lunt, *Financial Relations of the Papacy with England to 1327* (Cambridge, Mass., 1939), 197–205.

and Michaelmas feasts.[29] Equally, it was Henry's own very personal desire to bring first William and then Boniface of Savoy back to England as bishop of Winchester that turned that vacancy into a five-year *quarrelle célèbre* over royal interference in episcopal elections, and which in turn focused critical attention on Henry's more successful efforts to manipulate the elections at Coventry, Hereford, Durham, and Canterbury to the benefit of royal favourites. The financial rewards of such extended vacancies, although considerable, probably mattered less to Henry himself than did the opportunity to elect accommodating bishops.[30] But the king's ham-fisted attempts to browbeat the Winchester electors, and his increasingly personal campaign against William de Ralegh's postulation to the bishopric, helped to turn ecclesiastical liberties after 1238 into a rallying point for political opposition to the king. The consequence of this development would plague Henry until the end of his reign.

Episcopal vacancies were not, however, the only grievance which focused ecclesiastical opposition on the king during these years. In January 1240, frustration with the state of the Church produced a remarkable and dangerous indictment of Henry's policy toward Church liberties which did not even mention as a grievance the king's appeals against valid canonical elections.[31] Even more ominously, the bishops assembled at London declared these policies—the application of forest law to vacant bishoprics, the use of writs of prohibition to compel clerics to plead before secular courts, and to restrict the competence of Church courts—to be direct violations of Magna Carta. 'There were thirty heads in the complaints of the bishops against the king; and they proceeded so far as again to make a terrible denunciation of the sentence against all the counsellors of the king, who were endeavouring to turn his mind to the aforesaid enormities.'[32]

The substance of these charges is of less significance than their tone. To redress all the prelates' complaints in 1240 would have required Henry to abandon writs of prohibition almost entirely, a path neither he nor any other English king could follow. Even Grosseteste must

---

[29] Wardrobe account for 6 Feb. 1238 to 3 Feb. 1240 on Pipe Roll 23 Henry III (E. 372/83 rot. 7).

[30] See pp. 220–3 below for discussion of the financial importance of these vacancies.

[31] See the text of this council's decrees in *Councils and Synods, II*, 279–84, or in the Annals of Burton, *AM*, vol. i, 254–7. Matthew Paris made good the omission of electoral interference as a grievance in his account of the council: *CM*, vol. iv, 3.

[32] Giles, *Matthew Paris*, vol. i, 256, translating *CM*, vol. iv, 3. See also Annals of Dunstable, *AM*, vol. iii, 150.

have known that he and his episcopal colleagues were asking far more in their thirty articles than the king could reasonably deliver. Writs of prohibition were one of the continuing irritants in royal–ecclesiastical relations; but neither the king nor the church could entirely dispense with these writs. As such, they were a problem to be managed; and it is in the inability of the king and his council to manage ecclesiastical grievances through negotiation and compromise during these years that the primary significance of this episode lies. Instead, the prelates' complaints in 1240 appeared to fall on deaf ears, an impression which further heightened their sense of grievance toward the king and his legate, and further inflamed an already angry situation.

Collective action having failed, Archbishop Edmund Rich soon thereafter pronounced his own excommunication against all those persons who had advised the king to withhold from him custody of the lands of Ralph fitz Bernard, a lately deceased tenant-in-fee of the archbishopric.[33] Only the king and queen, Richard of Cornwall, and Stephen de Segrave were excluded from this sentence.[34] But it did no good either. Grosseteste's complaints about bribery and intimidation in the election of Peter d'Aigueblanche to the bishopric of Hereford had equally little effect.[35] The archbishop resolved to appeal personally to Rome yet again. But his journey this time was interrupted by illness, and he was forced to turn back at Pontigny, 'at which place his predecessor, St Thomas, had dwelt in his exile and employed himself in prayer and fasting'.[36] In November 1240 Edmund died at Soissy, and was almost immediately proclaimed a saint who had died in exile.[37] The pointed parallels to Becket's experience were obvious to all, not least in the complaints aired at London just prior to the archbishop's journey about royal violations of the independence of ecclesiastical courts. Such echoes could not help but point attention to the personal responsibility this new Henry bore for yet another Canterbury martyrdom.

Changes in the membership of the king's council emphasized still further Henry's personal responsibility for the paths his government was now following. In the spring of 1240, both Master Simon the Norman and Brother Geoffrey the almoner were dropped from the

[33] *Red Book*, vol. ii, 472, 725, 727, noticed in Lawrence, *St Edmund*, 171 and n. 4.
[34] Annals of Dunstable, *AM*, vol. iii, 150.
[35] Lawrence, *St Edmund*, 171, citing Grosseteste, *Epistolae*, 264–6.
[36] Giles, *Matthew Paris*, vol. i, 278, translating *CM*, vol. iv, 32.
[37] Lawrence has effectively disposed of the historical truth of this exile legend, and has done an equally good job of showing how it developed: *St Edmund*, 168–81.

council, for reasons which remain obscure in both cases.[38] Hugh de Pateshull, treasurer of the exchequer, left the court to become bishop of Coventry; Ralph de Nevill and William de Ralegh were of course already gone. In November 1239, William of Savoy, bishop-elect of Valence, died at Viterbo, still the object of Matthew Paris's bile. He was followed during 1240 by both the Earl Warenne (May) and by the earl of Lincoln (July), the latter after a lengthy illness which had removed him from court many months before.[39] Simon de Montfort returned to England in April 1240, but only to prepare for his crusade. He departed in June, accompanied by the king's senior steward Amaury de St Amand, and by a large number of Henry's own household troops. Richard of Cornwall embarked on his crusade in June also, accompanied by Thierry of Nussa, William Longsword, and a force of between fifty and seventy knights, many of them also drawn from among the king's retainers.[40]

In the absence of these great men, a very different kind of a council began to form around Henry, the likes of which had not been seen in England since John's reign. In the first place, the king's new councillors were much less eminent men than they had been before 1239. The reform council of 1236–9 had brought a great many changes to the king's government, but in terms of social prestige, its composition was entirely comparable in rank with the councils which had dominated the minority. In the autumn of 1237, Henry numbered among his councillors five earls or claimants to earldoms (Cornwall, Lincoln, Warenne, de Montfort claimant to Leicester, and William de Ferrers the heir to Derby), three bishops (Chichester, Carlisle, and the elect of Valence, whose social standing was undeniable regardless of his unpopularity), one archbishop (York), at least one baron of the first rank (John fitz Geoffrey), and a royal judge of acknowledged eminence

---

[38] Powicke, *Henry III*, 780–3. Contrary to Powicke's argument here, the fall of Master Simon and that of Brother Geoffrey do not appear to have been related. Geoffrey gave up his custody of the wardrobe on 3 Feb. 1240 (Pipe Roll 28 Henry III: E. 372/88 rot. 14), but on 25 Apr. he was appointed custodian of the vacant bishopric of Hereford (Originalia Roll 24 Henry III: E. 371/7 m. 1), a date almost certainly after the fall of Simon the Norman. Geoffrey's movements thereafter are very hard to trace. The new bishop of Hereford, Peter d'Aigueblanche, was granted his temporalities on 6 Sept. 1240 (*Cl.R.* 1237–42, 222), but the name of the keeper is not given, and no account for the vacancy was ever recorded. Brother Geoffrey may simply have retired from the king's service in 1240.

[39] *CM*, vol. iv, 34.

[40] Denholm-Young, *Richard of Cornwall*, 41. The names of the bannerets in each party are given in *CM*, vol. iv, 44. On the number of royal household knights who participated in the expedition, see pp. 183–6, below.

(William de Ralegh). Among the king's clerks, only Brother Geoffrey the almoner need be counted. Master Simon the Norman was a rising figure, but until 1239 his influence in England is hard to trace.[41] The king's stewards too were men of proven administrative and military experience, and while neither could claim the social distinction of fitz Geoffrey, Amaury de St Amand's son did hold a barony in Bedfordshire, and John fitz Philip was a considerable figure in Shropshire.[42]

After the conciliar changes of 1239–40, the situation was very different. Of the men who would dominate royal policy between 1240 and 1245, only the king's stewards, John fitz Geoffrey, William de Cantilupe, and perhaps Ralph fitz Nicholas (restored to his stewardship yet again in 1242), were of baronial rank. The other two stewards were lesser men. Bertram de Cryoll (appointed March 1239) was a shire knight from Kent, who had risen as a royal castellan at Dover and, incidentally, as a money-lender. Paulinus Peyvre (appointed December 1241) was a former steward to the elder William Cantilupe, himself a former steward to King John.[43] Richard of Cornwall and Simon de Montfort, the latter restored to favour again in 1242, were the only legitimate earls. Peter of Savoy was occasionally addressed as earl of Richmond, but he was never formally invested with that title. He held the lands of the honour of Richmond by gift of the king from May 1241.[44] John de Plessy was another royal creation whose only claim to an English earldom arose from the king's favour. He was a Poitevin, who rose initially through the king's military household.[45] In 1243, however, his fortunes took a magnificent turn when King Henry decided to marry him to the widowed countess of Warwick. Despite the lady's strenuous objections, Henry eventually prevailed, but even *jure uxoris*, John is rarely styled earl of Warwick before 1247.[46] He was entirely a man of the household, and a creation of the king. Among

---

[41] A point which Powicke does not make, but which emerges clearly from his account: cf. *Henry III*, 772–80.

[42] G. E. Cokayne, *Complete Peerage of England*, revised by Gibbs and Doubleday, 12 vols. (London, 1910–59), vol. xi, 295–6; Sanders, *English Baronies*, 26–7; Pipe Roll 21 Henry III (E. 372/81 rot. 4d); Robert W. Eyton, *Antiquities of Shropshire*, 12 vols. (London, 1853–60), vol. vi, 35–7; vol. xi, 1–2, 10–12; Meekings, *CRR* vol. 15, xxxviii.

[43] Meekings, *CRR* vol. 16, xxv–xxvi.

[44] Or perhaps from 20 Apr. 1240: cf. *Handbook of British Chronology*, ed. F. M. Powicke and E. B. Fryde, 2nd edn. (London, 1961), 445.

[45] *CPR 1225–32*, 227, 313, 358.

[46] Emma Mason, 'The Resources of the Earldom of Warwick in the Thirteenth Century', *Midland History* 3 (1975), 69–70; *The Beauchamp Cartulary Charters, 1100–1268*, ed. Emma Mason, PRS n.s. 43 (London, 1980), xl, nos. 249, 250; *Handbook of British Chronology*, 453 and n. 2.

the remaining councillors, Stephen de Segrave was the only other layman of rank. His eminence was unquestioned, but he died in October 1241, and was not replaced.[47] The remaining men on the council were clerics. Among the bishops, the archbishop of York and the bishop of Carlisle provided almost as much episcopal strength as the 1237 council had been able to boast. The great change, however, was in the position and importance of the king's clerks. Peter d'Aigueblanche had come to England in 1236 as the steward of William of Savoy, and rose swiftly after William's death. In February 1240 he was appointed keeper of the king's wardrobe; in August, Henry arranged his election as bishop of Hereford.[48] His diocese, however, exercised few claims upon his attentions, and he continued to spend most of his time at court. His episcopal diginity qualifies him for inclusion among the bishops on the council, but his interests and qualities make him a more natural associate of the king's clerks. Peter Chaceporc was another foreign clerk in the King's service, who also played an influential role on the council. He succeeded Peter d'Aigueblanche as keeper of the wardrobe in October 1241, and remained keeper until his death in 1254. Robert Passelewe and John Mansel were even more significant figures in advising the king, both of them English-born royal clerks, and each with a wealth of administrative and diplomatic experience behind him.

The second arresting feature of the king's new councillors, aside from their diminished social rank, is the number of them who were immigrants to England, and who had made their way there almost entirely through the king's favour. In determining social attitudes towards them, the second factor may be even more important than the first. The stewards were all Englishmen, as was the new chief justice *coram rege*, William of York.[49] But Peter of Savoy, Peter Chaceporc and Peter d'Aigueblanche were all quite recent arrivals to court and kingdom. John de Plessy had been in England rather longer, but he too owed his rise entirely to Henry's unfathomable favour, and not to any innate qualities, at least so far as we now can tell. Richard of Cornwall was of course a native, but after 1243 he was married to the

[47] Meekings, *CRR*, vol. 16, xxiii–xxiv.

[48] T. F. Tout, *Chapters*, vol. i, 261–2; *Handbook of British Chronology*, 229, for the date of his election. For Grosseteste's complaints about this election, see his *Epistolae*, 264–6.

[49] Meekings, *CRR*, vol. 16, xxiv–xxv. His career to 1241 can be traced through the index to Meekings's collected papers, *Studies in 13th-Century Justice and Administration*.

queen's sister, Sanchia of Provence. Henry had his reasons for bringing so many Savoyards and Poitevins to court during these years, reasons which we shall examine in Chapter 5. And in terms of administrative ability, men like John Mansel and Robert Passelewe were in no respect inferior to their predecessors on the king's council during the 1230s. What Henry's government lacked after 1238 was a man who could negotiate with the magnates and clergy in parliament in the way Ralegh had done between 1236 and 1238. Segrave might have filled this role, but he seems to have lacked the touch. He may also have lacked the nerve. He had, after all, been tarred and feathered by these magnates once before. But after Segrave's death, the king lacked even a credible candidate for such a role. By drawing his new councillors almost entirely from the ranks of his own private household, between 1239 and 1241 the king cut his lines of communication with his baronage. The consequences of this break were apparent when, in January 1242, King Henry announced his plans to mount a military campaign in Poitou. But they were presaged also in the new council's efforts between 1239 and 1242 to raise the funds which might make such an expedition possible. Having brought the custodial experiments to an end, and lacking the political support to raise another aid, the council under Segrave turned its financial attentions towards the Jews.

Before 1239, Jewish taxation had made a modest but fairly steady contribution to the king's finances of between 2000 and 3000 marks per year under Henry III.[50] In 1221, the Jews contributed between 1000 and 1500 marks toward an otherwise unknown aid to marry the king's sister Joan to the king of the Scots.[51] In 1223, they were assessed a tax of 3000 marks,[52] and in 1225–6 a tax of 6000 marks, which appears to have been paid in instalments up to Michaelmas 1228.[53] In 1229, a new tallage of 8000 marks was imposed on the Jews, undoubtedly in connection with the king's intended campaign in Brittany.[54] This tax

[50] What follows is a revised, shortened version of an article first published in the *Hebrew Union College Annual* 56 (1985), 175–249, entitled 'Royal Taxation and the Social Structure of Medieval Anglo-Jewry: The Tallages of 1239–42'. I am grateful to the editor for permission to reprint portions of this article. Further information and additional references may be found there.

[51] E. 401/4; Helena M. Chew, 'A Jewish Aid to Marry, A.D. 1221', *Transactions of the Jewish Historical Society of England* (hereafter *TJHSE*) 11 (1928), 92–111.

[52] E. 401/6, with some arrears on E. 401/7 rot. 1.

[53] E. 401/8,9; *Cl.R. 1227–31*, 411, 580; *CPR 1232–47*, 12–13.

[54] *Pipe Roll 14 Henry III*, 222; *CLR 1226–40*, 161; *Cl.R. 1227–31*, 580; *Cl.R. 1231–4*, 460.

too was apparently spread over several years, with receipts still coming in during 1231. In 1232, pressure on the Jews was intensified when the king's new ministers, Peter des Roches, bishop of Winchester, and Stephen de Segrave, the new justiciar, imposed a 10,000 mark tallage upon them as part of their efforts to restore the king's battered finances.[55] In March 1233, however, the Jews were granted permission to pay this tax by instalments of 1500 marks per year in 1233 and 1234, and of 3000 marks per year in 1235 and 1236.[56] Arrears on the levy were due initially at Michaelmas 1236, later extended to January 1237, with final quit-claims issued in June 1237.[57] In late 1236, the king continued these payments for another year by imposing an additional 3000 mark tallage, payable, at least in theory, a month from Easter 1237.[58] Meanwhile, Henry had also granted 3000 marks in tallage to his brother Richard, to assist his preparations for the crusade.[59] This grant was made in January 1237, but the funds had not yet been collected in November.[60] Payments toward this gift were probably still coming in during 1238.

With Segrave's return to office in 1239, however, this pattern of steady, moderate, effectively annual contributions to the king changed dramatically when Henry demanded from the Jews the third part of all their chattels, including the value of all unredeemed bonds. The financial motives behind this tax are relatively clear. With half to two-thirds of the proceeds of the thirtieth already gone, the Jews and a new general eyre (begun in October 1239) were the only remaining royal resources likely to produce a sum of ready cash large enough to replenish the king's depleted treasury.[61] No tallage had been imposed upon the Jews during 1238, and on the pattern which had been established since 1221, a contribution from the Jews was probably expected during 1239. What was unusual was the punitive nature of

[55] The schedule of payments given for this tallage in *CPR 1232–47*, 12–13 is obviously corrupt as it stands, but it does seem to require that the tallage be dated to 1232 and not to 1233 if the full 10,000 mark sum was to be met. On the financial problems which beset the king in 1232, see Ch. 1.

[56] Such at least is my interpretation of *CPR 1232–47*, 12–13; as the writ stands, the regnal years do not match the schedule of payments described in the writ.

[57] *Cl.R. 1234–7*, 302, 387, 404; *CLR 1226–40*, 244; *CPR 1232–47*, 187.

[58] Although the tax had been agreed by 17 Jan. 1237 (*CPR 1232–47*, 173), it was not assessed until Apr. (ibid., 178).

[59] *CPR 1232–47*, 173.

[60] *Cl.R. 1237–42*, 4.

[61] The royal demesne had already been tallaged in 1238, apparently as an alternative to paying the thirtieth on moveables: cf. Mitchell, *Studies*, 219–20.

the taxation imposed. The tax was cast in the form of a relief, which
for Jews generally amounted to a third of all their chattels and bonds,
and was apparently conceived as a fine whereby the Jews redeemed
their possessions from forfeiture to the king. Strengthening this
impression is the fact that the Jews were also assessed Queen's gold
on their payments against the third, the only known instance when
this was levied against Jewish taxation.[62] This fact strongly suggests
that the third was provoked by some real or imagined crime of which
the entire Jewish community was held to be guilty, and from which
the Jews were compelled to redeem themselves.

Specific evidence for such a charge is, however, hard to come by.
No central government record offers any explanation for levying the
third, although there is abundant evidence for its collection. Matthew
Paris is the only source which records such a crime, offering a characteristically colourful story of a secret murder perpetrated by the Jews
as the motive for this tax.[63] But both the structure of Matthew's story
and the absence of any specific details suggest that Matthew has here
combined his accurate knowledge of the tax itself with an uncor-
roborated murder story for which he had neither an accurate date
nor additional details. Without further information than Matthew
provides us, the immediate provocation for the third must therefore
remain mysterious.[64]

About the assessment of the third, we know relatively little. As was

---

[62] Queen's gold was an additional payment of 10 per cent on the monetary value of
every fine made with the king for his benevolence, collected at the exchequer by a special
official deputed for this purpose. Although regularly owed by Jews on the fines they
negotiated with the king, it was not owed on the proceeds from tallages or amercements.

[63] 'Et eodem anno, die Sancti Albani Anglorum prothomartyris [22 June 1239] et in
crastino, passi sunt Judei exterminium magnum et destructionem, eosdem arctante et
incarcerante et pecuniam ab eisdem extorquente Galfrido Templario, regis speciali
consiliario. Tandem vero post angarias, tertiam partem totius pecuniae suae, tam
debitorum quam catallorum, ut vita et pace ad tempus guaderent, miseri Judaei in
suam magnam ruinam et confusionem regi persolverunt. Hujus autem destructionis
seminarium suscitavit quoddam homicidium in civitate a Judaeis clanculo perpetratum.'
CM, vol. iii, 543.

[64] 'In order to punish the malice and falseness of the Jews', king and council in Dec.
1239 replaced the chirographers of London, suspended all interest on loans from 24
June to 25 Dec., and commanded all Jews to remain where they were living for one
year from Michaelmas 1239. The motive for these new measures is not specified, but
Segrave, Brother Geoffrey, Bertram de Cryoll, Master Simon the Norman, and Geoffrey
Despenser were all mentioned by name as responsible for these new provisions, which
may well have been connected with the imposition of the third: cf. *Liber de Antiquis
Legibus*, 237–8.

probably already traditional in making such assessments, the king ordered all the Jewish chests throughout England closed at some date prior to November 1239, while Bertram de Cryoll, the newest of the King's household stewards, and Brother Geoffrey the Templar, the king's almoner, toured these *archae*, totalled up the bonds they contained, and assessed the tax on the various communities.[65] The largest individual contributors, however, appear to have struck individual bargains with the king. Loss of the relevant receipt rolls makes it impossible to say with confidence how much the king collected from the third between the autumn of 1239 and the summer of 1240.[66] The returns appear, however, to have been disappointing. By the end of August 1240, approximately £1500 had been paid into the wardrobe or otherwise credited against the tax debts owed by the ten wealthiest Jews of England, each of whom had paid the king a fine to permit them to spread their remaining payments out over the next three to nine years.[67] With payments from the greatest contributors scheduled to trickle in over the next three to nine years, the king could expect relatively little from the remaining Jews, whose payments were due at Michaelmas 1240. By 4 September 1240, the exchequer had received a total of only 1000 marks from the king's Jewry, a sum which probably included payments by Christians on Jewish debts which had fallen in to the king, and by Jews purchasing royal writs or paying fines and amercements, as well as payments on the third.[68] The Michaelmas deadline came and went, with no further payments on the third. On 20 and 25 October, almost a month later, the king ordered the exchequer to distrain the Jews for their arrears, and on 30 October the first of these payments began to trickle into the exchequer.[69] A few Jews

---

[65] *Cl.R. 1237–42*, 156; *CLR 1240–5*, 106. For an example of the kinds of lists the inquisitors prepared, see WAM 6692, printed by V. D. Lipman in *The Jews of Medieval Norwich* (London, 1967), 245–59. This document is dated after 24 June 1239, a date significantly close to the date for the third given by Matthew Paris: cf. nn. 63 and 64.

[66] Our only clue to these receipts is *CLR 1226–40*, 488: 10 Aug. 1240, a liberate writ ordering that £100 of the 1000 marks (£666 13s. 4d.) from the Jewry should be paid to the keepers of the works at the Tower of London. A month later, the king ordered £400 'out of the £560 received by the treasurer and chamberlains from the King's Jewry' to be paid against the queen's expenses (ibid., 492: 4 September 1240). The coincidence of these two amounts makes it almost certain that we have here only one 1000 mark sum, successively diminished by £100 and £400.

[67] *CLR 1226–40*, 431, 439–40; *CLR 1240–5*, 96; *Cl.R. 1237–42*, 197; E. 368/13 rots. 1d, 7d; E. 372/83 rot. 7 (wardrobe account 6 February 1238–3 February 1240).

[68] See n. 66 above.

[69] E. 368/13 rot. 1d; *Cl.R. 1237–42*, 233; E. 401/13 m. 6.

secured temporary exemption from such distraint, but an unknown number were imprisoned in the Tower of London, and released only on 14 December after finding sureties that they would pay their arrears by the end of January 1241.[70] But despite these harsh measures, no more than about £600 was collected towards the third during Michaelmas and Hilary terms 1240–1, before the levy was abandoned; and of this amount, almost a third was paid in by Benedict Crespin and Elias l'Eveske of London, two of the remaining Jewish magnates, who had not previously fined with the king to extend the terms on their debts. Verifiable receipts from the third amounted to only about £2500 at most; it is therefore unlikely that total receipts could have exceeded £3000, even allowing for the incomplete nature of the extant returns.[71]

It was probably disappointment with the proceeds from the third which induced the king and his council to begin preparations for a much more thoroughgoing levy on Jewish wealth. In June 1240, the king ordered the *archae* closed again, and in July the council launched a full scale inquest into the wealth of the Jews of England. Procedure on this second set of inquests was apparently much more elaborate than that which had governed Brother Geoffrey's and Bertram de Cryoll's investigations the year before, with four separate teams of royal officials sent on circuit around the kingdom to record the contents of the chests.[72] The most extraordinary innovation, however, was the attempt in 1240 to compile an accurate census of all the Jews of England aged twelve years or more,[73] an unprecedented procedure which in 1240 probably reflects the conviction of the king and his council that many Jews had evaded payment of the third on chattels. Thereafter, however, such censuses appear to have become a fairly regular feature of Jewish taxation.[74]

---

[70] *Cl.R.* 1237–42, 343, 257.

[71] The documentary evidence on which these calculations are based is assembled in Stacey, 'Royal Taxation', app. I.

[72] *Cl.R.* 1237–42, 238–9; *CLR* 1226–40, 482–3. Some of these officials also enquired into the state of the royal demesne manors recently surrendered by Walter de Burgo: see pp. 87–91 above.

[73] *Cl.R.* 1237–42, 238–9. The text of one such census has been published by Cecil Roth as an appendix to 'The Ordinary Jew in the Middle Ages', in Meir Ben-Horin, Bernard D. Weinryb, and Solomon Zeitlin, eds., *Studies and Essays in Honor of Abraham A. Neuman* (Philadelphia, 1962), 435–7.

[74] A similar such census was prepared in 1275 by the chirographers of York: cf. R. B. Dobson, 'The Decline and Expulsion of the Medieval Jews of York', *TJHSE* 26 (1979), 43. This list is printed in H. G. Richardson, ed., *Calendars of the Plea Rolls of the Exchequer of the Jews*, vol. iv (1972), 16–17.

As a result of these inquisitions, by January 1241 the king and his council had quite an accurate idea of the financial strength of the Jews of England. This fact can only have increased the king's exasperation with the slow progress of the third.[75] There are also signs that by this time, Henry had begun to think again of mounting an expedition to recover the French lands his father and he had lost to the Capetians.[76] If Jewish resources were to provide the nucleus of the king's war chest, clearly a new approach to Jewish taxation would be required. The writs initiating this new approach issued on 25 January 1241, summoning representatives from every Jewish community in England to meet at Worcester on 10 February, to direct the collection of a one-year tallage of 20,000 marks.[77] Having determined on so striking a change of policy, the council wasted no time in executing it.

The elaborate arrangements made at the Worcester assembly to prevent favouritism or bribery from influencing the assessment of this tax have been described elsewhere.[78] The tallage itself was to be paid in two instalments, due respectively on 9 July and 29 October 1241.[79] Although the sheriffs were to assist in distraining for payment, the essential work of assessing and collecting the tallage was to be carried out by the Jews themselves, working under the supervision of a committee of royal auditors made up indifferently of exchequer and household officials.[80] Such special committees were a customary feature of taxation under Henry III; the employment of such a body to audit and direct a Jewish tallage merely indicates how regular a feature of Crown finance Jewish taxation had become by 1241.[81]

With these arrangements made, King Henry left Worcester on Ash Wednesday, to wend his way at a leisurely pace back to London. A week later, he officially brought to an end collection of the third on moveables.[82] He did, however, concede to the Jews that the sums they had already paid towards the third could be credited against the first

[75] Cf. *Cl.R. 1237–42*, 268.
[76] See pp. 183–5 below.
[77] *Cl.R. 1237–42*, 346–7.
[78] Stacey, 'Royal Taxation', 191–5.
[79] *Cl.R. 1237–42*, 312, 334.
[80] *Cl.R. 1237–42*, 281; *CPR 1232–47*, 247. Thomas of Newark and William of St Edmunds were justices at the Jewish exchequer; Jeremiah de Caxton had served as a sheriff, and became one of the junior justices *coram rege* in Jan. 1241; William Hardel was a king's clerk, and keeper of the mint; Peter Chaceporc was a wardrobe clerk, soon to become keeper of the wardrobe; Peter Grimbaud was one of the barons of the exchequer; and William de Haverhull was the king's treasurer.
[81] On these special exchequer committees, see Mitchell, *Taxation*, 1–62.
[82] *Cl.R. 1237–42*, 350.

term of their new debt of 20,000 marks.[83] Anticipating the beginning of a more satisfactory flow of cash from the Jews, in April 1241 Henry renewed his mid-January order setting such revenues apart from the rest of his treasure, and restricting their expenditure.[84] The first term's payments were due on 9 July 1241; the order to credit the Jews with the payments they had made on the third issued on 28 June; and on 1 August William de Haverhull was ordered to distrain all Jews whose tallage debts were still owing for their first term's payments. Defaulters were to be taken to London and imprisoned in the Tower until the king commanded otherwise. In addition, all those Jews who ought to have distrained their co-religionists to meet their terms were also to be imprisoned.[85] Thereafter, references to the tallage on the chancery rolls become scarce; but, from September 1241 until the effective end of the tallage in August 1242, we can rely on the exchequer receipt rolls to provide an exact record of the sums the king received from the Jews toward this tallage.[86]

A summary of the receipts recorded from this tallage is presented in Tables 4.1 and 4.2. There are a number of striking things about these results, but perhaps none more surprising than the apparent financial standing of the Jewish community of London in comparison with those of York and Oxford. Twenty years ago, Dr Lipman suggested in his 'Anatomy of Medieval Anglo-Jewry' that

in terms of taxable capacity, London represented about 30% of the community, York varied between 10% and 20%, Lincoln and Canterbury between 6% and 13%. In the range of 2% and 10% come Northampton, Gloucester, Winchester, and Cambridge. Between 1% and 5% are Norwich and Oxford; Bristol, Nottingham, Worcester, Hereford, and Exeter being rather smaller.[87]

Records for the levies of 1239–42 show a very different picture. York, London, and Oxford stand in a group by themselves at the top of the

---

[83] Ibid., 312.

[84] *CPR 1232–47*, 249; for the orders of mid-Jan., cf. *Cl.R. 1237–42*, 268.

[85] *Cl.R. 1237–42*, 322–3.

[86] Both chronological receipt rolls for 1241–2 survive, the only year before 1254 for which this is the case (E. 401/14, E. 401/15). They will be published in a forthcoming volume for the Pipe Roll Society entitled *Receipt and Issue Rolls, 26 Henry III*.

[87] Vivian D. Lipman, 'The Anatomy of Medieval Anglo-Jewry', *TJHSE* 21 (1968), 67.

TABLE 4.1　*Maximum recorded payments toward the 20,000-mark tallage*

Archa	Receipts on third	Receipts on 20,000 marks	Total receipts	% Total receipts
Bedford		£ 14 19s. 1d.	£ 14 19s. 1d.	0.1
Bristol		£ 31 5s. 4d.	£ 31 5s. 4d.	0.3
Cambridge		£ 82 18s. 8½d.	£ 82 18s. 8½d.	0.8
Canterbury	£ 113 6s. 10d.	£ 258 2s. 10d.	£ 371 9s. 8d.	3.5
Colchester		£ 15 10s. 6d.	£ 15 10s. 6d.	0.1
Gloucester	£ 9 8s. 4d.	£ 9 19s. 7d.	£ 19 7s. 11d.	0.2
Hereford	£ 130 13s. 4d.	£ 127 18s. 1½d.	£ 258 11s. 5½d.	2.4
Lincoln	5s.	£ 244 14s. 3d.	£ 244 19s. 3d.	2.3
London	£ 835 15s. 7d.	£1,503 13s. ½d.	£ 2,339 8s. 7½d.	21.8
Northampton		£ 73 19s. 4d.	£ 73 19s. 0d.	0.7
Nottingham		£ 299 0s. 0d.	£ 299 0s. 0d.	2.8
Norwich		£ 217 2s. 2d.	£ 217 2s. 2d.	2.0
Oxford	£ 176 6s. 1½d.	£1,150 14s. 0d.	£ 1,327 0s. 1½d.	12.3
Stamford		£ 175 15s. 6d.	£ 175 15s. 6d.	1.6
Warwick		£ 26 13s. 3d.	£ 26 13s. 3d.	0.2
Wilton	2s. 9d.	£ 25 19s. 9½d.	£ 26 2s. 6½d.	0.2
Winchester	£ 40 10s. 0½d.	£ 63 2s. 5½d.	£ 103 12s. 6d.	1.0
Worcester		£ 12 11s. 10d.	£ 12 11s. 10d.	0.1
York	£ 624 0s. 0d.	£4,485 18s. 1d.	£ 5,109 18s. 1d.	47.6
Totals	£1,930 8s. 0d.	£8,819 17s. 10½d.	£10,750 5s. 10½d.	100
Receipts on third before Sept 1240 (cf. n. 66)			£ 500 0s. 0d.	
Maximum receipts on third from Ilchester			£ 61 0s. 0d.	
Unlocated tallies for the third			£ 1 5s. 11d.	
Unlocated tallies for the 20,000 mark-tallage			£ 37 3s. 5d.	
Uncertain tallies, probably for 20,000 mark			£ 195 9s. 0d.	
Maximum possible recorded receipts, 1239–42			£11,545 4s. 2½d.	

table, York paying almost 50 per cent of the total assessment, London paying about 20 per cent, and Oxford around 13 per cent, with the three communities together paying more than 80 per cent of the entire tallage between them. Canterbury, Lincoln, Nottingham, Norwich, and perhaps Hereford[88] stand in a second group, each paying between 2 per cent and 4 per cent of the assessment, with Nottingham's position being due entirely to the wealth of David Lumbard and his family. In a third group, we find Stamford, Winchester, Cambridge, and Northampton, all paying between 0.5 per cent and 2 per cent; and in a final group, each paying less than 0.5 per cent, we find Bristol, Warwick, Wilton, Colchester, Bedford, Worcester, and Gloucester. Individual anomalies of course affect the position of any single

---

[88] If receipts from the third are included, Hereford's contributions rise to about 2.4 per cent of the total tallage.

TABLE 4.2 *Total communal contributions, 1239–42*

Below 0.5%	0.5% to 2.0%	2.0% to 3.5%	Over 3.5%
(19) Worcester 0.1	(12) Northampton 0.7	(8) Norwich 2.0	(3) Oxford 12.3
(18) Bedford 0.1	(11) Cambridge 0.8	(7) Lincoln 2.3	(2) London 21.8
(17) Colchester 0.1	(10) Winchester 1.0	(6) Hereford 2.4	(1) York 47.6
(16) Gloucester 0.2	(9) Stamford 1.6	(5) Nottingham 2.8	
(15) Wilton 0.2		(4) Canterbury 3.5	
(14) Warwick 0.2			
(13) Bristol 0.3			

community within a group—the surprisingly lowly position of Winchester, for example, is in part due to the inexplicable absence of its wealthiest citizen, Licoricia, from the extant returns to the tallage —but the pattern as a whole is clear and distinct, and requires some explanation.

The distorting element in the 1239–42 communal rankings is clearly the enormous personal wealth of Aaron and Leo of York, and of David of Oxford. The extent to which these three great men dominated Anglo-Jewry during these years is illustrated in Table 4.3, which compares their tallage assessments to those of the ten next wealthiest Jews in England. Between them, these thirteen men accounted for more than £8500 of the approximately £11,000 in known receipts which we can trace to a specific Jewish community. If the estimates in Table 4.3 of their assessments are correct, this group was expected to produce at least 15,000 of the 20,000 marks of the tallage personally.[89] Of this amount, Aaron and Leo of York, and David of Oxford themselves paid more than 10,000 marks. We have, of course, been taught to expect a medieval Jewish patriciate,[90] but not on this scale. Unless Dr Lipman's percentages mislead us about the usual thirteenth-century situation, and I do not believe they do, it appears that wealth within the Jewish community was concentrated in significantly fewer hands around the year 1240 than was the case either before 1225 or after about 1250. The patriciate's financial dominance of the Jewish

[89] Only the assessments marked as such in Table 4.3 are explicitly recorded; the rest are estimates. For Leo of York, see Fine Roll 26 Henry III (C. 60/39A m. 1); for Benedict Crespin, see *CLR 1240–5*, 98; and for Jacob Crespin, *Excerpta e Rotulis Finium*, vol. i, 380.
[90] R. B. Dobson, *The Jews of Medieval York and the Massacre of March 1190*, Borthwick Papers 45 (York, 1974), 42–3; Lipman, 'Anatomy', 68–70.

TABLE 4.3 *Largest contributors, 1239–42*

Name	Max. payments on third	Max. payments on 20,000 marks tallage	Unconfirmed tallies payments	Max. known total payments	Total (marks)	Assessment (marks)
Aaron of York	£440 0s. 0d.	£2,634 0s. 2½d.	£517 13s. 2½d.	£3,591 13s. 5d.	5,388	6,000
David of Oxford	£153 6s. 8d.	£993 13s. 4d.	£189 13s. 0d.	£1,336 13s. 0d.	2,005	2,200
Leo of York	£184 0s. 0d.	£1,073 0s. 0d.	—	£1,257 0s. 0d.	1,886	2,200[a]
Aaron Blund (London)	£219 6s. 8d.	£424 10s. 0d.	—	£643 16s. 8d.	966	1,200
Aaron son of Abraham (London)	£241 19s. 8½d.	£347 18s. 0d.	£23 0s. 0d.	£612 17s. 8½d.	919	1,200
David Lumbard (Nottingham)	—	£186 13s. 4d.	£102 13s. 4d.	£289 6s. 8d.	434	600
Benedict Crespin (London)	£133 6s. 8d.	£66 13s. 4d.	—	£200 0s. 0d.	300	300[a]
Elias l'Eveske (London)	£62 15s. 5½d.	£99 10s. 0d.	£3 0s. 0d.	£165 5s. 5½d.	248	300
Jacob, Moses and Isaac Crespin (London)	£33 6s. 8d.	£77 15s. 4d.	£11 9s. 0d.	£122 11s. 0d.	184	400[a]
Elias Blund (London)	£27 5s. 8d.	£68 5s. 1½d.	£3 8s. 2d.	£98 18s. 11½d.	148	200
Samuel son of Isaac of Norwich	—	£70 0s. 0d.	£1 6s. 8d.	£71 6s. 8d.	107	150
Leo Blund of Milkstreet (London)	£18 1s. 1½d.	£51 12s. 6½d.	—	£69 13s. 8d.	105	150
Josce, nephew of Aaron of York	—	£52 6s. 8d.	£3 6s. 8d.	£55 13s. 4d.	84	150
Total						15,050

[a] This assessment is known; cf. n. 89.

community in 1241–2 is extraordinary, and as such, requires some explanation.

In 1241–2, we find the Jewish communities where very great magnates did not dwell (i.e., all communities except York, London, and Oxford) to have paid rather less than half the amounts we would expect them to pay, had they contributed to the 20,000 mark tallage in accordance with Dr Lipman's percentages. They pay, in other words, the lump sum amounts we might expect them to pay on a tallage of perhaps 8000 marks. This may in fact be what occurred. The vast majority of the Jewish population of England may already have been stretched to the limit to meet a tax of 8000 marks, which before 1241 was the largest single tallage Henry III had ever imposed.[91] When this sum was increased to 20,000 marks, the resources of most Jews may simply have been insufficient to meet a 150 per cent increase in their assessments. The dozen or so greatest Jewish financiers may thus have been the only ones whose wealth could absorb this doubling of taxation, and so, therefore, the burden of the 20,000 mark tallage may have fallen disproportionately upon them. Disproportionately, that is, in comparison with the burdens they had borne in previous tallages.[92] The strain of meeting the 20,000 mark tallage did not ruin either David of Oxford or Leo of York, whose heirs in 1244 paid reliefs of 5000 marks and 7000 marks respectively to succeed to their estates.[93] But with Leo and David gone, the burden of the new 60,000 mark tallage, imposed in annual instalments between 1244 and 1250, probably fell even more heavily upon Aaron of York than it would have done had David and Leo been still alive.[94] This fact may help to

---

[91] I exclude here the 10,000 mark tallage of 1232–6 because it was spread over so many years. The 8000 mark tallage of 1229 was probably paid within two years: cf. pp. 143–4 above.

[92] Which David of Oxford, at least, thought were already too high in 1236: cf. *Cl.R. 1234–7*, 302.

[93] *Excerpta*, vol. i, 412, 418–19. In assessing the size of these reliefs, however, it is important to notice that these payments were not merely reliefs; in addition to the debts and chattels of the deceased, these fines purchased for the heirs exemption from any payments towards the 60,000 mark tallage which Henry levied on the Jews between 1244 and 1250. What the heirs in fact did was to compound for the relief and the tallage together. In view of the amounts paid by Leo and David toward the 20,000 mark tallage, the heirs would appear to have made a good bargain.

[94] Dobson, 'Decline and Expulsion', 36, is correct in asserting the reality of the 60,000 mark tallage, as against H. G. Richardson, *The English Jewry under the Angevin Kings*, (London, 1960), 214 n. 5, who described the tax as 'mythical'. Whether the king collected the entire 60,000 mark sum of the tallage is, of course, another matter.

explain how, by 1255, even Aaron of York had been reduced to penury,[95] and why the relative wealth of the various Jewish communities returns thereafter to its traditional levels as established by Dr Lipman.

It appears, therefore, that in the two decades before 1241 the greatest Jewish magnates may have been consistently underassessed for royal taxation relative to their wealth, a fact indirectly suggested also by the efforts made in 1241 to prevent the magnates from manipulating the new assessments in their favour. Disproportionate assessments prior to 1241 would also have left a larger share of the magnates' wealth in their own hands, while at the same time claiming for the king an excessively large share of the working capital of lesser men, thereby accentuating even further the gap between these magnates and the rest of the Jewish community. If this interpretation is correct, then it would appear that between 1221 and 1239 the king's policy of taxing the Jews at a modest, effectively annual rate may thus have played an important, perhaps even a decisive, role in the emergence of this small group of enormously wealthy financiers who are so prominent in the 1241–2 tallage returns. From the king's point of view, of course, such consequences were almost certainly accidental, although as a source of emergency loans and forced gifts, the presence of these great Jewish magnates cannot have been unwelcome. After 1239, however, the king and his council turned on the great men whose fortunes they had inadvertently fostered. The double blows of the 20,000 mark tallage of 1241–2 and the 60,000 mark tallage of 1244–50 ruined the Jewish magnates of England, and effectively decapitated the class structure of medieval Anglo-Jewry. By so doing, Henry broke the financial backbone of the English Jewish community, and permanently reduced its financial value to the Crown.

One can see something of these effects in the impact which the 20,000 mark tallage had upon the great men of some of the smaller Jewish communities. Jacob of Exeter and Bonefey of Bristol, the wealthiest members of their respective communities, both attempted to flee the

---

[95] Penury at least is alleged in the writs which excused him his 1255 tallage debts (*CPR 1247–58*, 441–4); but the claim is a surprising one in view of the rather large payments Aaron appears to have made between 1250 and 1254, and of the size of some of the debts still owing to him in 1255 and after: cf. Michael Adler, *Jews in Medieval England* (London, 1939), 156–61. As Dobson has noted ('Decline and Expulsion', 35), a new study of Aaron's career is badly needed.

tallage.[96] Bonefey was captured and imprisoned, but Jacob fled successfully, probably to France. Neither appears in any English records thereafter. Nor were they the only fugitives created by this tax. Almost every Jewish community registered some payments on behalf of paupers and fugitives who had fled the tallage; from Northampton alone there were at least six.[97] By the early 1250s, the effects of a decade of crippling royal taxation are similarly apparent in the Jewish community as a whole: Aaron of York a pauper, Elias L'Eveske ruined and finally a convert, David of Oxford, Leo of York, and David Lumbard all dead, each with heirs but none with a true successor in terms of financial importance. Dobson's remarks are apt: 'The corrosive effects of excessive tallage on the one side and of increased anti-Jewish propaganda and blood-libel accusations on the other seem to have made the mid-1250s a real watershed in the history of Anglo-Jewish relations.'[98] From an economic standpoint, I would be inclined to see the 1240s as the real watershed, which was followed during the subsequent decade by a marked increase in popular anti-Semitism. But there can be no doubt at all that Jewish fortunes in England changed dramatically and permanently between 1240 and 1260, and that this change was in large part a consequence of the new approach to Jewish taxation initiated by King Henry III and his council between 1239 and 1242.

Upon the king's non-Jewish subjects, the impact of the tallages of 1239–42 was less dramatic. One of the most remarkable features of the 20,000 mark tallage is that it appears to have been paid almost entirely in cash. A few bonds were handed over to the exchequer against the third on moveables, but these were specifically noted as such on the receipt rolls. Otherwise, it appears that the sums recorded on the receipt rolls against the tallage represent actual cash payments made into the lower exchequer. This impression is reinforced by the absence of any large number of new *debita Judeorum*[99] from the pipe

[96] For Bonefey, cf. E. 159/20 rot. 22d, E. 372/87 rot. 7d; for Jacob of Exeter, cf. E. 159/20 rot. 14d.

[97] For Northampton, cf. E. 159/20 rot. 9d; for payments on behalf of paupers and fugitives, see the accounts printed in Stacey, 'Royal Taxation', app. II.

[98] Dobson, 'Decline and Expulsion', 36 and *passim*.

[99] *Debita Judeorum* were Jewish debt instruments which had come into the king's hands through transfer or escheat, and which the Crown could therefore collect. Although seizure into the hands of the Crown had the effect of ending the accumulation of interest on the debt, it did also render the debtor liable to immediate royal distraint for the entire sum of the debt. Under Henry III, however, such debtors were usually allowed to make a fine with the king to pay off their debts over a term of years. See Ch. 6 below.

rolls between 1242 and 1245. By contrast, there are a very large number of such new debts on the pipe rolls for 1236–8, after the end of the 10,000 mark tallage of 1232–6, almost certainly as a result of debts handed over to the king for collection against this tallage.[100] Some debts certainly were handed over to the exchequer against the 20,000 mark tallage which do not appear on the receipt rolls.[101] We do know also that the exchequer sometimes handled such debts without recording them on the pipe rolls, either collecting them directly or else reselling the bonds at a discount to other lenders, Christian or Jewish.[102] It is therefore not possible to estimate the percentage of the tallage which may have been defrayed through the transfer of such bonds. It appears, however, that the great bulk of the tallage was borne directly by the Jews themselves, in cash, and thus was not passed on to the king's Christian subjects through the transfer of Jewish bonds to the exchequer. In turn, however, so large a cash transfer to the king must seriously have diminished the working capital through which the Jews, through new loans, might eventually have restored their losses to taxation. In this respect, the king's 'cash only' policy in 1241–2 may even have proved economically counter-productive in the long run. By concentrating the tax burdens on the Jews alone, instead of on the realm through the Jews, Henry choked one of his most effective conduits for the indirect taxation of the kingdom as a whole.

To the king himself, such long-range considerations probably mattered little in 1241–2. He was intent on accumulating as large a war chest as possible, in the shortest possible time. Cash on the nail suited his needs exactly. From December 1241, Henry's eyes were fixed entirely on Poitou.[103] Payments for the second term of the tallage ought

[100] E. 372/80 rot. 14d, rot. 16d; E. 372/81 rots. 1, 2, 3d, 4d, 5d, 6, 6d, 9d, 10, 12; E. 372/82 rot. 8d; and notice also the large number of debts owed by Christians to Jews which the king was attermining for payment between Jan. and July 1236: cf. Cl.R. 1234–7, 230–280, passim.

[101] For example, see E. 372/87 rot. 2d, a 120 mark debt owed by Thomas de Gresley to Aaron of York, newly in the king's hand, probably but not explicitly as a result of the 20,000 mark tallage; E. 159/20 rot. 10d for evidence of Arnold de Berkeley handling debita Judeorum handed into the exchequer against the tallage; and E. 159/20 rot. 6 for the involvement of John Mansel in the same business.

[102] The best description of how this was done is still Richardson, English Jewry under Angevin Kings, 70–6. Before his downfall in 1240, Master Simon the Norman was actively involved in this trade, acquiring many of the bonds himself: cf. E. 372/80 rot. 14d. Bertram de Cryoll apparently also participated in the trade, which made a useful complement to his money-lending: cf. E. 159/18 rot. 18 and p. 64 above.

[103] See Ch. 5 below.

to have been due at the end of October 1241, but in fact came steadily into the exchequer until April 1242.[104] A few large personal payments were deferred by prior arrangement until late April and early May 1242, when they were made directly into the wardrobe on the eve of the king's departure.[105] But already on 24 April, Henry had sent Peter Chaceporc to Westminster with a writ ordering the treasurer to hand over to Peter 20,000 marks 'from the Jewry as from other sources' for transport with the king to Poitou.[106] This sum suggests that the king already had nearly the full sum of the tallage due him.

For this supposition there is no certain proof, because the receipt rolls for the first term of the tallage are lost. However, even without the records of the first term's payments, we can account for between £10,500 and £11,500 in receipts towards the tallage.[107] This leaves only £2000 to £3000 to be raised from the first term's payments, after allowing for £2500 in credits for payments against the third. If Henry had not raised something close to this amount in the first term of such a major undertaking, it would be startling. For the Jews, it would probably have been disastrous. Arrears were certainly owing from the first term's payments. We can prove this by the imprisonments which Henry ordered in August 1241,[108] and by the fact that cash receipts on the receipt rolls and in the wardrobe after 29 September 1241 amounted to at least 12,000 marks, 2000 marks more than would have been owed for the second term had the first term's debts been paid in full. But that the arrears from the first term amounted to much more than 2000 marks may be doubted. Moreover, it is clear that after 29 April, most of the payments reaching the exchequer were the products of a subsidiary assessment, intended to make up arrears of the tallage only.[109] These payments were all fairly small, amounting to less than £240 in all. Predictably, Aaron of York paid the largest single sum, 50 marks, followed by Elias l'Eveske and Aaron Blund of London. A number of these subsidiary payments were explicitly on behalf of

---

[104] E. 401/14 and 15, *passim*. This may have been the usual pattern of payments on Jewish tallages, with terms tending to define when payments began rather than when they were to be completed. For discussion, see Stacey, 'Royal Taxation', 207 and n. 104.

[105] *CLR 1240–5*, 124–5, 127; E. 372/88 rot. 14 (wardrobe account 28 Oct. 1241 to 24 June 1245).

[106] *CLR 1240–5*, 121. This writ was paid in full: cf. E. 403/3 m. 5.

[107] This figure includes approximately £2500 in receipts for the third, plus the £8000 to £9000 recorded towards the 20,000 mark tallage. See Table 4.1.

[108] *Cl.R. 1237–42*, 322–3; E. 159/20 rot. 4.

[109] E. 401/15, *passim*; E. 159/20 rot. 14 makes explicit reference to such an assessment.

paupers and fugitives who had fled the tallage. None of this suggests that any large sums remained owing on the tax.

The tallage was not completely paid; we can follow in the memoranda rolls the exchequer's continuing attempts to collect its arrears.[110] But the king's officials themselves did not know how much was missing, and were forced to send writs to the sheriffs ordering them to bring all the tallies pertaining to the tallage to the exchequer, 'so that these same tallies being thereupon allocated, the King can know clearly, how much is owed to the king from the aforesaid tallage, and by whom'.[111] In at least one case, we can show that an individual charged by the exchequer with arrears had in fact paid his assessment in full.[112] And for several communities, writs of quittance are preserved on the memoranda rolls which attest to the entire payment of their assessments.[113] In other cases, where apparently a communal assessment had not been fully met, the exchequer had recourse yet again to the pledges appointed at Worcester two years before.[114] But the amounts involved, where we can trace them, are relatively small, and the names of those in arrears are usually obscure. The great Jewish magnates appear to have paid fully, and as we have seen, they paid the bulk of the tallage anyway.

The exchequer, of course, never knowingly overlooked any debt it regarded as outstanding, and it continued to pursue these arrears throughout 1243 and into 1244.[115] But after the summer of 1242, the additional amounts recovered from these debts probably did not repay the effort of collecting them. On 9 May 1242, when King Henry III set sail for Poitou, he carried with him the entire proceeds of the 20,000 mark tallage of the Jews. In so doing, he inaugurated a new and ultimately disastrous decade in the history of medieval Anglo-Jewry.

[110] E. 368/14 rots. 2, 3d, 5d, 20; E. 368/15 rots. 5, 5d, 6, 7.

[111] 'ut eisdem taliis ibidem tunc allocatis, Rex scire possit evidenter, quantum et a quibus Regi debebatur de tallagio praedicto.' E. 368/15 rot. 5, printed by Thomas Madox in *The History and Antiquities of the Exchequer of England* (2nd edn., London, 1769), vol. i, 224 n. (t). This order may explain how so many Hebrew tallies pertaining to this tax and to the third found their way to the exchequer. For a compilation of these tallies, see Michael Adler, 'Jewish Tallies of the Thirteenth Century', *Miscellanies of the Jewish Historical Society of England*, 2 (1935), 8–23.

[112] Benedict Crespin: cf. *Cl.R.* 1242–7, 39; *CLR* 1240–5, 98; and Table 4.3.

[113] E. 159/20 rot. 14d (Hereford), rot. 15d (Stamford).

[114] E. 368/15 rot. 5d.

[115] On 7 Feb. 1244 the king ended distraint for arrears owed by Jews on all previous debts, this respite to last until the Jews had finished paying the 60,000 mark tallage: Fine Roll 28 Henry III (C. 60/41 m. 9). This writ seems to have brought distraint for arrears of the 20,000 mark tallage to an end.

4. *King, Council and the Jews*   159

Henry had dreamt of this expedition for a dozen years; ultimately, it was the goal towards which all the conciliar reforms since 1236 had been directed. In providing so large a sum of cash for the enterprise, the council under Segrave could therefore claim a fair measure of success for its financial policies. In the long run, of course, Jewish revenues were not sufficient to make good the continuing shortfalls of revenue in relation to expenditure which became such a chronic feature of Crown finance in the years after 1245, and it was the attempt to make them so that largely ruined the Jewish community as a Crown financial resource. But had the 20,000 mark tallage of 1241–2 not been followed by an even more onerous levy of 60,000 marks between 1244 and 1250, the council's new approach to Jewish taxation after 1239 need not permanently have crippled the Jewish community's capacity to contribute to the king's coffers. Segrave himself died in October 1241. Although he helped initiate the first of these massive Jewish taxes, he cannot be held responsible for the disastrous policies of 1244 and after. Between 1239 and 1241, the council under his leadership had aimed only to produce a single infusion of cash which would make the king's military expedition possible. In this it succeeded. The causes of that expedition's failure must be sought elsewhere.

5

Diplomacy, War and Finance: The Campaign for Poitou

LEGALLY, King John forfeited his Continental fiefs by sentence of his lord King Philip's feudal court in 1202. Practically, John lost these lands because he could not command the native political and military support necessary to retain them in the face of a determined Capetian attack.[1] Once lost, the administrative centralization and social cohesiveness of these territories constituted an even more formidable obstacle to their successful reconquest than did the logistical difficulties of a military campaign. For most of the men who mattered in Anjou and Maine, the intermediate lordship of the king of England offered few compensations for the complications it caused them with their ultimate lord, King Philip. In Normandy, the tenurial ties across the Channel were stronger, in part because the Angevins had actively promoted new such ties through the arranged marriages of wards and heiresses.[2] Here there were relationships of fidelity and self-interest on which a successful reconquest might be built. Among the greatest men, however, even these relationships had been rather one-sided. Many of the English earls and barons had continued to hold important family lands in Normandy, but relatively fewer of the greatest Norman lords had important family holdings in England by 1204. Many of the Normans who did were expelled from Normandy by Philip Augustus, and so joined King John in English exile.[3] There was, thus, a reversionary Norman interest, on whose support King John and even his

[1] The classic account is by F. M. Powicke, *The Loss of Normandy*, 2nd edn. (Manchester, 1961). The best short narrative is Warren, *King John*, 51–99. There is important commentary on some of the general problems which led to the collapse in J. C. Holt, 'The End of the Anglo-Norman Realm', *PBA* 61 (1975), 223–65; Gillingham, *Richard the Lionheart*, 278–88, 303–4; and Holt's reply to Gillingham in *War and Government in the Middle Ages*, ed. Holt and Gillingham, 92–105.

[2] For an example of such ties being deliberately created by King Richard, see *CRR* vol. 15, no. 1717. See also Holt, 'End of the Anglo-Norman Realm', 262–3.

[3] Powicke, *Loss of Normandy*, 280–90, 328–58; Elizabeth M. Hallam, *Capetian France 987–1328* (London, 1980), 185–6.

son King Henry could rely; but its members were mostly English, and by 1214 mostly resident in England. There was no sizeable party of barons in Normandy after 1214 who were prepared to risk what they held from the king of France in order to restore the king of England to his Norman lordship. Two centuries of centralizing rule by their dukes had accustomed the barons of Normandy to acting in a united way in such critical matters as war and peace and feudal allegiance. After 1202, they had done so in transferring their allegiance to Philip Augustus.

In the two separate territories John did retain, the situation was different. Poitou was a feudal dependency of France, and as such fell under the same sentence of forfeiture as had Normandy, Brittany, Maine, and Anjou. Gascony, however, was an allod, held freely by the dukes of Aquitaine, and after the death of the Duchess Eleanor in 1204, by the kings of England as her heirs. Although Poitou and Gascony had been united since the mid-eleventh century in the hands of the Poitevin dukes of Aquitaine, the dukes did homage only for Poitou, when they bothered to acknowledge any feudal suzerain at all.[4] Neither territory had any long experience of effective ducal rule, despite the energetic efforts of Richard the Lionheart in the decade after 1174 to subordinate the turbulent local castellans and barons of the region.[5] As a result, the regional nobility throughout the twelfth century continued to pursue its local concerns and quarrels in essential independence of ducal administration.

Until the death of King Richard in 1199, power in Poitou therefore remained in the hands of about fifty or so fiercely independent castellans and minor barons.[6] Thereafter, however, the considerable wealth of Poitou was increasingly concentrated in the hands of the Lusignan counts of La Marche and (after 1220) Angoulême, of the viscounts of Thouars, and of the lords of Talmont and Parthenay, in whom it fuelled ambitions to establish extensive, cohesive regional lordships independent of close control by kings or dukes of any stripe. This process had begun during the struggles between King Richard and King Philip during the 1190s, and was in its origins largely the

---

[4] Pierre Chaplais, 'Le Traité de Paris de 1259 et l'inféodation de la Gascogne allodiale', *Le Moyen age* (1955), 121–37, and 'Le Duché-Paire de Guyenne: l'hommage et les services féodaux de 1259 à 1337', *Annales du midi* 69 (1957), 5–38, both reprinted in Chaplais's collected *Essays in Medieval Diplomacy and Administration* (London, 1981).

[5] Gillingham, *Richard the Lionheart*, 70–98; Warren, *Henry II*, 136–48.

[6] For what follows, see Robert Hajdu, 'Castles, Castellans and the Structure of Politics in Poitou, 1152–1271', *Journal of Medieval History* 4 (1978), 27–53.

product of ducal alienations and concessions to key supporters on both sides. But it quickly took on a life of its own, and after about 1220 had entirely transformed the political structure of Poitou.

·Gascony was a poorer land, more completely dependent for its prosperity on viticulture and its commercial proceeds than was Poitou, its bitter mercantile rival.[7] Lordships in Gascony tended to be smaller than in Poitou, and seem not to have experienced the gradual con-centration into the hands of a few great families which characterized Poitevin feudal geography after 1199. The Gascon lords were united primarily by their resentment at Poitevin hegemony in the region. Gascony and Poitou shared neither a common society nor a common language.[8] Aside from a common border, they shared only a common interest in the English wine market, from which both Bordeaux and La Rochelle aspired to exclude the other.[9]

Whatever their weaknesses as feudal principalities, during the late twelfth century Poitou and Gascony were ideal recruiting grounds for troops, and this remained their principal importance to King John. Normandy was by far the most valuable of the territories John had lost, and John never ceased to plan towards its recovery. The admin-istrative and political unity which made it so valuable, however, also made it unlikely that a direct English military assault on central Normandy would succeed. John seems therefore to have concluded that to recover Normandy, he had first to win a military victory over Philip Augustus elsewhere in France: a victory, moreover, which would be sufficiently decisive to convince the barons of Normandy to return *en masse* to their English allegiance, as they had departed from it between 1202 and 1204. Only then would military operations against

---

[7] There is a good description of Gascon geography in J. P. Trabut-Cussac, *L'Ad-ministration anglaise en Gascogne sous Henry III et Edouard I de 1254 à 1307*, Mémoires et documents publiés par la Société de l'École des Chartes 20 (Geneva, 1972), xi–xviii.

[8] Poitevin was a dialect of northern French, the *langue d'oeuil*; Gascon was a dialect of Provençal, and thus a part of the *langue d'oc*. The linguistic border appears to have been the Charente: cf. Gillingham, *Richard the Lionheart*, 40. This linguistic and political division appears also to have divided the two provinces socially; I have found little evidence of intermarriage between Gascon and Poitevin noble families, although a few Poitevin lords clearly did have interests in the south: cf. the example of Hugh de Vivona, p. 174 below. Such intermarriage as did occur was usually between border families: for an example, see the marriage of Maud of Tonnay-sur Charente with Senebrun lord of Lesparre in *CPR 1232–47*, 404.

[9] Gillingham, *Richard the Lionheart*, 46, 67–8; R. Dion, *Histoire de la vigne et du vin en France des origines au XIXᵉ siècle* (Paris, 1959), 353–87; *Histoire de Bordeaux*, vol. iii: *Bordeaux sous les rois d'Angleterre*, ed. Yves Renouard (Bordeaux, 1965), 53–9, hereafter cited as *Histoire de Bordeaux*, vol. iii.

the Capetian strongholds in central Normandy have any reasonable chance of success. This strategic vision dominated John's various Continental schemes. For the strategy to succeed, King John therefore required a Continental base of operations, from which troops could be recruited and attacks launched, and a system of alliances with other European powers prepared to participate in carving up Capetian France. John secured the first in 1206, when he recovered Poitou after a brief Capetian occupation. During the following eight years, he laboured to produce the second, resurrecting and reinvigorating the system of Rhineland alliances which his brother Richard had first constructed against the Capetians in 1194. John's strategy worked, and in 1214 forced King Philip to risk his kingdom on the outcome of the battle of Bouvines. The military defeat which John's allies there suffered should not obscure the conceptual soundness of the strategy which produced this battle. Philip's presence at Bouvines was a tactical triumph for John. Had the day gone differently, Normandy might well have been recovered by the Angevins.

King John's defeat at Bouvines, and the subsequent weakness of the English government at home and abroad during the decade thereafter, had profound effects on the structure of power in Poitou. The ducal demesne lands and castles had never been extensive anywhere in Aquitaine, but until the 1190s they had at least been adequate to establish the duke as the single greatest power in Poitou. In the struggles between King Richard and King Philip during the 1190s, however, ducal alienations and concessions to key supporters on both sides began to assist in the emergence of a small group of powerful regional lords, any one of whom was individually a match for the duke himself within Poitou.[10] This process was greatly accelerated after 1199, when the head of the house of Lusignan acquired also the lands and dignity of the county of La Marche as his price for supporting John's claims to the English throne.[11] In some significant sense, this concession to the Lusignans cost King John his Continental possessions.[12] In 1202, he married the heiress to the county of Angoulême himself, to prevent Hugh IX de Lusignan from marrying her, and becoming by this

---

[10] Hajdu, 'Castles, Castellans and ... Poitou', 34–40.

[11] Sidney Painter, 'The Houses of Lusignan and Chatellerault, 1150–1250', *Speculum* 30 (1955), reprinted in his collected essays *Feudalism and Liberty* (Baltimore, 1961), 79. For the background to the Lusignan claim to La Marche, see the same author's article on 'The Lords of Lusignan in the Eleventh and Twelfth Centuries', *Speculum* 32 (1957), reprinted in *Feudalism and Liberty*, 41–72.

[12] The narrative of events is best followed in Powicke, *Loss of Normandy*, 138–48.

marriage the dominant lord of the region. This breach of faith by King John toward his vassal (the lady was already affianced to Hugh) produced the sentence of forfeiture in King Philip's feudal court which justified the Capetian conquest of Normandy. And in the long run, King John's marriage did not even succeed in preventing the Lusignans from dominating Poitou. In 1220, Hugh X de Lusignan, count of La Marche, married the countess of Angoulême, John's widow, and thus fulfilled his father's ambition to become the effective arbiter of Poitou. Thereafter, neither the Angevins nor the Capetians could expect to control Poitou except through the Lusignans; and, by skilfully playing off the two royal houses against each other, the Lusignan counts of La Marche and Angoulême had a real chance to create a principality effectively independent of either overlord.

The regency government in England seems to have realized this, and by 1219 had virtually conceded the government of Poitou to the count of La Marche.[13] His 1220 marriage to the dowager queen of England only reinforced a hegemony he already enjoyed. All that the Lusignan domination lacked was control over one or both of the two major seaports in the region, La Rochelle and Bordeaux. Henry III's regents were prepared to promise Hugh a sizeable yearly pension out of the revenues of La Rochelle, but they were not willing to cede control over the city itself.[14] Louis VIII was prepared to offer more. Along with a yearly fee of £2000 Paris (approximately 1000 marks sterling), he promised the Lusignans a free hand against Bordeaux. This was the decisive consideration which propelled them into the Capetian camp in 1224.[15] And with the Lusignans opening their castles to Louis's invading army, Poitou simply could not be defended. Only at La Rochelle, that great boom town of the English wine trade, was an effective resistance mounted, and that effort was finally doomed by the failure of Hubert de Burgh's government to send speedy and sufficient reinforcements. While de Burgh and his factional allies diverted the king's army into an attack on their own domestic enemies at Bedford Castle, Poitou was lost to Louis.[16]

Once they crossed the Dordogne into Gascony, however, the Cape-

---

[13] *Foedera*, vol. i, pt. i, 155–6; *Diplomatic Documents*, nos. 35–7; and see also Norgate, *Minority of Henry III*, 132–7. Wherever possible, citations are to the more reliable versions in *Diplomatic Documents*, rather than to Shirley's edition of *Royal Letters*.

[14] Charles Petit-Dutaillis, *Étude sur la vie et le règne de Louis VIII* (Paris, 1894), 236.

[15] Ibid., 237–8.

[16] See above, pp. 29–32.

tian armies had conspicuously little success. Louis himself returned to Paris, leaving portions of his army with Hugh de Lusignan to attack Bordeaux. Had Bordeaux fallen, the rest of Gascony would soon have followed; but with the successful defence of their great port, the Gascons repulsed the Poitevin advance. A few border towns were lost, but only two of the major Gascon noblemen threw in their lot with King Louis.[17] Given the centuries of Gascon–Poitevin animosity, this fact should occasion no surprise. Moreover, by remaining loyal to Henry while Poitou fell to Louis, the Gascons could now look forward to a virtual monopoly of the lucrative English wine trade. In 1224 we are only at the beginning of the period in which Englishmen would discover a national taste for claret. The Gascon wine trade itself was still quite new, dating only from about the mid-twelfth century, and until 1224 the English market continued to be dominated by the white wines of Poitou, most of them shipped via La Rochelle.[18] But with the fall of La Rochelle to the French, claret's competitors disappeared from the English market as swiftly as the wines of Anjou and Normandy had done twenty years before. As duke of Aquitaine, the loss of Poitou to Louis was for Henry a disaster, which deprived him in a stroke of the wealthiest part of his duchy and the greatest portion of his ducal revenues. For the Gascons, it appears to have been an economic triumph and a political relief, which guaranteed them not only a monopoly of the English wine trade, but also the support of the English Crown in resisting Poitevin ambitions to dominate the region politically. That in future years the Gascons should have been unenthusiastic supporters of Henry's efforts to recover Poitou is only natural; seen from this perspective, what was more remarkable was their willingness to offer him any support at all for the project.

The loss of Poitou galvanized de Burgh's government into an uncharacteristic fit of energy. The 1225–7 military expedition dispatched to Gascony under the nominal command of Richard of

---

[17] Petit-Dutaillis, *Louis VIII*, 238–56, esp. 250–2; *Diplomatic Documents*, nos. 146–8. The two noblemen who joined the invaders were Elias Ridel of Bergerac, and Peter de Gaveretto, lord of St Macaire. Bergerac was a border fortress which was bound to be a focus for conflict if Poitou and Gascony followed separate lords: cf. the description in *Diplomatic Documents* no. 38. Peter de Gaveretto was in more or less continuous conflict with the men of Bordeaux; if they supported Henry, he was likely to be against him.

[18] Robert Boutrouche, *La Crise d'une société: seigneurs et paysans de Bordelais pendant la Guerre de Cent Ans* (Paris, 1947), 141–4; Gillingham, *Richard the Lionheart*, 46; Yves Renouard, *Études d'histoire médiévale* (Paris, 1968), 230, 238–41, 302–13; *Histoire de Bordeaux* vol. iii, 53–68.

Cornwall secured the borders of Gascony and opened up potentially useful relations with the neighbouring counts of Auvergne and Toulouse, but it had little effect on the balance of power in Poitou, which remained firmly in the hands of the Lusignans. Meanwhile, de Burgh renewed the search for Continental allies, reopening King John's relations with the duke of Lorraine, and proposing a marriage alliance between Henry and the daughter of the duke of Austria, to be complemented by a marriage between Henry's sister Isabella and the eldest son of Emperor Frederick II.[19] When these proposals came to nothing, de Burgh opened negotiations with the Lusignans' frequent ally, Peter of Dreux, duke of Brittany.[20] A draft treaty was prepared in mid-1226, and when Louis VIII died suddenly in November, it looked briefly as if de Burgh's diplomatic and military efforts might be rewarded. Hopes of regaining Poitou were quickly dashed, however, when the count of La Marche renewed his arrangements with the regency government of Louis IX. A few months later, the wavering duke of Brittany followed him into the new king's camp.[21] This ended any lingering English hopes of further gains outside Gascony. Having expended upwards of £50,000, Earl Richard concluded a two year truce with France and went home, leaving his titular county of Poitou in the hands of the French.

What was lacking from English policy after 1224 was not application, but a sense of a wider purpose. King John's purposes and strategy are fairly clear. He intended to recover the Angevin heartland of Normandy, Maine, and Anjou by attacking King Philip in Anjou, and, with the help of his German and Flemish allies, by defeating him in battle on the borders of Normandy. Poitou was for John a means to this larger end. After 1224, however, it is not at all clear what Henry III's larger ends on the Continent were. Henry's agents in Gascony saw little substance in Capetian control over Poitou, and assured the king that with enough money and a few troops, the province could be recovered.[22] The failure of the earl of Cornwall's expedition did not reduce their confidence; it merely reinforced the importance in English

---

[19] Norgate, *Minority of Henry III*, 253–4; Petit-Dutaillis, *Louis VIII*, 263–70.

[20] Sidney Painter, *Peter of Dreux*, 34–42, esp. 41–2.

[21] Ibid., 42–8.

[22] *Diplomatic Documents*, nos. 148, 176. A more accurate perception of the situation was conveyed to Henry in Nov. 1236 by Reynold de Pons, a baron of the Saintonge and one of Henry's most consistent supporters during these years. Reynold estimated that to control all of Aquitaine, including Poitou, would cost Henry 20,000 marks per year, and require the services of 1000 well-armed knights, excluding sergeants (ibid., no. 245). As the 1242–3 expedition would prove, Reynold was not far wrong in his estimates.

eyes of regaining the support of the count of La Marche. To the interests of the count of La Marche, however, Hubert de Burgh's proposed German alliances were a supreme irrelevance. An alliance between Henry and the duke of Brittany might have had more substantial effects on the balance of power in the region, but in 1227 that alliance too fell through. Nor was it guaranteed to bring the count of La Marche into the English camp. Despite the close personal relations between La Marche and the duke of Brittany, the Lusignans could not have been enthusiastic about the prospect of so ambitious a man as Peter of Dreux becoming a major power in Poitou.[23] Auvergne and Toulouse, on the other hand, might have been valuable allies in applying pressure to Poitou, but English alliances with both these counts remained insubstantial and ill-defined. In the truly decisive warfare between France and Toulouse which ended in the 1229 Treaty of Paris, English armies played no role. And with the remaining two major powers in the region, Aragon and Castile, de Burgh apparently had no contacts at all. Negotiations with Flanders, on the other hand, continued apace, and in 1230 Count Ferrand accepted an English pension of 500 marks per year.[24] All this left the primary focus of Henry's Continental ambitions in some doubt, both at home and abroad. Did Henry really intend to recapture Normandy, or were his ambitions primarily directed towards Poitou?

The pervasive sense of confusion which hangs over English policy after 1224 is not relieved by the one important clue we have to Henry's Continental strategy. In 1229, when Richard of Cornwall's truce with King Louis expired, Henry sent Ralph fitz Nicholas and the bishop of Coventry to negotiate with Louis IX the terms of a more lasting peace, if such could be had.[25] Both messengers were, of course, close factional allies of Hubert de Burgh, and fitz Nicholas at least seems to have shared de Burgh's opinions on Continental military strategy.[26] In 1228, Louis's supporters were at war among themselves, and the English had

---

[23] As Painter has pointed out, Peter of Dreux was duke of Brittany only until his son came of age; his own preoccupation during these years was thus to use his temporary position as duke to secure for himself lands and revenues which he could continue to enjoy after he had turned the duchy over to his son: cf. Painter, *Peter of Dreux*, 28–9, 32–3.

[24] *Patent Rolls 1225–32*, 322; *Diplomatic Documents*, no. 228. The fee may have been offered in 1227 (cf. *Patent Rolls 1225–32*, 143), but this is the first evidence for its payment.

[25] *Patent Rolls 1225–32*, 243–4: 5 April 1229. The negotiating proposals alluded to here are printed in *Diplomatic Documents*, no. 215.

[26] *Diplomatic Documents*, nos. 220, 223; and below, pp. 171–2.

resumed discussions with the discontented duke of Brittany. It is likely that a renewal of the 1226 marriage alliance proposed between Henry and Yolande of Brittany had already been agreed before the English ambassadors even departed for Paris.[27] Negotiating from a position of such relative strength, with circumstances propitious for a successful English military expedition, Henry must have pitched his demands high. Strikingly, however, even in these favourable circumstances, Henry's first offer to Louis was to abandon all English claims to Normandy, if Louis in return would cede to him the remainder of the Angevin lands, plus the dioceses of Coutances and Avranches in Normandy as a corridor of transit from England into Maine and Anjou. If Louis rejected this, Henry was prepared to forgo his demands for Coutances and Avranches. If this too proved unacceptable, Henry's final offer was to cede Normandy outright, and to marry his sister Isabella to Louis, with Maine and Anjou north of the Loire as Isabella's marriage portion. If Isabella and Louis had heirs of her body, these territories would remain to the heirs, who would also of course become kings of France. If Isabella died without issue by Louis, these lands would return to the kings of England. To secure any of these arrangements, Henry was prepared to pay monetary compensation, and himself to marry one of Louis' sisters, a condition which would immediately cast into doubt his proposed alliance with Brittany. Presumably, Henry and de Burgh thought the Breton alliance unnecessary if an agreement could be reached with Louis without a war.[28]

In these proposals, all the contradictions which plagued Henry III's Continental ambitions after 1224 are revealed. By 1229 at least, his closest advisers were convinced that Normandy was irretrievably lost; they preferred therefore to concentrate the king's military and diplomatic energies on the recovery of Anjou and Maine, but especially on Poitou, the only Angevin territory held by the French in 1229 which they were not prepared to offer to Louis under any circumstances. The reasons for this Poitevin preoccupation are fairly clear. Henry was himself three-quarters Poitevin, and there is no doubt that the loss of

---

[27] Painter placed the formal renewal of this marriage agreement in the summer of 1229 (*Peter of Dreux*, 60), just after Henry's negotiators returned from Louis's court. But it is likely that discussions of the renewal had been joined before the renewal itself was formalized. Peter of Dreux's disaffection from the French court dated back to at least 1228: ibid., 55–9.

[28] *Diplomatic Documents*, no. 215; Powicke, *Henry III*, 179–80. A broadly similar scheme may have been proposed to Louis VIII in 1225, but the document is too damaged for its specific proposals to be intelligible: cf. *Diplomatic Documents*, no. 174.

this province was a grievous personal blow. Du Burgh had been the principal man in charge of Poitevin affairs from at least 1220 until his downfall in 1232, and he too undoubtedly felt its loss as a personal responsibility. For Henry, Poitou was every bit as much a part of his inheritance as was Normandy; for de Burgh, with his own memories of Norman defeats under John, Poitou was the only area in which English armies stood a chance of success. Nor was Poitou without strategic importance. Although Toulouse was the great commercial centre which connected the Mediterranean and the Atlantic trade routes, Poitou blocked access between Toulouse and northern France. Capetian ambitions in southern France turned on control of Toulouse; in this respect, the 1224 conquest of Poitou was the essential prerequisite to the 1229 Treaty of Paris. If Henry could reverse the former, he stood a good chance of reversing the latter as well. And on its southern flank, Poitou controlled the navigation of the Gironde as well as the Atlantic coastline leading from England to Bordeaux. In this respect, English control over Poitou might even have been regarded as essential to preserving Henry's control over Gascony.

The division of territories which Henry proposed to Louis in 1229 was therefore in no way strategically foolish. But the diplomatic and military priorities which these 1229 proposals reveal—first the recovery of Poitou, then the recovery of Anjou and Maine, and perhaps finally the conquest of the border regions of Avranches and Coutances in Normandy—were precisely opposite to those of Henry's greatest men. The earls of Chester, Norfolk, Gloucester, Hereford, Warenne, Aumâle, Arundel, and Pembroke all had family claims to lands in Normandy.[29] Only Aumâle had any interests in Poitou.[30] The Gascons shared the prevailing disinterest in Poitou. They shared also a prevailing distaste for the Poitevin character, a distaste which since the 1160s had become deeply ingrained in the outlook of the English magnates as well. *Pictavenses* (Poitevins) and *proditores* (traitors) were virtual synonyms in England by 1230, and had been for perhaps half a century.[31] Individual Poitevins could and did rise to great office in

---

[29] Powicke, *Loss of Normandy*, esp. 328–58; and see also the extremely interesting letter written to Henry III by a citizen of Caen in 1227, printed in *Diplomatic Documents*, no. 206, and discussed by Holt, 'End of the Anglo-Norman Realm', 264–5. Wendy B. Stevenson, 'England and Normandy, 1204–1259' (unpublished Leeds University Ph.D. thesis, 1974) assembles detailed evidence on the continuing links between England and Normandy during this period.

[30] Turner, 'William de Forz', 222–4.

[31] Gillingham, *Richard the Lionheart*, 48–50, 55–7, 66, discusses the growth of this

England, but on the whole, the English shared the elder William Marshal's opinion, that the Poitevins were deceitful, conniving traitors, who were unworthy allies for any man.[32] This attitude was so widespread as to create an almost insuperable obstacle to the military support of Poitou by English troops. The barons of England simply would not participate in such a venture, as Henry would discover to his cost in 1242.

In the military campaign of 1230, however, the English magnates did participate, and they did so in force.[33] To a significant degree, this was true because the Poitevin focus of the king's strategy was by no means clear to the majority of the English baronage by the time the expedition departed. The alliances which de Burgh had sought in Germany suggested wider ambitions, which the Breton alliance reinforced to a great extent. The dukes of Brittany had traditional claims to territories on the Norman march, and Duke Peter himself held lands in Anjou, lands which he had lost to Queen Blanche in 1229.[34] At the time, he had no significant interests in Poitou.[35] The negotiations with Flanders, culminating in 1230 when Count Ferrand accepted an English pension, likewise suggested a northern focus for the forthcoming invasion. At his Christmas court in 1228, messages of support and encouragement had reached King Henry not only from Gascony and Poitou, but also from Normandy.[36] A number of the Norman ports sent ships to his service in 1230, and several important Norman barons promised to join Henry's army when it arrived in

---

prejudice. Matthew Paris made frequent use of this Latin conceit: cf. *CM*, vol. iii, 84; vol. iv, 496–7, for examples.

[32] *Histoire de Guillaume le Maréchal*, ll. 1577–80, 12521–50, and vol. iii, 24 n. 3; Gillingham, *Richard the Lionheart*, 56.

[33] The fullest account of this campaign is still Elie Berger, 'Les Préparatifs d'une invasion anglaise et la descente de Henri III en Bretagne', *Bibliothèque de l'École des Chartes* 54 (1893), 5–44. I have benefited from discussions with Dr John Maddicott about this expedition.

[34] Painter, *Peter of Dreux*, 37, 45–6, 62–5.

[35] Peter married the widow of the viscount of Thouars almost immediately after the death of her husband, that is to say, between Apr. and June 1230. The marriage brought him two important baronies in Poitou, and thus a stake in diverting King Henry's expedition southward, which he had not had when the expedition itself was being planned. His marriage also brought him into conflict with the Lusignans, and may therefore have played some role in dissuading the count of La Marche from joining Henry's cause in 1230. For details of the marriage, see Painter, *Peter of Dreux*, 65–6, 138–40.

[36] Roger Wendover, *Flores Historiarum*, ed. H. G. Hewlett (Rolls Series, London, 1886–9), vol. ii, 355–6; Painter, *Peter of Dreux*, 59 and n. 10.

Brittany.[37] Roger Wendover certainly seems to have thought that Normandy was the principal aim of the expedition,[38] and it is likely that the earls of Chester, Pembroke, Gloucester, and Warenne shared the same view. In France, the counts of Boulogne, St Pol, and Bar-le-Duc were known to be disaffected; Enguerrand de Coucy had even accepted an English pension.[39] In the 1230 invasion, Henry travelled with his crown, sceptre, and full coronation regalia.[40] To all appearances, he intended to make use of them in Normandy, Maine, and Anjou.

Henry's own intentions proved rather different. A few months previously, he had dispatched Hugh de Vivona on a secret mission to the count of La Marche in Poitou.[41] Henry and his closest advisers appear to have been confident that they would gain the count's support for the forthcoming expedition.[42] Upon his arrival in Brittany, Henry therefore delayed at Nantes for several weeks, waiting first for the arrival of the count of La Marche, who never came, and then receiving professions of loyalty from various other Poitevin barons. He was probably also waiting for King Louis's feudal army to disperse. The truce which had been signed in 1229 between the count of Champagne and his domestic enemies was due to expire on 1 July 1230, approximately the same date on which the French army's forty-day period of feudal military service would end.[43] When it did, Louis's army would dissolve into warring factions, and Henry's way would be clear into Anjou and Normandy. Anticipating his army's dissolution, in late June Louis began to withdraw towards Paris. A force of Norman knights under the command of Fulk Paynel arrived in Henry's camp at about the same time, pleading with the king to send an expedition into Normandy in their support. Yet at this critical moment, when the roads into Anjou and Normandy apparently lay open, Henry and de

[37] Berger, 'Préparatifs d'une invasion anglaise', 8–9, 10–11, 15, 19, 26. To this list should be added also Thomas de Gorges and his household, who joined the king once Henry had arrived in Brittany, in company with Robert de Bennecourt and Nicholas de Astin, who were probably also Normans: cf. *Patent Rolls 1225–32*, 405.

[38] Wendover, *Flores Historiarum*, vol. iii, 5–6.

[39] Painter, *Peter of Dreux*, 55–62; Berger, 'Les Préparatifs d'une invasion anglaise', 6; and for Coucy's English pension, *CLR 1226–40*, 161.

[40] Powicke, *Henry III*, 181.

[41] *Cl.R. 1227–31*, 309.

[42] Compare the confidence expressed in *Diplomatic Documents* no. 219 with the surprise in no. 220, when the count failed to join Henry's expedition. See also the letter of Geoffrey de Wulward, a king's clerk, written in late June, in which he still expressed confidence that the count would come over to Henry's side: ibid., no. 221.

[43] Berger, 'Les Préparatifs d'une invasion anglaise', 31–2.

Burgh chose instead to campaign in Poitou, a decision which guaranteed the military inconsequentiality of the entire expedition.[44]

The king spent six futile weeks in a vainglorious ceremonial procession through Poitou, collecting paper allies and dispensing extravagant fees to his new 'supporters', while Louis and the remnants of his army remained near Paris. By the time Henry's parade was over, his army was exhausted and thoroughly demoralized, his English supporters had begun to depart, and the king and his brother were both ill. He returned to Brittany in mid-September, and prepared to return to England, leaving the earls of Chester and Pembroke to continue the war along the Norman–Breton march. The only lasting success of the entire expedition was the recapture from the count of La Marche of Oléron, a strategically located island off the Poitevin coast which dominated the maritime approaches to La Rochelle, and which paid a farm of about £200 sterling per year.[45] To achieve this result, the king had spent a minimum of £20,000.[46] Except in Gascony, where it further strengthened the local defences against the Poitevins, the expedition had no other positive consequences whatsoever. The count of La Marche remained in the Capetian camp, and he remained in effective control of Poitou. Henry's Poitevin pensioners quickly returned to their former allegiances, where they had any, and the count of La Marche resumed his regional hegemony. So ephemeral was King Henry's Poitevin support that he appears not even to have bothered to appoint a seneschal to rule Poitou in his name. Without the support of the count of La Marche, even Henry must have realized there would be little left to rule. Three years later, after having received between £15,000 and £20,000 in English subsidies,[47] the duke of Brittany made his peace with King Louis, and the final strand in Henry's grand design unravelled.

In England, the expedition's failure had decisive effects. Politically, it confirmed the growing estrangement between de Burgh and the great

[44] The sequence of events can be followed in *Diplomatic Documents*, nos. 218–25. Henry's own attitude is clearest in document no. 224: once the count of La Marche had refused to join him, Henry saw Norman support for his expedition solely in terms of its utility in recovering Poitou.

[45] On the capture of Oléron, see Berger, 'Les Préparatifs d'une invasion anglaise', 37; for its value, see note 55 below.

[46] Mitchell, *Studies*, 181 shows direct expenditures of between 23,000 and 30,000 marks on this expedition. Henry's total expenses are likely to have been higher than this, certainly so if the subsidies he paid to the duke of Brittany between 1231 and 1234 are included: cf. Painter, *Peter of Dreux*, 86.

[47] Painter, *Peter of Dreux*, 86.

men of the land; militarily, it convinced the baronage that King Henry was at least as inept a general as his father had been. Most importantly, however, the campaign of 1230 marked the end of the Anglo-Norman realm as an English political ideal. To some extent, this was a consequence of mortality and the passage of time. By the end of 1232, the earls of Chester, Gloucester, and Pembroke were all dead; except for the Earl Warenne, they were the last of the earls who could themselves remember the Norman lands to which they laid claim. Primarily, however, the change was psychological. The campaign in 1230 convinced the aristocracy both in Normandy and in England that the separation between the two provinces would be permanent. Until 1230, families which had survived the first round of disseisins under John and Philip Augustus appear to have adopted a kind of 'wait and see' attitude toward resolving their cross-Channel claims and holdings. Between 1220 and 1230, we find relatively little new evidence of families deliberately 'rationalizing' their holdings by exchanging lands held on one side of the Channel for lands on the other side, all of which could then be held from a single king. After 1230, however, we find a steady stream of such arrangements, many of them involving members of Henry's own military household.[48] Many more such arrangements undoubtedly escape our notice, never having left a record on the royal rolls. In England, grants of land *in terre Normannorum* continued to be conditional, as they had been under John, 'until the lands of England and Normandy are one'. After 1230, however, there was no longer any confidence in the condition. King Henry had abandoned the Angevin patrimony in favour of Aquitaine, a land for which his barons had little concern and less sympathy. Their disinclination to participate in Henry's Continental military adventures thereafter reflects their specific opposition to this choice. South of the Loire, Henry would rule after 1230 on his own, out of the proceeds of his own resources, and supported by his own household troops. He could not rely on the support of his English subjects for his ambitions.

Royal revenues from Gascony were probably inadequate to meet the expenses of governing it even in the best of times, but during the 1230s these expenses were significantly higher than usual because Gascony was on an almost constant war footing. Henry's 1230

---

[48] The d'Albinis, the Chaworths, the Courtenays, the Trublevills, and the Talebots were all involved in such arrangements during the 1230s, as were a number of lesser men like Philip de Charteray and Philip de Cartred: cf. *Patent Rolls 1225–32*, 438; CPR *1232–47*, 33, 81, 105–6, 169, 172, 254, 261; *Cl.R. 1231–4*, 519.

truce with King Louis ensured that French royal armies would not take the field against Gascony, but it did not guarantee the conduct of the Poitevins or the Navarrese, both of whom continued to harass the Gascon borderlands throughout the 1230s. Moreover, until 1234 the seneschal of Gascony also had to lead expeditions in support of the count of Brittany's continuing conflicts with his own Breton vassals and private enemies.[49] To meet these obligations, Henry de Trublevill, the most successful of Henry's seneschals, appears to have tried to create a body of reliable military retainers in Gascony by granting out in fee many of the revenue-producing lands which remained to him.[50] This policy was reversed in 1233 when Trublevill, a Norman, was replaced by Hugh de Vivona, a Poitevin with connections to the Poitevin bishop of Winchester, Peter des Roches. As a local man, Vivona had local interests to foster in Gascony, which he did with some success, acquiring several important wardships and custodies for his own use.[51] This fact probably increased his difficulties with the Gascons. Trublevill's constables proved unwilling to hand over their castles to the new seneschal until they had been paid for their custodies, and the citizens of Bordeaux entirely refused to surrender to him the castle of St Macaire, despite his custody of its heir, the son of Peter de Gavaretto.[52] Vivona's policy was probably less costly than Trublevill's—there are, at least, fewer records of loans made to him while in office—but it was also far less ambitious. Henry de Trublevill was by far the most able military man to rule Gascony during the 1230s; with the fall of the Poitevin regime in England, Trublevill returned as seneschal to Gascony, and picked up where he had left off in 1233.[53]

With Trublevill's second term of office in Gascony (May 1234 to February ? 1237), we begin to get some indication of the size of the Gascon revenues. Bordeaux was by far his most valuable single resource, largely because of the income from customs duties assessed on the wine shipped through there. Moreover, the value of the wine trade appears to have been steadily increasing during the 1230s, and

[49] *Cl.R.* 1234–7, 169–70.

[50] *Patent Rolls 1225–32*, 507; *CPR 1232–47*, 6, 194–5, 318.

[51] Vivona acquired custody of the Mauleon heir (*CPR 1232–47*, 40–1), the Erald heir (ibid., 81), and the Gavaretto heir to St Macaire, whom he married to his daughter (ibid., 88; *Cl.R. 1234–7*, 504).

[52] *CPR 1232–47*, 135, 139.

[53] Trublevill's letters of reappointment as seneschal of Gascony are dated 23 May 1234 (ibid., 47). The connection with the fall of the Poitevins in England is too exact to be accidental: cf. Meekings in *CRR* vol. 15, xxiii–xxvii.

with it, the value of Bordeaux to the seneschal. By 1238, the farm of Bordeaux was valued at at least £700 sterling per year.[54] The island of Oléron was worth an additional £200 sterling per year, also largely from the customs charged on shipping.[55] During Trublevill's second term of office, he also had custody of the Channel Islands; when he gave up their custody in 1240, the king farmed them for 400 marks sterling per year.[56] Outside Oléron, the royal demesne lands were of no great significance, although there were some rents to be collected in Entre-Deux-Mers.[57] The seneschal also collected the farms of the towns of La Réole, Bayonne and Labourd, Bazas, St Émilion, and Dax.[58] Although any such estimate is guesswork, it is probably unlikely that these remaining towns and the king's demesne manors added more than perhaps £600 sterling to the seneschal's resources. Without the Channel Islands, the total value of Gascony may thus have been around £1500 sterling per year. The seneschal's actual yearly revenues were significantly smaller. Most of the value of Oléron went in fees to the king's supporters, and collecting the king's other rents and revenues was never easy, even in Bordeaux. The lack of a capable royal bureaucracy further limited the seneschal's income, by making it necessary to farm out most of the king's revenues. Seneschals, therefore, were constantly in debt. Trublevill owed 6000 marks from his first term in office,[59] and between July 1235 and July 1236 he borrowed an additional £2075 sterling beyond his provincial revenues.[60] Although the first debt was assigned for repayment out of the farm of Bordeaux, the new loans had to be repaid from the English exchequer.[61] 1235–6 was a war year, and so expenses were significantly higher than usual. Nevertheless, none of Henry's Gascon seneschals seems to have been able to survive without borrowing fairly heavily, even in peacetime. Between 1224 and 1245, Gascony therefore remained a continuous

---

[54] *CPR 1232–47*, 137, 187; *Cl.R. 1237–42*, 121. In all conversions, I presume that £5 Bordeaux is equivalent to £1 sterling. Occasionally one can find a 4 : 1 ratio being employed (*CLR 1226–40*, 256, for example), but this was unusual, and may conceal interest payments on loans. 5 : 1 is the usual ratio.

[55] *CPR 1232–47*, 116–17, 119. I presume here an exchange rate of £4 Tours to £1 sterling, which is the ratio employed in these writs.

[56] Pipe Roll 25 Henry III (E. 372/85 rot. 7d).

[57] *CPR 1232–47*, 193; *Cl.R. 1234–7*, 561–2.

[58] *ClR. 1234–7*, 561–2

[59] *CPR 1232–47*, 49; it is unclear whether these were marks sterling or marks of Bordeaux.

[60] I have computed this sum from the following entries: *CPR 1232–47*, 113–14, 132, 136, 143; *CLR 1226–40*, 256.

[61] *CPR 1232–47*, 49; and the references in n. 60 above.

drain on the king's purse, even if one excludes from its costs the annual fees which Henry paid to his Gascon supporters and various of his Poitevin admirers. When these fees are added to the king's other expenses, the drain becomes a financial haemorrhage, which may have amounted to as much as £3000 sterling per year between 1230 and 1241.[62]

Despite a chronic lack of funds, however, there was a vigour to Trublevill's Gascon policies after 1234 which had not been seen since Richard of Cornwall's expedition a decade before. Trublevill resumed his grants of lands in fee to his local supporters, and carried through a number of disseisins of persons whose loyalty he questioned. Although this policy appears to have had King Henry's general approval, a number of these disseisins were later reversed on appeal to the king in England.[63] Nonetheless, Trublevill pressed on with his policies. He showed a particular zeal in enforcing his control over castles. Some of these castles he purchased, others he acquired by exchange.[64] Most of them, however, he appears to have acquired by insisting on the rendability of all Gascon castles in time of need, a royal prerogative which had long been customary in England and in northern France, but which was distinctly not the custom in Aquitaine. It is likely that Trublevill's insistence on the rendability of castles and his reluctance to remove his garrisons once the immediate danger was past lie behind many of the complaints of disseisin which were raised against him.[65]

Of the danger itself, however, there can be no doubt. Henry's truce with Louis expired in 1234. Both sides seem to have expected a new war, but Henry's domestic difficulties and a timely change of sides by

---

[62] I have arrived at this figure by estimating an approximately £1000 per annum shortfall in local revenues vs. expenses, an amount suggested by Trublevill's rate of borrowing, and by the £1000 p.a. fee granted to subsequent seneschals; plus annual payments of fees amounting to about £2000 per year, including the £200 paid to the count of La Marche in exchange for Oléron.

[63] Henry's approval of Trublevill's policy is suggested by CPR 1232–47, 137; for royal reversals of Trublevill's disseisins, see ibid., 118, 138, 156, 195.

[64] Taillecheval, for example, Trublevill purchased in return for an annual fee of £60 Bordeaux and two robes per year: Cl.R. 1237–42, 121. Coutures-sur-le-Cropt he acquired by exchange with the archbishop of Bordeaux: Cl.R. 1234–7, 518. For the very similar policy towards castles followed by Edward after 1254, see Trabut-Cussac, L'Administration anglaise, xx-xxi.

[65] CPR 1232–47, 113, 118, 120, 138, 195. On the importance of the rendability of castles, see Hajdu, 'Castles, Castellans and ... Poitou', 41–2. Henry insisted on the rendability of castles in his 1242–3 campaign (CPR 1232–47, 401, 405), and again in 1254 (Trabut-Cussac, L'Administration anglaise, 211–12).

the duke of Brittany convinced him to renew the truce for five more years. During the interval between the expiration and the renewal of the truce, however, a riot in the border town of La Réole came within an inch of turning control of that town over to the French.[66] Even after the truce was sworn, the problems in Gascony continued. The count of La Marche seems not to have considered himself bound by the agreement between the two kings, and in 1235 seized the Ridels' important border castle at Blaye, along with its lord and his sons.[67] Eventually, King Henry was forced to purchase the Lusignans' adherence to the truce by agreeing to pay the count £800 Tours (£200 sterling) per annum in compensation for Oléron,[68] but not before the Ridels had concluded a private agreement with their captor by which they recovered their freedom and their castle. Both King Henry and his seneschal were deeply suspicious of this agreement, and although the king's local supporters assured him that the agreement was not to his prejudice, Henry seems to have remained uncertain of the Ridels' loyalty for several years thereafter.[69] Trublevill's refusal to return to them the castle of Bélin, which the Ridels claimed to hold by charter of Earl Richard of Cornwall, probably reflects these continuing suspicions, as well as providing another link in the chain of royal castles which Trublevill was trying to create in Gascony.[70]

Trublevill's castle strategy was effective, but expensive. It also raised opposition in Gascony itself. Much of the trouble at St Émilion seems to have been connected with Trublevill's castle-building there,[71] and it is possible that the same was true of the disturbances at La Réole.[72] The La Réole troubles were linked in turn to an even more complicated dispute at Bordeaux involving among other issues a factional dispute between the city's ruling families.[73] But in Bordeaux too it appears that opposition to Trublevill also played an important part in the riots.[74]

---

[66] CPR 1232–47, 129; *Diplomatic Documents*, nos. 240–42; *Histoire de Bordeaux* vol. iii, 49–51.

[67] *Diplomatic Documents*, no. 245; *Foedera*, vol. i, pt. 1, 217, 219; *Royal Letters*, vol. i, 559–60, which reveals, among other things, how closely the papacy was involved in the effort to arrange a new truce between the Kings of France and England.

[68] CPR 1232–47, 84, 111–12, 116, 119.

[69] *Diplomatic Documents*, no. 245; *Gascon Register A*, ed. G. P. Cuttino, 3 vols. (London, 1975–6), vol. ii, 521–2; CPR 1232–47, 201–2, 192–3, 318, 328.

[70] CPR 1232–47, 118, 120, 138, 201–2; *Royal Letters*, vol. ii, 47–8.

[71] Cf. *Cl.R.* 1234–7, 457.

[72] CPR 1232–47, 242.

[73] *Diplomatic Documents*, nos. 240–42.

[74] Although the general interpretive framework offered by Frank Burr Marsh, *English Rule in Gascony, 1199–1259* (Ann Arbor, 1912) has been justly criticized, his suggestion

Trublevill protected Gascony during the difficult period between 1234 and 1236 when an extension of the truce between Louis and Henry was being negotiated. By the end of 1236, the border threats had subsided, and King Henry decided to replace Trublevill with a less aggressive, and perhaps also less expensive, seneschal. Trublevill appears to have departed from Gascony in February 1237.[75] In July, the archbishop of Bordeaux is addressed as seneschal,[76] but by mid-August Hubert Hoese had been named as Trublevill's permanent replacement,[77] probably at a great convocation of Gascon magnates which Henry held in London during the summer of 1237.[78] Hoese had served as one of the royal arbiters appointed in late 1236 to decide a conflict between the Abbey of the Holy Cross, Bordeaux, and Bernard de Beauville, son of Peter de Gavaretto, over the secular justice of St Macaire.[79] He may also have attempted to mediate between Trublevill and some of his opponents at the same time.[80] This mission appears to have been his only experience with Gascony prior to his appointment as seneschal. Like Trublevill, Hoese was a member of the king's military household and an important West Country baron in England. He seems also to have continued most of Trublevill's Gascon policies, especially with respect to castles.[81] For most of his tenure in office, however, the patent rolls are lost, and so we can say relatively little with confidence about his activities. In contrast to Trublevill, who appears to have served in Gascony at his own expense, Hoese received an annual fee of £1000 at the English exchequer for his services as

---

that Trublevill had allied himself with the Bordeaux political faction led by the Solers family seems to me to have considerable merit. There is an important review of Burr's book by Charles Bémont in *Revue historique* 114 (1913), 382–3. See also *Histoire de Bordeaux*, vol. iii, 46–51.

[75] Trublevill was recalled from Gascony for consultation with the king in England in Nov. 1236 (*CPR 1232–47*, 169), but probably did not leave Gascony until at least Feb. 1237 (cf. *Cl.R. 1234–7*, 416). The last clear reference to Trublevill as seneschal is on 13 July 1237 (*Cl.R. 1234–7*, 472), the same day on which the archbishop of Bordeaux is addressed as seneschal (*CPR 1232–47*, 189). Both men were probably in England at this time. The list of Gascon seneschals published by Shirley in *Royal Letters*, vol. ii, 399–400 is unreliable.

[76] *CPR 1232–47*, 189.

[77] *CPR 1232–47*, 194; *Cl.R. 1234–7*, 486, 561–2.

[78] References to this assembly may be found in *CPR 1232–47*, 193; *CLR 1226–40*, 285, 286; and *Gascon Register A*, vol. ii, 521–2.

[79] *CPR 1232–47*, 169, 192; *Gascon Register A*, vol. ii, 419, 420.

[80] *CPR 1232–47*, 169.

[81] Ibid., 245; *Cl.R. 1237–42*, 121; *CLR 1226–40*, 353, 361.

seneschal.[82] The fee was paid with fair regularity, but arrears were still owing when Hoese retired from office.[83] The last reference to Hoese as seneschal is in June 1240, but the first reference to a new seneschal is not until September 1241, when Rostand de Solers, leader of the dominant civic faction in Bordeaux, assumed the office.[84] It is therefore not entirely clear when Hoese retired as seneschal. Hoese was certainly back in England by July 1241, when he was involved in Henry's war on the Welsh Marches.[85] So far as we can judge, he appears to have been a success as a seneschal.[86] He and Trublevill left Gascony a much more peaceful and secure province in 1241 than it had been a decade before.

Henry's diplomacy also played a role in the gradual solidification of English control in Gascony during these years. The defection of the duke of Brittany at the end of 1234 left Henry without a major Continental ally, just as the truce with King Louis expired. A truce with Navarre helped to relieve the pressure on Gascony's southern flank, while Henry renewed the truce with Louis.[87] In 1236, Henry helped further to strengthen his seneschal's position in Gascony by agreeing to pay a yearly fee to the count of Auvergne.[88] Henry also reopened discussions with the count of Toulouse, although once again these do not appear to have produced any useful results.[89] In 1241, Toulouse was still regarded as one of the powers likely to move war against the seneschal of Gascony.[90] Despite Henry's and Count

---

[82] *CLR 1226–40*, 361. Payments on this fee sometimes passed through the wardrobe: cf. E. 372/83 rot. 7.

[83] *CPR 1232–47*, 313; *CLR 1240–5*, 154.

[84] *Cl.R. 1237–42*, 196 is the last reference to Hoese as seneschal. The first references to a new seneschal are *CPR 1232–47*, 259; *Cl.R. 1237–42*, 333.

[85] *CLR 1240–5*, 60.

[86] Matthew Paris claims that in 1240 the seneschal of Gascony arrived in England, having been virtually driven out of Gascony, to report that the king stood in imminent danger of losing control over the entire province (*CM*, vol. iv, 15). I have found no confirmation for this story elsewhere.

[87] *CPR 1232–47*, 87.

[88] Ibid., 137.

[89] Ibid., 129. Henry did his chances no good by siding with the church against Count Raymond of Toulouse and his seneschal, William Arnaldi de Tantalon, in an excommunication case centring on possession of secular justice in Le Mas d'Agenais, which Raymond claimed against the local prior. Henry ordered his own seneschal to distrain on the lands of Raymond and William until they had made satisfaction to the church: *CPR 1232–47*, 202–3. The contrast with Louis IX's well-known refusal to bring secular sanctions to bear against persons excommunicated in secular disputes, without first rehearing the case in his own court, is instructive.

[90] *CPR 1232–47*, 259.

Raymond's common interest in checking Capetian expansion into southern France, it was not until the autumn of 1242 that a formal alliance was concluded between them.

In northern Europe, Henry's pursuit of Continental alliances was more successful. Early in 1235, he proposed to marry the heiress to the county of Ponthieu, a small but strategically valuable county which lay between Flanders and Normandy. Understandably, Louis IX took a dim view of the proposal, and prevailed upon the pope to quash the match on grounds of consanguinity.[91] Later that year, however, Henry scored perhaps the greatest diplomatic success of his reign when he married his sister Isabella to Emperor Frederick II of Germany. The match cost Henry a dowry of £20,000, but it provided him with the most powerful ally he could have against the Capetians. And Matthew Paris, at least, was in no doubt that this alliance was directed against Louis IX.[92] Henry's efforts to attract the duke of Lorraine and the count of Guisnes were less successful, despite the king's offer to restore to the duke the honour of Eye in England.[93] But in the emperor, Henry had an ally whose connections and claims to overlordship stretched from Jerusalem to Denmark, and from the Alps to Aquitaine. The marriage opened up to Henry the prospect of forging a truly Continental alliance by which to recover his own ancestral lands. This dream of such a European-wide alliance continued to animate Henry's diplomacy right up until the eve of his 1242 Poitevin expedition.

The king's January 1236 marriage to Eleanor of Provence was probably intended to forward such plans, partly by checking the gains which Louis IX had made into the Rhône valley by marrying Eleanor's elder sister Margaret, and partly by establishing closer connections between King Henry and the important imperial vassals in Savoy and Provence.[94] Henry was not unaware of the strategic importance to Louis IX of the Alpine passes of Provence, and he may have hoped eventually to trade his own Provençal claims against other concessions from Louis. It was, none the less, an odd choice. Although the count of Provence had only daughters to succeed him, Eleanor brought no automatic rights of inheritance with her. At best Henry might hope to

[91] *Foedera*, vol. i, pt. 1, 216; *Diplomatic Documents*, no. 238; Powicke, *Henry III*, 160 and n. 2.

[92] *CM*, vol. iii, 324–5.

[93] On the count of Guisnes, see *CPR 1232–47*, 86, 94, 97; on the duke of Brabant and Lorraine, see ibid., 96, 103, 108, 110, 136. The honour of Eye was apparently restored to the duke, at least briefly, in late 1224: cf. *Diplomatic Documents*, no. 151 and n. 4.

[94] Cox, *Eagles of Savoy*, 47, comes to much the same conclusion, on different grounds.

divide the county between himself and the husbands of the other three sisters, among whom King Louis of France would be the first. The count promised a dowry of 5000 marks to Henry with his daughter, but this was a paltry sum in comparison to the dowry King Henry had paid to the emperor, and even this poor sum was never paid.[95] The marriage also complicated Henry's already difficult relations with the count of Toulouse, who had a long-standing claim to be the imperial marquis of Provence, and who was, therefore, an established enemy of the count of Provence.[96] If the recovery of Poitou was indeed Henry's primary interest, a Spanish marriage, which might have given him an ally against Poitou and potential claims in the Languedoc, would seem to have been a more promising alternative. It was not until the 1250s, however, that Henry began to turn his attentions toward resolving Spanish claims to Gascony through a marriage alliance between his son Edward and Eleanor of Castile.[97] Until that date, neither Aragon nor Castile appear to have played any important role in Henry's Aquitainian plans. Such a lack of interest was in no way traditional at the English court;[98] rather, it is a specific reflection of the general ignorance about Continental affairs which characterized Henry's council during these years.

The new queen of England did bring with her one significant advantage, however, upon which Henry quickly seized. Through her mother Beatrice of Savoy, the queen was niece to Count Amadeus of Savoy and his six extraordinary brothers.[99] One of these brothers, William of Savoy, bishop-elect of Valence, came to England with the queen, and within four months had established himself as the titular head of the king's council.[100] In 1237, Thomas of Savoy married the widowed countess of Flanders, and became its count *jure uxoris*. Philip of Savoy was beneficed in England in 1236; by 1241, Peter of Savoy had been granted the earldom of Richmond and established as the dominant

---

[95] Henry had sought a dowry of 20,000 marks, but had authorized his envoys to accept a dowry of 15,000, 10,000, 7000, 5000, or 3000 marks, or none at all: *Foedera*, vol. i, pt. 1, 220. Louis IX had been promised 10,000 marks with Eleanor's elder sister, Marguerite, but this dowry was never paid either: cf. Cox, *Eagles of Savoy*, 44.

[96] Cox, *Eagles of Savoy*, 27–8, 44–5, 96–7.

[97] Trabut-Cussac, *L'Administration anglaise*, xxxiv–xxxvi; compare Powicke, *Henry III*, 232–3, who treats Castilian claims less seriously.

[98] Gillingham, *Richard the Lionheart*, shows clearly how important Richard's negotiations with the kings of Aragon, Navarre, and Castile were in the context of his diplomacy. Much the same point could be made about Henry II and Edward I.

[99] On this family, see Cox, *Eagles of Savoy*, *passim*.

[100] See pp. 96–8 above.

figure on England's south coast, and Boniface of Savoy had been elected archbishop of Canterbury. Indeed, between 1236 and 1241 it is not too much to speak of Henry pursuing a consciously 'Savoyard' diplomatic strategy. William of Savoy brought to Henry's court a knowledge of European affairs which had been sorely lacking hitherto. His death in 1239 deprived the king of his most acute diplomatic mind. Peter of Savoy travelled on a number of diplomatic missions for Henry, seeking alliances for the king in Burgundy, as also did Peter d'Aigueblanche, bishop of Hereford after 1240 and yet another Savoyard.[101] Count Thomas of Flanders, however, was the real hinge to Henry's Continental plans during these years. In 1239 he accepted the annual fee of 500 marks per year which the counts of Flanders had traditionally received from the kings of England; Henry may also have attempted to grant him a special customs levy on English wool exports.[102]

Once again, Henry seems to have dreamed of reviving his father's strategy of 1214; but once again, the strategy simply did not fit the circumstances. Despite the importance of maintaining good commercial relations with England, Count Thomas would never risk possession of Flanders for a fee of 500 or even 1000 marks per year. Had the emperor chosen to march against Louis, it is possible then that Count Thomas might have marched with him;[103] but after 1237 the emperor was entirely engaged in his Italian campaigns and with the troubles his 1239 excommunication created for him. Until 1241, Henry may have continued to hope that the emperor's problems with the Church might yet be resolved, thus freeing Frederick to engage in a joint campaign against France. But with the death of Pope Gregory IX in 1241, and Frederick's subsequent capture of a papal fleet full of cardinals, Henry's last hope of imperial support against Louis was dashed. And with this hope went any last, lingering ambitions which Henry might have treasured to attempt the reconquest of Normandy or Anjou. It was against this background of frustrated diplomatic hopes and disappointed dreams of a Continent-wide campaign that King Henry embarked upon his second invasion of Poitou in 1242.

In reality, Poitou was never far from Henry's thoughts, even while

---

[101] Cox, *Eagles of Savoy*, 112; and above, p. 142.

[102] For discussion, see Powicke, *Henry III*, 780–3.

[103] As a member of the House of Savoy, Thomas was an imperial vassal, who like all of his brothers had to play a very delicate game in his relations with the emperor. Cox, *Eagles of Savoy*, 95–107, 121–33, 179–88, makes this point clearly.

he was negotiating Rhineland alliances with Flanders and Germany. The king's 1236 agreement to pay the count of La Marche £200 per year in compensation for his wife's dower claims to Oléron smoothed relations between the king and his troublesome step-father. A year later, Henry was hoping to build on these beginnings by offering the count the marriage of the minor earl of Gloucester for one of his daughters.[104] In 1238, Henry devoted at least 2300 marks from the proceeds of the thirtieth to paying off the arrears he owed to his various Poitevin stipendiaries. Thereafter, he made an obvious effort to keep these payments up to date.[105] Most of these fees went to the barons of the Saintonge, a strategic strip of land between the Charente and the Gironde which offered Henry an ideal base from which to push into Poitou, and which, in hostile hands, might close down the Gironde wine trade altogether. By 1241, all but two of these lords were receiving English pensions.[106]

The regularity with which these Poitevin fees were paid after 1238 reflects not only the financial freedom which reform and taxation had provided King Henry, but also the king's quickening interest in a second Poitevin expedition. Nevertheless, it is extremely difficult to determine when Henry first began to plan actively toward another invasion. The 1240 revolt of Raymond Trençavel in Languedoc apparently took Henry by surprise. Indeed, he appears to have renewed his truce with Louis for five more years while the Trençavel revolt was still in progress. Even if Henry had wanted to assist Trençavel in 1240, however, the absence of Richard of Cornwall, William Longsword, and Simon de Montfort on crusade, along with a sizeable contingent of Henry's own household knights, must seriously have weakened his capacity to mount a military expedition. Henry's support for this crusade and the absence of any evident preparations to renew the war at the expiration of the 1235–40 truce, suggest that the king was not yet planning a new campaign.

By January 1241, however, Henry was attempting to gather together a special fund which has the look of an embryonic war chest.[107] The

---

[104] *CPR 1232–47*, 199–200, and above, p. 118.

[105] Ranulf Jakelin is a good example. Granted a fee of £12 10s. per year in 1230, he received payment of four full years' arrears in Mar. 1238. Thereafter, however, his fee was paid regularly: *Patent Rolls 1225–32*, 398; *CLR 1226–40*, 317, 503; *CLR 1240–5*, 44.

[106] The two exceptions were the Count of La Marche (who did receive £200 for Oléron), and Geoffrey de Rançon, lord of Taillebourg.

[107] *Cl.R. 1237–42*, 268. This order was renewed in mid-April: cf. *CPR 1232–47*, 249, and above, p. 149.

stimulus for these preparations was probably King Louis's announced plans to fulfil the terms of the 1229 Treaty of Paris by investing his brother Alphonse as count of Poitou at the forthcoming Midsummer court.[108] As brother and overlord to the rightful count of Poitou, Henry could not let such a usurpation pass unnoticed, especially while his brother was on crusade. Henry's opposition was as nothing, however, to that of the Poitevin nobles themselves, led as usual by the count of La Marche.[109] For thirty years, the great regional lords and their vassals had ruled Poitou without any supervening comital authority, prospering as they did so from usurped or alienated comital revenues. The arrival of this resident, foreign count, backed by the armies and financial resources of the Capetians, would cast into doubt all that the Lusignans and their neighbours had accomplished in Poitou. Trouble was inevitable, and cannot have caught either Henry or King Louis by surprise. In June 1241 the Poitevins attended Count Alphonse's investiture, but already they appear to have been plotting their alternatives.[110] By December 1241, a written agreement had been reached between King Henry and the count of La Marche,[111] and the king began to prepare in earnest for a new expedition.

The alliance between Henry and the count of La Marche was sealed in late November 1241; in December, the king summoned a parliament to meet on 28 January, to consider an aid for the expedition.[112] None the less, the count's insulting behaviour at Louis's Christmas court, which precipitated the revolt of the Poitevins, was probably not pre-arranged between the count and Henry. Henry's serious preparations for the invasion really only began with the conclusion of the treaty with La Marche. As things stood, he had neither the men nor the money to launch an immediate invasion of Poitou. And even if the January parliament were to grant an aid, the tax itself could not be

[108] The exact date of Louis's announcement is uncertain, but the Christmas court of 1240 is the most likely occasion. Louis may even have delayed making this announcement until after the truce with England had been extended. It was well known, however, that 1241 was the year of Alphonse's twenty-first birthday. All that was at issue was the date of his formal investiture as count of Poitou.

[109] Our best source for events in Poitou during these months is an anonymous letter first printed by Leopold Delisle, 'Mémoire sur une lettre inédite addressée à la Reine Blanche par un habitant de La Rochelle', *Bibliothèque de L'École des Chartes* 17 (1856), 513–33. The letter itself appears on pp. 525–9.

[110] Delisle, 'Mémoire sur une lettre inédite', 525–7; Cox, *Eagles of Savoy*, 115, for the negotiations between the Counts of La Marche and Toulouse in 1241.

[111] *CPR 1232–47*, 268.

[112] *CM*, vol. iv, 180.

assessed before Easter. Receipts from the tax would not be available until Midsummer at the earliest. Seen from this perspective, the count's Christmas revolt was a singularly stupid piece of work, which probably took King Henry by surprise, and which certainly gave King Louis an unnecessary five-month head start in mounting his campaign. So premature was the count's revolt that news of it may not yet even have reached England when the parliament met in January, a supposition which would explain, for example, why discussions in that parliament centred so exclusively on whether King Henry should break unilaterally a truce which still had three years left to run.[113] None the less, the pivotal role of the count of La Marche in Henry's schemes must have been clear to the assembly, even if news of the actual revolt had not yet arrived.[114] Indeed, even before the parliament met, the English magnates clearly knew that something was up; a number of them took a mutual oath before the discussions began to refuse any requests which the king might make for taxation.[115] The parliamentary discussions themselves, however, seem to have focused primarily on the existence of the truce with Louis. In their formal reply to the king's demands, the barons did not even mention Henry's request for financial assistance, urging him only to observe the truce until Louis violated it, and then to consult with them again about a remedy if such a breach should occur.[116] The magnates' opposition to any further involvement in Poitou could not have been clearer. Henry would have to fund this expedition on his own, and fight it with his own household troops and retainers. Denied both financial and military support, King Henry was thrown back upon his own resources. The 1242 expedition was therefore to be the acid test of the king's reformed financial system.

Henry's military retainers formed the backbone of his army. Between 1236 and 1245, the king paid yearly fees to approximately seventy-five

[113] See the account of this parliament in *CM*, vol. iv, 181–8. In assessing these discussions, it is particularly important to distinguish what was actually said and written down at the parliament (which I take to be the material on 181–2, 185, 187–8) from Paris's own contributions (182–4, 186–7).

[114] *CM*, vol. iv, 181.

[115] Ibid., 181. Such mutual oaths were not uncommon in times of perceived crisis, such as 1258 and 1308; but this is the first such oath which was associated specifically with the impending business of a parliament.

[116] Ibid., 185. As remarked in n. 113 above, it is important to notice that the rest of this answer is probably Matthew Paris talking, and not the barons. The questions which the king raised subsequently with the barons, and to which the barons responded ibid., 187–8, have nothing to do with the other points Paris raises, but relate specifically to the 'written' response which Paris includes on p. 185. This is likely to be the only portion of the response Paris gives which actually reached the king.

knights each year, at an annual cost of about £1000 excluding their robes.[117] Although a few fees were higher, most of these knights received fees of between £5 and £20 per annum for their services. On campaign, they also received wages of 2s. per day. In addition, Henry maintained a number of knights at daily wages without fees, in garrison at the royal castles. Very few household knights held lands from the king in place of exchequer fees, although some knights did hold lands and pensions jointly. Altogether, the king could probably count on the service of about 100 knights *de familia regis* at any given time. Royal sergeants were probably as numerous, but they are much more difficult to trace. In contrast to the knights, however, the number of sergeants could be easily and rapidly increased in an emergency. It is therefore unlikely that Henry retained more than about 100 sergeants continuously in his service. Of this number, thirty to fifty would probably have been mounted sergeants, receiving wages of between 9d. and 12d. per day. The rest would have been foot-sergeants, who received about half the wages of a horse-sergeant. In a peacetime castle garrison, no more than one or two knights would generally have been in residence; even at an important castle like Windsor, the king's sergeants bore the bulk of garrison duty.[118] At Westminster, Henry also maintained a squad of crossbowmen, who travelled in the king's entourage. Their constables were sometimes significant figures at court,[119] but the squad itself probably rarely numbered more than twenty. Like other types of sergeants, crossbowmen could be hired when the need arose, especially in Gascony. There was no need to retain them continuously in service.

Henry's household thus constituted a respectable nucleus for an invasion force, but it could not hope to compete on its own with the vast numbers of feudal troops available to Louis IX. Fortunately, however, Henry was convinced he would not need to bring large forces with him from England. With sufficient money, he intended to hire the troops he would need in Poitou itself. Matthew Paris wrote scornfully of this plan, remarking that it was 'as though the king of England were

---

[117] The information which follows is taken from a larger study in progress of Henry's military household. The only previous study of this subject is by Walker, 'Anglo-Welsh Wars,' Ch. 2 and *passim*.

[118] In May 1242, Henry left a garrison at Windsor of one constable, four knights, and seven watchmen (*CPR 1232–47*, 286). In 1244, the garrison consisted of one knight, five sergeants, and three watchmen (*CLR 1240–5*, 213).

[119] Halingrat, the Gascon constable of Henry's crossbowmen during the 1240s, was not only an influential figure at court, but also an important money lender to the king. References to his career can be traced through the close, patent, and liberate rolls.

a banker, exchanger, or huckster, rather than a king and a noble leader and commander of knights'.[120] But the strategy itself was sound, *if* the king could raise sufficient funds, and *if* the king could rely on his Poitevin allies to supply the troops. It was, therefore, to the gathering of funds that Henry devoted most of his energies between the collapse of the January parliament and his departure for Poitou in May.

The parliament had refused to grant the king an aid, but the great men of the realm could not safely deny the king the military service they owed him if he summoned them to his service. Henry could, however, as a matter of grace agree to pardon their service overseas in return for a fine *pro passagio*.[121] Although by custom a tenant-in-chief had an effectively free choice between performing his military service or paying scutage in lieu of his service, Henry continued to regard permission to pay scutage as a grace, for which his barons ought to pay as for any other royal concession. In Henry's eyes, these fines *pro passagio* therefore purchased two separate privileges for each fining magnate: personal exemption from his own obligation to do military service, and permission to pay the king scutage instead of furnishing the *servitium debitum* he owed from his lands. The terms of such fines were, however, negotiable, and although most of the lesser tenants-in-chief appear to have paid fines in addition to their scutage, Henry permitted a number of the magnates to compound for the fine and the scutage together, in a single lump sum payment to the crown.[122] Such a combined payment had two advantages for the magnates. It allowed them to retain for their own use the entire amount of the scutage owed by their sub-tenants, and it allowed them to avoid a potentially dangerous conflict with the king, who in 1242 was attempting to collect scutage from all the knights' fees in England, irrespective of the traditional quotas which previously had determined scutage obligations.[123] From the amount of resistance which this attempt engendered, it seems unlikely that Henry increased his

[120] Giles, *Matthew Paris*, vol. i, 405; Latin version, *CM*, vol. iv, 191: '... acsi potius rex Anglorum esset nummularius, trapezita, vel institor, quam rex et militum dux et praeceptor magnificus ...'.

[121] The best introduction to the literature on these fines is Helena M. Chew, 'Scutage under Edward I', *EHR* 37 (1922), 321–36, reprinted in condensed form in her book, *The English Ecclesiastical Tenants-in-Chief and Knight Service* (London, 1932), 46–56.

[122] Mitchell, *Studies*, 228–31. The exchequer clerks did not distinguish on the pipe rolls between fines paid in addition to the scutage and fines paid as compositions for the scutage. The terms of the fines must be recovered individually, usually from the fine rolls.

[123] Mitchell, *Studies*, 223, 233–4.

revenues from the scutage to any great extent by this new procedure, although the threat which it represented may have increased the willingness of the magnates to purchase exemption from it. Indirectly, then, the effect of this new procedure may be reflected in higher revenues from the purchase of fines and compositions rather more than in the direct returns from the scutage itself. From these fines and compositions, Henry raised about £1500.[124] Returns from the scutage are harder to judge, because no records of its collection have survived.[125] It is unlikely, however, that the king raised more than £2000 from the scutage, despite assessing it at its maximum rate of 40s. per fee.[126] The bishops claimed to be exempt from summonses to perform military service overseas, but paid the king an aid on their traditional *servitia debita* at the scutage rate of 40s. per fee.[127] If all the bishops paid fully, as they apparently did, this 'aid of the prelates' should have produced £651.[128] Pressure on the monastic houses to contribute toward a voluntary aid for the king beyond their scutage

[124] I have computed this sum directly from the pipe rolls.

[125] The aid of 1245 and the scutage of Gannoc in 1245–6 were both enrolled on the pipe rolls, but the 1242 scutage was apparently enrolled on a foreign roll, which has not survived. The scattered records which remain are printed in *Book of Fees*, vol. ii, 1138–46. When the arrears from the 1242 scutage were transferred to the pipe rolls in 1244 and 1245, they amounted to approximately £550.

[126] Henry's tenants-in-chief recognized the service of about 6000 knights' fees in England (cf. the assessment of the 1245 aid to marry the king's daughter in Mitchell, *Studies*, 242–4), but on average the king did not assess scutage on more than about 2000 of these 6000 fees: cf. the returns for the scutages of 1229, 1230, 1232, and 1246 in Mitchell, *Studies*, 185, 191, 197, 246–8. Presumably, the lords of the remaining 4000 fees would have performed their military service and collected their scutage themselves. Although fewer tenants-in-chief served Henry in 1242 than had done in 1230, a large number of lords did compound with the king to have their scutage in 1242 without serving personally. It therefore seems unlikely that Henry could have assessed scutage on more than about 2000 fees in 1242, despite his efforts to extend its incidence to previously unrecognized fees. Moreover, actual receipts from a scutage were always substantially less than the amounts assessed; often, only about half the assessments were in fact collected, as the accounts in Mitchell illustrate.

[127] On the background to this claim, see Chew, *Ecclesiastical Tenants-in-Chief*, 37–46. Henry and the bishops agreed that this aid should not form a precedent, the bishops because they denied any obligation to contribute such an aid, the king because he denied their claim to be exempt from doing military service overseas. Henry issued letters patent to the bishops, specifying that the aid should not be drawn into a precedent, but the letters were never enrolled on the patent rolls. They were recorded on the exchequer memoranda rolls, from which they have been reprinted by Madox, *History and Antiquities of the Exchequer*, vol. i, 609 n. (c).

[128] I accept Walker's computation of the bishops' *servitia debita* at 460½ fees ('Anglo-Welsh Wars', 58), from which I have deducted the fees of Canterbury (60), Winchester (60), and Coventry (15). Since all three sees were vacant in 1242, Henry would have collected the 40s. scutage directly from the sub-tenants on these estates.

produced an additional £1600 or so for the king, most of which was paid into the wardrobe.[129] All in all, then, these exactions amounted to a rather small sum, in all likelihood somewhat less than £6000.[130]

Nor did King Henry have any large amount of treasure in reserve from which to fund his expedition. Only about £3000 remained from the thirtieth of 1237, and of this amount, Henry sent £2000 overseas to the count of La Marche in March 1242.[131] At the Temple, he apparently had about £8000 in his special fund, the great bulk of which had come from the Jews.[132] From the treasury, Henry withdrew 4000 marks in late March; a month later, when he emptied his treasury immediately before his departure, the king withdrew 20,000 marks from the proceeds of the Jewish tallage, and an additional 4000 marks from other sources.[133] Direct receipts into the wardrobe from monastic

[129] The accounts for this aid are printed in *Book of Fees*, vol. ii, 1130–38, although a few additional payments made into the wardrobe can be recovered from *Cl.R.* 1237–42, 420–1. From these two sources, one can show that of the £1771 6s. 8d. in total promised 'gifts', at least £1615 had been paid by the time these accounts were made up. Of this amount, at least £1086 was paid directly into the king's wardrobe before he sailed to Poitou. Like the fines *pro passagio* paid by lay tenants, these 'gifts' appear sometimes to have included a composition for the scutage owed by the house, and sometimes to have been paid in addition to the scutage. Sometimes the arrangement was even more complicated. The abbot of Hyde, for example, owed scutage on twenty fees, for a total of 60 marks. He paid a gift of 50 marks, and was pardoned his scutage on five fees, but still owed 45 marks scutage on the remaining fees. Including the gift, the abbot thus wound up paying 35 marks more than he would have paid on the scutage alone, without the additional gift (cf. *Book of Fees*, vol. ii, 652).

[130] The wardrobe accounts (E. 372/88 rot. 14) show that Henry had received £1912 6s. 8d. by May 1242 from these monastic gifts and from the aid of the bishops. He had also received £1840 13s. 4d. 'de donis diversorum' in addition to the £1127 he received in the wardrobe from the fines *pro passagio* and from other fines and amercements, producing total receipts of £4880 exclusive of the scutage.

[131] For earlier expenditure from the thirtieth, see pp. 125–8 above. £1638, apparently from the thirtieth, was delivered from Bristol in Mar. 1242 (*Cl.R.* 1237–42, 392; *CLR* 1240–5, 107; *CPR* 1232–47, 284), along with £522 10s. from the thirtieth of Wiltshire, which had been stored at Devizes (*Cl.R.* 1237–42, 392; *CLR* 1240–5, 116). Of this sum, £2013 6s. 8d. went with Nicholas de Bolevill to Poitou; the remaining £147 3s. 4d. was handed over to the king (*CLR* 1240–5, 132). When the king cleared his treasury in late Apr., only 1247 marks 2s. 10½d. (£831 9s. 6½d.) remained from the thirtieth (*CPR* 1232–47, 281).

[132] *CPR* 1232–47, 281. The 10,000 marks from the Jewry mentioned in this writ is a suspiciously round number, doubly so because none of this money came from the proceeds of the 1241–2 tallage, which was withdrawn separately: cf. *CLR* 1240–5, 121; E. 403/3 m. 5. But because the issue rolls of the lower exchequer do not show withdrawals from the New Temple, there is no way to verify the figures given in the patent roll enrolment.

[133] The issue rolls of the lower exchequer (E. 403/3 mm. 4, 5; E. 403/4 m. 1) confirm the evidence of *CLR* 1240–5, 121, 128. No chancery writs exist to authorize the first 4000 mark sum, which was paid out in two instalments of 2000 marks each.

and other gifts, the aid of the prelates, and the fines *pro passagio* amounted to about £5000;[134] Henry also collected about £1000 in payments from his sheriffs and manorial bailiffs, for which they received writs of computate to the exchequer.[135] In addition to an enormous supply of provisions, Henry also drew about £2500 in cash from the vacant bishoprics, particularly from Canterbury and Winchester.[136] These two bishoprics continued to supply the royal army throughout the fifteen-month expedition. Altogether, Henry may thus have sailed from Portsmouth with as much as £35,000 in his cash barrels. This was a substantial sum, but it was only about half the amount he had hoped to accumulate by the time of his departure.[137] Even this amount, however, had strained the king's resources to their limits. Between May and October, the regents in England were able to raise only about £3500 in additional cash for the king, despite Henry's urgent pleas for at least 50,000 marks.[138] The king had antici- pated his revenues so successfully that he left almost nothing for his regents to collect after his departure.

At heart, however, Henry's problems in organizing this expedition were less financial than political. A great deal of medieval English government depended upon the willingness of unpaid barons and shire knights to execute royal commands speedily. It was not so much that unpopular orders were deliberately and defiantly disobeyed. This did occasionally happen, but the instances were rare, and were invariably indications of serious political unrest in the countryside.[139] More often, the execution of unpopular commands would simply be delayed, and delayed, and delayed yet again, until finally the king gave up the project altogether, or else succeeded by successive distraints in compelling obedience to his will. In organizing a military expedition, however, a king who was forced to distrain obedience had already lost the game. Speed was essential to military success, and distraint was a slow

---

[134] See the wardrobe account for the period from 28 Oct. 1241 to 24 June 1245 on Pipe Roll 28 Henry III (E. 372/88 rot. 14); and n. 130 above.

[135] E. 372/88 rot. 14.

[136] Ibid.

[137] Henry ordered sufficient money barrels constructed to hold £60,000: *Cl.R. 1237– 42*, 390.

[138] E. 403/4 m. 2, confirming *CLR 1240–5*, 143; and *Cl.R. 1237–42*, 459, for the shipment of treasure to the king. For Henry's orders to send him 50,000 marks, see *Cl.R. 1237–42*, 522.

[139] The outright resistance in 1261 to the newly reappointed royal sheriffs is an example of such discontent: cf. Treharne, *Baronial Plan of Reform*, 263–8.

and increasingly cumbersome procedure.[140] Yet this was precisely the dilemma in which Henry found himself in the spring of 1242. The truce with Louis was still in effect, and the barons had flatly refused to sanction its unilateral breach by Henry. Henry was determined to mount a military expedition, but could not openly declare his intentions. Ostensibly, he travelled abroad in May 1242 merely to secure from Louis amends for alleged French violations of the truce. Only if Louis failed to offer such amends would there be a *casus belli*. And only at that point would Henry be in a position to compel attention to his military summons without resorting to the time-consuming and ultimately counter-productive processes of distraint. Fundamentally, Henry was up against a problem of consent to his policies, expressed not so much in the will of parliament (which was as yet in no sense an institution) as in the reluctance of the shire knights and barons to co-operate with the king's requests. This fact was brought home to Henry by the minimal response from his tenants-in-chief when he summoned them to meet him at Winchester on 27 April, armed and ready to accompany him to Poitou.[141] Henry responded to this poor showing by ordering distraint, and also by launching an inquest into the total knight service owed him by his English tenants-in-chief.[142] This latter order proved entirely unenforceable, despite several attempts by the regency government to do so.[143] Those who had opposed the expedition in the first place were unlikely to be softened in their opposition by so threatening an inquest, while those who had supported the expedition thought the inquest a poor reward for their labours. Henry was eventually compelled to abandon it.[144] Efforts to distrain those individuals who held £20 of land or more to become knights were similarly unavailing, although this order did produce a small income for the king from the sale of writs of respite or exemption from it.[145]

Despite such opposition, however, Henry did have some success in

[140] Changes in the laws of distraint and replevin during the thirteenth century may have contributed to the increasing ineffectiveness of shrieval distraint. Paul Brand's promised book on the law of replevin should clarify many points; in the meantime see for some suggestions T. F. T. Plucknett, *Legislation of Edward I* (Oxford, 1970), 55–8.

[141] *Cl.R.* 1237–42, 431, 435.

[142] Ibid., 486; *Book of Fees*, vol. ii, 637–652; for the extant returns to these inquests, see ibid., ii, 654–1130.

[143] Mitchell, *Studies*, 233–4.

[144] Memoranda Roll 27 Henry III (E. 368/14 rot. 6d), cited in Mitchell, *Studies*, 234 n. 44.

[145] M. R. Powicke, *Military Obligation in Medieval England*, (Oxford, 1962), 73–4.

recruiting his greatest tenants-in-chief to his banner.[146] The earls of
Cornwall, Leicester, Essex and Hereford, Pembroke, Devon, and
Norfolk all served personally, as did Peter of Savoy, styled earl of
Richmond, and William Longsword, claimant to Salisbury. Including their retinues, these earls probably contributed a total of about
fifty knights to the king's forces.[147] Twenty barons also departed with
the king in May, and several others sent their knight service. From the
shire knights, however, Henry drew very little response. Excluding
the forty-three members of his military household, only about twenty
or so identifiable knights sailed with the king to Poitou in May. Among
the approximately 200 persons issued protections to depart with the
king, I have been unable to identify fifty-eight; presuming that most
of these persons were knights or sergeants rather than non-combatant
household servants, and presuming also that for the most part,
members of comital retinues did not appear on this royal protection
list, Henry may have sailed with as many as 200 knights. His forces
were certainly no larger than this, and probably were considerably
smaller.[148]

To the king's military purposes, this force was entirely inadequate.
Less than a month after his arrival in Poitou, Henry sent an urgent
letter back to England, ordering the regents to send him reinforcements
of 200 knights, 100 sergeants, 500 Welsh foot-soldiers, and as much
further money as could be found.[149] For an expedition whose ostensible
purpose was merely to seek amends for breaches of the truce, however,
the force Henry took with him in May was more than adequate. No
one was likely to be fooled by the king's dissembling as to the purposes
of the expedition, least of all King Louis. Henry, however, took the
ploy seriously enough to leave nine of his household knights and a
significant number of his baronial supporters in England during May
and early June. When the truce collapsed, Henry summoned this force

---

[146] The information which follows is derived from the protection lists for Henry's
army in *CPR 1232–47*, 294–7, 336–7; the scutage lists in *Cl.R. 1237–42*, 489–93; and the
scutage roll for the expedition, drawn up in Gascony in late June 1242 (C. 72/6).

[147] This estimate is based on the service these earls did on other military campaigns
between 1217 and 1280, as given in Walker, 'Anglo-Welsh Wars', 54.

[148] Although such fighting clerks as John Mansel are excluded here from the ranks
of the knights, the estimate of 200 knights is still more likely high than low. Among the
persons issued protections, only eight can be positively identified as royal servants, and
only eleven as sergeants. Only by presuming that all of the fifty-eight unidentified persons
were knights can we raise Henry's total force to 200; and this is a very unlikely
presumption. For John Mansel's fighting qualities, see *CM*, vol. iv, 236–7.

[149] *Cl.R. 1237–42*, 496–7.

immediately from England, professing surprise that the truce had been broken by Louis, and noting that he was at present 'insufficiently provided with the good men and most powerful men of our realm of England, on whom we specially rely to fight the king of the French'.[150] In addition, he sent a renewed summons to forty English barons, assuring them that he had not expected the truce to lapse, and imploring them to come with all haste to his assistance, since war had now been declared.[151] Henry probably hoped that once the truce had been broken by Louis, the household knights he had left in England would immediately be able to lead out a large body of baronial reinforcements to the king in Poitou. These hopes were not entirely frustrated. Of the forty barons Henry summoned on 15 June, at least sixteen either served personally or sent their service to Poitou. Unfortunately for Henry, all of the important fighting in the campaign was over before any of this rearguard force could arrive. Even so, however, their numbers were inadequate to have altered the outcome of the expedition.

The existence of the truce continued to plague Henry's campaign even after he arrived in Poitou.[152] Louis had summoned his own army to meet at Chinon on 28 April. He began almost immediately to besiege the Lusignans' castles in central Poitou, having already brought the dominant noble in northern Poitou, Amaury viscount of Thouars, over to his side. Henry did not even arrive in Poitou until 12 May. By 20 May, he had arrived at Pons in the Saintonge, where he waited another five days for Louis to appear to discuss the truce violations Henry alleged against him.[153] Louis did not show up. Only then did Henry summon his Gascon and Poitevin allies to service.[154] Five days later, Henry sent ambassadors to Louis, who were received by the king, but secured no satisfaction.[155] On 8 June, Henry and his council declared the truce at an end, and the king then sent urgent requests to his

---

[150] '... minus sufficienter muniti simus bona gente et potissime gente regni nostri Anglie de qua specialius confidimus ad ipsum [regem Francorum] impugnandum', *Cl.R. 1237–42*, 498.

[151] Ibid., 527–8.

[152] The best account of this campaign is by Charles Bémont, 'La Campagne de Poitou (1242–1243): Taillebourg et Saintes', *Annales du Midi* 5 (1893), 289–314. Details and references can be traced there.

[153] Henry's itinerary while in Gascony has been compiled by Charles Bémont in *Rôles gascons: supplément au tome premier 1254-1255* (Paris, 1896), xxvii–xxviii.

[154] *Cl.R. 1237–42*, 524–7.

[155] Matthew Paris claims that Louis told these messengers he was prepared to return Poitou and Normandy to Henry III, but that King Henry then refused the offer. This is extremely unlikely, but it does at least reflect continuing English interest in Normandy: *CM*, vol. iv, 202–5.

remaining forces in England to come to his assistance.[156] By mid-June, when the scrupulous Henry was finally free to declare war on Louis, the French king had already besieged and taken the Lusignan castles at Montreuil, Beruges, Fontenay-le-Comte, and Vouvent, and Henry's Poitevin allies had already begun to desert his cause.[157] English chroniclers were quick to condemn them for their treachery, but in fact the Poitevin lords had little choice. Faced with the loss of their lands to Louis, they could either submit and hope to retain them from Count Alphonse, or fight on and forfeit them forever. Predictably, few chose the latter alternative; those few that did generally had to make a new life for themselves in England after the war.[158]

King Henry, meanwhile, devoted the rest of June to assembling his army, concluding alliances with the counts of Auvergne and Toulouse and with the emperor, and continuing the discussions the count of Toulouse had initiated with the kings of Aragon and Castile.[159] In mid-June, Henry's chances were still sufficiently promising to bring promises from the count of Auvergne to join his side. In return for the count's promises, Henry agreed to support 100 of the count's knights in service for a year, at wages of a shilling a day, from the moment the count entered the war against Louis.[160] In the end, however, only the count of Toulouse actually joined the hostilities, and his armies did not take the field until autumn, by which time Henry's own campaign was effectively over.[161] In the six weeks Henry delayed at Pons and Saintes, he lost the war to Louis.

Throughout the first weeks of July, Louis's relentless advance continued. Outside the Saintonge, Henry had only two significant Poitevin allies: his father-in-law the count of La Marche and William l'Arceveske lord of Parthenay, whose chief castle Henry garrisoned with a detachment of English troops.[162] Perhaps for this reason, Louis ignored Parthenay, and continued to besiege the Lusignans. The La

---

[156] *Cl.R.* 1237–42, 495–9.

[157] Bémont, 'Le Campagne de Poitou', 294–5.

[158] Guy de Rocheford, lord of Villiers, was one of these. He received a fee of £120 per year in England in exchange for the lands he lost in Henry's service, but it was several years before he received any English lands. Cf. *CPR* 1232–47, 310, 395; *CLR* 1240–5, 229, 237, 275, 300, 326; *Charter Rolls* 1226–57, 323, 329, 363, 390, 411, 462, 473.

[159] Bémont, 'Le Campagne de Poitou', 297 n. 11; see also Cox, *Eagles of Savoy*, 115; *CM*, vol. iv, 204; and *CPR* 1232–47, 308–9.

[160] *CPR* 1232–47, 308.

[161] Bémont, 'Le Campagne de Poitou', 293.

[162] *CPR* 1232–47, 307, 310, 316, 318.

Marche stronghold at Frontenay fell to the French and was destroyed, along with their castles at Villiers, Tonnay-sur-Boutonne, and Matha. Henry remained at Saintes, on the opposite side of the Charente, where a steady stream of dispossessed Poitevin lords joined his camp. Most of the exiles were granted annual fees in compensation for the lands they had lost, but few can have regarded such an exchange as satisfactory on any long term basis.

Henry's only foray north of the Charente was to Taillebourg, where he concluded an alliance with its lord, Geoffrey de Rançon. Taillebourg guarded the most important bridge across the Charente.[163] Strategically, it was the gateway to the Saintonge, and Henry was determined to hold it. Henry's relations with Geoffrey de Rançon had long been ticklish, however, and he may have been reluctant to risk antagonizing Geoffrey by taking command of his castle away from him. Whatever the explanation, when Henry advanced again to Taillebourg to check the advance of the French army, he positioned his army on the left bank of the river, and left Taillebourg itself in Geoffrey's hands to defend. Geoffrey, however, had a long-standing personal quarrel with the count of La Marche, and when Louis IX arrived at Taillebourg, he promptly turned the town, the castle, and the stone bridge over to Louis. Installed now on the right side of the river, opposite Henry III's army, Louis then began a flanking movement, sending a detachment of sergeants to construct a makeshift wooden bridge further down the Charente. Realizing that they were outnumbered and that their only escape route was about to be cut off, Richard of Cornwall disarmed himself, grabbed a pilgrim's staff, and walked across the stone bridge to meet King Louis. Using the personal credit he had gained on his crusade when he freed many of the knights now in Louis's army from imprisonment in Egypt,[164] Richard secured a twenty-four-hour truce from the French. Henry's army, led by the king, then beat a pell-mell retreat back to Saintes, leaving Louis to cross the Charente unopposed. Outside Saintes, a detachment of Louis's foragers clashed with the rearguard of Henry's army in the only direct fighting which occurred between the two forces. The engagement was indecisive; it salvaged a small bit of English pride, but did nothing to slow the speed of Henry's retreat.[165] Once Louis was across the Charente, Henry was in as great

---

[163] For what follows, see Bémont, 'Le Campagne de Poitou', 299–305, who also assesses the sources for this incident.

[164] Denholm-Young, *Richard of Cornwall*, 42–3.

[165] Matthew Paris's account of this retreat is particularly colourful: cf. *CM*, vol. iv, 212–13.

danger of being surrounded at Saintes as he had been at Taillebourg. The English withdrawal therefore continued, from Saintes to Pons, from Pons to the Ridel stronghold at Blaye, and from Blaye finally to Bordeaux. The only remnant of Henry's army which remained in Poitou after the end of July was the garrison assigned to Parthenay, which was now entirely cut off from assistance. When the lord of Parthenay went over to Louis in mid-August, the English garrison withdrew from the castle and made its way through hostile country back to the king at Bordeaux.[166]

By 1 August, English involvement in the military aspects of the campaign was effectively over. Although Henry continued to attempt to resurrect his army, the fighting between August 1242 and April 1243 was largely between the count of Toulouse and Louis IX.[167] In late July, the count of La Marche went over to Louis's side, and on 1 August made his submission, ceding to the king in perpetuity all the lands and castles Louis had captured during the war. This settlement broke the power of the house of Lusignan forever,[168] and with it went any further hopes King Henry might have had of recovering Poitou from the French. Although Henry remained in Gascony a further year, until September 1243, he was thereafter engaged almost entirely in resolving internal Gascon quarrels.[169] In April 1243, a few months after the conclusion of the war between Louis and Count Raymond of Toulouse, Henry signed a new five-year truce with King Louis. Of the thirty-two Poitevin signators to the agreement on Louis's side, half had been English pensioners in 1241-2.[170] For the French the real conquest of Poitou began in 1242;[171] for Henry, 'The Treaty of Paris (1259) would do little more than render legal the de facto situation established by the victory at Saintes.'[172]

The reasons for Henry's defeat in 1242 are fairly clear: he began the

---

[166] CPR 1232-47, 316, 318; CLR 1240-5, 158.

[167] The only major military action on the English side was the blockade and siege of La Rochelle, but this was mostly a Gascon enterprise.

[168] Hajdu, 'Castles, Castellans and ... Poitou', 40-3.

[169] The only extended discussion of Henry's activities in Gascony during these months is in Marsh, English Rule in Gascony, 86-110.

[170] CPR 1232-47, 401-2. This figure excludes the counts of Toulouse and Auvergne, since they were not Poitevins, and does not count among Henry's previous supporters such persons as Benedict of Mortagne-sur-Gironde and Geoffrey de Rançon, whom Henry had wooed with gifts, but to whom he had never paid an annual fee.

[171] Petit-Dutaillis, Louis VIII, 278.

[172] 'Le traité de Paris (1259) ne fera guère que rendre légale la situation de fait établie par la victoire de Saintes.' Bémont, 'Le Campagne de Poitou', 314.

expedition too late, he moved too slowly once he finally arrived in Poitou, and he was constantly outnumbered. Although by July 1242 Henry was probably able to mount an army of between 500 and 1000 knights,[173] his forces were still seriously outnumbered by the feudal levies available to Louis IX. Louis's financial resources were certainly greater than Henry's, but in 1242 this disparity alone was probably not decisive.[174] Louis's great advantage was the enormous number of feudal troops he could muster through the *arrière-ban*. A professional army capable of waging a prolonged campaign could counteract this advantage by outlasting the initial French assault and then counter-attacking, but in 1242 Henry had no such resource at his disposal. His household forces were only the nucleus of such an army. The bulk of his troops were drawn from among the men whose lands were most directly threatened by King Louis's advance into Poitou. Had Henry been able to seize the offensive immediately, he might have turned this fact to his advantage. His troops did, at least, have a great deal to lose if defeated. But once Louis's initial successes had forced Henry onto the defensive, Henry's Poitevin supporters were concerned principally to strike the best individual bargains they could with the victorious French king. Henry himself blamed his defeat on the treachery of Geoffrey de Rançon, Hugh de Lusignan, and Reynold de Pons,[175] but in fact his own military inaction had placed them in an impossible position. The Poitevins, of course, contributed to their own demise by launching the revolt prematurely, thus allowing Louis IX to seize the initiative in the campaign; the Gascons, meanwhile, had never been keen to fight for Poitou in the first place. The siege of La Rochelle caught their fancy,[176] offering a chance to cripple a commercial rival,

---

[173] Beyond the perhaps 150 English knights he brought with him, Henry also summoned 526 Gascon and Poitevin knights to his service on 25 May (*Cl.R. 1237–42*, 524–7). Although this list does not include the count of La Marche's forces, which certainly accompanied Henry to Taillebourg, it is very unlikely that all the knights summoned on 25 May actually served in Henry's army. There is direct evidence for the service of only about half the individuals summoned on 25 May. Judging from the surviving writs for wages, Henry's army was down to perhaps 300 knights between Sept. and Dec. 1242.

[174] Figures for Louis IX's annual income are mostly conjectural. In the Ascension term 1238, he had gross receipts of about £25,000 sterling, excluding the one time payment of Thomas of Savoy's relief for Flanders: cf. Hallam, *Capetian France*, 241. Over three terms, this would suggest a gross annual income of around £75,000 sterling. Henry's expendable revenues (cash receipts plus credits) in an average year were about £33,000, although the proceeds of taxation could raise them substantially: see Ch. 6.

[175] See his letters to the emperor in Sept. 1242 and Jan. 1243: *Cl.R. 1237–42*, 530–2; *CPR 1232–47*, 399.

[176] In planning the revolt, a siege of La Rochelle was one of the few proposals on

but on land their military resistance stiffened only at Blaye, where Gascony's border with Poitou began.

Henry also ran out of money at a very inopportune moment. Between 12 May and mid-July, Henry spent over £22,000 in fees and wages for his army, and in gifts to his supporters.[177] By the time he arrived at Taillebourg to confront King Louis, his coffers were empty and he had begun to borrow from his own supporters.[178] This fact probably increased the growing sense of panic among Henry's Poitevin allies which Louis's military successes had already begun. When Henry retreated from Taillebourg in disarray, barely escaping encirclement and capture, the morale of his army collapsed, and the retreat became a rout which was not arrested until the remnants of the army reached Gascony. Between July and October 1242, Henry borrowed at least 5000 marks sterling, and issued bonds to cover an additional 3700 marks in debts.[179] The 5000 marks which arrived from England in mid-October did not even suffice to pay the king's debts,[180] much less the continuing wages of the king's army, which still numbered at least 250 knights and fifty sergeants, and was probably somewhat larger.[181]

Henry's finances continued in this parlous state until his departure from Gascony a year later. Between October 1242 and September 1243, the king received £20,000 in treasure from England beyond the approximately £35,000 he had brought with him in May 1242.[182] The real financial costs of the expedition were, however, substantially more than £55,000. When Henry finally departed from Gascony, he left behind him unpaid bonds for almost £5000 in loans he had received while overseas.[183] These loans all had to be repaid from the exchequer

---

which the Gascons and the count of La Marche could immediately agree: cf. Delisle, 'Mémoire sur une Lettre Inédite', 527–9.

[177] Wardrobe account (E. 372/88 rot. 14).

[178] Cf. CPR 1232–47, 313–14.

[179] My total, from the records in CPR 1232–47, 313–34.

[180] A fact obvious from the total of his debts as established above, and on which the king himself remarked in notifying the regents that the treasure had arrived: Cl.R. 1237–42, 519.

[181] I have computed this total from the writs for wages which Henry issued to his army while awaiting further funds from England.

[182] 10,000 marks arrived from England in Dec. 1242 (CPR 1232–47, 355; CLR 1240–5, 147, 148, 150); 12,000 marks in Apr. 1243 (CPR 1232–47, 372; CLR 1240–5, 171–2, 178–9); 2000 marks from Ireland in July 1243 (CPR 1232–47, 384); and 6000 marks in late Aug. 1243 (CPR 1232–47, 394). For some reason this final shipment of treasure took more than three months to get from England to Gascony: cf. CLR 1240–5, 180, 181, 187; Cl.R. 1237–42, 101, 102, 104, 110, 111, 38–9.

[183] Wardrobe account (E. 372/88 rot. 14).

during the 1243–4 financial year. In addition, between May 1242 and September 1243, Henry had issued from Gascony writs of liberate (for payments from the exchequer) or of computate (for payments by the keepers of episcopal vacancies) which totalled more than £15,000 beyond his loans. Of this amount, almost £12,000 had been drawn between the end of October 1242 and September 1243; more than £9500 between March 1243 and September.[184] The total cost of the expedition was thus at least £75,000. This sum, however, includes neither the value of the provisions Henry drew in kind from the vacant bishoprics, nor the cost of the pardons on royal debts which Henry granted to his supporters while on campaign. Such pardons alone alienated more than £5000 in potential future revenue.[185] When the value of the provisions is also included, the final cost of the Poitevin campaign to the king must have been at least £80,000. Of this sum, £15,000 was probably still owing when Henry returned to England in 1243. It would appear, therefore, that Henry mortgaged or alienated about half a year's total revenues to pay for the Poitevin campaign. 'Et haec tantum ad regis cesserunt emolumentum.'[186]

None the less, despite these expenditures and pardons, Henry does not seem fatally to have mortgaged his financial future to support the campaign for Poitou. The exchequer was clearly under strain in the autumn of 1243; the king's debts exceeded his revenues to such an extent that the exchequer adopted a policy of paying only half, or in some cases a quarter, of the actual amount specified in Gascon writs of liberate presented to it for payment.[187] The remaining half of these writs was to be paid in the following Easter term. The issue roll for

---

[184] The clerks who kept the Gascon liberate roll for 27 Henry III (printed by Francisque Michel in *Rôles Gascons*, vol. i (Paris, 1885), 220–62 totalled these writs up to 11 Mar. 1243, reporting their sum from the beginning of the regnal year (28 Oct. 1242) and from the king's arrival in Poitou (12 May 1242): cf. ibid., 227. I have accepted these scribal totals up to 11 Mar. Thereafter, I have computed these sums directly from the rolls. Between 11 Mar. and 14 Sept., Henry's liberate writs totalled about £9700; between 12 Aug. (the approximate date on which Henry's final shipment of treasure reached him) and 14 Sept., they totalled about £3700.

[185] Of this sum, more than £2000 went to Simon de Montfort and his wife, by three separate writs: cf. Pipe Roll 27 Henry III (E. 372/87 rot. 14). An additional 2000 marks in prests were pardoned to Peter of Savoy: *CLR 1240–5*, 317.

[186] Matthew Paris's verdict on the Poitevin expenditures: *CM*, vol. iv, 254. Giles, *Matthew Paris*, vol. i, 455 translates: '[And] this was all the benefit the king got.'

[187] *CPR 1232–47*, 407; see also the marginal notations of payment on the issue roll of the lower exchequer for Michaelmas term 1243 (E. 403/5), *passim*, and the enrolments of the writs which authorized these payments on the exchequer liberate roll for the same term (E. 401/17), *passim*.

Easter term 1244 is unfortunately lost, and so we cannot follow the final disposition of these writs, but it appears that most of the king's remaining Gascon debts were resolved by the end of 1244. We do, at least, find little evidence after 1244 of Gascons continuing to present their ageing writs of liberate at the exchequer for payment.[188]

Militarily, the combination of financial and conciliar policies pursued from 1239–42 was a failure. They did not provide Henry with either the men or the money he needed to recover Poitou by force of arms. Financially, however, what is much more significant than the failure of the Poitevin expedition is the resilience of the king's revenues in the two years following the expedition. Despite the further expenses of a Scottish muster and a Welsh campaign, despite the costs of yet another royal marriage and a new building programme at Westminster Abbey, Henry was not critically short of cash in 1244 and 1245. This was in marked contrast to his experience in the early 1230s, when the far less costly Breton expedition nearly bankrupted him, and suggests therefore the relative financial strength of Henry's position in the mid-1240s, a strength for which the 1236–9 reforms deserve some credit. In the chapters which follow, we shall assess this surprising financial strength, and its implications for the history of Henry's reign.

---

[188] A few writs were still coming in during 1245: cf. *CLR 1240–5*, 293; *CPR 1232–47*, 446; but the next surviving issue roll, for Easter term 1246, shows no payments for 1242–3 Gascon debts, which suggests that by this date at least they had all been resolved.

6

Receipts and Expenditure, 1240–1245

Despite the existence of an almost unbroken series of thirteenth-century pipe rolls, estimates of royal revenues throughout the century can only be approximate.[1] Historically, the pipe rolls developed as a record of the sheriffs' yearly account for the financial issues of their shires. Royal receipts not handled by the sheriffs were therefore not likely to appear on the rolls. The great diversification of royal financial resources accomplished under Henry II probably rendered the pipe rolls an even less adequate measure of yearly royal receipts than they had been under Henry I. The emergence of foreign accounts membranes under Richard and John brought some of these new Angevin resources back within the confines of the pipe rolls, albeit not into the shire accounts. These foreign rolls, as we shall henceforth call them, continued as a regular feature of pipe roll accounting throughout the thirteenth century. But even with the addition of these miscellaneous accounts of escheats, custodies, vacancies, and aids, an unknown portion of the king's receipts continued to escape pipe roll accounting. Much of this non-pipe roll income, from fines, forests, forced gifts, and other gratuitous payments 'pro gratia regia', went directly into the king's wardrobe, which had its own separate administrative and accounting tradition.[2] How many of these payments were actually recorded on the household rolls is difficult to say, as very few such rolls survive from before the reign of Henry III. Even if these rolls had survived, however, the absence of comparable financial records from the Angevin territories in France would render any effort to estimate the total financial resources of these monarchs a hazardous enterprise.[3]

With respect to the reign of Henry III, the prospects for estimating

---

[1] Sir James H. Ramsay, *A History of the Revenues of the Kings of England, 1066–1399*, 2 vols. (Oxford, 1925) was a pioneering attempt, which foundered on an insufficient acquaintance with the records: see the review by Mabel H. Mills in *EHR* 41 (1926), 429–31. It is fair to add that there are now a great many more records in print than when Ramsay wrote.

[2] *Foreign Accounts Henry III*, v.

[3] See Ch. 5 n. 1 above.

royal revenues are somewhat better. As we have seen, Gascony was a continuing financial drain on the king; for all intents and purposes, Henry's positive income after 1224 was limited to England and Ireland. The Irish accounts unfortunately perished in the early part of the present century, but through the wardrobe accounts and the English chancery records, we can accurately trace all shipments of treasure from Ireland to Henry between 1240 and 1245. Our computations of net revenues can therefore be limited to the king's English resources. Even here the pipe rolls are not a complete account of the king's receipts, although there are signs that from 1235, some at least of Henry's councillors and exchequer barons thought that perhaps they should be. Aside from an anomalous gap between February 1240 and October 1241, the pipe rolls preserve a continuous series of enrolled wardrobe accounts from 1234 until 1252, which record, in surprising detail, all the wardrobe's receipts from the exchequer or from other sources. However, except in 1241–2, when extraordinary taxation swelled wardrobe receipts unaccounted on the pipe rolls to more than £5000, the wardrobe received on average less than £500 per year between 1241 and 1245 which had not first passed through the exchequer and the treasury.[4] And while it remains possible that the king might personally have collected some further payments of fines or amercements which were never enrolled on the wardrobe accounts, it is unlikely that any large sum of money would have been handled in this way. Persons making such payments would usually have wanted a record of the payment entered on the wardrobe rolls as a kind of receipt. Similarly, the wardrobe clerks themselves appear to have been particularly anxious during these years to ensure that their records were as complete as possible, entering even the smallest receipts which passed through the king's hands on their rolls. It appears, therefore, that between the pipe and the wardrobe rolls, we have a reasonably complete record of the king's receipts during these years.

Some accounts, of course, continued to be left off both the pipe and the wardrobe rolls. The records of Jewish tallages were kept separately at the exchequer, as were the accounts for the thirtieth of 1237, although we do have an unofficial record of its final proceeds.[5] Between 1238 and 1240 we are also missing the patent rolls, as well as the foreign roll on which Walter de Burgo accounted for his final two

---

[4] See Table 6.5 and also Pipe Roll 28 Henry III (E. 372/88 rot. 14).
[5] *Red Book*, vol. iii, 1064.

years' custody of the southern demesne manors. These losses make it virtually impossible to calculate Henry's probable annual income between 1236 and 1240. Between 1240 and 1245, however, our records for such extraordinary revenues are substantially complete. Until 1244, we have accurate figures for the king's receipts from Jewish taxation. Thereafter, however, we must guess, because there are almost no known records of receipt from the 60,000 mark tallage of 1244–50.[6] With respect to other tax records, only the account for the 1242 Gascon scutage is missing, but its returns can be estimated with reasonable accuracy.[7] Records from the 1245 aid to marry the king's daughter, and from the 1245–6 scutage of Gannoc, are both enrolled complete on the pipe rolls. The dissolution of Walter de Burgo's custodial experiment in 1240 returned the royal demesne manors in the south to the regular shire accounts on the pipe rolls, where their receipts can be easily traced. Although Robert de Crepping continued to hold some of the northern manors in custody between 1240 and 1245, his accounts are complete on the foreign rolls. Only Warner Engayne's account for the few manors which remained in his possession after 1238 is missing, and his net receipts per year are unlikely to have reached £100. In estimating the king's annual receipts, they can therefore be discounted.

There are also very few signs during these years of Henry antici-pating his income by assigning the collection of specified revenues directly to his various debtors.[8] Henry could, and frequently did, order persons who owed him money to pay the sums they owed directly to a named third party, but such payments were always allowed to the original accountant on the pipe rolls by writs of allocate.[9] Otherwise, the only royal resource for which I have not been able to find a regular account rendered either at the exchequer or in the wardrobe was for the town of Stamford in Lincolnshire, which Henry held after 1240 in custody as part of the Earl Warenne estate. Henry granted custody of the rest of the earldom's lands to the countess at farm, but appears to have retained Stamford in his own hands, although in 1240 he did

[6] References on the chancery rolls give only vague hints as to the king's receipts from this tallage: cf. *CLR 1240–5*, 206, 209, 239, 256; *CPR 1232–47*, 445.

[7] See Ch. 5, above.

[8] This was done frequently with the issues from ecclesiastical vacancies during the 1250s, but not before: cf. Margaret Howell, *Regalian Right in Medieval England* (London, 1962), 154–9.

[9] Writs of allocate could be issued to the exchequer barons for any account for which they were responsible, including payments toward Jewish tallages. Their use was not restricted to pipe roll accounting.

contemplate granting the town at farm to its men for £239 per year.[10] Very few of its issues reached the king in cash; for the most part, Henry preferred to assign its issues either to pay the fees of his household knights, or to repay merchants for goods purchased from them for the king's use.[11] Otherwise, I can find no evidence during these years of any 'chamber manors', the issues from which were paid directly to the king without appearing on the pipe or foreign rolls.[12]

The most significant potential distortions which might result from using the pipe rolls to estimate Henry's yearly receipts lie in the relationship between the receipts accounted on the pipe roll, and the cash payments actually made into the lower exchequer as these are recorded on the receipt rolls. Sheriffs and the king's other accountants were expected to appear at the exchequer twice a year to make payments against their debts. The financial year ran from Michaelmas to Michaelmas; at Easter the sheriff made a partial payment towards the current year's debts (known as the proffer), and at Michaelmas, at the end of the financial year, he returned to the exchequer to pay the remainder of his debts for the year just ended (the adventus). In fact, by 1240 the lower exchequer was open almost the entire year, and while receipts did peak around Michaelmas and Easter, money came in fairly steadily throughout the year.[13] The upper exchequer also worked throughout the year, auditing the shire accounts. Thus, although the payments from a particular shire for 25 Henry III (1240–1) were theoretically due at the lower exchequer by Michaelmas 1241, the upper exchequer might not be able to audit the sheriff's account for 25 Henry III until as late as Easter 26 Henry III, by which date the sheriff should already have made his proffer for the debts which would be audited after Michaelmas 1242. Lacking a complete series of receipt rolls, it is thus impossible to distinguish cash payments made towards

[10] For the grant to the Countess Warenne, see *Pipe Roll 26 Henry III*, ed. Cannon, 210; for the proposed farm of Stamford, see Fine Roll 25 Henry III (C. 60/37 m. 15). Contrary to the claim on the fine roll, the grant to the men of Stamford was never enrolled on the patent rolls, nor was it entered on the originalia roll: cf. E. 371/8A m. 2. The farm is exceptionally high, and may even be a clerical error, but since the fine roll is the only enrolment, this cannot be checked. It is evident, however, that the grant never took effect.

[11] In 1245, 130 marks from Stamford's issues were paid into the wardrobe (E. 372/88 rot. 14; *CLR 1240–5*, 296). Otherwise, its issues were assigned to repay the king's debts: cf. for example *CLR 1240–5*, 226, 254, 296.

[12] Excepting, of course, the queen's lands, the value of which has not been included in the calculations which follow.

[13] See my introduction to *Receipt and Issue Rolls, 26 Henry III*, PRS, forthcoming.

the 1241–2 account from those made to clear the 1240–1 account. Nor was it important to the upper exchequer to do so. The exchequer barons audited each sheriff's account by comparing the summonses they had issued with the exchequer tallies he presented. Debts which had not been cleared were transferred to the following year's roll, and summoned again. If the sheriff presented a tally to clear the account, it was of no importance to the upper exchequer when that payment had been made. It was thus possible for a debt to have been paid into the lower exchequer several years before the sheriff finally presented his tally at the upper exchequer and had the debt cleared from his account. One cannot therefore be sure that the pattern of receipts revealed on the pipe rolls between 1240 and 1245 reflects the actual rise and fall of the king's supply of expendable cash as received into the lower exchequer. It could reflect merely the sheriffs' convenience in presenting their tallies for audit.

On the whole, however, it appears that variations in the pipe roll receipts from year to year do in fact reflect variations in the king's annual cash revenues. Revenues from the general eyres were always paid promptly into the exchequer; indeed, the speed with which judicial receipts came into the king's hands was one of the great advantages of this kind of revenue. In times of financial strain, as in the preparations for the 1245 Welsh campaign, Henry might also order his sheriffs and the men of his demesne manors to pay their farms directly into his wardrobe, issuing writs of allocate to the exchequer barons in their name. In this way, the king did have some control over the timing of his receipts. Moreover, receipts into the lower exchequer during 1241–2 (the only year for which both terms' receipt rolls survive) correspond almost exactly with the cash receipts for the year as computed from the pipe roll for 26 Henry III.[14] It should also be noted that except in 1241–2, the variations in the king's yearly receipts on the pipe rolls are not particularly large, never exceeding £5000 on total yearly receipts of around £33,000 in cash and credits. If anything, then, the pipe roll records may tend to disguise the extent to which Henry's expendable cash varied from year to year. They certainly do not seem to have magnified such variations.

[14] The receipt roll totals for the year, excluding receipts from the 20,000 mark tallage, amounted to about £27,400. The pipe roll receipts for the year, excluding direct wardrobe receipts and shipments of Irish treasure (neither of which would have passed through the lower exchequer, and which would therefore not appear on the receipt rolls) amount to about £28,250. The two sums vary by only 3 per cent.

In calculating the king's total revenues, one must also remember that the king spent a certain portion of his pipe roll income every year before it reached the lower exchequer, through writs sent directly to the local receivers of these funds. Such expenditures are listed in the revenue tables below as 'credits', in so far as they were expended sums credited against the total receipts for which each accountant responded on the pipe roll. Credits could thus be allowed against various categories of royal income. Because the sheriffs were the most frequent recipients of orders to expend cash, most of these expenditures were credited against the shire farms and profits. But it was entirely up to each accountant to decide the debts against which he wished his credit to be entered. Expenditures could be credited against judicial revenues or any other receipts which the sheriff had handled during the year. The percentages in Table 6.1 therefore do not accurately reflect the proportional importance of the resources from which the king derived his total gross income. Rather, they reflect the proportional importance of Henry's various resources to his cash income as it reached the lower exchequer.

TABLE 6.1   *Percentage contribution to total cash receipts*

	1240–1	1241–2	1242–3	1243–4	1244–5
Shire issues	6.0	3.8	7.9	3.9	6.6
Demesne issues	17.2	14.0	19.5	17.4	25.3
Debts and prests	7.3	5.6	8.6	6.1	6.4
Jews	10.5	22.8	1.1	12.7	10.8
Custodies and seisins	9.0	12.2	19.4	15.7	15.0
Vacancies	23.6	10.0	22.3	22.7	2.2
Judicial issues	20.0	9.9	7.9	9.7	19.7
Taxation	2.0	15.9	2.6	0.6	8.7
Mint issues	2.2	1.4	4.3	4.7	3.8
Irish treasure	2.2	3.6	5.0	6.3	1.5
Other issues	—	0.8	1.4	0.2	—
	100.0	100.0	100.0	100.0	100.0

If we except 1241–2, when taxation of both Christians and Jews swelled Henry's income by more than £17,000, Henry's cash revenues averaged about £28,000 per year between 1240 and 1245.[15] If we

[15] Hereafter, unless otherwise noted, all figures cited in the text can be verified from Tables 6.1–6.6. Shire-by-shire analyses of receipts from each of the categories of revenue on Tables 6.1 and 6.2 (shire farms, royal demesne, justice, etc) are presented in Tables 6.7–6.14 at the end of the chapter.

include the sums disbursed locally at the king's command, his total expendable income[16] during these years averaged about £33,000 annually, a sum substantially higher than the estimate of about £25,000 per year which scholars, following Ramsay, have been forced to use for lack of any more accurate measure.[17] Neither figure includes the approximately £5500 which was paid out annually from the shire farms in fixed alms, fees, and wages, and in allowances for *terris datis*. Taxation, of course, could increase royal receipts considerably, and in 1241–2, the year of Henry's Gascon campaign, his cash revenues climbed to more than £45,000, and his total expendable income to more than £50,000. Otherwise, however, the king's total receipts are surprisingly regular, despite great fluctuations in almost all the component parts of those receipts. Except in 1241–2, Henry's gross yearly receipts did not vary more than about £5000 between 1240 and 1245, for an average yearly fluctuation of about 15 per cent. This is particularly surprising in view of the enormous yearly fluctuations which characterized almost all of the component categories of this income. Between 1240 and 1245, there is not a single royal resource the yield from which did not fluctuate by at least 33 per cent between 1240 and 1245. Most fluctuations were of the order of 50 per cent. That the king's net receipts should have remained relatively constant in the face of such wide variations in their constituent parts suggests that while the royal revenues may have been acutely sensitive to exchequer pressure, such pressure could not be applied everywhere at once. When the exchequer intensified its efforts to collect one type of royal revenue, receipts from that source went up, but at the expense of another resource, the receipts from which would tend to decline. Clearly this explanation will not suit all the king's resources: the issues of the mint, for example, fluctuated directly with the volume of foreign exchange which passed through it. But fluctuations in the issues of the royal demesne and from the collection of old debts and prests between 1240 and 1245 probably do reflect the relative intensity of exchequer efforts to collect them.

In gross, the shire farms, profits, and increments produced about

[16] I use the term 'expendable income' to refer to the total of Henry's receipts excluding the value of fixed credits assigned for yearly payment against the shire farms: see Table 6.2.

[17] Meekings, *1235 Surrey Eyre*, vol. i, 135–6; Maddicott, 'Magna Carta and the Local Community', 47. Powicke, *Thirteenth Century*, 36, appears to have estimated Henry's annual income at more than £30,000, but gives no indication as to how he arrived at this figure.

TABLE 6.2 *Total receipts*

	1240–1	1241–2	1242–3	1243–4	1244–5
Cash					
Shire issues	£ 1,839 17s. 0d.	£ 1,768 13s. 0d.	£ 2,125 10s. 0d.	£ 1,040 2s. 0d.	£ 1,792 15s. 0d.
Demesne issues	£ 5,228 11s. 0d.	£ 6,451 2s. 0d.	£ 5,251 8s. 0d.	£ 4,618 18s. 0d.	£ 6,907 15s. 0d.
Debts and prests	£ 2,212 3s. 0d.	£ 2,610 15s. 0d.	£ 2,310 12s. 0d.	£ 1,613 13s. 0d.	£ 1,753 9s. 0d.
Jews	£ 3,193 1s. 0d.	£ 10,527 11s. 0d.	£ 306 18s. 0d.	£ 3,378 2s. 0d.	£ 2,953 8s. 0d.
Custodies and seisins	£ 2,758 15s. 0d.	£ 5,648 0s. 0d.	£ 5,222 14s. 0d.	£ 4,177 16s. 0d.	£ 4,111 0s. 0d.
Vacancies	£ 7,196 0s. 0d.	£ 4,635 0s. 0d.	£ 5,982 0s. 0d.	£ 6,017 0s. 0d.	£ 601 0s. 0d.
Judicial issues	£ 6,083 12s. 0d.	£ 4,574 18s. 0d.	£ 2,128 13s. 0d.	£ 2,563 16s. 0d.	£ 5,376 1s. 0d.
Taxation	£ 609 13s. 0d.	£ 7,341 11s. 0d.	£ 695 2s. 0d.	£ 147 15s. 0d.	£ 2,387 7s. 0d.
Mint issues	£ 665 0s. 0d.	£ 640 0s. 0d.	£ 1,163 10s. 0d.	£ 1,255 0s. 0d.	£ 1,044 0s. 0d.
Irish treasure	£ 666 13s. 0d.	£ 1,666 13s. 0d.	£ 1,333 7s. 0d.	£ 1,666 13s. 0d.	£ 397 10s. 0d.
Other issues	—	£ 378 3s. 0d.	£ 367 14s. 0d.	£ 56 15s. 0d.	—
	£30,453 5s. 0d.	£46,242 6s. 0d.	£26,886 18s. 0d.	£26,535 10s. 0d.	£27,324 5s. 0d.
Credits[a]					
	£ 4,182 13s. 0d.	£ 5,115 11s. 0d.	£ 3,535 10s. 0d.	£ 5,004 2s. 0d.	£ 6,960 18s. 0d.
Total expendable income	£34,635 18s. 0d.	£51,357 17s. 0d.	£30,422 8s. 0d.	£31,539 12s. 0d.	£34,285 3s. 0d.
Fixed credits in corpus comitatuum					
	£ 5,488 6s. 0d.	£ 5,700 12s. 0d.	£ 5,667 10s. 0d.	£ 5,651 6s. 0d.	£ 5,624 14s. 0d.
Total notional income	£40,124 4s. 0d.	£57,058 9s. 0d.	£36,089 18s. 0d.	£37,190 18s. 0d.	£39,909 17s. 0d.

[a] Excluding fixed credits made out of the body of the shire.

TABLE 6.3 *Total credits*

	1240–1	1241–2	1242–3	1243–4	1244–5
Credited expenditures outside corpus					
Fees, wages and gifts to laymen outside corpus	£1,368 18s. 10d.	£1,110 3s. 4d.	£1,316 7s. 0½d.	£1,463 12s. 0½d.	£2,432 18s. 11½d.
Alms, wages and gifts to clerics outside corpus	£508 0s. 0d.	£570 17s. 9½d.	£483 1s. 6½d.	£732 2s. 10½d.	£620 16s. 1½d.
Construction and maintenance on houses, castles	£1,574 3s. 0½d.	£1,331 10s. 6½d.	£865 2s. 0d.	£1,177 18s. 3½d.	£1,776 6s. 5½d.
Castle garrisons, munitioning and costs of war	£164 8s. 3d.	£1,644 16s. 6½d.	£351 7s. 6d.	£1,136 4s. 9d.	£1,214 12s. 0d.
Provisioning of royal household	£482 16s. 8½d.	£296 4s. 8½d.	£341 16s. 7d.	£358 8s. 11½d.	£521 7s. 2d.
Administrative costs	£84 5s. 10½d.	£161 17s. 7½d.	£177 14s. 11½d.	£135 15s. 1½d.	£197 12s. 7½d.
Royal land purchases	—	—	—	—	£197 3s. 4d.
Total expenditures outside corpus	£4,182 12s. 8½d.	£5,717 10s. 6½d.	£3,535 9s. 7½d.	£5,004 2s. 0½d.	£6,960 17s. 8d.
Fixed credits in corpus comitatuum					
Laymen	£3,977 8s. 10d.	£4,184 16s. 1½d.	£4,157 19s. 3½d.	£4,125 12s. 3½d.	£4,095 2s. 11d.
Clerics	£1,404 9s. 6d.	£1,409 7s. 10d.	£1,403 2s. 10d.	£1,419 5s. 4d.	£1,421 2s. 10d.
Total	£5,381 18s. 4d.	£5,594 3s. 11½d.	£5,561 2s. 1½d.	£5,544 17s. 7½d.	£5,516 5s. 9d.
Pardons on pipe rolls					
Pardons to laymen	£588 7s. 5d.	£1,251 7s. 5d.	£3,873 6s. 7d.	£580 9s. 4½d.	£451 8s. 6d.
Pardons to clerics	£6 13s. 4d.	£86 13s. 4d.	£134 5s. 0d.	£67 18s. 10d.	£27 8s. 0d.
Total pardons	£595 0s. 9d.	£1,338 0s. 9d.	£4,007 11s. 7d.	£648 8s. 2½d.	£478 16s. 6d.

TABLE 6.4 Total cash receipts

	1240–1	1241–2	1242–3	1243–4	1244–5
Pipe roll shire accounts					
Shire farm, profits and increments	£ 1,839 17s. 0d.	£ 1,768 13s. 0d.	£ 2,125 10s. 0d.	£ 1,040 2s. 0d.	£ 1,766 2s. 0d.
Demesne issues	£ 4,518 11s. 0d.	£ 5,846 2s. 0d.	£ 4,530 19s. 0d.	£ 4,147 18s. 0d.	£ 6,299 8s. 0d.
Debts and prests	£ 2,212 3s. 0d.	£ 2,610 15s. 0d.	£ 2,310 12s. 0d.	£ 1,613 13s. 0d.	£ 1,753 9s. 0d.
Debita Judeorum	£ 193 1s. 0d.	£ 527 11s. 0d.	£ 306 18s. 0d.	£ 99 0s. 0d.	£ 286 15s. 0d.
Custodies, wards, reliefs and seisins	£ 1,202 15s. 0d.	£ 3,583 0s. 0d.	£ 3,697 14s. 0d.	£ 3,078 16s. 0d.	£ 2,497 7s. 0d.
Judicial revenues	£ 6,083 12s. 0d.	£ 4,574 18s. 0d.	£ 2,128 13s. 0d.	£ 2,563 16s. 0d.	£ 5,376 1s. 0d.
Taxation and fines for service	£ 609 13s. 0d.	£ 2,461 11s. 0d.	£ 550 13s. 0d.	£ 147 15s. 0d.	£ 2,351 10s. 0d.
War booty	—	£ 20 0s. 0d.	£ 327 14s. 0d.	£ 43 16s. 0d.	—
Total	£16,659 12s. 0d.	£21,392 10s. 0d.	£15,978 13s. 0d.	£12,734 16s. 0d.	£20,330 12s. 0d.
Pipe roll foreign accounts					
Demesne issues	£ 710 0s. 0d.	£ 605 0s. 0d.	£ 485 0s. 0d.	£ 471 0s. 0d.	£ 595 0s. 0d.
Custodies and seisins	£ 1,556 0s. 0d.	£ 2,065 0s. 0d.	£ 1,525 0s. 0d.	£ 1,099 0s. 0d.	£ 1,527 0s. 0d.
Vacancies	£ 7,196 0s. 0d.	£ 4,635 0s. 0d.	£ 5,982 0s. 0d.	£ 6,017 0s. 0d.	£ 601 0s. 0d.
Mint issues	£ 665 0s. 0d.	£ 640 0s. 0d.	£ 1,163 0s. 0d.	£ 1,255 0s. 0d.	£ 1,044 0s. 0d.
Total	£10,127 0s. 0d.	£ 7,945 0s. 0d.	£ 9,155 0s. 0d.	£ 8,832 0s. 0d.	£ 3,767 0s. 0d.
Wardrobe receipts not accounted above	no account	£ 5,238 3s. 0d.	£ 419 18s. 0d.	£ 635 7s. 0d.	£ 162 10s. 0d.
Irish treasure received	£ 666 13s. 4d.	£ 1,666 13s. 4d.	£ 1,333 6s. 8d.	£ 1,666 13s. 4d.	£ 397 10s. 6d.
Jewish taxation	£ 3,000 0s. 0d.	£10,000 0s. 0d.	—	£ 2,666 13s. 4d.	£ 2,666 13s. 4d.

£3000 per year in expendable revenues for the king. In cash, Henry's annual receipts from this resource were never more than about £2000 per year, and between 1240 and 1245 they were sometimes as low as £1000.[18] For the most part, this discrepancy reflects the expenditures made by the sheriffs at the king's command out of the shire issues, which were then credited to them by writ. In fact, shire issues were the most regularly accounted of all the king's revenues. On average, no more than about £500 in shire issues remained owing on any single year's account from all the sheriffs combined. In the rare instances where one does find a sheriff running up a large debt at the exchequer, this is usually a sign that he had a large construction project under way, for which he had not yet submitted his tallies.[19] Indeed the dependability with which shire issues could be collected may have been one reason why the king's council raised the shire profits so relentlessly during the 1250s.

Demesne issues on average produced about 20 per cent of the king's total cash income during these years. Most of the revenue came from the farms of the royal demesne manors and boroughs, with forest issues making only a minor contribution to the receipts.[20] In 1244 and 1245, however, the royal council set out deliberately to increase the king's forest receipts, ordering the newly appointed justices of the forest to take in hand all unlicensed assarts and purprestures, and appointing Geoffrey de Langley to administer these confiscated lands to the king's profit.[21] The sums which could be raised from fines and rents for assarted lands were as nothing, however, in comparison to the amercements which could be imposed upon the nobility for forest offences, especially for taking venison without licence. The success of the 1244–5 forest justices in imposing such amercements is reflected in the chroniclers' accounts of the unparalleled harshness of this eyre,

[18] In addition to Tables 6.4 and 6.5, see also Tables 6.7 and 6.8 at the end of the chapter for a shire-by-shire analysis of these figures.

[19] The only exception to this between 1240 and 1245 was Nicholas de Haversham, sheriff of Wiltshire from 1240 until 1246, who owed almost £400 in debts by the end of 1245: Pipe Roll 29 Henry III (E. 372/89 rot. 5). His shire profits were set at an unrealistically high level: cf. above, p. 63 and n. 67.

[20] Issues from timber sales out of the royal forests did not usually appear on the pipe rolls, however. Probably they were paid directly into the wardrobe, although no such sales appear on the surviving wardrobe accounts between 1235 and 1245.

[21] *CPR 1232–47*, 427, 442, 459, 462. On Geoffrey de Langley, see P. R. Coss, 'Sir Geoffrey de Langley and the Crisis of the Knightly Class in Thirteenth-Century England', *Past and Present* 68 (1975), 3–37.

TABLE 6.5   *Direct cash receipts into wardrobe not already*
accounted on the pipe rolls

1240–1

---

no account

1241–2

£1912 6s. 8d.	Aid of the Prelates
£1127 0s. 0d.	Fines *pro passagio*, plus other fines and amercements
£1840 13s. 4d.	Various gifts
£ 238 19s. 5½d.	Issues of the Great Seal
£ 119 3s. 6d.	Perquisites of the marshalcy and of mariners
£5238 2s. 11½d.	

1242–3

£ 11 3s. 3d.	Customary payment for hospitality, La Réole
£ 215 8s. 8d.	Focage of Gascony
£ 44 8s. 11d.	Customary payments, Bordeaux
£ 17 15s. 7d.	Issues of Oléron
£ 2 4s. 6d.	Other Gascon issues
£ 26 11s. 0d.	Perquisites of marshalcy
£ 2 7s. 4½d.	Profits from exchanging money
£ 100 0s. 0d.	Customary payment by Londoners to king on his return from overseas
£ 419 18s. 3½d.	

1243–4

£ 127 12s. 0d.	Chattels of Leo of York, Jew
£ 318 3s. 0d.	Chattels of David of Oxford, Jew
£ 166 13s. 4d.	Aaron of York, on 60,000 mark Jewish tallage
£ 10 0s. 0d.	Bardney Abbey vacancy
£ 6 5s. 6d.	Royal hospitality at Mortlake, by elect of Canterbury
£ 6 13s. 4d.	Royal hospitality at Mortlake, by prior of Thetford
£ 635 7s. 2d.	

1244–5

£ 13 6s. 8d.	Sheriff of Cambridgeshire
£ 13 6s. 8d.	Sheriff of Essex
£ 86 13s. 4d.	Issues of Stamford fair (Warenne custody)
£ 13 6s. 8d.	Farm of Plympton (Devon custody)
£ 2 10s. 0d.	Aid to marry daughter, from abbot of Bristol
£ 33 6s. 8d.	Aid to marry daughter, from prior of Winchester
£ 162 10s. 0d.	

and also in the noticeable rise in demesne issues between 1243–4 and 1244–5 evident in Table 6.4.[22]

The king's judicial revenues were almost entirely dependent upon the operation of the general eyre. Even in years when no eyre was in progress, the great bulk of judicial receipts came from the collection of amercements imposed by the preceding eyre. It is perhaps not surprising that Bench and *coram rege* issues should have been low during 1240 and 1241, while the eyre was in progress, since during much of this time the Bench was not in session. But even in 1242–3, when no eyre was in progress and when the king was out of the country, newly entered Bench amercements produced only about £300 in total issues, a yield comparable to that from Robert de Lexinton's and William of York's novel disseisin circuits through Lincolnshire, Kent, Northamptonshire, Essex, and Hertfordshire in the same year. Directly or indirectly, most of the remaining £1500 in judicial receipts for the year arose from eyre amercements.

This extraordinary financial dependence upon the eyre is reflected in the council's 1245 decision to send the eyre justices around again to the four shires (Norfolk and Suffolk, Lincolnshire, and Yorkshire) from which the king derived the largest judicial revenues. Until 1245, these counties had been visited only as part of the programme of a general eyre; but between 1245 and 1248, hardly a year went by in which the eyre justices did not visit at least a few shires.[23] This altered pattern in part reflects the demand for justice in the shires; it was not merely a royal scheme to increase receipts. None the less, this change did ultimately produce a good deal of popular resentment against the eyres, which in 1258 gave rise to a renewed insistence on enforcing an alleged custom of the realm that forbade the eyre justices to visit a county more than once every seven years.[24]

In considering such resentments, however, it is important to keep in mind that not all the proceeds of an eyre were directly judicial. Every shire the justices visited was traditionally assessed a common fine of 50 to 100 marks, and many local bailiwicks paid similar,

[22] CM, vol. iv, 400, 426–7; Young, *Royal Forests*, 77.

[23] David Crook, *Records of the General Eyre*, PRO Handbooks no. 20 (London, 1982), 105 and *passim*.

[24] Treharne, *Baronial Plan of Reform*, 398–406 presents a detailed consideration of the evidence for such a custom. His conclusions, however, will need to be rethought in the light of Crook's revised listing of the eyre visitations and their dates.

smaller fines, before any strictly judicial judgements were delivered.[25] In essence, such fines were a form of taxation; they were assessed on all the suitors of the court concerned (shire, borough, or hundred),[26] and until 1245 seem generally to have been promptly paid. Although it is possible that the size of these fines was increasing after 1245,[27] the speed with which they were paid until that date suggests that the men of the shires had not found them too oppressive. Thereafter, however, as the eyre visitations and their attendant common fines became more frequent, and as the eyre justices extended the incidence of *murdrum* fines to cases of accidental as well as felonious death,[28] Henry's subjects did come to see the eyre as yet another royal money-making scheme. This, however, is a development which was only beginning in 1245. Like so many of the king's offensive financial policies, it did not become seriously oppressive until the 1250s.

It is not always easy to distinguish judicial issues from other types of debts and fines recorded on the pipe rolls. For the most part, however, in compiling the tables presented here I have tended to treat doubtful issues as judicial payments. Except in the rare cases where serious distortions would result, I have therefore classified as judicial issues all lump sum payments made by the sheriffs which cleared a number of previously enrolled debts with a single payment. The constituent debts which made up this final sum would be marked on the preceding pipe roll with a 't' in the left-hand margin, but such debts were not re-enrolled individually when they were paid and cleared in this manner.[29] The majority of these individual debts were

[25] Meekings, *1235 Surrey Eyre*, vol. i, 136–9 has an excellent discussion of these common fines. The level of these fines in the 1239–41 eyre shows no increase over the 1234–6 assessments; in several counties they were somewhat lower. In no county, however, do the fines vary by more than 25 marks from their 1234–6 level.

[26] This fact may be one reason why, especially after 1245, so many persons sought exemption from doing suit of court. Such exemptions are not uncommon before that date, but they became much more common between 1245 and 1258, finally producing the situation complained of in clause 28 of the 1258 *Petitio Baronum*: Treharne and Sanders, *Documents of the Baronial Movement*, 88–9.

[27] Norfolk, which had paid a common fine of 60 marks in the 1234–6 and 1239–41 eyres, paid 160 marks in 1245; Suffolk, which previously had paid 30 marks, paid 60 marks in 1245: cf. Pipe Roll 29 Henry III (E. 372/89 rot. 2d)

[28] Paul A. Brand, 'The Contribution of the Period of Baronial Reform (1258–1267) to the Development of the Common Law in England', (unpublished Oxford University D. Phil. thesis, 1974), 246–59; Maddicott, 'Magna Carta and the Local Community', 47. I am grateful to Dr Brand for permission to use his thesis.

[29] For discussion of this method of clearing a number of pipe roll debts by a single payment, see C. A. F. Meekings, 'The Pipe Roll Order of 12 February 1270', in *Studies Presented to Sir Hilary Jenkinson*, ed. J. Conway Davies (Oxford, 1957), 222–53,

in fact judicial, but due to the deterioration of some of the pipe roll margins, it is not always possible to determine all the individual amercements, debts, and fines which composed these lump sum payments.

This method of treating lump sum shrieval payments will also compensate to some extent for the judicial issues which lie concealed in the rather arbitrary category of 'debts and prests'. Prests were loans which the king had made at some previous date, and which the recipients were now paying back, either by instalments or, more rarely, in a single payment. Strictly speaking, they were not new income, but they did contribute to the king's supply of expendable cash in any given year, and so I have chosen to treat them as part of the royal revenues.[30] 'Debts' are not so easily categorized. Principally, these are payments made yearly by an accountant against a variety of different types of debts (judicial amercements, fines, farms, prests) which the exchequer had gathered together into a single sum and attermined for payment, but I have also included in this category payments made against scutage debts which pre-date 1236. Individually, each of the constituent parts of such an attermined debt would thus deserve to be classified with another category of issues; but because these constituent debts cease to be distinguishable after the exchequer combined them into a single sum, I have not distinguished them.

The terms granted to individuals to resolve such combined debts varied enormously, reflecting more or less directly their influence with the king.[31] John fitz Geoffrey, the king's steward, owed more than £600 in debts, which he was paying off at £10 per year.[32] Robert Lupus, the sheriff of Lincolnshire, owed almost £400 in debts, which were attermined for repayment at 100 marks per year.[33] Rarely, however, were the terms of repayment onerous. This is especially true with

reprinted in *Studies in Thirteenth-Century Justice and Administration*. The 't' stood for 'totum reddiderunt'.

[30] Such payments rarely amounted to more than perhaps £500 per year. They certainly did not balance the sums the king loaned out during these years, especially during the Poitevin campaign.

[31] Policy in the 1250s was basically similar, but perhaps even more permissive towards the debts owed by the king's court circle: cf. D. A. Carpenter, 'Kings, Magnates, and Society: The Personal Rule of King Henry III, 1234–1258,' *Speculum* 60 (1985), 52–7.

[32] *Pipe Roll 26 Henry III*, 115; *Cl.R. 1237–42*, 516; Pipe Roll 29 Henry III (E. 372/89 rot. 3d).

[33] Fine Roll 25 Henry III (C. 60/37 m. 16); Pipe Roll 25 Henry III (E. 372/85 rot. 2). The king was clearly angry with Robert, whose debts derived mostly from his tenure as sheriff of Lincolnshire, a position he gained in return for a debt owed to him by King John for his services: cf. Fine Roll 20 Henry III (C. 60/35 m. 16), and above p. 52 n. 28).

respect to the enormous fines which a number of magnates still owed
for agreements they or their ancestors had made with King John. Such
fines had been put in charge and summoned since the earliest days of
the minority, but by the late 1230s (and probably much earlier) most
had been attermined for repayment at less than £1 per year.[34] *Debita
Judeorum* were also repaid on easy terms. The newer Jewish debts
coming into the exchequer tended to be fixed for repayment on terms
of ten years or less,[35] but some of the long-standing debts were being
resolved at the rate of a mark or even a half-mark per year, which
would extend their repayment well into the following century. Most
of these extended terms appear to have been products of the king's
minority. The exchequer was not prepared to give up its claims to
collect these debts, but it could not risk incurring again the kind of
resentment which John's draconian policies towards such debts had
produced. De Burgh's government therefore settled for a compromise
which preserved the king's rights, but which guaranteed that he would
gain little profit from their exercise. By and large, Henry III's Jewish
revenues came through taxation, not through the direct collection of
debita Judeorum. By themselves, Jewish debts produced only about
£300 per year for the king between 1240 and 1245.

It is possible, however, that Henry's apparently mild approach to
collecting Jewish debts may be misleading, at least with respect to the
pressure which such debts could place on the men who owed them.
Some at least of the Jewish debts signed over to the exchequer as a
result of royal taxation were never enrolled on the pipe rolls for
collection, being instead resold to another lender, almost certainly at
a discount.[36] Such purchasing of Jewish debts may have been a major
business for some of Henry's curial officials, who with their court
connections would have been able to secure prompt and effective
distraint on their newly acquired debtors.[37] If so, Henry's own rela-

[34] I have classified all such payments against debts from King John's reign as judicial
issues in the tables, unless specifically designated as being for custodies purchased.

[35] Thomas Gresley's debt to Aaron of York is typical of these newer debts. On 29
Dec. 1243, 20 marks of the 120 mark debt were pardoned, and the remaining 100 marks
attermined at 50 marks per year: Fine Roll 28 Henry III (C. 60/41 m. 10).

[36] See pp. 155–6 above.

[37] It is possible that this situation may lie behind the complaints in 1244 that many
unjust writs had been issued over the king's seal because of the absence of a justiciar
and a chancellor. The nature of these writs was not specified in the 1244 complaints (on
which see below, pp. 247–8), and the recorded chancery writs for the period do not
provide any obvious examples of injustice. Writs for distraint were not recorded on the
chancery rolls, however, although they did go out over the Great Seal.

tively generous approach to collecting such debts may not have saved him from the opprobrium directed at his courtiers.[38] But it is only rarely that we can actually catch the courtiers at their obnoxious work.

Although in theory a debtor who failed to meet the terms set for repayment of such long-standing debts was liable to immediate distraint for their full amount, Henry routinely granted exceptions to this rule, allowing debtors to continue their yearly payments notwithstanding a previous default. The king was also usually prepared to allow a debtor to add new indebtedness to his existing total, without increasing his yearly payments. In practice, therefore, such long-standing debts rarely became important until the debtor died, at which time all his debts fell due to the king, along with possession of his chattels, including stock, ploughs, and standing grain. The right of every magnate to make a will was accepted without cavil by the 1240s,[39] but the king would not release the chattels of the deceased to his executors until the executors had given security to resolve the debts owed by the deceased to the king. Such debts took precedence over all the executors' other testamentary obligations, including debts owed to the Church. If the deceased's chattels were not sufficient to pay off his debts to the king, the remaining debts would be held over on the pipe rolls, to be charged against his heir when he reached his majority. If the deceased left no heirs, his debts would sometimes be assessed against his tenants, at modest terms, or against his pledges, if any could be found. Such debts were almost never abandoned by the exchequer as uncollectable.

The collection of such long-term debts was an important aspect of Henry's approach to administering his custodies and escheats, but financially speaking, such debts were always of secondary importance to the direct issues he derived from custodies, marriages, and reliefs. Magna Carta had set the maximum allowable reliefs at £100 for an earldom or a barony, and at £5 per knight's fee up to that amount. Without exception, Henry held scrupulously to these limits. Magna Carta had said nothing, however, about the size of the fines the king could charge an heir for seisin of the royal crops, ploughs, and stock present on the estate when he paid his relief; nor had it imposed a

---

[38] See the complaints about this practice in the 1258 *Petitio Baronum* in Treharne and Sanders, *Documents of the Baronial Movement*, 86–7. Contrary to the note the editors provide, it is by no means clear that 'the burden of Jewish debts fell on the lower ranks of society'. See also Coss, 'Geoffrey de Langley', 18–19, 23–5, and the references given there.

[39] Although cautious persons might still seek the king's permission before doing so: cf. CPR 1232–47, 184, 480.

limit on the fines the king could charge a wife (or an interested third party) to have custody of her husband's land and children, or to control her own and her children's marriages. For favours such as these, Henry continued to charge and to collect fines of a magnitude comparable to those of his father's day. Joan, daughter of Nicholas de Stuteville and heiress to the Stuteville baronies of Cottingham, Yorkshire, and Liddel Strength, Cumberland, offered Henry a fine of 10,000 marks to have custody of all the lands of her husband, Hugh Wake baron of Bourne in Lincolnshire, along with the marriage of their son and heir, and the right to marry herself to whom she chose. She paid off this fine at a rate of 700 marks per year, with stiff penalties threatened for any default.[40] Next to this fine, the £100 relief she paid for Cottingham was inconsequential. Emma, widow of Ralph baron of Sudeley, Gloucestershire, paid 1000 marks for similar privileges.[41] In 1245, Simon de Montfort offered a 10,000 mark fine for custody of the lands and marriage of the heirs of Gilbert de Umfraville baron of Prudhoe, Northumberland.[42] Payment on this fine was to be 500 marks per year, to be credited against the 500 marks per year which Henry had granted Simon for his wife's dowry, and which Simon was collecting at the exchequer until the king could find him lands to the same value. Initially, the fine therefore cost Simon nothing; but as he received the promised lands, he was to remit a corresponding portion of the fine to the exchequer. If the heirs came of age before the twenty-year term on the fine had expired, de Montfort was to be quit of the remaining fine. Meanwhile, Roger de Clare, heir to the earldom of Gloucester, and John fitz Alan, heir to the Shropshire barony of Oswestry, paid fines of 1200 and 1500 marks respectively to retain the royal crops, stock, and chattels on their estates when they came of age.[43] Both fines were to be paid off within two years, although both men had already endured many years of direct royal exploitation of their estates while in the king's custody. Whether they agreed to such large fines because in fact the royal stock and crops were worth so much, or rather because they wished to prevent the king's officials from stripping the manors

[40] Fine Roll 26 Henry III (C. 60/38 m. 11), printed in *Excerpta e Rotulis Finium*, vol. i, 364–5; Sanders, *Baronies*, 37, 107–8, 129.
[41] Fine Roll 26 Henry III (C. 60/38 m. 3), printed in *Excerpta e Rotulis Finium*, vol. i, 376.
[42] Fine Roll 29 Henry III (C. 60/42 m. 8), printed in *Excerpta e Rotulis Finium*, vol. i, 436–7. Umfraville's son eventually became earl of Angus through his mother: cf. Sanders, *Baronies*, 73.
[43] CLR 1240–5, 283, 299.

on their departure, one cannot say. Aside from the inferential evidence of such fines, however, there is little other evidence during these years that the king's escheators mistreated the manors in their possession.

For the most part, Henry sold the custodies which fell in to him to persons around his court, although he was certainly prepared to sell custodies and marriages to others if they offered enough for the privilege. Only the largest honours were retained in hand for direct exploitation, and even these were often let at farm after a few years, at values determined by very careful manorial extents.[44] It is possible that Henry's courtiers were more heavy-handed than was the king himself in administering the custodies they acquired, but there is very little evidence from the 1240s by which to judge this. Much must have depended on the purposes for which the courtiers acquired these custodies. If their motives were purely pecuniary, no doubt the temptation to commit waste must have been considerable; but when a courtier acquired the marriage of an heir or heiress for the use of a member of his own family, his treatment of the lands in custody was probably exemplary.

The king enjoyed an extraordinary number of large custodies between 1240 and 1245, including the proceeds of five earldoms,[45] but aside from Henry's reluctance to allow noble widows to choose their own husbands without paying him a fine, it is difficult to find fault with his administration of them, or to see in it any obvious violations of the Great Charter. The complaints voiced in 1264 about the treatment of custodies appear to pertain specifically to the practices of the 1250s, and need not impugn his policies up to 1245.[46] Indeed, it is worth noting in this respect that in 1259 the reform council intended to continue selling such custodies, just as Henry had done to that date. The baronial reformers objected not to the sales themselves, but rather to the identity of the recent purchasers, and especially to the king's Poitevin relatives.[47]

[44] The earldom of Gloucester lands remained continuously under direct royal exploitation until the heir's majority, but this was exceptional. The administration of the Lincoln earldom lands was much more typical. After a period of about two years under direct royal management, they were leased, after a careful series of extents, to the archbishop of York: cf. Fine Roll 26 Henry III (C. 60/38 m. 2); Pipe Roll 27 Henry III (E. 372/87 rot. 13d). On the care with which such extents were examined, see p. 74 n. 96 above.

[45] Lincoln, Gloucester, Arundel, Warenne, and Devon.

[46] Treharne and Sanders, *Documents of the Baronial Movement*, 270–1.

[47] Treharne and Sanders, *Documents of the Baronial Movement*, 150–3; and on the 1258 opposition, Carpenter, 'What Happened in 1258?', *passim*.

Except at Winchester, the evidence is much the same with respect to Henry's treatment of ecclesiastical vacancies. Although Matthew Paris charged him with wasting the lands of the bishopric of London between 1241 and 1244 by deliberately extending the vacancy,[48] the delay in filling this see was only indirectly the king's fault. Fulk Basset, dean of York, was elected and approved by the king within three months of his predecessor's death. But with the archbishopric of Canterbury vacant along with the papal chair, Basset could not secure ecclesiastical confirmation until 1244. Miss Howell has suggested that the keeper of the bishopric between 1242 and 1244, Ralph Dayrell, was a particularly harsh administrator;[49] but a comparison of his accounts with those of the previous year's keepers (one of whom was the abbot of Evesham) does not bear out this charge. Dayrell's average yearly issues were 50 per cent higher than those of the previous keepers (about £900 as against about £600 per year) because the first year's keepers sold no grain. Evidently, all the grain they raised was still in the barns when Ralph Dayrell took over custody of the bishopric. Otherwise, his issues are entirely comparable with those of the first year's keepers, and do not appear to justify Matthew Paris's allegations.[50]

Henry claimed and exercised the right to tallage once each bishopric that came into his possession,[51] and his keepers also imposed fines *de terris retinendis* on episcopal tenants, just as Walter de Burgo had done on the royal demesne estates. But the figures collected by Howell do not suggest that such tallages were heavier during the 1240s than in other decades of the reign. Indeed, in several cases they were substantially less onerous than those which de Burgh's government had imposed during the 1220s.[52] And while Henry might justly be charged with extending the vacancy at Canterbury through his successful efforts to secure the election of Boniface of Savoy to the archbishopric, Henry's motives in so doing were only incidentally financial. His primary concern was to ensure that a man with close ties to the royal family sat on the throne at Canterbury. He did

---

[48] CM, vol. iv, 170.

[49] Howell, *Regalian Right*, 142.

[50] Pipe Roll 27 Henry III (E. 372/87 rot. 3).

[51] Howell, *Regalian Right*, 122–5.

[52] See app. A in Howell, *Regalian Right*, 211–33, especially the accounts for Ely, Exeter, and Salisbury.

not wish to repeat his experience with Archbishop Edmund, and he succeeded in that aim.[53]

At Winchester, the picture is rather different, and here there seems to be little question that Henry did deliberately lay waste the lands of the bishopric as punishment for the obduracy of the monks, who insisted on electing William de Ralegh to the see rather than Henry's preferred nominees.[54] Winchester remained vacant for more than six years due to the king's opposition to Ralegh's election, although, as at London, the dispute was much prolonged by the three-year papal vacancy. And since Winchester was by far the richest of the English bishoprics, financial considerations must have played some role in the king's continuing appeals against Ralegh. On the other hand, however, there is no doubt that relations between Henry and Ralegh after 1240 were hostile in an unusually personal way. Henry claimed in 1243 that 'the king reputes the bishop to be his strongest enemy, and long ago ordained that, by reason of the rancour which he conceived against the bishop, the latter should not appear before the king's majesty'.[55] Ralegh was fully the king's equal in venom. In his response to Henry's charges against him, Ralegh heaped scorn on the king's proposal to submit their dispute to the masters of Paris, remarking that

as there are in both laws most experienced men in the realm, it is not fitting to invoke those of another country, as that imputes either that the king distrusts the fealty of his own [men], or reputes their counsel insufficient ... , which is not becoming to the king's highness, which ... should be distinguished not only by arms but by laws, especially as in times past the great princes of the world in their doubtful causes used to seek the counsel of the king's predecessors, and in all things accept what was formulated in the convocation of even the unlearned men of England. ...[56]

[53] There is an interesting, if perhaps too laudatory, account of Boniface's career by Leland Edward Wilshire, 'Boniface of Savoy, Carthusian and Archbishop of Canterbury, 1207–1270', *Analecta Cartusiana* 31 (University of Salzburg, 1977), 4–90.

[54] CLR *1240–5*, 195; Howell, *Regalian Right*, 104–9, 144–5.

[55] CPR *1232–47*, 410.

[56] Ibid., 440. I have altered slightly the punctuation of this passage. Ralegh's historical allusion is to Henry II's role in 1177 in mediating a dispute between the kings of Navarre and Castile, on which see Roger of Howden, *Gesta Regis Henrici Secundi*, ('Benedict of Peterborough'), ed. William Stubbs, 2 vols. (London, 1867), vol. i, 138–54. That Ralegh should have known about this incident, and that he expected others to catch the reference also, is an interesting reflection on the historical knowledge around Henry III's court.

In a single, perfect blow, Ralegh rubbed salt in Henry's Poitevin wounds, and portrayed him both in arms and in wisdom as the unworthy descendant of a regal line. Nothing could have wounded Henry's pride more deeply. It can be little wonder that compromise should have proved difficult between two such combatants as these.

Even without the extended vacancy at Winchester, Henry enjoyed an extraordinary number of episcopal vacancies between 1236 and 1245. This fact was not lost on Matthew Paris, who believed that the revenue from these alone should have sufficed to make the king a wealthy man. As usual, Paris overstated the case, but the financial importance of these vacancies is obvious and undeniable. Between 1236 and 1240, Henry collected approximately £15,000 from this source, more than two-thirds of this sum between 1238 and 1240. From 1240 to 1244, he received about £23,000 from episcopal vacancies, presuming a notional value of £1500 per year for Canterbury, for which no account survives during these years. Except in 1241–2, when significant portions of the issues from Winchester were sent in kind to the king in Gascony, and so did not pass as cash through the exchequer, episcopal vacancies between 1240 and 1244 accounted for more than 20 per cent of the king's annual cash revenues. In 1244–5, however, revenues from this resource dropped precipitously, from around £6000 per year to less than £500, reflecting the final resolution of the vacancies at Winchester, Canterbury, and London. Between 1245 and 1249, Henry received less than £1000 total from all his ecclesiastical vacancies combined.[57]

The king's true financial advantages from episcopal vacancies were, however, substantially greater than the direct monetary revenues which could be drawn from them. Henry made a number of grants of timber from the forests of Winchester and Canterbury between 1241 and 1244,[58] but because these trees were never turned into cash, their value does not appear on the rolls. Similarly, the extensive provisions Henry drew from these two bishoprics to support the 1242 Poitevin expedition do not appear as cash receipts on the tables below, because most of these were consumed directly by the army.[59] By far the most important of these 'unquantifiable' resources, however, was the supply of ecclesi-

[57] With a few adjustments, these figures are all derived from Appendix B of Howell, *Regalian Right*. The calculations are my own.

[58] Howell, *Regalian Right*, 144–5 collects some of these references.

[59] Provisions which were later sold in Gascony, after having been sent in kind from Winchester, have however been included in the tables, on the basis of the purchase price as given in the wardrobe account on Pipe Roll 28 Henry III (E. 372/88 rot. 14).

astical patronage which an episcopal vacancy made available to the king. Only about one in five of the advowsons Henry required to support his clerks and household officials belonged directly to the Crown; the remainder of these positions came into the king's hands through ecclesiastical vacancies and noble custodies.[60] Henry was well aware of their importance. Even when he sold a noble custody, he usually retained in his own hands the advowsons pertaining to it. In this respect, episcopal vacancies and lay custodies literally made royal administration possible.

The most important of all the king's unquantifiable financial resources was, however, the king's own will. So long as retaining that goodwill could make a crucial difference in a magnate's fortunes, kings were always potentially richer than a mere listing of their revenues might suggest. This fact emerges particularly clearly from the taxation Henry was able to raise to support the 1242 Poitevin expedition. The largest single contribution to his coffers was of course made by the Jews through the 20,000 mark tallage, but the king collected an additional £2500 or so from the scutage assessed on his lay tenants-in-chief, and from the aid of the prelates. The fines *pro passagio* are an interesting mixture of negotiation and compulsion, in which the king's will played a significant role. Henry extracted from them about £1500. He also negotiated individually with the monastic houses, who were brought to contribute another £1600. In addition, Henry also collected £1840 13s. 4d. 'from the gifts of various people'.[61] Who contributed these gifts is nowhere stated, but they are unmistakable evidence of the fiscal importance which the royal will retained for Henry III. Similar such gifts, in cash, plate, and jewels, were also collected on the birth of the lord Edward in 1239, and upon the king's return from Gascony in 1243.[62]

Except when resistance reached a point of virtual rebellion, Henry always had the capacity to raise such gifts. In contrast to fourteenth-century practice, however, there are no signs before 1245 that Henry attempted to levy forced loans; and when in 1245 Henry did finally

---

[60] Howell, *Regalian Right*, 171–7.

[61] 'de donis diversorum'. For all these figures, see Ch. 5 above, and also the wardrobe account on Pipe Roll 28 Henry III (E. 372/88 rot. 14).

[62] See *CM*, vol. iii, 539–40 for Matthew Paris's account of the gifts Henry solicited on the birth of the lord Edward, and ibid., vol. iv, 255 for gifts on his return from Gascony. On the latter occasion, Henry also collected £100 from the Londoners, which he claimed as a customary sum due from them whenever the king returned from overseas: cf. Pipe Roll 28 Henry III (E. 372/88 rot. 14).

try to do so, his claims were directed against the foreign merchants doing business in the realm, and not against his own subjects.[63] The likely explanation for this is that Henry probably did not feel it necessary to pretend that he ever intended to pay back such gifts as he collected. Forced loans suggest a king less certain of his claims to profit by the royal will than was Henry, who seems generally to have solicited and accepted gifts from his subjects as his due.

Considered as a whole, Henry's financial resources between 1240 and 1245 were better balanced and considerably more extensive than has previously been supposed, providing the king with a base annual expendable income of at least £33,000, which could be increased by as much as 50 per cent through Jewish taxation, new judicial eyres, and voluntary aids or scutages. Undoubtedly the king had been lucky during these years also. He had enjoyed an unusually large number of episcopal vacancies, including three of the wealthiest sees in the realm (Durham, Winchester, and Canterbury); and when these came to an end after 1244, a new windfall of vacant earldoms and baronies helped cushion the immediate impact on the king's revenues. Except with respect to Jewish taxation, it therefore does not appear that Henry's efforts to amass a war chest for his Poitevin expedition weakened his revenue base in any permanent way; and even with respect to Jewish taxation, these effects were not felt seriously until the end of the decade, when the 60,000 mark tallage had completed the work of destruction begun in 1241–2. Overall, the king's revenues remained relatively buoyant after 1243, despite largely yearly fluctuations in their constituent parts (see Table 6.1). But before pronouncing Henry's finances healthy, we need to look also at the balance between expenditure and receipt. Barring the costs of a major war, were royal resources adequate to Henry's needs in the decade prior to 1245, or was Henry running a continuing deficit as a result of his expenditures?

Unfortunately, it is easier to raise this question than to answer it. Records of actual expenditure during the reign are much less complete than those for receipts, and even where the records are complete, they do not tell us all we wish to know. The pipe rolls, of course, record expenditure only incidentally, in cases where a pipe roll accountant had been ordered to make a payment out of his receipts, before he delivered his account before the exchequer barons. Only a small percentage of Henry's total annual expenditures was made in this

---

[63] For discussion of this incident, see p. 246 below.

manner. For the most part, Henry's cash revenues were disbursed from the treasury, through writs of liberate sent by the king to the exchequer barons. Such writs were recorded on the chancery liberate rolls, which in theory ought to have recorded all such orders. In fact, they do not;[64] moreover, even the orders they do record were not always acted upon by the exchequer. To determine whether a liberate writ was paid in full, in part, or not at all, one needs to consult the issue rolls of the lower exchequer, which recorded the actual disbursement of the sums along with a short abstract of the authorizing writ. Sometimes it is also necessary to consult the so-called 'exchequer liberate rolls', on which the exchequer clerks copied the entire authorizing writ, along with special notations about its payment. A complete set of chancery and exchequer liberate rolls, along with the related issue rolls, survives only for 1241–2; otherwise, issue rolls survive only for Michaelmas terms 1240 and 1243. Any conclusions as to the king's total annual expenditures, except during 1241–2, must necessarily involve a good deal of guesswork.

Even if we had a complete run of liberate and issue rolls, however, we would still be some way from a complete accounting of the king's expenditures. Each year, the king sent a number of writs ordering the keepers of ecclesiastical vacancies to make payments out of their receipts to specified individuals or projects. Such writs, known as writs of computate, allocate, or contrabreve, depending on the first word in their opening formula, were particularly important in funding royal construction projects, and in directing cash into the king's wardrobe. Such writs were also, however, particularly likely to go unpaid, usually because the keepers did not have the cash in hand to fulfil the king's orders. To ascertain whether in fact these expenditures were made, we have to check the chancery writs which authorized such payments against the pipe roll enrolments of the keepers' accounts. This is not an easy job, since the enrolled accounts often lump several such authorizing writs together, or abbreviate their terms so drastically as to render them unrecognizable. Moreover, as has already been noted, the enrolled accounts for the 1240–4 Canterbury vacancy are entirely missing from the pipe rolls, and although we can make a fairly accurate estimate of the net cash value of this vacancy to the king, we have no way at all of knowing how many of the writs ordering expenditures out of the Canterbury receipts were in fact honoured by the keepers

[64] See Ch. 5, n. 133 above.

of the vacancy. Even more than payments out of the exchequer, then, expenditures by writs of computate or allocate involve a great deal of guesswork, and can only be approximately accurate.

The final complication in analysing the king's expenditure concerns the wardrobe accounts. In an average year, somewhere between a quarter and a half of the king's annual cash income would pass through the royal wardrobe, where it would be disbursed in a variety of ways. Household receipts and expenditures are both recorded on the wardrobe accounts, sometimes, as between 1235 and 1240, in great detail.[65] Between February 1240 and October 1241, however, no wardrobe accounts were compiled; and when these accounts resume in 1241, expenditure is recorded in far less detail than previously, perhaps because after 1241, the keeper of the wardrobe was no longer responsible for issues of cloth and fur from the 'great wardrobe', these being now under the supervision of the king's tailor.[66] As a result of this administrative change, we no longer know after 1241 how much the king spent on robes for himself and his household. Nor can we determine easily how much he spent through the wardrobe on the annual fees of his retainers, on gifts to his magnates, or on wages to his fighting men, all three categories of expenditure being now lumped together into a single sum on the rolls, which in 1241–2 amounted to £22,485, and in 1242–3 to £17,551. From the wardrobe accounts, we can say how much the king spent through the household, but we cannot say very much about the purposes for which he spent it.

Calculations of total royal expenditures between 1240 and 1245 are therefore considerably less reliable, all in all, than are the figures for royal income. But subject to these caveats, a broadly convincing picture does emerge from the records of Henry's spending.[67] In 1240–1 and 1241–2, Henry's income appears to have exceeded his expenditures by about £3600 in the first year, and about £5300 in the second year. In 1242–3, he appears to have run a deficit of around £2300, although uncertainty as to whether liberate writs drawn in Gascony were paid out of the wardrobe overseas, or out of the treasury at Westminster, renders expenditure calculations particularly unreliable for this year. In 1243–4, the lingering effects of the king's overseas expenses are evident in the £9000 deficit between expenditures and receipts. For this year, the surviving issue roll for Michaelmas and Hilary terms 1243–4

---

[65] E. 372/80 rot. 2d; E. 372/81 rots. 13, 13d; E. 372/83 rot. 7.
[66] Tout, *Chapters*, vol. i, 258–9.
[67] For what follows, see Table 6.6.

TABLE 6.6 *Cash expenditures and receipts, 1240–5*

	Liberate	Computate	Total	Cash receipts	Balance
1240–1	£20,000	£6,900	£26,900	£30,500	£3,600
1241–2	£38,200	£2,700	£40,900	£46,200	£5,300
1242–3	£26,700	£2,500	£29,200	£26,900	(£2,300)
1243–4	£30,000	£5,500	£35,500	£26,500	(£9,000)
1244–5	£24,500	£4,400	£28,900	£27,300	(£1,600)
Overall balance					(£4,000)

Note: All figures rounded to the nearest £100.

allows us to calculate the actual sums paid out of the treasury during the first half of the fiscal year, when many Gascon writs from the preceding year were presented to the exchequer for payment. By 1244–5, however, the financial situation was starting to return to normal. Despite the costs of the king's 1245 war in Wales, Henry ran a deficit of only about £1600 on the year, although he also drew an additional £1600 in writs during September and October 1245 which were to be payable during the 1245–6 fiscal year. The effect of the 1242–3 war in Poitou is obvious in the overall deficit of approximately £4000 which these figures reveal between 1240 and 1245. On first sight, this result might go far to justify a view that the Poitevin expedition left the king with a mountain of debt which he was never able to surmount thereafter, and thus helped prepare the way for the rebellion of 1258.

Such a conclusion would, however, be misleading. Some of the writs of liberate and computate included here under expenditure were probably never paid; but because no issue rolls survive after March 1243, we cannot tell which ones were paid and which ones were not. Total expenditure figures for 1243–5 are therefore almost certainly too high. Moreover, this £4000 deficit does not include the £6000 in receipts which remained to Henry in 1241 from the 1237 thirtieth on moveables. Henry drew £2700 from this treasure in August 1241, and the remaining £3000 in March and April 1242.[68] This alone is enough to balance the overall account. And although it cannot do much to negate the deficits in 1244 and 1245, we should keep in mind also that our estimates for

[68] See Ch. 3, n. 190 above.

Henry's receipts from Jewish taxation during these years may be seriously too low. Between 1244 and 1250, Henry attempted to impose a tallage of 60,000 marks on the English Jewish community. No records of exchequer receipts from this tax are known to survive, and even chancery enrolments pertaining to it are scanty. But if all the liberate writs drawn against this tallage during 1244 were in fact paid, Henry's receipts from this source amounted to at least 9100 marks during this year alone.[69] Because no records of receipt survive at all for this tallage from 1245, I have elected to include only 4000 marks per annum as the yield of this tax during 1243–4 and 1244–5, but this estimate could be too low by at least half. If so, the deficit between 1243 and 1245 would be reduced from £10,600 to only about £5000, which may still be too high if, as seems possible, the accounts for 1242–3 at Westminster in fact should show not a deficit, but perhaps even a small surplus. No further sums were despatched to the king in Gascony after May 1243;[70] receipts at Westminster between late May and October 1243 should therefore have provided a modest financial surplus with which to begin the 1243–4 financial year, which would reduce even further the 1243–4 deficit shown above.

No precise computations of the king's debts in 1243 or 1245 is possible, because the records of royal expenditure during these years permit only the roughest approximations. What is clear, however, is the burden the Poitevin debts represented to the king's administrators in the two years following his return. In the final chapter, we shall examine Henry's response to his defeat, the measures he took in order to resolve these debts, and the consequences of these decisions for the history of the reign.

---

[69] *CLR 1240–5*, 209, 238, 243, 256; *CPR 1232–47*, 445.
[70] Cf. p. 198 and n. 182 above.

TABLE 6.7 Net value of shire farms

	1240–1	1241–2	1242–3	1243–4	1244–5
Berks.	—	(−£ 3 3s. 4d.)	(−£ 3 3s. 4d.)	(−£ 3 3s. 4d.)	(−£ 3 3s. 4d.)
Bucks. and Beds.	£ 130 9s. 10d.	£ 130 9s. 10d.	£ 130 9s. 10d.	£ 130 9s. 10d.	£ 130 9s. 10d.
Cambs. and Hunts.	£ 100 15s. 7d.	£ 100 15s. 7d.	£ 101 10s. 7d.	£ 102 5s. 9d.	£ 102 5s. 9d.
Cheshire	—	—	—	—	—
Cornwall					
Cumberland	£ 62 0s. 4d.	£ 62 0s. 4d.	£ 62 0s. 4d.	£ 62 0s. 4d.	£ 62 0s. 4d.
Devon	£ 7 15s. 3d.	£ 7 15s. 3d.	£ 7 15s. 3d.	£ 7 15s. 3d.	£ 25 9s. 1d.
Essex and Herts.	£ 188 16s. 2d.	£ 188 16s. 2d.	£ 188 16s. 2d.	£ 188 16s. 2d.	£ 188 16s. 2d.
Gloucs.	£ 23 11s. 0d.	£ 23 11s. 2d.	£ 23 13s. 8d.	£ 23 11s. 2d.	£ 23 11s. 2d.
Hants.	(−£ 13 3s. 7d.)	(−£ 12 1s. 4d.)	(−£ 4 11s. 8d.)	(−£ 12 1s. 4d.)	(−£ 12 1s. 4d.)
Hereford	(−£ 16 10s. 11d.)	(−£ 13 15s. 1d.)	(−£ 12 15s. 1d.)	(−£ 12 15s. 1d.)	(−£ 11 4s. 10d.)
Kent	£ 112 5s. 10d.	£ 107 14s. 7d.	£ 132 14s. 7d.	£ 155 4s. 7d.	£ 155 4s. 7d.
Lancs.	£ 2d.	£ 2d.	£ 2d.	£ 2d.	£ 2d.
Lincs.	£ 279 8s. 7d.	£ 279 8s. 7d.	£ 279 8s. 7d.	£ 279 8s. 7d.	£ 279 8s. 7d.
London and Middx.	£ 266 3s. 3d.	£ 266 3s. 3d.	£ 266 3s. 3d.	£ 266 3s. 3d.	£ 268 8s. 10½d.
Norfolk and Suffolk	£ 116 0s. 0d.	£ 114 17s. 2d.	£ 113 12s. 2d.	£ 113 12s. 2d.	£ 113 12s. 2d.
Northants.	(−£ 3 9s. 1½d.)	(−£ 3 9s. 1½d.)	(−£ 3 9s. 1½d.)	(−£ 4 1s. 7d.)	(−£ 5 17s. 11d.)
Northumberland	£ 34 7s. 11d.	£ 34 7s. 11d.	£ 34 7s. 11d.	£ 34 7s. 11d.	£ 34 7s. 11d.
Notts. and Derby	(−£ 9 14s. 10d.)	(−£ 9 14s. 10d.)	(−£ 9 14s. 10d.)	(−£ 7 17s. 5½d.)	(−£ 9 14s. 10d.)
Oxon.	£ 44 14s. 1½d.	£ 44 14s. 1½d.	£ 44 14s. 1½d.	£ 44 14s. 1½d.	£ 44 14s. 1½d.
Salop and Staffs.	£ 89 3s. 10d.	£ 89 3s. 10d.	£ 89 3s. 10d.	£ 89 3s. 10d.	£ 89 3s. 10d.
Som. and Dorset					
Surrey	(−£ 6 10s. ½d.)	(−£ 6 10s. ½d.)	(−£ 6 10s. ½d.)	(−£ 6 10s. ½d.)	(−£ 6 10s. ½d.)
Sussex	£ 26 0s. 0d.	£ 26 0s. 0d.	£ 26 0s. 0d.	£ 26 0s. 0d.	£ 26 0s. 0d.
Warks. and Leics.	£ 97 2s. 10d.	£ 97 2s. 10d.	£ 97 2s. 10d.	£ 97 2s. 10d.	£ 97 2s. 10d.
Westmorland	—	—	—	—	—
Wilts.	£ 106 17s. 11½d.	£ 106 17s. 11½d.	£ 106 17s. 11½d.	£ 106 17s. 11½d.	£ 106 17s. 11½d.
Worcs.	(−£ 7 4s. 1d.)	(−£ 7 4s. 1d.)	(−£ 7 4s. 1d.)	(−£ 9 13s. 11d.)	(−£ 9 13s. 11d.)
Yorks.	£ 59 8s. 4d.	£ 54 18s. 6d.	£ 54 18s. 6d.	£ 54 18s. 6d.	£ 54 18s. 6d.
	£1,688 8s. 5d.	£1,678 19s. 5d.	£1,712 1s. 7d.	£1,726 9s. 8d.	£1,744 6s. 6d.

TABLE 6.8 *Cash receipts from shire farms, profits and increments*

	1240–1	1241–2	1242–3	1243–4	1244–5
Berks.	£ 35 14s. 11½d.	£ 37 8s. 0d.	£ 62 15s. 2d.	£ 46 7s. 1d.	£ 250 15s. 0½d.
Bucks. and Beds.	£ 265 10s. 2½d.	£ 269 3s. 6d.	£ 284 4s. 7d.	£ 265 17s. 3d.	£ 13 6s. 8d.
Cambs. and Hunts.	£ 88 18s. 6d.	£ 96 5s. 7½d.	£ 123 18s. 2½d.	£ 66 16s. 10½d.	£ 180 0s. 0d.
Cheshire	£ 232 10s. 0d.	—	—	—	—
Cornwall	—	—	—	—	—
Cumberland	£ 40 0s. 0d.	£ 40 0s. 0d.	£ 43 9s. 11½d.	£ 20 0s. 0d.	£ 40 0s. 0d.
Devon	£ 48 0s. 0d.	£ 70 5s. 7d.	—	—	£ 59 8s. 0d.
Essex and Herts.	£ 142 11s. 6d.	£ 132 13s. 4d.	£ 195 17s. 5d.	£ 141 3s. 7½d.	£ 160 7s. 1d.
Gloucs.	—	—	£ 45 5s. 0d.	£ 38 19s. 7d.	—
Hants.	£ 29 10s. 0d.	£ 8 11s. 6d.	£ 0 16s. 3¼d.	—	£ 15 19s. 8d.
Hereford	—	—	—	—	—
Kent	£ 109 6s. 5d.	£ 6 3s. 3d.	£ 26 16s. 2d.	£ 20 0s. 0d.	£ 19 5s. 7½d.
Lancs.	£ 433 18s. 1d.	£ 409 15s. 4d.	£ 486 9s. 7d.	£ 165 10s. 2d.	£ 473 11s. 5d.
Lincs.	£ 23 11s. 3d.	£ 15 3s. 1d.	£ 179 14s. 9d.	£ 2 17s. 3d.	£ 72 8s. 7d.
London and Middx.	£ 3 13s. 3½d.	£ 48 5s. 5d.	£ 268 16s. 0d.	£ 100 0s. 0d.	—
Norfolk and Suffolk	£ 16 13s. 4d.[a]	£ 16 13s. 4d.[a]	£ 44 4s. 2d.	£ 31 8s. 2½d.	£ 49 15s. 2d.
Northants.	£ 25 7s. 3½d.	£ 40 10s. 10d.	£ 36 16s. 0d.	£ 33 6s. 8d.	£ 63 6s. 8d.
Northumberland	£ 66 13s. 4d.	£ 66 13s. 4d.	£ 11 5s. 5d.	£ 19 14s. 0d.	—
Notts. and Derby	£ 29 19s. 0d.	£ 26 12s. 0d.	£ 26 12s. 0d.	—	—
Oxon.	£ 79 12s. 2d.	£ 30 0s. 0d.	£ 27 9s. 5d.	—	—
Salop and Staffs.	—	—	—	—	—
Som. and Dorset	£ 26 13s. 4d.	£ 32 13s. 4d.	—	—	—
Surrey	—	—	—	—	—
Sussex	£ 64 8s. 4d.[a]	£ 174 11s. 3d.	£ 23 6s. 8d.	—	—
Warks. and Leics.	£ 23 0s. 6½d.	£ 138 10s. 0d.	£ 49 17s. 6d.	—	£ 364 16s. 6d.
Westmorland	—	—	—	—	—
Wilts.	£ 6 10s. 0d.	£ 3 11s. 3d.	£ 50 15s. 2d.	—	£ 3 2s. 0d.
Worcs.	£ 47 15s. 0d.	£ 104 19s. 2¾d.	£ 137 6s. 8d.	£ 88 1s. 8d.	—
Yorks.	—	—	—	—	—
	£1,839 16s. 6½d.	£1,768 13s. 2d.	£2,125 10s. 1¾d.	£1,040 2s. 4½d.	£1,766 2s. 5d.

[a] Two-year account.

TABLE 6.9 *Demesne revenues: cash*

	1240–1	1241–2	1242–3	1243–4	1244–5
Berks.	£ 29 19s. 8d.	£ 418 13s. 8d.	£ 260 9s. 6d.	£ 211 15s. 7d.	£ 166 13s. 6d.
Bucks. and Beds.	£ 124 6s. 0½d.	£ 111 15s. 10½d.	£ 169 7s. 7½d.	£ 83 9s. 1½d.	£ 283 7s. 11½d.
Cambs. and Hunts.	£ 287 16s. 11½d.	£ 362 8s. 5½d.	£ 298 18s. 4d.	£ 280 12s. 7d.	£ 407 1s. 5d.
Cheshire	—				
Cornwall	—				
Cumberland	£ 301 7s. 7d.	£ 132 11s. 8½d.	£ 137 9s. 8d.	£ 168 7s. 11½d.	£ 145 0s. 10d.
Devon	£ 205 14s. 6d.	£ 128 15s. 11d.	£ 66 10s. 1d.	£ 26 10s. 1d.	£ 76 10s. 9d.
Essex and Herts.	£ 178 7s. 8d.	£ 241 16s. 0½d.	£ 230 17s. 10d.	£ 210 13s. 0d.	£ 663 7s. 10d.
Gloucs.	£ 314 14s. 3d.	£ 570 3s. 0d.	£ 481 16s. 6d.	£ 442 13s. 0½d.	£ 249 10s. 2d.
Hants.	£ 416 17s. 2d.	£ 288 3s. 4d.	£ 248 13s. 3½d.	£ 171 8s. 8d.	£ 655 3s. 7d.
Hereford	£ 4 0s. 0d.	£ 277 13s. 0d.	£ 127 6s. 6d.ᵃ	£ 127 6s. 6d.ᵃ	£ 8 0s. 0d.
Kent	£ 50 8s. 8d.	£ 203 12s. 9d.	£ 55 13s. 4d.	£ 137 8s. 5d.	£ 165 5s. 1d.
Lancs.	£ 13 6s. 8d.	£ 96 15s. 4d.	£ 29 2s. 3d.	£ 89 1s. 6d.	£ 83 18s. 9½d.
Lincs.	£ 237 14s. 6½d.	£ 265 2s. 11d.	£ 259 12s. 3d.	£ 52 19s. 9½d.	£ 486 18s. 5d.
London and Middx.	£ 14 13s. 6d.	£ 14 13s. 6d.	£ 14 0s. 4d.	£ 14 0s. 4d.	£ 14 0s. 4d.
Norfolk and Suffolk	£ 300 4s. 2½d.	£ 248 12s. 8d.	£ 240 6s. 3d.	£ 177 9s. 8d.	£ 313 19s. 8d.
Northants.	£ 434 13s. 10d.ᵃ	£ 434 13s. 11d.ᵃ	£ 412 16s. 10d.	£ 508 14s. 11d.	£ 835 4s. 1½d.
Northumberland	£ 149 5s. 1½d.	£ 183 12s. 10d.	£ 161 0s. 7d.	£ 61 17s. 8d.	£ 156 0s. 10d.
Notts. and Derby	£ 346 17s. 6d.	£ 264 12s. 8d.	£ 282 4s. 4d.	£ 266 12s. 10½d.	£ 271 11s. 10d.
Oxon.	£ 90 8s. 3d.	£ 186 14s. 2d.	£ 73 15s. 11d.	£ 84 13s. 4d.	£ 153 4s. 0d.
Salop and Staffs.	£ 161 11s. 4½d.	£ 231 13s. 11½d.ᵃ	£ 180 15s. 4d.	£ 132 15s. 8½d.	£ 132 15s. 9d.
Som. and Dorset	£ 182 17s. 10d.ᵃ	£ 182 17s. 10d.ᵃ	£ 136 10s. 0d.	£ 342 2s. 1d.	£ 305 1s. 2d.ᵃ
Surrey	£ 62 7s. 6d.	£ 51 16s. 0d.	£ 51 15s. 8d.	£ 50 16s. 5½d.	£ 52 6s. 6d.
Sussex		£ 4 6s. 8d.	£ 85 12s. 2d.		
Warks. and Leics.	£ 81 14s. 6d.ᵃ	£ 82 18s. 4d.	£ 18 19s. 2d.	£ 21 16s. 8d.	£ 17 0s. 0d.
Westmorland					
Wilts.	£ 141 18s. 3d.	£ 180 6s. 6d.	£ 37 18s. 4d.	£ 157 8s. 5d.	£ 95 0s. 3d.
Worcs.	£ 125 10s. 7d.	£ 125 18s. 10d.	£ 88 1s. 0d.	£ 61 18s. 4d.	£ 29 2s. 4d.
Yorks.	£ 261 15s. 4d.	£ 555 12s. 0d.	£ 381 6s. 2d.	£ 265 5s. 6d.	£ 533 3s. 4d.
	£4,518 11s. 6d.	£5,846 1s. 10½d.	£4,530 19s. 3d.	£4,147 18s. 2½d.	£6,299 8s. 1½d.

ᵃTwo-year account.

TABLE 6.10 *Judicial revenues: cash*

	1240–1	1241–2	1242–3	1243–4	1244–5
Berks.	£ 350 10s. 7½d.	£ 64 4s. 3d.	£ 51 5s. 11d.	£ 14 5s. 0d.	£ 37 4s. 10½d.
Bucks. and Beds.	£ 541 5s. 0½d.[a]	£ 69 19s. 6d.	£ 102 11s. 4d.	£ 87 2s. 9½d.	£ 59 4s. 9d.
Cambs. and Hunts.	£ 128 2s. 8d.	£ 22 3s. 8d.	£ 88 17s. 10d.	£ 31 12s. 8d.	£ 40 1s. 11½d.
Cheshire	—	—	—	—	—
Cornwall	—	£ 27 0s. 0d.	£ 46 10s. 0d.	£ 2 0s. 0d.	£ 7 13s. 7½d.
Cumberland	£ 124 2s. 0d.	£ 381 7s. 11d.	£ 67 6s. 8d.	£ 545 16s. 5d.	£ 430 2s. 10d.
Devon	£ 151 4s. 4d.	£ 93 3s. 5d.	£ 114 14s. 11d.	£ 96 0s. 0d.	£ 109 10s. 0d.
Essex and Herts.	£ 256 18s. 0½d.	£ 169 1s. 10½d.	£ 22 19s. 0d.	£ 34 3s. 4d.	£ 4 6s. 8d.
Gloucs.	£ 398 8s. 5d.	£ 135 15s. 11½d.	£ 165 1s. 11d.	£ 34 16s. 8½d.	£ 54 11s. 8d.
Hants.	£ 11 0s. 0d.	£ 79 6s. 3d.	£ 27 14s. 6½d.[a]	£ 64 16s. 8½d.[a]	£ 20 1s. 6d.
Hereford	£ 15 10s. 0d.	£ 13 13s. 2d.	£ 51 18s. 8d.	£ 27 14s. 6½d.[a]	£ 15 1s. 8d.
Kent	£ 13s. 4d.	£ 328 8s. 5d.	£ 168 5s. 3d.	£ 45 4s. 6d.	£ 1,844 9s. 7½d.
Lancs.	£ 1,000 6s. 5d.	£ 563 7s. 8d.	£ 256 14s. 0d.	£ 25 17s. 3½d.	£ 60 9s. 0d.
Lincs.	£ 5 11s. 8d.	£ 179 2s. 8d.	£ 5 15s. 0d.	£ 154 3s. 9d.	£ 1,588 19s. 10½d.
London and Middx.	£ 473 19s. 1d.	£ 16 11s. 8d.	£ 289 13s. 11d.	£ 170 10s. 2d.	£ 41 11s. 2½d.
Norfolk and Suffolk	£ 119 4s. 1d.[a]	£ 485 18s. 1d.	£ 67 6s. 8d.	£ 94 4s. 9½d.	£ 25 3s. 4d.
Northants.	£ 260 13s. 4d.	£ 119 4s. 1d.[a]	£ 64 13s. 4d.	£ 40 14s. 6d.	£ 425 6s. 8d.
Northumberland	£ 399 11s. 7d.	£ 114 16s. 8d.	£ 38 7s. 10d.	£ 34 8s. 8d.	£ 64 16s. 2d.
Notts. and Derby	£ 203 9s. 2½d.	£ 36 5s. 4d.	£ 25 16s. 8d.	£ 103 18s. 10½d.	£ 6s. 8d.[a]
Oxon.	£ 173 13s. 2d.	£ 50 4s. 9d.	£ 61 17s. 6d.	£ 66 5s. 0d.	£ 43 10s. 6d.
Salop and Staffs.	£ 37 15s. 7d.[a]	£ 45 19s. 0d.	£ 28 3s. 4d.	£ 6s. 8d.[a]	£ 19 11s. 4½d.
Som. and Dorset	£ 172 14s. 11d.	£ 37 15s. 7d.[a]	£ 86 19s. 4d.	£ 645 11s. 11d.	£ 69 10s. 11½d.
Surrey	£ 3 16s. 4d.	£ 76 19s. 0d.	£ 13 16s. 8d.	£ 48 12s. 1d.	£ 100 3s. 8½d.
Sussex	£ 214 2s. 8d.[a]	£ 403 17s. 11½d.	£ 104 0s. 1d.	£ 87 12s. 10d.	
Warks. and Leics.		£ 181 7s. 11d.		£ 22 10s. 10d.	
Westmorland		£ 349 6s. 7d.			
Wilts.	£ 331 19s. 6½d.	£ 53 9s. 0d.	£ 73 6s. 8d.	£ 49 9s. 8½d.	£ 3 13s. 4d.
Worcs.	£ 150 13s. 8d.	£ 52 19s. 3d.	£ 65 11s. 4d.	£ 6 6s. 4d.	£ 34 9s. 10d.
Yorks.	£ 558 6s. 0d.	£ 423 8s. 1d.	£ 39 4s. 4d.	£ 71 6s. 8d.	£ 275 15s. 2d.
	£6,083 11s. 8½d.	£4,574 17s. 8½d.	£2,128 12s. 8½d.	£2,563 16s. 0d.	£5,376 0s. 11½d.

[a] Two-year account.

TABLE 6.11 *Debts and prests: cash*

	1240–1	1241–2	1242–3	1243–4	1244–5
Berks.	£74 6s. 8d.	£49 18s. 4d.	£45 0s. 0d.	£4 13s. 4d.	£21 0s. 0d.
Bucks. and Beds.	£101 11s. 2d.[a]	£35 0s. 0d.	£59 16s. 8d.	£77 14s. 8d.	£81 12s. 2d.
Cambs. and Hunts.	£117 11s. 2d.	£85 0s. 0d.	£68 16s. 8d.	£42 6s. 8d.	£9 0s. 0d.
Cheshire	—	—	—	—	—
Cornwall	—	£101 10s. 0d.	—	—	—
Cumberland	£19 12s. 11d.	—	—	—	—
Devon	£95 8s. 3d.	£87 5s. 1d.	£62 6s. 8d.	£55 6s. 8d.	£79 6s. 8d.
Essex and Herts.	£287 16s. 2d.	£260 12s. 0d.	£341 18s. 8d.	£124 7s. 1½d.	£228 19s. 6½d.
Gloucs.	£23 6s. 8d.	£36 13s. 4d.	£14 0s. 0d.	£3 6s. 8d.	—
Hants.	£78 7s. 3d.	£119 13s. 4d.	£215 14s. 4d.	£107 16s. 8d.	£44 1s. 8½d.
Hereford	£7 11s. 9¾d.	£138 13s. 4d.	—	—	£79 6s. 8d.
Kent	£3 0s. 0d.	£199 15s. 2d.	£9 11s. 10d.	£64 3s. 8d.	£77 14s. 5d.
Lancs.	—	£80 0s. 0d.	£40 0s. 0d.	£40 0s. 0d.	£40 0s. 0d.
Lincs.	£208 0s. 7½d.	£187 19s. 5d.	£207 14s. 3d.	£133 16s. 8d.	£209 17s. 8½d.
London and Middx.	£56 18s. 4d.	£23 3s. 2d.	£97 18s. 4d.	£117 18s. 4d.	£51 11s. 8d.
Norfolk and Suffolk	£84 18s. 9d.	£199 7s. 7d.	£111 7s. 2d.	£78 10s. 5d.	£46 4s. 0d.
Northants.	£47 5s. 2d.[a]	£47 5s. 2d.[a]	£109 10s. 8d.	£38 1s. 2d.	£33 15s. 0d.
Northumberland	£25 3s. 4d.	£30 6s. 8d.	£10 8s. 10d.	£7 15s. 6d.	£3 13s. 4d.
Notts. and Derby	£284 16s. 8d.	£166 2s. 4d.	£144 10s. 0d.	£132 10s. 0d.	£126 13s. 4d.
Oxon.	£21 12s. 7d.	£74 6s. 8d.	£83 10s. 0d.	£14 10s. 0d.	£81 0s. 0d.
Salop and Staffs.	£33 2s. 5d.	£94 0s. 0d.	£37 7s. 0d.	£55 4s. 2d.[a]	£55 4s. 2d.[a]
Som. and Dorset	£50 0s. 0d.[a]	£50 0s. 0d.[a]	£42 0s. 0d.	£128 0s. 0d.	£61 13s. 4d.
Surrey	£6 13s. 4d.	—	£5 4s. 8d.	—	£28 8s. 6d.
Sussex	£3 17s. 8d.	£36 17s. 7½d.	£4 0s. 0d.	£21 3s. 5d.	£9 10s. 0d.
Warks. and Leics.	£253 4s. 11d.	£80 7s. 4d.	£41 5s. 0d.	£20 11s. 8d.	£13 6s. 8d.
Westmorland	—	—	—	—	—
Wilts.	£12 6s. 8d.	£16 3s. 4d.	£5 8s. 0d.	£112 3s. 4d.	£115 14s. 10d.
Worcs.	£60 0s. 0d.	£108 6s. 8d.	£128 13s. 4d.	£233 13s. 4d.	£255 15s. 2d.
Yorks.	£255 10s. 1d.	£302 8s. 7d.	£424 10s. 2d.	—	—
	£2,212 2s. 7d.	£2,610 15s. 5½d.	£2,310 12s. 3d.	£1,613 12s. 11½d.	£1,753 8s. 10½d.

[a] Two-year account.

TABLE 6.12 *Debita Judeorum: cash*

	1240–1	1241–2	1242–3	1243–4	1244–5
Berks.	—	£8 13s. 4d.	—	—	—
Bucks. and Beds.	£11 11s. 8d.ᵃ	£12 3s. 4d.	£10 6s. 8d.	£12 6s. 8d.	£22 6s. 8d.
Cambs. and Hunts.	£4 6s. 8d.	£4 8s. 2d.	£2 9s. 8d.	£1 17s. 6d.	£4 10s. 8d.
Cheshire	—	—	—	—	—
Cornwall	—	—	—	—	—
Cumberland	—	—	—	—	—
Devon	£24 3s. 4d.	£12 16s. 4d.	£17 3s. 4d.	£10 13s. 4d.	£3 12s. 0d.
Essex and Herts.	—	£3 6s. 8d.	£3 7s. 8d.	£1 10s. 8d.	£19 19s. 8d.
Gloucs.	£1 0s. 0d.	£59 17s. 4d.	£4 6s. 8d.	£3 6s. 8d.	£3 7s. 8d.
Hants.	£1 6s. 8d.	£20 13s. 4d.	£8 0s. 0d.ᵃ	£1 10s. 0d.	£2 2s. 8d.
Hereford	—	£5 0s. 0d.	£1 13s. 4d.	£8 0s. 0d.ᵃ	£8 0s. 0d.
Kent	—	—	—	—	—
Lancs.	—	—	—	—	—
Lincs.	£25 17s. 4d.	£90 12s. 11d.	£7 13s. 4d.	£9 2s. 9d.	£61 11s. 8d.
London and Middx.	£6 6s. 4d.	£2 17s. 11d.	£50 14s. 4d.	£2 5s. 0d.	£5 18s. 6d.
Norfolk and Suffolk	£47 15s. 4½d.ᵃ	£226 16s. 8d.	£39 11s. 1d.	£24 10s. 6d.	£46 3s. 0d.
Northants.	£8 13s. 10d.ᵃ	£8 13s. 11d.ᵃ	£8 11s. 0d.	£—	£—
Northumberland	—	—	—	—	—
Notts. and Derby	—	£2 0s. 0d.	£52 0s. 0d.	£ 6s. 8d.	£56 13s. 4d.
Oxon.	—	£29 13s. 4d.	£46 1s. 8d.	£2 13s. 4d.	—
Salop and Staffs.	£3 0s. 0d.ᵃ	£3 0s. 0d.ᵃ	£3 13s. 4d.	—	£11 13s. 4d.
Som. and Dorset	—	£2 0s. 3d.	—	—	—
Surrey	£16 0s. 0d.	£12 0s. 0d.	—	£8 0s. 0d.	£21 0s. 0d.
Sussex	£12 19s. 5d.	£7 11s. 2d.	£6 11s. 2d.	£4 3s. 2d.	£6 13s. 4d.
Warks. and Leics.	£10 0s. 0d.	£5 0s. 0d.	—	—	—
Westmorland	—	—	—	—	—
Wilts.	—	£3 0s. 0d.	£2 0s. 0d.	£2 0s. 0d.	£2 0s. 0d.
Worcs.	£20 0s. 0d.	£7 6s. 8d.	£42 13s. 4d.	£6 13s. 4d.	£11 2s. 4d.
Yorks.	—	—	—	—	—
	£193 0s. 7½d.	£527 11s. 4d.	£306 18s. 4d.	£98 19s. 7d.	£286 14s. 10d.

ᵃ Two-year account.

TABLE 6.13 *Custodies, reliefs and seisins: cash*

	1240–1	1241–2	1242–3	1243–4	1244–5
Berks.	£ 3 6s. 8d.	£ 83 6s. 8d.	£ 13 6s. 8d.	—	£ 17 0s. 0d.
Bucks. and Beds.	£ 103 15s. 9d.[a]	£ 42 3s. 4d.	£ 89 13s. 4d.	£ 24 0s. 0d.	£ 41 18s. 7d.
Cambs. and Hunts.	£ 20 0s. 0d.	£ 83 6s. 8d.	—	—	£ 16 13s. 4d.
Cheshire	—	—	—	—	—
Cornwall					
Cumberland	£ 53 13s. 9d.	£ 213 6s. 8d.	£ 413 6s. 8d.	£ 460 5s. 8d.	£ 13 6s. 8d.
Devon	£ 88 19s. 8½d.	£ 137 1s. 8d.	£ 49 18s. 9d.	£ 13 6s. 8d.	£ 50 0s. 0d.
Essex and Herts.	£ 295 18s. 10½d.	£ 301 15s. 4d.	£ 42 0s. 8d.	£ 81 3s. 4d.	£ 82 3s. 4d.
Gloucs.	£ 42 13s. 8d.	£ 287 6s. 8d.	£ 92 0s. 0d.	£ 144 6s. 8d.	£ 305 13s. 0d.
Hants.	£ 117 2s. 2½d.	£ 88 17s. 9d.	£ 10s. 6¼d.	£ 23 6s. 8d.	£ 7 9s. 4d.
Hereford	—	£ 5 9s. 2d.	£ 78 6s. 8d.	£ 6 13s. 4d.	—
Kent	£ 61 0s. 0d.	£ 217 6s. 8d.	£ 23 12s. 9d.	£ 14 9s. 11½d.	£ 20 2s. 6d.
Lancs.	—	£ 8 10s. 7d.	£ 28 17s. 7d.	£ 16 13s. 4d.	£ 15 6s. 8d.
Lincs.	£ 16 13s. 4d.	£ 120 0s. 0d.	—	—	—
London and Middx.	—	—	£ 432 11s. 0d.	£ 465 16s. 7d.	£ 681 2s. 4d.
Norfolk and Suffolk	—	£ 33 6s. 8d.	£ 16s. 8d.	£ 6 13s. 4d.	£ 9 6s. 8d.
Northants.	£ 17 10s. 0d.[a]	£ 17 10s. 0d.[a]	£ 24 9s. 11d.	£ 28 16s. 9d.	£ 40 0s. 0d.
Northumberland	£ 92 0s. 0d.	£ 28 6s. 8d.	£ 244 9s. 8d.	£ 16 13s. 4d.	£ 8 0s. 0d.
Notts. and Derby	£ 40 0s. 0d.	£ 40 0s. 0d.	£ 7 10s. 0d.	£ 16s. 0d.	—
Oxon.	£ 10 0s. 0d.	£ 10 0s. 0d.	£ 150 13s. 1d.	—	—
Salop and Staffs.	£ 20 0s. 0d.	£ 377 7s. 8d.	£ 25 0s. 0d.	—	—
Som. and Dorset	£ 99 3s. 4d.[a]	£ 99 3s. 4d.[a]	—	£ 196 2s. 3d.[a]	£ 196 2s. 3d.[a]
Surrey	£ 34 13s. 4d.	£ 22 16s. 0d.	£ 34 6s. 8d.	£ 5 0s. 0d.	£ 203 6s. 8d.
Sussex	£ 16 17s. 5d.	£ 22 10s. 0d.	—	£ 13 0s. 0d.	£ 20 0s. 0d.
Warks. and Leics.	£ 1 0s. 0d.[a]	£ 30 0s. 4d.	£ 5 0s. 0d.	—	£ 23 13s. 4d.
Westmorland	—	—	—	—	—
Wilts.	£ 61 13s. 4d.	£ 13 6s. 8d.	—	—	—
Worcs.	—	—	—	—	—
Yorks.	£ 6 13s. 4d.	—	—	—	—
	£ 1,202 14s. 8½d.	£ 1,300 1s. 1½d.	£ 1,941 3s. 2d.	£ 1,561 12s. 2½d.	£ 743 2s. 2d.
		£ 3,582 19s. 7½d.	£ 3,697 13s. 9½d.	£ 3,078 16s. 1d.	£ 2,497 6s. 10d.

[a] Two-year account.

Table 6.14 Taxation and fines for service: cash

	1240–1	1241–2	1242–3	1243–4	1244–5
Berks.	—	£ 1 13s. 4d.	£ 2 0s. 10d.	—	£ 106 0s. 0d.
Bucks. and Beds.	£ 20 0s. 0d.	£ 75 7s. 0d.	£ 16 0s. 8d.	£ 10 7s. 11d.	£ 4 5s. 2¼d.
Cambs. and Hunts.	£ 81 1s. 8d.	£ 4 6s. 8d.	£ 16 13s. 4d.	—	£ 3s. 8d.
Cheshire					
Cornwall	—	£ 21 14s. 8d.	£133 13s. 4d.	—	—
Cumberland	—	£ 67 0s. 0d.	£ 2 10s. 0d.	—	£ 3 10s. 0d.
Devon	—	£ 10 13s. 4d.	£ 2 10s. 0d.	—	£ 203 11s. 8d.
Essex and Herts.	£ 9 9s. 6d.	£211 7s. 11d.	£ 35 4s. 6d.	£ 1 10s. 0d.	£ 7 6s. 8d.
Gloucs.	—	£ 59 0s. 0d.	£ 1 11s. 0d.	£ 14s. 9¾d.	£ 200 7s. 10½d.
Hants.	£ 4 16s. 10d.	£ 76 0s. 0d.	£ 6 6s. 0d.	£ 12 5s. 4d.	£ 166 9s. 6½d.
Hereford					£ 51 10s. 8d.
Kent	—	£ 7 2s. 0d.	£ 66 13s. 4d.	£ 1 16s. 7d.	£ 1 12s. 6¾d.
Lancs.	£ 62 5s. 4d.	—	£ 20 0s. 0d.	£ 66 13s. 4d.	£ 3 12s. 6½d.
Lincs.	£ 49 6s. 8d.	£120 2s. 1d.	£ 48 13s. 4d.	—	£ 252 10s. 4d.
London and Middx.	£121 14s. 3½d.	£949 13s. 4d.	£ 41 0s. 0d.	£ 8 0s. 6d.	£ 3s. 4d.
Norfolk and Suffolk	—	£210 14s. 6d.	£ 12 16s. 6½d.	£ 17 6s. 8d.	£ 217 4s. 8d.
Northants.	£ 95 13s. 0d.[a]	£ 95 13s. 0d.[a]	£ 10 0s. 0d.	—	£ 118 7s. 6d.
Northumberland	£100 19s. 4d.	£135 0s. 0d.	£ 24 13s. 4d.	£ 8 13s. 4d.	£ 72 16s. 6d.
Notts. and Derby	£ 7 3s. 8d.	£ 35 10s. 3d.	£ 66 0s. 0d.	£ 4 0s. 0d.	£ 101 5s. 8d.
Oxon.		£ 17 13s. 4d.	£ 2 0s. 0d.	£ 15 0s. 0d.	£ 66 1s. 0d.
Salop and Staffs.		£ 58 13s. 4d.			£ 77 5s. 8d.
Som. and Dorset		£ 86 13s. 4d.			£ 353 19s. 7d.
Surrey		£ 6 13s. 4d.			
Sussex		£ 13s. 4d.		£ 1 6s. 8d.	£ 35 13s. 4d.
Warks. and Leics.		£ 3 6s. 8d.			
Westmorland					
Wilts.	£ 16s. 4d.	£ 40 0s. 0d.	£ 14 3s. 2d.		£ 56 0s. 0d.
Worcs.			£ 20 0s. 0d.		
Yorks.	£ 51 6s. 8d.	£167 0s. 0d.	£101 13s. 4d.		£ 251 11s. 8½d.
	£609 13s. 3½d.	£2,461 11s. 5d.	£550 12s. 8½d.	£147 15s. 1½d.	£2,351 9s. 8d.

[a] Two-year account.

7

Crown Finance and the Grievances of the Realm

Like his father thirty years before, Henry returned to England in late September 1243 to confront the consequences of his Poitevin defeat. Financially, Henry's debts from the expedition amounted to some £15,000 in direct loans and promissory writs, which the exchequer worked extremely hard to repay during the autumn and winter of 1243–4. Between Michaelmas and Christmas 1243, almost £10,000 passed out of the treasury, the great bulk of it to pay off war-related debts. Between Christmas 1243 and 1 March 1244, a further £4500 followed, with payment on an additional £1700 in war debts deferred until after Easter. Beyond these direct military expenses, however, Henry had also to fulfil some rather expensive obligations to his wartime supporters, both Gascon and English. Geoffrey Ridel of Blaye, for example, was by now an old man.[1] In 1243, he retired to England with Henry, where he remained until his death, leaving his lands in Gascony to his son, Geoffrey Ridel the younger. Over the next two years, Henry paid the elder Geoffrey almost 1000 marks in fees and back debts owing to him from the 1242–3 war.[2] To Peter of Geneva, a Savoyard who had come to Henry's service in Gascony, the king had promised a landed endowment in England and a fee of £100 per year; to Guy de Rocheford, who had come to England after losing his Poitevin lands in Henry's service, the king owed £120 per year compensation until he could grant him lands to that value.[3] Eleanor de Montfort, meanwhile, had never been properly dowered out of the Marshal lands of her first husband. Because King Henry had acted as surety for these arrangements, he was responsible to make good their failure. Nor had he ever granted his sister a dowry for her second

---

[1] CPR 1232–47, 434.

[2] CLR 1240–5, 204, 265, 269.

[3] On Peter of Geneva, see CPR 1232–47, 306, 421, 429; CLR 1240–5, 220, 245, 249, 255, 291. On Guy de Rocheford, see CPR 1232–47, 395; CLR 1240–5, 229, 237, 275, 300, 326.

marriage. To resolve these claims, Henry in 1245 promised de Montfort and his wife 500 marks per year out of the exchequer, until he could grant them the equivalent in land; and to guarantee the arrangement, he granted them custody of the lands and heirs of Gilbert de Umfraville in payment of the 500 mark fee.[4]

Characteristically, however, Richard of Cornwall made off with the largest prizes. In December 1243, Earl Richard married Sanchia of Provence, third daughter of Count Raymond of Provence, and sister to both the French and the English queens. This marriage was an important element in Henry's Continental plans, which during the following six years were to focus almost entirely on Provence and Savoy.[5] The bride's impecunious father could give her no dowry, but Henry made good this lack by promising his brother £3000 in cash with the marriage.[6] Also, in a rash moment of overwhelming gratitude after Richard had engineered his wartime escape from Taillebourg, Henry had promised Richard lifetime possession of Gascony to go along with his title of count of Poitou.[7] Had this grant been effected, it would have been manifestly to the disinheritance of the Lord Edward, to whose landed endowment Henry began to devote considerable attention during 1244.[8] To soothe Earl Richard's feelings after revoking the grant, Henry gave him an additional 1000 marks per year at the exchequer, until he could find him £500 in lands, to hold to himself and his heirs forever.[9] During these same months, Henry also made a final gesture to the memory of William of Savoy, the queen's uncle, by resolving William's remaining £1000 in debts.

Financially speaking, these new grants were roughly equal in value to the annual fees which before 1242 Henry had paid to the Poitevin nobles who had now abandoned him. The difficulty was that these new obligations mostly called for grants of land, and as regards alienable manors and estates Henry was decidedly short of land after 1243. In a small way Henry attempted to remedy this situation through land purchases;[10] but the 1244 *terre Normannorum* inquests were his

    [4] See above, p. 218, for discussion of this grant.
    [5] Michael Clanchy, *England and Its Rulers*, (London, 1983), 235; Denholm-Young, *Richard of Cornwall*, 51–4.
    [6] *CLR* 1240–5, 198.
    [7] Denholm-Young, *Richard of Cornwall*, 48–51; *CPR* 1232–47, 437. For the events at Taillebourg, see pp. 195–6 above.
    [8] *CPR* 1232–47, 418, 420, 422.
    [9] Ibid., 415, 437.
    [10] Ibid., 446, 451, 458; *CLR* 1240–5, 297, 302, 319; and Pipe Roll 29 Henry III (E. 372/89 rots. 7d, 9, 12d).

most thoroughgoing response to the problem. The inquests did, of course, have a financial motive also: the fines which might be paid to retain such lands were not inconsequential, especially during a period of fiscal stringency. And there may also have been an element of reprisal in the campaign, since it appears that Louis IX had recently ordered the confiscation of all French lands still held by English families.[11] Never the less, although Henry's initial writ spoke only of inquests into lands belonging to persons in the power of the king of France, in fact the inquests ranged much more widely, and inquired into possession of all *terre Normannorum* lands dating back to the reign of King John. Many of the individuals whose lands were listed by the inquest as confiscatable had been resident in England for years, and could not by any stretch of the imagination have been regarded as being 'in the power of the king of France'.[12] Henry's real hope in ordering these inquests was probably to recover lands held without proper warrant, so as to redistribute them to the new claimants pressing upon him, a motive suggested also by his grant to the Lord Edward of half the recovered lands.[13] The revival of these inquests, for the first time since their abandonment in 1237, is a sign both of the urgency and of the arrogance of the king's administrators during these years.

Increasing expenditure also contributed to Henry's problems during these months. Almost immediately upon his return, Henry set off upon an elaborate round of alms-giving and court pageantry designed to restore his battered prestige as a monarch. Ordinarily, Henry's alms-giving in the decade after 1236 was relatively modest. In daily gifts, his almoner distributed between £100 and £200 per year from the wardrobe: 2s. to 3s. during Mass, and 5s. afterwards on feast days, 2d. or 3d. during Mass, and 4d. or 5d. afterwards on non-feast days.[14] During the 1240s, Henry also fed 500 poor people a day, a custom which added £700 to £800 per year to the cost of his alms-giving.[15]

---

[11] *CM*, vol. iv, 288. On the extent of these holdings by 1244, see Stevenson, 'England and Normandy', 199–237, 379–485.

[12] See the returns printed in *Book of Fees*, vol. ii, 1142–57, esp. 1144–7. Both William de Fednes and William Talbot had served as military retainers in Henry's household, while the Stutevilles and the Balliols were among the most important baronial families in the north.

[13] *CPR 1232–47*, 418.

[14] An almoner's roll survives for 1238–9 (C. 47/3/44). These yearly totals can also be confirmed from the wardrobe accounts for the period.

[15] *Cl.R. 1237–42*, 496–7; *CLR 1240–5*, 160, 169, 180; Hilda Johnstone, 'Poor Relief in the Royal Households of 13th-Century England', *Speculum* 4 (1929), 154–6. This

But beyond these sums, Henry's annual fixed and discretionary alms amounted only to about £600 to £800 in additional gifts. Between 1240 and 1245, Henry's total annual giving to churchmen and the poor thus averaged about £1500 to £1700 yearly; before 1240, it was probably about half this level. In 1243–4, however, in spite of all the other claims on the king's purse, it topped £3000.

Some of this increase derived from parting gifts to religious houses in Gascony, but the bulk of it was the result of Henry's English devotions and enthusiasms. Throughout his reign, Henry cultivated the sacral aura of monarchy in a very self-conscious manner, crossing himself like a priest, carrying candles like a cleric in religious processions and ceremonies, having the *Christus vincit* sung before him on every conceivable occasion, and carrying out an elaborate round of ritualized charitable works.[16] Such image-making did not, of course, succeed ultimately in staving off a baronial revolt; but in shaping popular attitudes toward the monarchy, especially in the wake of the disasters of John's reign, the political significance of Henry's alms-giving and public ceremonial should not be too quickly dismissed. And in the uncertain months following the Poitevin débâcle, Henry turned to such displays in a major way. In an ordinary year after 1240, Henry provided about 180,000 meals to the poor. In 1244, however, he provided almost 80,000 meals beyond this, sponsoring a series of mass feedings at Westminster (20,000), St Paul's (15,000) and Oxford (1600). Fifty-five thousand of these extra meals came in the first five months after the king's return.[17] During these same months, Henry also staged two ceremonial solemn entries into London, the first upon his own return from Gascony, the second only two months later, to welcome his mother-in-law the countess of Provence on her arrival for her daughter's wedding.[18] He also gave lavishly to the shrine of St Thomas of Canterbury during these months,[19] although his devotion to the martyr did nothing to soften his opposition to Ralegh's postulation at Winchester. Despite papal confirmation of Ralegh's position in

custom may only have begun around 1240. Except for two groups of 300 paupers fed on Christmas Eve and Maundy Thursday, there is no evidence for the custom on the 1238–9 almoner's roll (C. 47/3/44). On the chancery rolls, the first references to the mass feeding of poor people begin in 1239–40, when meals were sponsored at Windsor, probably on behalf of the infant Lord Edward: cf. *CLR 1226–40*, 433, 435, 446, 459.

[16] Michael Clanchy, 'Did Henry III have a Policy', *History* 54 (1968), 207–10.

[17] *CLR 1240–5*, 204, 210, 220, 281, 306–7; *Cl.R.* 1242–7, 140, 145, 150, 152, 164, 199.

[18] *CM*, vol. iv, 254–5, 261. At his own entry, Henry extracted a £100 gift from the Londoners, alleging this to be a custom of the realm: cf. E. 372/88 rot. 14.

[19] *CLR 1240–5*, 196, 200, 212.

September 1243, Henry continued this quarrel at Rome for another nine months, expending at least £500 in fruitless diplomatic costs, before finally accepting Ralegh's postulation in May 1244. Meanwhile, Henry had also to replace the more material accoutrements of monarchy during these months, having been forced to sell off his stores of cloth, plate, jewels, and furs in Gascony prior to his return.[20]

At Christmas 1243, Henry brought the ceremonial refurbishing of his kingship to a climax with the marriage of Earl Richard of Cornwall to the queen's younger sister, Sanchia of Provence. To celebrate the occasion, Henry entertained his magnates at an extraordinary feast, the splendour of which shines through all Matthew Paris's conventional deprecations of its worldliness.[21] And he surrounded these festivities with a further round of familial gift-giving which underscored the links which now bound together the ruling houses of England and Provence. Already responsible for her daughter's dowry, Henry also paid the countess's travelling expenses from Provence to England, and granted her a fee of £400 per year for seven years from the Vieuxpont custody.[22] At the feast of the Circumcision, when Henry customarily presented his household knights with rings and favoured magnates with brooches or jewelled belts, he presented his mother-in-law also with an elaborate gold eagle, which cost him over £100; while on her departure, Henry spent an additional £64 12s. on candles to light the churches of Canterbury against her arrival, and paid her travelling expenses back to Provence.[23]

The pace of Henry's alms-giving and ceremonial display declined after Easter, but his expenditure on building rose to match it, thus negating any benefit the exchequer might have had from the king's restraint. During the autumn and winter of 1243–4, Henry's construction expenses were surprisingly modest, no doubt in deference to the other claims upon his purse. Between 1236 and 1245, Henry's construction costs averaged about £2500 per year. Between Michaelmas 1243 and 1 March 1244, however, he spent less than £300 from the exchequer on building. Thereafter, however, his construction costs soared. By Michaelmas 1244, they had topped £6000 for the year, half drawn directly from the exchequer, the other half drawn from

[20] Ibid., 200, for one example among many; see also E. 403/5.
[21] CM, vol. iv, 263.
[22] CLR 1240–5, 200; E. 403/5; CPR 1232–47, 414.
[23] CLR 1240–5, 213, 211, 215. Records of Henry's gifts on the feast of the Circumcision are contained in the wardrobe accounts.

the revenues of the vacant bishoprics and from the king's pipe roll accountants. Henry's construction expenditures had reached £6000 at least once before, in 1240–1, but between 1241 and 1243 these had totalled only about £2100 per year. To some extent, then, Henry's enormous expenditures in 1243–4 were an attempt to catch up on projects left unfinished during the war years. But since his building expenses dropped back again in 1244–5 to their usual level of around £2500 per year, we are probably entitled to see these 1244 expenditures as yet another of Henry's attempts to rebuild monarchical prestige in the wake of his military defeats.

The necessity for such expenditure is not easy to evaluate. There is no doubt that in artistic and architectural matters, Henry was a connoisseur; equally, there is no doubt that a great deal of rebuilding was required in the decade after 1236 to accommodate the queen and her children, and to bring the king's houses and castles up to the rapidly rising European standards for monarchical elegance. In the absence of comparable figures for other decades and other monarchs, it is very hard to judge whether £2500 per year in construction costs was a reasonable or an unreasonable amount.[24] In 1244, for example, Henry spent about £2000 in constructing a chamber for the king's knights at Westminster.[25] A considerable sum, surely; but how can one measure the effect which such expenditures may have had upon the loyalty and affection of the king's military household for their lord? At the Tower of London, Henry's large expenditures between 1238 and 1241 were a clear military necessity, at what was arguably the most important single castle in the kingdom;[26] at Winchester and Windsor, his rebuilding was a mixture of domestic expansion and military improvement, which served the king well during the baronial wars of the 1260s. Rebuilding at Nottingham Castle showed a similar mixture of domestic and military concerns, the utility of which was clearly evident in 1244, when hostilities threatend between King Henry and the King of Scots. Elsewhere, Henry's domestic modifications to his

[24] Colvin, for example, notes that Henry's annual average expenditures on building were two to three times those of John: *The History of the King's Works*, vol. i, ed. R. A. Brown, H. M. Colvin, and A. J. Taylor, (London, 1963), 109; but one must reckon here not only with rising standards, but also with the incompleteness of the surviving records for John's expenditures. Only about half Henry's annual expenses for construction were recorded on the pipe rolls; this may well have been true for John as well, but the chancery rolls are inadequate to prove it.

[25] *CLR 1240–5*, 239.

[26] *King's Works*, vol. ii, 711–15, for details of this construction.

residences and hunting lodges during these years simply were not that expensive. Despite the loving detail of the liberate roll entries which describe them, such works rarely cost more than a few hundred pounds per project. Next to the expenditures at Winchester, Windsor, Westminster, and the Tower, they pale into insignificance.

After 1245, however, one's verdict on Henry's architectural 'extravagance' may be different. The rebuilding of Westminster Abbey alone added £2000 per year to the king's construction costs between 1245 and 1261,[27] and it seems doubtful whether in the eyes of his subjects, the king bought £30,000 worth of prestige with these sums. Indeed, by taking over what had been a favoured local project, Henry's rebuilding of the Abbey may even have inspired some local Westminster resentment towards him.[28] As usual, King Louis IX would appear to have obtained better value for his money with the Sainte Chapelle. But the era of such massive and continuing expenditure on architectural display only began in 1245, when the king took over the Abbey works; and like so many of the outlandish financial commitments of the 1250s, construction costs did not begin seriously to undermine the Crown's financial health until around 1250. Before that date, the demands of war played a far more determinant role in Crown finance than did the demands of the king's good taste.[29]

But whatever the verdict on such 'extravagance', there is no doubt that this combination of Poitevin debts, compensatory fees to wartime supporters, ceremonial alms-giving, and public display would by itself have been enough to put crown finance under serious strain during 1243–4. New diplomatic and military expenses, however, compounded these problems enormously. The count of Provence was known to be unwell; his death would leave as heiresses his four daughters, the eldest married to Louis IX, the next two now married to Henry and his brother Richard, and the youngest still unmarried. It was probably to strengthen his hand in the likely event of a disputed succession to Provence that Henry agreed in January 1244 to loan his impecunious father-in-law 4000 marks on the security of five Provençal castles.[30] Just what Henry intended to do with these castles is unclear, but they were chosen with care, and were of considerable strategic importance

---

[27] *King's Works*, vol. i, 155–7; I include the cost of the shrine.
[28] Local contributions to the Abbey works virtually disappear after 1245, although they had been common until that date: cf. A. G. Rosser, 'The Essence of Medieval Urban Communities: the Vill of Westminster, 1200–1540', *TRHS*, 5th s. 34 (1984), 102.
[29] Colvin's verdict is similar: cf. *King's Works*, vol. i, 109.
[30] *CLR 1240–5*, 213; *CPR 1232–47*, 416, 418; Cox, *Eagles of Savoy*, 119–20, 149–54.

in the region. At the very least, Henry probably hoped to use these castles to forestall further French gains in this vital area while Count Raymond was still alive. He may also have hoped that control over these castles might keep Provence out of French hands when Count Raymond died, or at least allow him to trade possession of these castles, and the mountain passes they controlled, against more proximate concessions by King Louis. Alternatively, Henry may also have hoped that by establishing himself as a power in the Alpine foothills, he could act as mediator in the war between the pope, now based in Lyons, and Emperor Frederick II of Germany. Despite the recent death of Henry's sister Isabella, Frederick remained his most important potential ally on the Continent, and Henry could ill afford a complete imperial collapse on the south-eastern borders of France. In the end, however, the castles proved worthless to all these ends. Henry was simply too far away from Provence to control them. When the count of Provence died in 1245, the countess turned over her youngest daughter and her county to Louis IX, to whose brother the heiress was promptly married. Henry's interests in the area continued none the less. On behalf of his queen, he appealed several times to Louis to grant her her rightful portion of Provence, while in January 1246 Henry accepted the homage of Count Amadeus of Savoy, transferring to him certain of his own local claims in the region, and promising to pay the count £1000 for his homage, plus an annual fee of 200 marks.[31] As with Henry's other Alpine schemes, the purposes of this arrangement remain obscure. Peter d'Aigueblanche was its leading proponent on the council, but it was discussed in detail by the entire council before any offer to the count was made.[32] The arrangement must have offered some advantages which were clearer at the time than they are to us.

Ultimately, however, the renewed demands of war were what turned 1244 from a year of unavoidable stringency into a year of distinct financial crisis. In Gascony, a border war erupted between Bayonne and Navarre during the spring of 1244, and continued for almost a year, bringing with it further chaos in Gascony, and a new round of compensatory fees for dispossessed royal supporters. The total costs of this war are hard to calculate, but from the English exchequer alone

---

[31] CPR 1232–47, 469; CM, vol. iv, 550; Denholm-Young, *Richard of Cornwall*, 51–3; Clanchy, *England and its Rulers*, 230–5.

[32] *Diplomatic Documents*, no. 260; although dated 1246, this must in fact pertain to 1245: cf. CPR 1232–47, 469.

during 1244 they amounted to at least 4000 marks.[33] Trouble was also brewing in Scotland, where relations between Louis IX and King Alexander were becoming dangerously close. To forestall the threat of such an alliance, Henry summoned his military forces in the summer of 1244 and marched north to confront Alexander. Assisted by a large force of Flemish knights led by Thomas of Savoy count of Flanders, Henry was clearly prepared to fight. But at the last moment, the king of Scots came to Henry at Newcastle, and agreed to make no alliance with Henry's enemies. This arrangement averted the threat of war in the north, but preparations for the expedition cost Henry a minimum of £4000, three-quarters of this sum going to the king's Flemish troops in gifts, fees and wages.[34]

Along with these Gascon and Scottish problems, a bloody and destructive war also broke out in Wales during 1244, which threatened to undo all the gains Henry had made there in 1241. The war began with simmering hostility and sporadic border raids, which during the autumn of 1244 intensified into an all out Welsh attack on the lands of the marcher lords and on the new royal castles still under construction at Dyserth and Deganwy. The marcher lords, as usual, bore the brunt of the initial onslaught, along with the skeleton forces which Henry maintained in garrison at Montgomery and the Three Castles of White, Skenfrith and Grosmont.[35] At first, Henry apparently thought the Welsh could be contained without a full scale expedition. During the summer of 1244, he therefore detached two bodies of household troops to assist the marcher lords, the southern force commanded by John of Monmouth, and the northern force under Herbert fitz Matthew, a former seneschal of Gascony.[36] But when the northern force was mauled by the Welsh, and fitz Matthew killed, Henry began in January 1245 to make plans to lead out an army himself the following summer.[37] Summoning assistance from Ireland and from his English tenants-in-chief, the king spent more than two months in Chester and Wales during 1245, completing the construction of Deganwy (Gannoc) Castle and harrying the Welsh countryside. Although the war dragged on through 1246, the destruction by an Irish

[33] CPR 1232–47, 422, 445; CLR 1240–5, 247, 267–8, 271, 274–5.
[34] CLR 1240–5, 264; Pipe Roll 28 Henry III (E. 372/88 rot. 14); CM, vol. iv, 359, 378, 381–5.
[35] CM, vol. iv, 323–4, 358; CLR 1240–5, 275.
[36] CPR 1232–47, 427, 431; CLR 1240–5, 259, 260, 263, 271; CM, vol. iv, 385–6.
[37] CLR 1240–5, 287 gives the first hint that Henry was planning to lead out a summer expedition. For fitz Matthew's death, see CM, vol. iv, 407–9.

force of the Welsh grain fields in Anglesey was ultimately decisive, and with the death of the Welsh leader David ap Llewellyn in late 1246, the war wound down to a reasonably successful close, at least from Henry's standpoint. The 1247 Treaty of Woodstock returned his position in Wales to what it had been in 1241, restoring the territorial *status quo ante bellum* and guaranteeing him the direct homage and fealty of all the local Welsh rulers, thus excluding the intermediary authority of any 'prince of Wales', such as Llewellyn the Great and David ap Llewellyn had sought to become.[38] Given the modesty of his ambitions in Wales, this was, for Henry, a highly satisfactory outcome.

That Henry could mount such a series of military campaigns so soon after the Poitevin débâcle says much about the fundamental strength and resilience of the crown's financial resources during these years, despite the undeniable signs of financial strain. By the summer of 1244, the exchequer was entirely out of cash, with no further receipts expected until Michaelmas,[39] a fact which forced the king into a series of short-term expedients to confront the crises facing him. The Gascon expenses were met by loans raised in Gascony, but repayable at the English exchequer after Michaelmas 1244. Payments on the king's wine purchases during the summer of 1244 were similarly delayed until after Michaelmas, while the royal household struggled along on loans from Richard of Cornwall and from the reluctant Italian merchants, whom Henry finally threatened to expel in 1245 if they would not lend him money.[40] But aside from the 1245 scutage of Gannoc, which by 1247 had produced less than £1000,[41] Henry financed all three of these military expeditions from his regular revenues, supplemented by new Jewish taxation, a tallage on the royal demesne, and by loans. Remarkably, this system succeeded in keeping armies in the field. Although the Welsh expedition encountered some supply problems,[42] there are no signs that the king ran out of money to finance it. It is clear, however, from the loans he had to raise to equip this campaign that Henry had no cash reserves left to sustain him, despite his efforts

[38] Walker, 'Anglo-Welsh Wars', 7. I am heavily indebted to Walker for the structure of the narrative as it appears above. See also J. E. Lloyd, *A History of Wales from the earliest times to the Edwardian conquest*, 2 vols. (London, 1939), vol. ii, 700–8.
[39] See the letter from William de Haverhull to the king in Ancient Correspondence (S. C. 1/3/90).
[40] *Cl.R. 1242–7*, 314–15.
[41] Mitchell, *Studies*, 246.
[42] See the letter written from Gannoc while the king was encamped there, in *CM*, vol. iv, 481–4.

throughout 1244 to create such a fund.[43] By the end of 1245, his financial affairs were thus firmly established on the hand-to-mouth footing which would continue to characterize them until the end of the reign.

It need not have been so. By November 1244, when the king approached his baronage in parliament to seek an aid on moveables, he ought to have been able to see the Welsh war coming. Indeed, the war itself was already fully launched. All that remained in question was the role which Henry himself would choose to play in it. Had Henry based his request for funds on the need to thoroughly subjugate the Welsh, and agreed to the demands made at the parliament to afforce his council with additional members, the king might well have recovered the political initiative and re-established his financial equilibrium. Characteristically, however, Henry based his request for funds, which he made personally to the parliament,[44] not on the costs of the Scottish and Welsh campaigns, but on the debts he had incurred in Poitou, which he disingenuously claimed to have undertaken on the advice of the magnates.[45] The effect of such a claim on the magnates can be easily imagined. With William de Ralegh in attendance as the newly installed bishop of Winchester, the assembled prelates sought the co-operation of the lay magnates in returning a joint response to the king. The laity agreed, and a committee of four bishops, four earls, two barons, and two abbots was selected to deal with the king's request.

The unity of the lay and clerical opposition to Henry, revealed by this joint response, was the most significant political consequence of the policies the king had pursued since 1239, and marks the most ominous contrast between this parliament and the one which had met in similar circumstances in 1237. By 1244, however, Henry's long resistance to Ralegh's postulation, his blatant manipulation of canonical elections at Hereford and Canterbury, and his attempt to have his financial administrator Robert Passelewe confirmed at Chichester,

---

[43] CLR 1240–5, 209, 229, 230, 238; CPR 1232–47, 424, 437, 457.

[44] CM, vol. iv, 362. The king's appeal, *ore proprio*, was a new ploy, in marked contrast to the role which William de Ralegh had played in 1237, and William of York in 1242, as the king's spokesmen to the parliament. After the failure of 1242, Henry may have decided he could do a better job himself. Certainly by this date he had no administrator of any greater stature than William of York on his council who could have acted as spokesman for him.

[45] Unless otherwise noted, all information on the proceedings during this parliament is derived from CM, vol. iv, 362–8, 372–4.

had convinced the prelates that the liberties of the church were now
fundamentally threatened; while to the lay magnates, Henry's 1244
terre Normannorum inquests and confiscation were only the latest in
a long series of threats to the security of seisin dating back to at least
1233.[46] As in 1237, Henry's critics found their rallying point in Magna
Carta, which they alleged Henry had never observed, despite his oaths
to Archbishop Edmund Rich, yet another Canterbury martyr, whom
Henry's actions thus posthumously betrayed. Along with his alleged
violations of the Charter, the committee further complained to the
king that the aids they had already granted him had not profited the
realm as they should have done had they indeed been spent on the
necessitas regni for which they had been granted.[47] They complained
also that unjust writs had been issued over the king's seal because of
the absence of a chancellor and a justiciar.[48] They therefore sought to
have new such officials appointed, who would become permanent
members of the council. Henry, in reply, refused to appear to act under
compulsion, but promised to remedy the complaints he had heard. To
this the spokesmen responded that if the king would select such
councillors and deal with the *jura* of the realm so as to content the
magnates, they would gather again in late February to make some
response to the king's request, provided that any funds then granted
ad commodum regni should be expended only under the supervision
of the twelve spokesmen.

Henry, however, had no intention of making concessions to such
complaints; once again, the contrast with Ralegh's management of the
1237 parliament is clear. Instead, he sought first to weaken the
assembled magnates by several additional days of pleading. When that
failed, he dismissed the lay magnates, but retained the clergy for
another day, communicating to them a letter from the pope in support
of his requests, and sending special messengers to press his case. These
messengers included the earl of Leicester who, despite being a member
of the committee of twelve which had refused the king's request, now
tried to convince the clergy to make an immediate grant. It was
apparently only at this point, after the lay magnates had departed,
that the king's messengers raised the issue of the Welsh war as grounds
for granting an aid. The king himself, however, appears to have taken

[46] For the disseisin of Gilbert Basset in that year, see pp. 38–9 above.
[47] For the significance of this language, see Harriss, *King, Parliament, and Public
Finance*, 27–39.
[48] For discussion see p. 216 and n. 37 above.

little interest in this particular argument, which may explain why it played such a minor part in the proceedings. In his personal appearance before the detained clerics, Henry laid stress not on the Welsh but on his own honour, which, he argued, ought to be as dear to the clergy as was their honour to him.[49] In view of all the references to the fate of Archbishop Rich, and in an assembly which included William de Ralegh, this may not have been Henry's strongest debating point. None the less, there were signs that the clergy were starting to waver, until Bishop Robert Grosseteste brought them back into line, quoting scripture to the effect that if they allowed themselves to be separated from their common stand with the magnates, they would all perish separately in consequence. On this mournful note, the prelates too adjourned until February, to await the outcome of events.

In view of the amount of ink spilt already over the proposals enshrined in the paper constitution, it is important to keep in mind the relative moderation of the proposals which were actually presented to the king in 1244. The paper constitution itself is a more radical document, which proposes an elaborate system of co-optation for the four new councillors it wished to add to the king's council, and which envisioned these four 'conservators of liberties' supervising all of the king's financial affairs. But despite the heading Matthew Paris gives to the document, which implies that it was agreed to by the king, I am inclined to believe, with Cheney, that it was only a draft proposal, which was never actually presented to Henry.[50] The committee's proposal to supervise the expenditure of the proposed aid recalls the offer made in 1237 by William de Ralegh to the assembled magnates as part of the terms on which he sought a thirtieth for the king.[51] This was probably not coincidental: Ralegh was one of the six clerical spokesmen on the 1244 committee of twelve. Except for Grosseteste, however, he was the only member of the twelve who could conceivably have been considered a royal opponent. Among the earls, Cornwall, Leicester, and Norfolk all had court connections; Walter Marshal's sentiments are not known, but had Henry been willing to use the aid to suppress the Welsh, it is hard to imagine the Marshal opposing him. The archbishop of Canterbury was the king's uncle, Boniface of Savoy. The bishop of Worcester, Walter Cantilupe, was a respected canon lawyer and a friend of Grosseteste, but he was also a member of an

---

[49] CM, vol. iv, 365: '... quod honor eorum honor suus foret, et e converso'.
[50] Cheney, 'Paper Constitution', 213–21.
[51] See p. 112 above.

important marcher family with close connections to the court. His brother William was one of Henry's household stewards, and was chosen, along with Leicester and several other household men, as one of the king's special messengers to the detained clergy. Neither the two barons, Richard de Muntfichet and John de Balliol, nor the abbots of St Edmunds and Ramsey, are likely to have played a major role in the deliberations, whatever their sentiments may have been towards the king. This was not a body of men likely to propose a revolution, or even a continuing, baronially controlled royal council. None the less, the king was unyielding, and when the magnates returned in 1245, they found his administration and its financial policies to be exactly as they had left them in November.

Henry's failure to seize the opportunity which the Welsh war presented to unite the magnates in a popular, common cause, and his refusal to make even token concessions towards the 1244 complaints, thus ensured that the 1245 parliament would be little more successful than its predecessor. In the end, the assembly did vote the king an aid at a rate of 20s. on the knight's fee to marry his eldest daughter, who was still an infant. Even this was a Pyrrhic victory, however. Legally, the king did not require magnate consent to levy such an aid in the first place. By giving it, the assembly not only staked a claim to revive a provision of Magna Carta 1215 which had been dropped from all subsequent reissues; it also restricted the assessment of the aid to the customary *servitia debita*, thus short-circuiting Henry's longstanding attempt to bring the entire knight service of England under contribution to aids and scutages. Victories such as these cost the king at least as much as he gained from them; but without more negotiating talent than either he or his present council possessed, Pyrrhic victories were all the king could win over his magnates during these years.

Much of the opposition the king encountered in this parliament was a direct product of his fiscal and administrative policies over the preceding year. As in 1236–7, Henry had put the realm under great pressure during 1244 in an attempt to pay his debts. In January, he began the *terre Normannorum* inquests, thus reviving a threat the magnates thought they had disposed of in 1237.[52] In February, he also initiated a series of inquests into sergeanties alienated without license, at first confiscating such holdings, and then returning them to their holders at an annual rent.[53] During April, this pressure intensified.

[52] *CPR 1232–47*, 418; *Book of Fees*, vol. ii, 1142–57; *CM*, vol. iv, 288.
[53] *Cl.R. 1242–7*, 236–7, 213, 258–9; *Book of Fees*, vol. ii, 1163–1258.

Robert Passelewe began another round of inquests in the royal forests, searching out unlicensed assarts for confiscation or arrentation, investigating the rights of the king's foresters to their offices, and adding acreage to the king's forests in contravention of the Forest Charter.[54] A new proclamation, which Matthew Paris thought was intended specifically to punish the Cistercians' refusal to grant an aid for the Gascon expedition, prohibited the sale of wool out of the realm without the king's license, while another forbade all merchants to lend money.[55] At the same time, Henry also renewed his 1242 efforts to distrain the £20 freeholders of the realm to take up knighthood.[56] Most ominous of all these measures, however, was the king's proclamation to his sheriffs, also in April 1244, that henceforward no liberties of any sort were to be recognized unless they had been warranted by the king or his predecessors, or else were held by ancient tenure and had been exercised prior to the meeting at Runnymede in 1215.[57] Throughout his reign, Henry remained convinced that many valuable royal rights had been lost during his minority, and in times of financial exigency he was particularly inclined to search these out for recovery.

Against this background, it is plausible to read the paper constitution's references to 'liberties' as having both a general reference to Magna Carta and a more specific reference to the franchisal rights threatened by the king in 1244.[58] And in this respect as in others, there is a suggestive parallel, both in the king's policies and the magnates' response, to the circumstances which had produced the reconfirmation of Magna Carta in 1237 in exchange for the thirtieth on moveables. As in 1236–7, the king had resorted during 1244 to a series of administrative measures which asserted and enforced acknowledged royal rights, but which in doing so gave rise to far more resentment and annoyance than their meagre cash yields could justify. And in each case too, the resulting grievances had produced a serious political confrontation in the ensuing parliament. As an approach to resolving the king's debts, such policies made sense only if the king could trade

---

[54] CPR 1232–47, 442; Cl.R. 1242–7, 243–4, 253; CM, vol. iv, 400–1, 426–7, and for the articles of the inquest, CM, vol. vi, 94–9. On the addition of acreage to the forests, see Young, *Royal Forests*, 77, citing C. 47/11/3/9.

[55] Cl.R. 1242–7, 240, 242; CM, vol. iv, 324.

[56] Cl.R. 1242–7, 242.

[57] Cl.R. 1242–7, 242; cf. also ibid., 212, where the earl of Leicester's liberties are guaranteed notwithstanding the fact that they had not been exercised in times past.

[58] Notice especially the reference to the need to reform the state of those whose liberties had been injured since the last concession: CM, vol. iv, 366.

redress of these resulting grievances against a grant of voluntary taxation from the magnates; and in 1244 as in 1237, it was clearly the king's intention to seek an aid. The difference was that in 1244 Henry had no one on his council whom the magnates in parliament trusted enough to bargain with for such a grant; while the king himself, who carried the burden of the negotiations personally, seems not to have been inclined to bargain at all. Had he done so, the results might well have been different. If one lays aside the demands of the paper constitution, and focuses instead on the demands actually advanced by the magnates, it seems clear that the magnates were not asking very much more in 1244 than Ralegh had been prepared to concede them in 1237: the appointment of a chancellor and a justiciar; the addition of a few new members to the council; and magnate supervision over the expenditure of any such aid as should be granted.[59] These were not radical demands. Moreover, even without the satisfaction of their grievances, the magnates were still willing to grant the king a feudal aid to marry his daughter, knowing full well that this was simply a device to raise money for the king. In 1237, the magnates had purchased concessions from the king by paying him a thirtieth on moveables. In 1244, they were probably prepared to do so again. What they were not prepared to do was grant taxation without purchasing anything at all from the king. They had already purchased the general liberties of the realm in 1225, and had confirmed their purchase, with further liberties, in 1237. They would not buy Magna Carta, by itself, again. The language of commercial exchange is writ large across these 1244 negotiations: unless the king had something new to sell, the magnates had nothing new to buy, and therefore saw no reason to pay a tax.

Behind the failure of these negotiations, however, lay deeper grievances than the king's 1244 administrative exactions and his stubbornness. Fundamentally, what had broken down was the king's relationship with his magnates, a fact manifest by 1244 both in the magnates' deep-seated distrust of Henry's councillors, and in the unity which had emerged between the king's lay and ecclesiastical critics. Both these developments were products of the financial and administrative policies Henry had pursued since 1239. Partly as a way to forward his Poitevin schemes without hindrance, and partly because of the personal animosities which had wrecked the 1236–9 council's efforts, Henry had drawn his councillors since 1239 almost entirely

[59] Ibid., 362–3.

from the ranks of his household administrative officials. As a result, by 1244 he and his household were dangerously isolated from the greatest portion of the earls and barons.[60] Among the great men of the realm, only Cornwall, Leicester, and Peter of Savoy were consistently influential figures at court during 1244, and they were hardly less closely identified with the household than were the king's clerks. Indeed, this household element on the council had been even further strengthened during 1244 with the death of the chancellor Ralph de Nevill and the emergence of John Mansel and Paulinus Peyvre as the king's leading councillors.[61] Along with Robert Passelewe, who also emerges prominently during 1244, these three men were principally responsible for the administrative policies which helped provoke the 1244–5 opposition. They also neatly symbolized the abuses which had unified Henry's lay and ecclesiastical opponents. Peyvre, a layman, had been the keeper of the Winchester vacancy; John Mansel, one of the king's fighting clerks, had figured in a lengthy and violent squabble with Robert Grosseteste over the prebend of Thame, to which the king had presented him; while Henry's nomination of his forest admin-istrator Passelewe to the see of Chichester had been turned down flat just months before by Grosseteste, who declared the candidate unfit for episcopal office. These were the administrators at the centre of the lay and ecclesiastical opposition in 1244.

In fact, however, this opposition was less united than at first it might appear. The prelates' grievances against the council had to do with extended ecclesiastical vacancies, with manipulated episcopal elections, with the circumscribed jurisdiction of the Church courts, and increasingly after 1243, with the demands of papal taxation. The earls and greatest barons blamed the council for the king's alarming threats to seisin and to franchises, and for the miserable advice which had taken him to Poitou; but except when papal claims threatened their own rights over benefices and advowsons, the grievances of the clergy were not of pressing concern to them. The grievances of lesser

---

[60] The extent of this isolation is revealed by the witness list to the Dec. 1243 charter confirming Richard of Cornwall's resignation of his claims to Gascony. This agreement, of fundamental importance to the realm, was witnessed by four bishops (York, Nevill the chancellor, Mauclerc the former treasurer, and Peter d'Aigueblanche), four stewards (Cantilupe, fitz Geoffrey, fitz Nicholas, and Cryoll), two household bannerets (Hugh de Vivona and Philip Basset), five royal clerks (Passelewe, John Mansel, Henry de Susa, Guy de Russilun, and Artaud de St Romano), and by the chief justice *coram rege*, William of York: *CPR 1232–47*, 437. This was a pattern characteristic of all the king's business in the years after 1239.

[61] *CM*, vol. iv, 294.

men, the knights and men of the shires, were different again, and tended to be more directly related to the obnoxious fiscal policies to which indebtedness drove the king's administrators. Distraint to knighthood, the arrentation of sergeanties and assarts, the revocation of disafforested forest land, and the traffic in encumbered estates resulting from excessive Jewish tallages, all bore most heavily upon these smaller men. In 1244, all three of these groups came together to deny the king the aid he sought, and to root their sense of grievance in the king's alleged breaches of Magna Carta. But the Charter meant very different things to these three groups in 1244, as the divergent nature of their grievances should indicate.[62] And in the years after 1245, Henry was able to play upon these differences to divide the united opposition which had frustrated him in 1244.

The unity between the lay and ecclesiastical opposition was in some respects the most remarkable aspect of the 1244–5 resistance, but it also proved the most evanescent. On such matters as the proper jurisdiction of church courts the two groups would never see eye to eye, and in his 1247 regulations defining and restricting such juris-diction, Henry shrewdly exploited the differences between them.[63] In other respects, however, Henry did his best to mollify ecclesiastical complaints. In part because there were very few episcopal vacancies between 1244 and 1250, there was only one extended vacancy, at Bath. And while the king's clerks continued to be elected to the vacancies which did occur, Henry's candidates during these years were worthy ones, and excited no alarm.[64] Although the king eventually backed down, he did also make some efforts during 1245 and 1246 to protect the church from the pope's financial demands.[65] Despite his lack of resolution, Henry was still the church's only hope in trying to resist papal taxation, and in the years between 1244 and 1250, ecclesiastical attention was therefore more often focused on papal excesses than on Henry's.

The key to Henry's difficulties in 1244 and 1245, however, lay in his tenuous relations with his magnates, especially the earls; and in the years following this parliament, he set about systematically to recon-struct his links with his greatest men. The death of the last Marshall

[62] Maddicott, 'Magna Carta and the Local Community', *passim.*

[63] *CM,* vol. iv, 614.

[64] Silvester de Everdon was elected to Carlisle and William of York to Salisbury in 1246, and Walter de Kirkham went to Durham in 1249. This changes again, of course, with the Nov. 1250 election of Aymer de Lusignan to Winchester.

[65] Lunt, *Financial Relations of the Papacy with England to 1327,* 206–19.

Earl of Pembroke in late 1245 helped his cause considerably. Henry's relations with the Marshals had always been uneasy, and with their passing, he was able to distribute their vast holdings among more pliant men. Cornwall, Leicester, and Peter of Savoy were already comfortably within the court circle in 1244; but during the following years, through marriages, gifts, and favours, Henry laboured assiduously to bring the earls of Gloucester, Norfolk, and Hereford also into his orbit. By and large he succeeded. Gloucester and Norfolk had grown up at Henry's court, while Hereford's large debts, acquired with his inheritance, made it especially important for him to curry the king's favour. The earl of Norfolk became the new Earl Marshal, and served frequently on diplomatic missions abroad, while the newly invested earl of Gloucester emerged after 1245 as the preponderant power in the Marches of southern Wales. So successfully did Henry integrate his comital supporters with his household administrators that by 1251 the king's justices could describe the earl of Gloucester as John Mansel's partner in the rule of the kingdom.[66] Although ultimately disastrous in its results, Henry's introduction of his Poitevin relations into England after 1246 was also part of this same attempt to bind the greatest nobles of the realm more closely to the king and his court.[67] Here as elsewhere, however, Henry failed to reckon with the depth of English prejudice against the Poitevins.

The king cemented these new alliances with a lavish use of patronage. Aside from the usual gifts, grants, and marriages, however, Henry also relaxed the normal rules of judicial and administrative equity in dealing with his new court party. The consequences of such laxity became steadily more apparent throughout the 1250s. By 1258, a series of unofficial and unsanctioned liberties had emerged on these favoured magnates' lands, wherein the king's writ did not run, and his officials did not enter.[68] Towards the men outside this charmed court circle, however, Henry's government was anything but lax in the decade prior to the 1258 revolt. The king renewed his campaigns against unauthorized franchises in 1250, and again in 1255; and on the marchers' lands at least, the impact of these campaigns was felt, except of course by the earl of Gloucester and his agents.[69] Even greater pressure

---

[66] Maddicott, 'Magna Carta and the Local Community', 60.

[67] Carpenter, 'Personal Rule', 57–60 makes this point clearly.

[68] Carpenter, 'Personal Rule', 62–70; Maddicott, 'Magna Carta and the Local Community', 50–61.

[69] Michael Clanchy, 'The Franchise of Return of Writs', *TRHS* 5th s. 17 (1967), 64–9 and *passim*; R. R. Davies, 'Kings, Lords and Liberties in the March of Wales, 1066–

was brought against ecclesiastical claims to the issues from eyre amercements, and against the boroughs' claims to return the king's writs.[70] Henry's pressure on franchises was too inconsistent to be termed a policy; but on those who fell victim to it, it could have a considerable effect, not least because more favoured individuals never suffered such oppressions at all.

The king's success in turning the greatest men of the realm into a body of court supporters entirely transformed the nature of the political opposition the king would face in the decade prior to the 1258 rebellion; and when finally the court did break apart in 1258, Henry's council fractured along the factional lines which divided the Poitevins from their court opponents. It did not divide into a household and a comital camp. Such successes were not, however, an adequate response to the problem of Crown finance. The aid granted the king in 1245 was probably sufficient to repay the debts remaining from the preceding three years of war, but it left no surplus against future emergencies. The profits of the 1247–9 recoinage, combined with the last receipts from the 60,000 mark Jewish tallage, probably sufficed to keep the king's accounts in balance up to the end of the decade. But thereafter, the king's financial situation quickly became desperate. Henry's expenditures were rising from the late 1240s on, due to the increasing costs of construction (especially at Westminster Abbey), diplomacy (connected first with the crusade, and then with the Sicilian negotiations), and war (especially in Gascony). His revenues, meanwhile, were almost certainly declining. Receipts from the royal demesne had been reduced by the fees granted out after 1245 to his wartime supporters and to his Poitevin relations. The extraordinary tallages of the 1240s had effectively bankrupted the Jewish community, and permanently reduced its financial value to the Crown. Edward's endowment was an increasing strain on the budget, which became a haemmorhage after his 1254 marriage; while the baron's continuing refusal to grant the king an aid reflected the rising tide of local resentment against the king's exactions, and revealed the earls' very limited capacity to command the assent of the wider baronage in parliament.[72]

1272', *TRHS* 5th s. 29 (1979), 56–60; and see Carpenter, 'Personal Rule', 49–52 and n. 62 for some suggested modifications to Davies's argument.

[70] Carpenter, 'Personal Rule', 49–52 and n. 51; Clanchy, 'Return of Writs', 64–9.

[71] Carpenter, 'What Happened in 1258?', *passim*.

[72] This is especially striking in the negotiations for an aid in 1254: cf. Maddicott, 'Magna Carta and the Local Community', 46.

Even the revenues which were theoretically rising were consistently mismanaged. Although the profits imposed on the shires rose gradually after 1245, and markedly from about 1250, the king's council regularly failed to notify the exchequer of the new amounts to be collected. Between 1245 and 1250, such administrative failures combined with the sheriffs' inability to collect the higher amounts to nullify the financial advantage the king ought to have derived from the new increases. All that seems to have risen substantially was the level of shrieval oppression in the countryside. In the shires, Henry's justices began a systematic campaign during the late 1240s to increase the incidence of *murdrum* fines assigned on eyre, while the sheriffs, under increasing pressure from the exchequer, raised new obligations to frankpledge, suit of court, and a host of other petty exactions and oppressions. Grievances over forest boundaries went unanswered, while the traffic in encumbered estates around the court went on unchecked.

With respect to the management of the royal demesne, the situation was only slightly better. When the leases assigned to the manors in 1240 expired in 1245, the council made no effort to investigate the present value of these manors, or to assign revised farms to them. Additional manors were granted out to the king's supporters and relations, but otherwise the demesne manors in 1250 were held on the terms established in 1240. The only change in their administration was the serious and mounting confusion at the exchequer as to the identity of the persons holding them, and the terms on which they were held. Some of this confusion is probably attributable to the death of Alexander de Swereford in 1246, but the king's council must bear much of the responsibility. The exchequer simply could not function if it was not kept properly informed, and this the king's council manifestly failed to do with respect to the shire farms and the royal demesne lands.[73]

The trouble with such policies was, of course, that like so many of Henry's fiscal expedients, they raised much more political annoyance than expendable cash; and it was precisely because the king had not met their existing grievances over forest boundaries, distraint of knighthood, and the confiscation of sergeanties and assarts, that the lesser baronage particularly would not grant him an aid. The financial policies pursued by the king's administrators after 1243 could only

[73] Pipe Rolls 30–35 Henry III (E. 372/90–95), *passim*.

exacerbate such local grievances, and thus render the likelihood of any voluntary aid increasingly remote. This pattern of abuse and annoyance, leading on to the refusal of an aid, which in turn produced more abuse and more annoyance, set Henry's relations with the localities on a collision course with disaster during the 1250s. But this result was not foreordained, even in 1245, and it certainly was not the inevitable product of the financial reforms which Ralegh had set under way in 1236. Between 1236 and 1245, the king's finances were fundamentally sound. It was only the coincidence of rising expenses and declining revenues from the late 1240s on, combined of course with the utter lunacy of the Sicilian obligations, which brought Crown finance to its 1258 state of collapse. And even then it is significant that political rebellion broke out only when the king's carefully constructed court party broke into warring factions as a result of the immoderate favour the king had shown towards his despised Poitevin relations. After 1245, Henry's adroit handling of his magnates left the festering grievances of the shire knights without political leadership, and kept his lay and ecclesiastical critics divided, right until the eve of the 1258 rebellion. Financially, too, his position was fundamentally sound, probably until his return from his second Gascon expedition in 1253–4. Thereafter, however, matters quickly became desperate.

It is traditional to paint Henry III as an inept monarch, whose fundamental inadequacies led the realm inevitably towards revolt. This is unfair to Henry, and in so far as it implies that a few root causes led more or less directly from 1227, or 1236, to the rebellion of 1258, it is positively misleading. Henry was a king who learned from mistakes, both his father's and his own. His reign is a complicated one because of this fact. Henry's policies as a king changed frequently, in response to new problems or, more often, to new complaints about his previous policies. Nowhere is the reactive quality of his kingship clearer than with respect to Crown financial policy. Between 1236 and 1239, his administration attempted to respond to the problems created by the factional conflicts of the minority. Under Ralegh's leadership, these were the only years when a truly long-range view was taken toward the development of the Crown's financial resources. Richard of Cornwall's revolt brought Ralegh's control over the council to an end; between 1239 and 1245, the king adopted a very different approach to Crown finance, focusing his ambitions on Poitou and Provence, and exploiting the revenues from ecclesiastical vacancies and Jewish taxation to support them. After 1245, Henry changed course again, and embarked on a systematic attempt to repair the damage done to his relations with his magnates during the preceding six years of household government. This approach too created its own set of problems, which after a further series of twists and turns, led on to the curial explosion of 1258, to the consolidation of the king's opponents into a briefly united party, and ultimately to rebellion and civil war.

The financial and political crises of the 1250s thus came as a short, sharp shock, not as the necessary consequences to three decades of abuse. Had Ralegh's 1236–9 reforms survived to become the foundation on which Henry's financial and political strategies were to be based, the disasters which overtook Henry during the 1250s might well have been avoided. At the very least, they would have assumed a different shape, because Ralegh's reforms were founded on a perception that baronial consent to the king's policies, foreign and domestic, was essential to Crown finance and to effective kingly rule. Like his father before him, Henry was not prepared to be bound by such limitations. The recovery of Poitou was simply too important to him. But it was not until the 1250s that the king's unpopular ambitions at home and abroad decisively outdistanced his capacity to finance them through the traditional fiscal prerogatives of the Crown. Then, and only then, was he faced with a revolt. By 1258, therefore, Henry was indeed sitting on a volcano. But it was a relatively new volcano, which he himself had created in the decade immediately prior to 1258. It was not the inevitable product of thirty years of rising grievance and complaint.

SELECT BIBLIOGRAPHY

MANUSCRIPT SOURCES

Public Record Office, London

C. 47	Chancery Miscellanea
C. 60	Fine Rolls
C. 72	Scutage Rolls
E. 40	Ancient Deeds
E. 101	Exchequer King's Remembrancer, Accounts, Various
E. 159	Memoranda Rolls, KR
E. 163	Miscellanea of the Exchequer
E. 199	Sheriffs' Accounts
E. 352	Chancellor's Rolls
E. 364	Foreign Accounts
E. 368	Memoranda Rolls, Lord Treasurer's Remembrancer
E. 370	Miscellaneous Rolls, LTR and Pipe Office
E. 371	Originalia Rolls, LTR
E. 372	Pipe Rolls
E. 401	Receipt Rolls of the Lower Exchequer
E. 403	Issue Rolls of the Lower Exchequer
JI 1	Eyre and Assize Rolls
KB 26	Plea Rolls, Bench and Coram Rege
SC 1	Ancient Correspondence

Bodleian Library, Oxford

Rawlinson B 150	Battle Abbey Chronicle

British Library, London

Cotton MS Faustina A. VIII	Annals of Southwark
Cotton MS Julius D. V	Chronicle of St Martin's Priory, Dover

PRINTED SOURCES

Annales Monastici, ed. Henry R. Luard, 5 vols., Rolls Series (London, 1864–9).

'The Annals of Southwark and Merton', ed. M. Tyson, *Surrey Archaeological Collections* 26 (1925), 24–57.

The Beauchamp Cartulary Charters, 1100–1268, ed. Emma Mason, PRS n. s. 43 (London, 1980).

Bracton: De Legibus et Consuetudinibus Angliae, ed. G. E. Woodbine, revised and translated by S. E. Thorne, 4 vols. (Cambridge, Mass., vols. i and ii 1968, vols. iii and iv 1977).

Bracton's NoteBook, ed. F. W. Maitland, 3 vols. (London, 1887).

Building Accounts of King Henry III, ed. Howard M. Colvin (Oxford, 1971).

Calendar of Charter Rolls, Volume I. Henry III, 1226–1257, PRO (London, 1903).

Calendar of Inquisitions Miscellaneous, vol i, PRO (London, 1916).

Calendar of Inquisitions Post Mortem, vol. i, PRO (London, 1904).

Calendar of Liberate Rolls, Henry III, 6 vols. PRO (London, 1917–64).

Calendar of Patent Rolls, Henry III, vols. 3–6, PRO (London, 1906–13).

Calendars of the Plea Rolls of the Exchequer of the Jews, 4 vols., ed. J. M. Rigg, Hilary Jenkinson, and H. G. Richardson (London, vol. i. 1905, vol. ii 1910, vol. iii 1929, vol. iv 1972).

Carte Nativorum: A Peterborough Abbey Cartulary of the Fourteenth Century, ed. C. N. L. Brooke and M. M. Postan, Northamptonshire Record Society 20 (1960).

Cheshire in the Pipe Rolls, 1158–1301, ed. R. Stewart-Brown, Lancashire and Cheshire Record Society 92 (1938).

Chronica Rogeri de Houedene, ed. William Stubbs, 4 vols., Rolls Series (London, 1868–71).

Chronica Rogeri de Wendover. Liber qui dicitur Flores Historiarum ab anno Domini MCLIV annoque Henrici Anglorum Regis Secundi primo, ed. H. G. Hewlett, 3 vols., Rolls Series (London, 1886–89).

The Chronicle of Jocelin of Brakelond, ed. H. E. Butler (London, 1949).

Close Rolls of the Reign of Henry III, 15 vols., PRO (London, 1902–75).

Councils and Synods, with other documents relating to the English Church, Volume II. ed. F. M. Powicke and C. R. Cheney (Oxford, 1964).

Crown Pleas of the Wiltshire Eyre, 1249, ed. C. A. F. Meekings, Wiltshire Archaeological and Natural History Society 16 (1961).

Curia Regis Rolls, 16 vols., PRO (London, 1922–79).

De Antiquis Legibus Liber: Cronica Maiorum et Vicecomitum Londoniarum, ed. Thomas Stapleton, Camden Society (London, 1846).

Descriptive Catalogue of Ancient Deeds, 6 vols. PRO (London, 1890–1915).

Dialogus de Scaccario, ed. Charles Johnson (London, 1950).

Diplomatic Documents, vol. i, 1101–1272, ed. Pierre Chaplais, PRO (London, 1964).

Documents of the Baronial Movement of Reform and Rebellion, 1258–1267. ed. R. F. Treharne and I. J. Sanders (Oxford, 1973).

Domesday Book, ed. Henry Ellis and Abraham Farley, 4 vols., Record Commission (London, 1783–1816).

English Historical Documents, vol. ii, 1042–1189, ed. D. C. Douglas and G. W. Greenaway, 2nd edn. (London, 1981).

Excerpta e Rotulis Finium in Turri Londinensi Asservati, Henry III, 1216– 1272, ed. Charles Roberts, 2 vols., Record Commission (London, vol. i, 1835, vol ii, 1836).

Fitznells Cartulary, ed. C. A. F. Meekings, Surrey Record Society 16 (1968).

Flores Historiarum, ed. H. R. Luard, 3 vols., Rolls Series (London, 1890).

Foedera, Conventiones, Litterae, etc.; or Rymers Foedera, 1066–1383, ed. Adam Clarke, J. Caley, J. Bayley, F. Holbrooke and J. W. Clarke, Record Commission (London, 1816–69).

Foreign Accounts, Henry III, 1219–1234, ed. Fred A. Cazel, Jr., PRS n. s. 44 (London, 1982).

Gascon Register A, ed. G. P. Cuttino, 3 vols., (London, vols. i and ii 1975, vol iii 1976).

Gesta Regis Henrici Secundi ('Benedict of Peterborough'), ed. William Stubbs, 2 vols., Rolls Series (London, 1867).

Glanvill: Tractatus de Legibus et consuetudinibus regni Anglie qui Glanvilla vocatur, ed. G. D. G. Hall (London, 1965).

Histoire de Guillaume le Maréchal, ed. Paul Meyer, 3 vols., Société de l'histoire de France, (Paris, 1891–1901).

Liber Feodorum: The Book of Fees commonly called *Testa de Nevill* (1198– 1293), 3 vols., PRO (London, 1921–31).

Liber Rubeus de Scaccario. The Red Book of the Exchequer, ed. Hubert Hall, 3 vols., Rolls Series (London, 1896).

A Lincolnshire Assize Roll for 1298, ed. W. S. Thomson, Lincoln Record Society 36 (1944).

The London Eyre of 1244, ed. Helena M. Chew and Martin Weinbaum, London Record Society 6 (1970).

Manorial Records of Cuxham, Oxfordshire, circa 1200–1359. ed. P. D. A. Harvey, Historic Manuscripts Commission Joint Publications Series 23; Oxfordshire Record Society 50 (London, 1976).

Matthaei Parisiensis Chronica Majora, ed. H. R. Luard, 7 vols., Rolls Series (London, 1872–84).

Memoranda Roll 1 John, ed. H. G. Richardson, PRS n.s. 21 (London, 1943).

Memoranda Roll 10 John, ed. R. Allen Brown, PRS n.s. 31 (London, 1957).

Memoranda Roll for Michaelmas 1230–Trinity 1231, ed. Chalfant Robinson, PRS n.s. 11 (London, 1933).

Memoriale Walteri de Coventria, ed. William Stubbs, 2 vols., Rolls Series (London, 1872–73).

Patent Rolls, Henry III, vols. i–ii, PRO (London, 1901–3).

Pipe Rolls:

Magnum Rotulus Scaccarii de anno 31° Henrici I, ed. Joseph Hunter, Record Commission (London, 1833); revised by Charles Johnson, (1929).

The Great Rolls of the Pipe, 5 Henry II to 14 Henry III, 60 vols., PRS (1884–1976).

The Great Roll of the Pipe for 26 Henry III, ed. H. L. Cannon (New Haven, 1918).

The Pipe Roll for 1295, Surrey Membrane, ed. Mabel H. Mills, Surrey Record Society 21 (1924).

Pleas of the Crown for the County of Gloucester, A.D. 1221, ed. F. W. Maitland (London, 1884).

Radulphi de Coggeshall Chronicon Anglicanum, ed. Joseph Stevenson, Rolls Series (London, 1875).

Receipt and Issue Rolls, 26 Henry III (1241–1242), ed. Robert C. Stacey, PRS, forthcoming.

'Robert Grosseteste at the Papal Curia, Lyons 1250: Edition of the Documents,' ed. Servus Gieben, *Collectanea Franciscana* 41 (1971), 340–93.

Roberti Grosseteste Epistolae, ed. H. R. Luard, Rolls Series (London, 1861).

Rôles Gascons, 26–38 Henry III (1242–1254), ed. Francisque Michel, documents inédits sur l'histoire de France (Paris, 1885).

Rôles Gascons: Supplement au Tome Premier, 1254–1255, ed. Charles Bémont, documents inédits sur l'histoire de France (Paris, 1896).

Rotuli de Dominabus et Pueris et Puellis, ed. J. H. Round, PRS 35 (London, 1913).

Rotuli Hundredorum, ed. W. Illingworth and J. Caley, 2 vols., Record Commission (London, 1812–18).

Rotuli Litterarum Clausarum in Turri Londinensi Asservati, ed. Thomas Duffus Hardy, 2 vols., Record Commission (London, 1833–44).

Rotuli Litterarum Patentium in Turri Londinensi Asservati, ed. Thomas Duffus Hardy, Record Commission (London, 1835).

Rotulorum Originalium in Curia Scaccarii Abbreviatio, ed. Henry Playford, 2 vols., Record Commission (London, 1805–10).

'Un Rotulus Finium Retrouvé (1242–1243)', ed. Charles Bémont, *Bulletin Philologique et Historique de Comité des Travaux Historiques et Scientifiques* (1924), 225–40.

Royal and Other Historical Letters Illustrative of the Reign of Henry III, ed. Walter W. Shirley, 3 vols., Rolls Series (London, 1844–62).

Select Cases in the Exchequer of Pleas, ed. Hilary Jenkinson and Beryl E. R. Formoy, Selden Society 48 (London, 1932).

Select Charters and Other Illustrations of English Constitutional History, ed. William Stubbs, 9th edn., revised by H. W. C. Davis (Oxford, 1966).

Select Pleas, Starrs and Other Records from the Rolls of the Exchequer of the Jews (1220–1284), ed. J. M. Rigg, Selden Society 15 (London, 1901–2).

Starrs and Jewish Charters Preserved in the British Museum, ed. Israel Abrahams, Henry P. Stokes, and Herbert Loewe, 3 vols. (London, 1930–2).

The 1235 Surrey Eyre, Volume I, ed. C. A. F. Meekings, Surrey Record Society 31 (1979).

Thesaurus Novus Anecdotorum. ed. E. Martene and U. Durand (Paris, 1717).

SECONDARY SOURCES

Adler, Michael, 'Jewish Tallies of the Thirteenth Century', *Miscellanies of the Jewish Historical Society of England* 2 (1935), 8–23.

——, *Jews in Medieval England* (London, 1939).

——, 'The Testimony of the London Jewry against the Ministers of Henry III', *Transactions of the Jewish Historical Society of England* 14 (1941), 141–85.

Barraclough, Geoffrey, *The Earldom and County Palatine of Chester*, (Oxford, 1953).

Bazeley, Margaret Ley, 'The Extent of the English Forest in the Thirteenth Century', *TRHS* 4th s. 4 (1921), 140–72.

Bean, J. M. W., *The Decline of English Feudalism, 1215–1540* (Manchester, 1968).

Bémont, Charles, 'La Campagne de Poitou (1242–1243): Taillebourg et Saintes', *Annales du Midi* 5 (1893), 289–314.

——, Review of Frank Burr Marsh, *English Rule in Gascony, 1199–1259*, in *Révue Historique* 114 (1913), 382–3.

——, *Simon de Montfort, Earl of Leicester*, trans. Ernest F. Jacob (Oxford, 1930).

Berger, Elie, 'Les Préparatifs d'une invasion anglaise et la descente de Henri III en Bretagne', *Bibliothèque de l'École des Chartres* 54 (1893), 5–44.

Booth, P. H. W., *The Financial Administration of the Lordship and County of Chester*, Chetham Society 28, 3rd s. (Manchester, 1981).

Boutrouche, Robert, *La Crise d'une société: seigneurs et paysans du Bordelais pendant la Guerre de Cent Ans* (Paris, 1947).

Brand, Paul, A., 'The Contribution of the Period of Baronial Reform (1258–1267) to the Development of the Common Law in England', unpublished Oxford University D.Phil. thesis (1974).

——, 'The Control of Mortmain Alienation in England, 1200–1300', *Legal Records and the Historian*, ed. J. H. Baker (London, 1978), 29–40.

——, 'Ireland and the Literature of the Early Common Law', *The Irish Jurist* n.s. 16 (1981), 95–113.

Bridbury, A. R., 'Thirteenth-Century Prices and the Money Supply', *Agricultural History Review* 33 (1985), 1–21.

Brown, Alfred L., 'The Authorization of Letters under the Great Seal', *BIHR* 37 (1964), 125–56.

Buck, M. C., 'The Reform of the Exchequer', *EHR* 98 (1983), 241–60.

Callus, D. A., ed., *Robert Grosseteste* (Oxford, 1969).

Cam, Helen M., *Studies in the Hundred Rolls* (Oxford, 1921).

——, *The Hundred and the Hundred Rolls* (London, 1930).

——, *Law-Finders and Law-Makers in Medieval England* (London, 1962).

Carpenter, David A., 'Sheriffs of Oxfordshire and their Subordinates, 1194–1236', unpublished Oxford University D. Phil. thesis (1973).

——, 'The Decline of the Curial Sheriff in England, 1194–1258', *EHR* 91 (1976), 1–32.

——, 'The Fall of Hubert de Burgh', *Journal of British Studies* 19 (1980), 1–17.

——, 'What Happened in 1258?', *War and Government in the Middle Ages: Essays in Honour of J. O. Prestwich*, ed. John Gillingham and J. C. Holt (Cambridge, 1984), 106–19.

——, 'Kings, Magnates, and Society: The Personal Rule of King Henry III, 1234–1258', *Speculum* 60 (1985), 39–70.

Cazel, Fred A., Jr., 'The Fifteenth of 1225', *BIHR* 34 (1961), 67–81.

Chaplais, Pierre, *Essays in Medieval Diplomacy and Administration* (London, 1981).

Cheney, C. R., 'The "Paper Constitution" Preserved by Matthew Paris', *EHR* 65 (1950), 213–21.

Chew, Helena M., 'Scutage under Edward I', *EHR* 37 (1922), 321–36.

——, 'A Jewish Aid to Marry, AD 1221', *Transactions of the Jewish Historical Society of England* 11 (1928), 92–111.

——, *The English Ecclesiastical Tenants-in-Chief and Knight Service* (London, 1932).

Chrimes, S. B., *An Introduction to the Administrative History of Medieval England*, 3rd edn. (Oxford, 1966).

Clanchy, Michael T., 'Magna Carta, Clause 34', *EHR* 79 (1964), 542–8.

——, 'The Franchise of Return of Writs' *TRHS* 5th s. 17 (1967), 59–82.

——, 'Did Henry III Have a Policy?', *History* 54 (1968), 203–16.

——, *From Memory to Written Record: England, 1066–1307* (Cambridge, Mass., 1979).

——, *England and its Rulers, 1066–1272* (London, 1983).

Clementi, D. R., 'The Documentary Evidence for the Crisis of Government in England in 1258', *Parliaments, Estates and Representation* 1 (1981), 99–108.

Cokayne, George E., *Complete Peerage of England, Scotland, Ireland, Great Britain, and United Kingdom*, revised and enlarged by Vicary Gibbs, H. A. Doubleday, *et al.*, 12 vols. (London, 1910–59).

Colvin, Howard; Brown, R. Allen; and Taylor, A. J., *The History of the King's Works*, vol. i (London, 1963).

Coss, P. R., 'Sir Geoffrey de Langley and the Crisis of the Knightly Class in Thirteenth-Century England', *Past and Present* 68 (1975), 3–37.

Cox, Eugene, *The Eagles of Savoy: The House of Savoy in Thirteenth-Century Europe* (Princeton, 1974).

Cramer, Alice C., 'The Jewish Exchequer: An Inquiry into its Fiscal Functions', *American Historical Review* 45 (1939–40), 327–37.

Crook, David, 'The Struggle over Forest Boundaries in Nottinghamshire, 1218–27', *Transactions of the Thoroton Society* 83 (1979).

——, 'The Early Remembrancers of the Exchequer', *BIHR* 53 (1980), 11–23.

——, *Records of the General Eyre*, Public Record Office Handbooks 20 (London, 1982).

Darby, H. C., and Versey, G. R., *Domesday Gazetteer* (Cambridge, 1975).

Davies, J. Conway, 'The Memoranda Rolls of the Exchequer to 1307', *Studies Presented to Sir Hilary Jenkinson* (London, 1957), 97–154.

Davies, R. R., 'Kings, Lords and Liberties in the March of Wales, 1066–1272', *TRHS* 5th s. 29 (1979), 41–61.

Delisle, Leopold, 'Mémoire sur une lettre inédite addressée à la Reine Blanche par un habitant de La Rochelle', *Bibliothèque de l'École des Chartes* 17 (1856), 513–33.

Denholm-Young, Noël, *Seignorial Administration in England* (Oxford, 1937).

——, 'A Letter from the Council to Pope Honorius III, 1220–1221', *EHR* 60 (1945), 88–96.

——, *Richard of Cornwall* (Oxford, 1947).

——, 'The "Paper Constitution" Attributed to 1244', *EHR* 58 (1943), 403–23; reprinted in *Collected Papers of Noël Denholm-Young* (Cardiff, 1969), 133–54.

Dibben, L. B., 'Chancellor and Keeper of the Seal under Henry III', *EHR* 27 (1912), 39–51.

Dion, Roger, *Histoire de la vigne et du vin en France des origines au XIXe siècle* (Paris, 1959).

Dobson, R. B., *The Jews of Medieval York and the Massacre of March 1190*, Borthwick Papers 45 (York, 1974).

——, 'The Decline and Expulsion of the Medieval Jews of York', *Transactions of the Jewish Historical Society of England* 26 (1979), 34–52.

Elman, Peter, 'The Economic Causes of the Expulsion of the Jews in 1290', *Ec.H.R.* 7 (1937), 145–54.

English, Barbara, *The Lords of Holderness, 1086–1260* (Oxford, 1979).

Eyton, Robert W., *Antiquities of Shropshire*, 12 vols. (London, 1853–60.

Flahiff, G. B., 'The Use of Prohibitions by Clerics against Ecclesiastical Courts in England', *Mediaeval Studies* 3 (Toronto, 1941), 101–16.

——, 'The Writ of Prohibition to Court Christian in the Thirteenth Century', *Mediaeval Studies* 6, 7 (Toronto, 1944, 1945), 261–313, 229–90.

Galbraith, V. H., 'The Death of a Champion (1287)', *Studies in Medieval History Presented to F. M. Powicke* (Oxford, 1948), 283–95.

Giles, J. A., ed., *Matthew Paris' English History*, 3 vols. (London, 1852–4).

Gillingham, John, *Richard the Lionheart* (New York, 1978).

Gillingham, John, and Holt, J. C., *War and Government in the Middle Ages: Essays in Honour of J. O. Prestwich* (Cambridge, 1984).

Gransden, Antonia, *Historical Writing in England, 550–1307* (London, 1974).

Select Bibliography 267

Green, Judith A., 'Some Aspects of Royal Administration in England during the Reign of Henry I' unpublished Oxford University D.Phil. thesis (1975).

——, 'William Rufus, Henry I and the Royal Demesne', *History* 64 (1979), 337–52.

——, 'The Last Century of Danegeld', *EHR* 96 (1981), 241–58.

——, '"Praeclarum et Magnificum Antiquitatis Monumentum": the Earliest Surviving Pipe Roll', *BIHR* 55 (1982), 1–17.

Hajdu, Robert, 'Castles, Castellans and the Structure of Politics in Poitou, 1152–1271', *Journal of Medieval History* 4 (1978), 27–53.

Hall, G. D. G., 'The Early History of Entry sur Disseisin', *Tulane Law Review* 42 (1968), 584–602.

Hallam, Elizabeth M., *Capetian France, 987–1328* (London, 1980).

Harris, Brian E., 'King John and the Sheriffs' Farms', *EHR* 79 (1964), 532–42.

Harriss, Gerald, *King, Parliament and Public Finance in Medieval England to 1369* (Oxford, 1975).

Hart, Cyril, *Royal Forest: A History of Dean's Woods as Producers of Timber* (Oxford, 1966).

Harvey, Barbara, *Westminster Abbey and its Estates in the Middle Ages* (Oxford, 1977).

Harvey, P. D. A., *A Medieval Oxfordshire Village: Cuxham, 1240–1400*, Oxford Historical Series, 2nd s. (Oxford, 1965).

——, 'The English Inflation of 1180–1220', *Past and Present* 61 (1973), 3–30.

——, 'The Pipe Rolls and the Adoption of Demesne Farming in England', *Ec. H. R.*, 2nd s. 27 (1974), 345–59.

Holt, J. C., 'Philip Mark and the Shrievalty of Nottinghamshire and Derbyshire', *Transactions of the Thoroton Society* 56 (1952).

——, 'The Barons and the Great Charter', *EHR* 70 (1955), 1–24.

——, 'King John's Disaster in the Wash', *Nottingham Medieval Studies* 5 (1961), 75–86.

——, *The Northerners: A Study in the Reign of King John* (Oxford, 1961).

——, 'The St. Albans Chroniclers and Magna Carta', *TRHS* 5th s. 14 (1964), 67–88.

——, 'A Vernacular French Text of Magna Carta, 1215', *EHR* 89 (1974), 346–64.

——, 'The End of the Anglo-Norman Realm', *PBA* 61 (1975), 223–65.

——, *Magna Carta* (Cambridge, 1975).

Howell, Margaret, *Regalian Right in Medieval England* (London, 1962).

Hoyt, Robert S., *The Royal Demesne in English Constitutional History, 1066–1272* (Ithaca, 1950).

Hunt, R. W., Pantin, W. A., and Southern, R. W., eds. *Studies in Medieval History Presented to Frederick Maurice Powicke* (Oxford, 1948).

Hurnard, Naomi D., 'Magna Carta, Clause 34', *Studies in Medieval History Presented to F. M. Powicke* (Oxford, 1948), 157–79.

Hurnard, Naomi D., 'Did Edward I Reverse Henry II's Policy upon Seisin?', *EHR* 69 (1954), 529–53.

——, *The King's Pardon for Homicide before* AD *1307* (Oxford, 1969).

Hyams, Paul, R., 'Origins of a Peasant Land Market in England', *Ec.H.R.* 2nd s. 23 (1970), 18–31.

——, 'The Jewish Minority in Mediaeval England, 1066–1290', *Journal of Jewish Studies* 25 (1974), 270–93.

——, Review of S. F. C. Milsom, *The Legal Framework of English Feudalism*, in *EHR* 93 (1978), 856–61.

——, *Kings, Lords and Peasants in Medieval England: The Common Law of Villeinage in the Twelfth and Thirteenth Centuries* (Oxford, 1980).

——, 'The Origins of the English Common Law', paper presented to the 1981 Bristol Legal History Conference.

Jacob, Ernest F., *Studies in the Period of Baronial Reform and Rebellion, 1258–1267* (Oxford, 1925).

——, 'The Reign of Henry III: Some Suggestions', *TRHS* 4th s. 10 (1927), 21–53.

Jenkinson, A. V., 'The Jewels Lost in the Wash', *History* 8 (1923), 161–8.

Jenkinson, Hilary, 'Financial Records of the Reign of King John', *Magna Carta Commemoration Essays*, ed. H. E. Malden (London, 1917), 244–300.

——, 'The Records of Exchequer Receipts from the English Jewry', *Transactions of the Jewish Historical Society of England* 8, 9 (1918, 1922), 19–54, 188–92.

Johnstone, Hilda, 'Poor Relief in the Royal Households of Thirteenth-Century England', *Speculum* 4 (1929), 149–67.

Jolliffe, J. E. A., *The Constitutional History of Medieval England* 4th edn. (London, 1961).

——, *Angevin Kingship*, 2nd edn. (London, 1963).

King, Edmund, *Peterborough Abbey, 1086–1310: A study in the Land Market* (Cambridge, 1973).

Kirby, J. L., 'The English Exchequer of Receipt in the Later Middle Ages', *Annali della fondazione italiana per la storia amministrativa* 4 (1967), 78–87.

Knowles, Clive H., *Simon de Montfort, 1265–1965*, Historical Association (London, 1965).

——, 'The Resettlement of England after the Barons' War, 1264–67', *TRHS* 5th s. 32 (1982), 25–41.

Langmuir, Gavin I., 'The Jews and the Archives of Angevin England: Reflections on Medieval Anti-semitism' *Traditio* 19 (1963), 183–244.

——, 'The Knight's Tale of Young Hugh of Lincoln', *Speculum* 47 (1972), 459–82.

Larson, A. T., 'Some Aspects of the Medieval Exchequer Memoranda Rolls', *BIHR* 16 (1938–39), 12–18.

Lawrence, Clifford Hugh, *St Edmund of Abingdon* (Oxford, 1960).

Lipman, V. D., *The Jews of Medieval Norwich* (London, 1967).

——, 'The Anatomy of Medieval Anglo-Jewry', *Transactions of the Jewish Historical Society of England* 21 (1968), 64–77.

Little, A. G. and Powicke, F. M. eds., *Essays in Medieval History Presented to Thomas Frederick Tout* (Manchester, 1925).

Lloyd, J. E., *A History of Wales from the Earliest Times to the Edwardian Conquest*, 2 vols. (London, 1939).

Lunt, William E., *Financial Relations of the Papacy with England to 1327* (Cambridge, Mass., 1939).

Lydon, James F., *The Lordship of Ireland in the Middle Ages* (Dublin, 1972).

Maddicott, John R., 'Law and Lordship: Royal Justices as Retainers in Thirteenth- and Fourteenth-Century England', *Past and Present* Supplement 4 (1978).

——, 'Magna Carta and the Local Community, 1215–1259.' *Past and Present* 102 (1984), 26–65.

Madox, Thomas, *The History and Antiquities of the Exchequer of England*, 2nd edn. (London, 1769).

Maitland, F. W., *Collected Papers*, ed. H. A. L. Fisher, 3 vols. (Cambridge, 1911).

Malden, Henry E., ed., *Magna Carta Commemoration Essays* (London, 1917).

Marsh, Frank Burr, *English Rule in Gascony, 1199–1259* (Ann Arbor, 1912).

Mason, Emma, 'The Resources of the Earldom of Warwick in the Thirteenth Century', *Midland History* 3 (1975), 67–75.

Mate, Mavis, 'Profit and Productivity on the Estates of Isabella de Forz (1260–92)' *Ec.H.R.* 2nd s. 33 (1980), 326–34.

McKechnie, William S., *Magna Carta*, 2nd edn. (Glasgow, 1914).

Meekings, C. A. F., 'Analyses of Calendars of Charter Roll Witness Lists', unpublished manuscript, PRO.

——, *Studies in Thirteenth-Century Justice and Administration* (London, 1981).

Meisel, Janet, *Barons of the Welsh Frontier* (Lincoln, 1980).

Miller, Edward, 'England in the 12th and 13th Century: an Economic Contrast?' *Ec.H.R.* 2nd s. 24 (1971), 1–14.

——, 'Farming of Manors and Direct Management', *Ec.H.R.* 2nd s. 26 (1973), 138–40.

——, and Hatcher, John, *Medieval England: Rural Society and Economic Change, 1086–1348* (London, 1978).

Mills, Mabel H., 'Adventus Vicecomitum, 1258–1272', *EHR* 36 (1921), 481–96.

——, 'Adventus Vicecomitum, 1272–1307' *EHR* 38 (1923), 331–54.

——, 'Exchequer Agenda and Estimates of Revenue, Easter Term, 1284', *EHR* 40 (1925), 229–34.

Mills, Mabel H., 'Experiments in Exchequer Procedure, 1200–1232', *TRHS* 4th s. 8 (1925), 151–70.

——, Review of J. H. Ramsay, *A History of the Revenues of the Kings of England*, *EHR* 41 (1926), 429–31.

——, 'The Reforms at the Exchequer, 1232–1242', *TRHS* 4th s. 10 (1927), 111–33.

Milsom, S. F. C., *The Legal Framework of English Feudalism* (Cambridge, 1976).

Mitchell, Sydney Knox, *Studies in Taxation under John and Henry III* (New Haven, 1914).

——, *Taxation in Medieval England* (New Haven, 1951).

Morris, William A., *The Medieval English Sheriff to 1300* (Manchester, 1927).

Norgate, Kate, *The Minority of Henry III* (London, 1912).

Oschinsky, Dorothea, *Walter of Henley and Other Treatises on Estate Management and Accounting* (Oxford, 1971).

Painter, Sidney, *William the Marshal: Knight-errant, Baron, and Regent of England* (Baltimore, 1933).

——, *The Scourge of the Clergy: Peter of Dreux, Duke of Brittany* (Baltimore, 1937).

——, *Studies in the History of the English Feudal Barony* (Baltimore, 1943).

——, *The Reign of King John* (Baltimore, 1949).

——, *Feudalism and Liberty: Articles and Addresses of Sidney Painter*, ed. Fred A. Cazel, Jr (Baltimore, 1961).

Palmer, Robert C., *The County Courts of Medieval England, 1150–1350* (Princeton, 1982).

Petit-Dutaillis, Charles, *Étude sur la vie et le Règne de Louis VIII* (Paris, 1894).

Plucknett, T. F. T., *Legislation of Edward I* (Oxford, 1970).

Pollock, Sir Frederick, and Maitland, F. W., *The History of English Law*, 2 vols., 2nd edn. (Cambridge, 1968).

Postan, M. M., 'Investment in Medieval Agriculture', *Journal of Economic History* 27 (1967), 576–87.

——, *Essays on Medieval Agriculture and General Problems of the Medieval Economy* (Cambridge, 1973).

Powicke, F. M., 'The Chancery in the Minority of Henry III', *EHR* 23 (1908), 220–35.

——, 'Per iudicium parium vel per legem terrae', *Magna Carta Commemoration Essays* (London, 1917), 96–121.

——, *Stephen Langton* (Oxford, 1928).

——, 'The Oath of Bromholm', *EHR* 56 (1941), 529–48.

——, *King Henry III and the Lord Edward: The Community of the Realm in the Thirteenth Century*, 2 vols. (Oxford, 1947).

——, *Ways of Medieval Life and Thought: Essays and Addresses by F. M. Powicke* (London, 1949).

——, *The Loss of Normandy, 1189–1204*, 2nd edn. (Manchester, 1961).

——, *The Thirteenth Century* (Oxford 1962).

——, and Fryde, E. B., *Handbook of British Chronology*, 2nd edn. (London, 1961).

Powicke, Michael R., *Military Obligation in Medieval England* (Oxford, 1962).

Prestwich, Michael, *War, Politics and Finance under Edward I* (London, 1972).

Public Record Office, Lists and Indexes, vol. ix: *List of Sheriffs for England and Wales from the Earliest Times to* AD 1831 (London, 1898). Revised edn. (New York, 1963).

——, Lists and Indexes, vol. xv. *List of Ancient Correspondence of the Chancery and Exchequer*, revised edn. (London, 1969).

Ramsay, James H., *The Dawn of the Constitution, 1216–1307* (London, 1908).

——, *A History of the Revenues of the Kings of England, 1066–1399*, 2 vols. (Oxford, 1925).

Reed, C. G., and Anderson, T. L., 'An Economic Explanation of English Agrarian Organization in the 12th and 13th Centuries', *Ec.H.R.* 2nd s. 26 (1973), 134–7.

Renouard, Yves, *Études d'histoire Médiévale*, 2 vols. (Paris, 1968).

——, ed., *Histoire de Bordeaux, vol. iii: Bordeaux sous les rois d'Angleterre* (Bordeaux, 1965).

Richardson, H. G., *The English Jewry under the Angevin Kings* (London, 1960).

Rosser, A. G. 'The Essence of Medieval Urban Communities: the Vill of Westminster, 1200–1540', *TRHS* 5th s. 34 (1984), 91–112.

Roth, Cecil, *Jews of Medieval Oxford* (Oxford, 1951).

——, 'The Ordinary Jew in the Middle Ages', *Studies and Essays in Honor of Abraham A. Neuman*, ed. Meir Ben-Horin, Bernard D. Weinryb, and Solomon Zeitlin (Philadelphia, 1962), 431–7.

——, *A History of the Jews in England*, 3rd edn. (Oxford, 1964).

Sanders, Ivor J., *English Baronies: A Study of their Origin and Descent*, 1086–1327 (Oxford, 1960).

Sayles, G. O., *The King's Parliament of England* (London, 1975).

Snellgrove, Harold S., *The Lusignans in England, 1247–1258* (Albuquerque, 1950).

Southern R. W., 'The Place of Henry I in English History', *PBA* 47 (1962), 127–70.

——, *St. Anselm and his Biographer* (Cambridge, 1966).

Stacey, Robert C., 'Crown Finance and English Government under Henry III, 1236–1245', unpublished Yale University Ph.D. thesis (1983).

——, 'Royal Taxation and the Social Structure of Medieval Anglo-Jewry: The Tallages of 1239–1242', *Hebrew Union College Annual* 56 (1985), 175–249.

——, 'Agricultural Investment and the Management of the Royal Demesne Manors, 1236–1240', *Journal of Economic History*, 46 (1986) 919–34.

Stamp, A. E., 'Some Notes on the Court and Chancery of Henry III', *Historical Essays in Honour of James Tait*, ed. J. G. Edwards, V. H. Galbraith, and E. F. Jacob (Manchester, 1933), 305–11.

Stenton, D. M., *English Justice Between the Norman Conquest and the Great Charter, 1066–1215* (London, 1965).

Stephenson, Carl, *Medieval Institutions: Selected Essays*, ed. Bryce D. Lyon (Ithaca, 1967).

Stevenson, Wendy B., 'England and Normandy, 1204–1259', unpublished Leeds University Ph.D. thesis (1974).

Stewart-Brown, Ronald, 'The End of the Norman Earldom of Chester', *EHR* 35 (1920), 26–54.

——, *The Sergeants of the Peace in Medieval England and Wales*, (Manchester, 1936).

Stokes, H. P. *Studies in Anglo-Jewish History* (Edinburgh, 1913).

Stones, E. L. G. *Anglo-Scottish Relations, 1174–1328* (Oxford, 1970).

Strayer, Joseph R., *The Reign of Philip the Fair* (Princeton, 1980).

Stubbs, William, *The Constitutional History of England*, 3 vols., 4th edn. (Oxford, 1883).

Summerson, H. R. T., ed., *Crown Pleas of the Devon Eyre of 1238* (Devon and Cornwall Record Society, n. s. 28, 1985).

Sutherland, Donald W., *Quo Warranto Proceedings in the Reign of Edward I, 1278–1294* (Oxford, 1963).

Thomson, S. Harrison, *The Writings of Robert Grosseteste* (Cambridge, 1940).

Tout, T. F., 'Wales and the March During the Barons' Wars, 1258–67', *Historical Essays by Members of Owens College, Manchester*, ed. T. F. Tout and James Tait (Manchester, 1907), 76–136.

——, *Chapters in the Administrative History of Mediaeval England*, 6 vols. (Manchester, 1920–33).

Trabut-Cussac, J. P., *L'Administration anglaise en Gascogne sous Henry III et Edouard I de 1254 à 1307*. Mémoires et documents publiés par la Société de l'École des Chartres 20 (Geneva, 1972).

Treharne, R. F., *The Baronial Plan of Reform, 1258–1263* (Manchester, 1971).

Turner, G. J., 'The Sheriff's Farm', *TRHS* n.s. 12 (1898), 117–49.

——, 'The Minority of Henry III,' *TRHS* n.s. 18 (1904), 245–95; 3rd s. 1 (1907), 205–62.

Turner, Ralph V., *The King and his Courts* (Ithaca, 1968).

——, 'William de Forz, Count of Aumâle: An Early Thirteenth-Century Baron', *Proceedings of the American Philosophical Society* 115 (1971), 221–49.

——, 'Roger Huscarl, Professional Lawyer in England and Royal Justice in Ireland, c. 1199–1230' *The Irish Jurist* 16 (1981), 290–8.

——, *The English Judiciary in the Age of Glanvill and Bracton, c. 1176–1239* (Cambridge, 1985).

Vaughan, Richard, *Matthew Paris* (Cambridge, 1979).

Vinogradoff, Paul, 'Clause 39', *Magna Carta Commemoration Essays* (London, 1917), 78–95.

Walker, R. F. 'The Anglo-Welsh Wars, 1217–1267 with special reference to English Military Developments', unpublished Oxford University D. Phil. thesis (1954).

——, 'Hubert de Burgh and Wales, 1218–1232', *EHR* 87 (1972), 461–94.

Walker, Sue Sheridan, 'The Action of Waste in the Early Common Law', *Legal Records and the Historian*, ed. J. H. Baker (London, 1978), 185–206.

Warren, W. L. *King John* (London, 1961).

——, *Henry II* (Berkeley, 1973).

Whitwell, R. J. 'The Revenue and Expenditure of England under Henry III' *EHR* 18 (1903), 710–11.

Wilkinson, Bertie, 'The Council and the Crisis of 1233–4', *Bulletin of the John Rylands Library* 27 (1943–4), 384–93.

——, *The Constitutional History of England, 1216–1399*, with select documents, 3 vols. (New York, 1948–58).

Willard, James F., 'The Memoranda Rolls and the Remembrancers, 1282–1350', *Essays in Medieval History Presented to T. F. Tout*, ed. A. G. Little and F. M. Powicke, (Manchester, 1925), 215–29.

Williamson, Dorothy, 'Some Aspects of the Legation of Cardinal Otto', *EHR* 64 (1949), 145–73.

Wilshire, Leland Edward, 'Boniface of Savoy, Carthusian and Archbishop of Canterbury, 1207–1270', *Analecta Cartusiana* 31 (University of Salzburg, 1977), 4–90.

Wolffe, Bertram P., *The Royal Demesne in English History: The Crown Estate in the Governance of the Realm from the Conquest to 1509* (London, 1971).

Young, Charles R., *The Royal Forests of Medieval England* (Philadelphia, 1979).

INDEX

Abthorpe (Northants) 55 n., 88, 90

Acornbury (Hereford) 55 n., 56, 88, 90, 91 n.

Aigueblanche, Peter de 91 n., 92, 134, 136, 139, 142, 182, 244, 253 n.

Albini, Philip de 13, 24

Alton (Hants) 55 n., 87, 88

Amounderness (Lancs): see Wirresdale, Lonsdale, and Amounderness

Andover (Hants) 55 n., 68, 88

Angoulême: see La Marche, count of

Anjou 160–1, 165, 166, 168–9, 171, 182, 193

Aquitaine 161, 166 n.

Aragon 167, 181, 194

Arceveske, William le 194, 196

archbishop of Canterbury: see Becket, St Thomas; Langton, Stephen; Rich, St Edmund; Savoy, Boniface of

Aumâle, William de Forz, count of 13, 15, 22–4, 28, 31, 94, 169

Austria, duke of 166

Auvergne, count of 166, 167, 179, 194, 196

Aylesbury 101, 103

Aylsham (Norfolk) 59 n.

Balliol, John de 239, 250

Bamborough Castle 59 n.

Barton Gloucester (Glos) 55 n., 86, 88, 91 n.

Basingstoke (Hants) 55 n., 77, 88, 91 n., 136

Basset, Alan 13, 67–8

Basset, Fulk: see London, Fulk Basset, bishop of

Basset, Gilbert 38–9, 94

Basset, Philip 253 n.

Basset, Richard 48

Bath, bishopric of 254

Bath, Henry of 64–5

Bath, Jocelin, bishop of 31–2, 93

Bayonne 175, 244–5

Bazas 175

Beauville, Bernard de 178

Becket, St Thomas, archbishop of Canterbury 48, 139

Bedford Castle, siege of 30–2, 164

Bélin 177

Bergerac 165

Blakeford, Robert de 102 n.

Blanche of Castile, queen of France: see Louis IX, king of France

Blaye 177, 196, 198, 237

Bolevill, Nicholas de 128 n.

Bolsover (Derby) 115

Bordeaux 162, 164–5, 169, 174–5, 177, 179, 196

Bouvines, battle of 163

Bracton 41

Bray (Berks) 55 n., 85, 86, 88

Breauté, Fawkes de 1, 11, 12, 13, 14–15, 18, 19, 24, 25, 28, 30–2

Breauté, William de 31

Brescia 126, 127, 128

Brewer, William 24, 27

Bridport (Dorset) 55 n., 79, 88

Brigstock (Northants) 55 n., 85, 86, 88, 90, 91 n., 103

Brill (Bucks) 55 n., 85, 86, 88, 90

Bristol Castle 14

Brito, Ranulf 136

Brittany: 1230 expedition 36, 143, 170–2; subsidies to 42; see also Dreux, Peter of

Brocton (Lancs) 55 n.

Bromsgrove (Worcs) 55 n., 77, 85–6

Brother Geoffrey the Templar, royal almoner 77, 115, 122 n., 133–4, 139–40, 141, 145 n., 145–6

Burgh, Hubert de: during the regency 1, 4 n., 11, 12; and the siege of Rockingham and Sauvey Castles 15–16; his rise to power in the minority 16–19, 23–32; marriage to Margaret of Scotland 21–2; and revolt of the count of Aumâle 22–4; and the siege of Bedford Castle 30–2; and siege of La Rochelle 164; and 1225–7 Gascon expedition 165–6; earl of Kent 35; financial management 32–4; and profits on shire farms 51–2;

MA

I